Quicken® for Windows User's Guide

Version 4

New version created by
Eli Abbe
Ken Chiu
George Hansen
John Pattinson
Noah Shaffer
Tim Villanueva
Joe Wells
Daryl Yee

Intuit®

First Printing, September 1994.
ISBN: 0-929804-64-3

Intuit Inc.
P. O. Box 3014
Menlo Park, CA 94026

Manuals, Help, Qcards, Quick Tour Mike Barden, Jennie Tan, Karen Tingey

Development team Kate Atwood, Li Chan, James Del Favero, Matt Glickman, James Hackleman, Mari Ivener, Roland Kwong, Dave McMurtry, Steve Ollanik, Rowena Pelayo, Mark Pierce, Mardi Poulin, Robin Sahai, Tom Schulenburg, Simone Shapiro, Hermanese Sims, Greg Sofos, Lisa Tam, Terry Tierney, Erik Torres, John Vahsholtz, Jimmy Wu, Lisa Yee, DJ Young, Jim Zalesny

Special thanks to Corby Anderson, Pete M. Antunes, Alan Ashton, Barbara Bernstein, Claudia Carpenter, Mark Chen, Eric Dunn, Doug Eberman, Deborah Gordon, David Gurevich, Jesper Helweg, Dawn Hughan, Miriam Kelman, Ray Kundra, Jeff Lombardi, Jeanette Lunt, Cesar Managad, Eleanor Mayfield, Adrian McCarthy, Earnest Nation, Gabriella Piccioni, John Rathbone, Lew Risica, John Sieraski, Wade Temple, John Unruh, Doug Van Gordon, Jim Voos, Bob Walters, Tim Walters, Michael Wells, Lun Yuen

Contents

Analyzing your data

Using Quicken online

Appendixes

1 Working with accounts and data files

The difference between an account and a data file

Generally, if you are using Quicken to track the finances of a single person or household, you'll need only one *data file*. In it, you create all the *accounts* (such as checking accounts, savings accounts, credit card accounts, and loans) that you want to keep track of. The data file also contains lists of categories, transactions, and other information that can be shared by all the accounts in that file. When you first start Quicken, it creates the file QDATA.QDT, and helps you set up your first account. The following section explains how to create more accounts in QDATA.QDT. Quicken displays the name of the file you have open in the title bar of the main Quicken window.

Setting up additional Quicken accounts

You can create up to 64 related accounts in a single Quicken file. (To increase this number up to 255 by copying the file, see page 303.)

1 **If you have more than one file, be sure to open the one you want before setting up the new account.**

In most cases, you'll want to set up all your accounts in the same file so you can create reports based on data from all of them. However, in some cases you might want separate Quicken files. When you set up a new account, Quicken adds it to the current Quicken file.

For information about when and how to create more than one Quicken file, see "Setting up additional files" on page 299.

See “Using Quicken HomeBase” on page 10 in the *Getting Started Guide*.

2 **From the Activities menu, choose Create New Account.**

Or, from the Account list, click New. You can also create a new account by clicking Create Accounts in Quicken HomeBase.

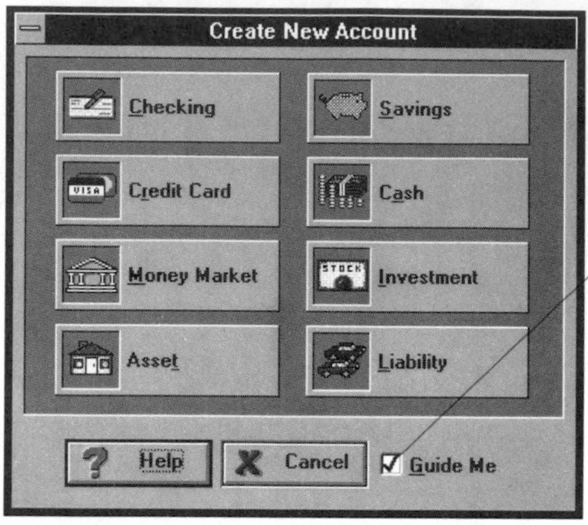

Select the Guide Me checkbox to have Quicken interview you about the account information.

Liability accounts:
To set up a liability account to track an amortized loan such as a house mortgage, see Chapter 10, *Tracking loans and mortgages,* on page 105 first. That chapter explains how Quicken sets up a liability account for you as part of setting up the loan.

3 **(Optional) Select the Guide Me checkbox.**

Quicken will help you set up your first account by interviewing you about the account information step by step.

4 **Click the type of account you want.**

5 **If you selected the Guide Me checkbox, complete the interview.**

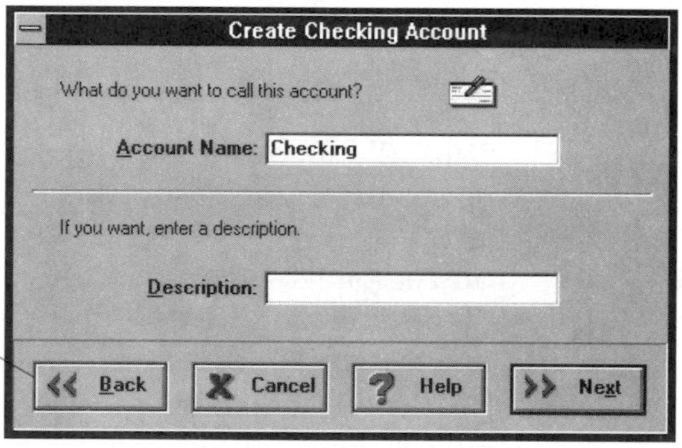

Throughout the New Account interview, click Back to return to the previous window, click Next to continue with the interview, or click Help for extra information about the window. Click Cancel to stop the interview without creating an account.

Otherwise, enter information in the Create Account window.

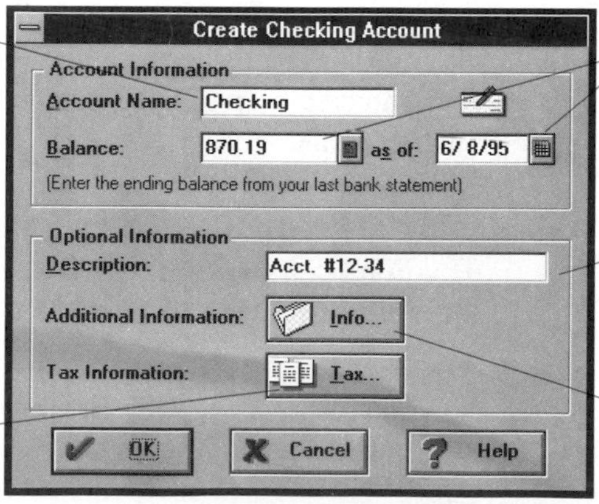

Enter a unique name for the account, up to 15 characters long. Use your own name, your bank name, or a descriptive name such as Checking, VISA, or Mortgage. The name can include letters, numbers, spaces, and any characters except these: ^ | / : [ ]

See the table on the next page to enter the correct information in these fields.

The description in this box is optional. Enter up to 21 characters.

Click here to make this a tax-deferred account, or to assign tax schedule line items to transfers in and out of the account.

(Optional) Click Info to enter some background details about the account.

Account type	Enter this in the Balance field	Enter this in the Date field
Checking, Savings, or Money Market	The ending balance shown on your last bank statement	The date of your last bank statement
Cash	The amount of cash you have on hand	Today's date
Credit card	The balance due shown on your last credit card statement	The date of your last credit statement
Asset	The current value of the asset	Today's date
Liability	The current principal amount owed on the loan	Today's date
Investment	Not applicable	Not applicable

Windows Tip
To move to the next box in a window, click the box or press Tab.

6 **Enter other information in the Create Account window.**

- To enable electronic payments for a bank account, see Chapter 26, *Paying bills online,* on page 277.
- To enable IntelliCharge for a credit card account, see "Setting up a credit card account to use IntelliCharge" on page 261.
- To track a savings goal, see "Creating a savings goal" on page 241.
- To enter additional information about the account for your own benefit (for example, the account number or interest rate), click Info. Fill in the boxes of the Additional Account Information window and click OK to close the window.
- To make this a tax-deferred account or to assign tax schedule line items to transfers in and out of the account, click Tax. Complete the boxes in the Tax Schedule Information window and click OK.

Windows Tip
You can press Enter instead of clicking OK.

7 **Click OK.**

8 **(Optional) If this is a liability account, Quicken asks if you would like to set up an amortized loan. If you click Yes, be sure to read Chapter 10, *Tracking loans and mortgages,* on page 105.**

Quicken creates the new account.

Selecting an account to use

You can work with many accounts at one time by opening multiple account windows on your desktop. There are three ways to open the Account list:

- From the Lists menu, choose Account.
- Press Ctrl+A.
- Click the Accts (Accounts) icon on the iconbar.

The Account list contains information about the accounts in the current file. It shows the name, type, description, number of transactions in each account, and the ending balance for each account.

If you have checks to be printed, the Account list also displays a checkmark in the Chks column for that account.

There are four ways to open the account you want to use:

- To open an account, choose it from the Account list.

Click one of these tabs to see only that type of account, or click All Types to see all your accounts.

Double-click the account you want to open.

OR

Select the account and then click Open. (To select an account, either click its name or move the highlight bar using the Up Arrow and Down Arrow keys.)

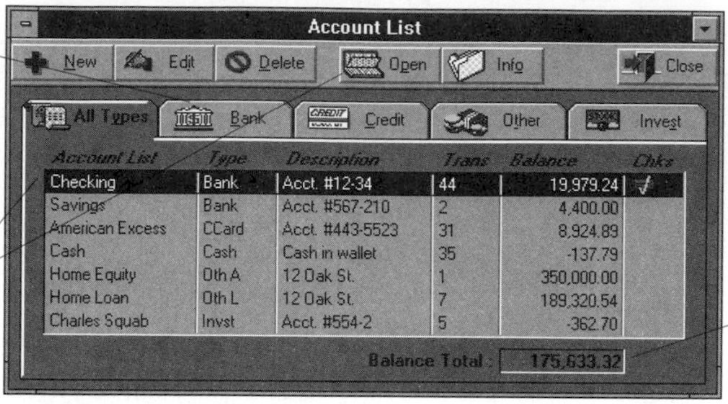

This shows the total of the balances of all your accounts.

- If the account is already open, click on it to make it active.

In this example, the Category & Transfer List window is active. (The title bar of an active window is highlighted.) Click anywhere in the Bank Account window to make it active and see its register.

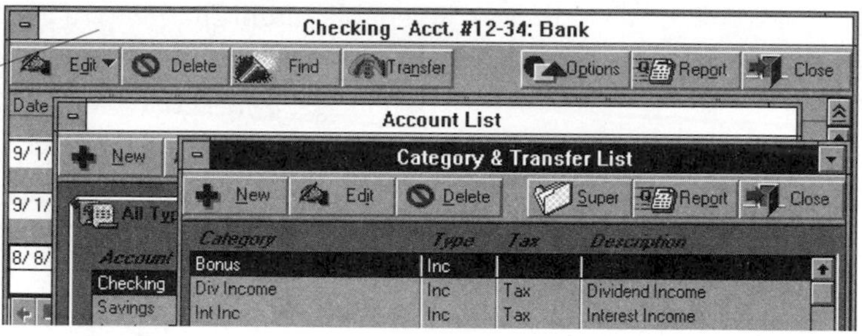

- If the account is already open, but obscured by other windows, choose the account name from the Window menu.

The bottom part of the Window menu lists all the Quicken windows that are open.

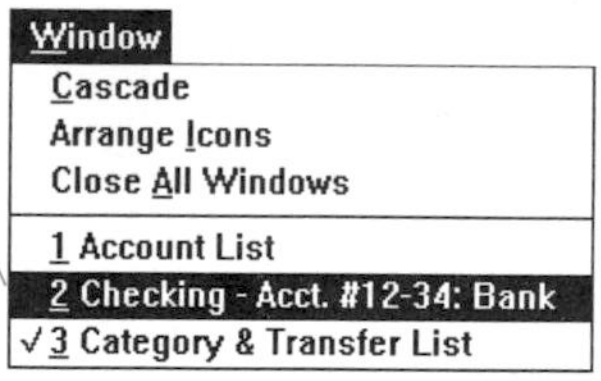

- If another account's register is already open, click on the button at the bottom of the register to select the account you want to open.

Click one of these buttons to go to that account. (Investment accounts are not listed in non-investment registers.)

You can rearrange these buttons by dragging them with the mouse.

Editing account information

After setting up and using an account, you can change its name, description, opening balance, tax-deferred status, or credit limit (if it's a credit card account).

Or press Ctrl+A

1 **From the Lists menu, choose Account.**

2 **Select the account you want to edit.**

The savings account is selected in this Account list.

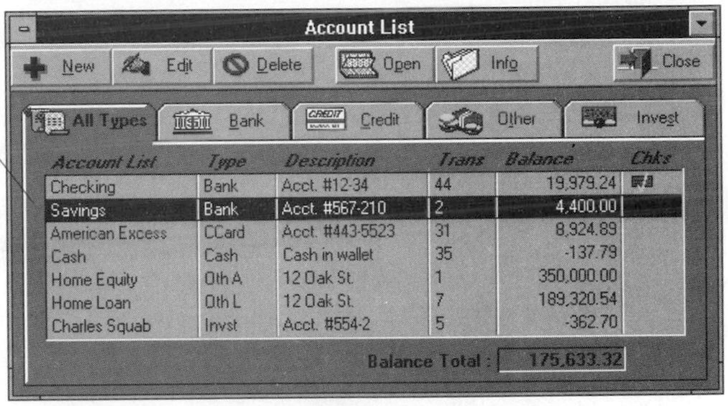

Or press Ctrl+E

3 **Click Edit.**

Enter up to fifteen characters for an account name.

Click Info to change the additional information for the account.

Click Tax to change the tax-deferred status of the account, or to change tax schedule assignments to transfers in and out of the account.

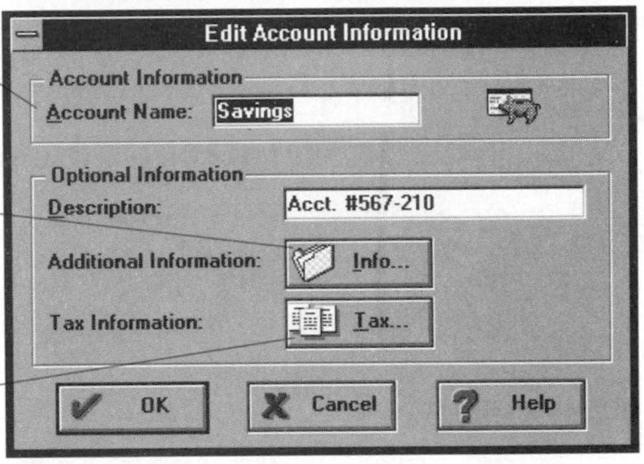

Windows Tip
To move to the next field in the window, click the field or press Tab.

4 **Change the account name or description.**

If you change the name of an account, Quicken automatically updates any transactions linked to this account through transfers to show the new name. (For more information about account transfers, see "Transferring money between accounts" on page 22.)

5 **(Optional) If this is a credit card account, change the credit limit and click OK.**

You can also enable or disable the account for IntelliCharge.

For more information about IntelliCharge, see "About IntelliCharge" on page 261.

6 **(Optional) Click Info to change the additional information about the account, then return to the Edit Account Information window.**

7 **(Optional) Click Tax to change the tax-deferred status of the account, or to change tax schedule assignments to transfers in and out of the account.**

8 **Click OK.**

Windows Tip
You can press Enter instead of clicking OK.

Quicken makes the changes and updates the name of the account in the Account list and in the Category & Transfer list.

Changing the opening balance

See Chapter 3, *Using the register,* on page 17, on how to enter and edit transactions in the register.

See "Having Quicken adjust for differences" on page 90.

To change the opening balance for an account after the account is set up, go to the Opening Balance transaction in the register and change the date or amount of the transaction. Enter the revised opening balance into the deposit column over the previous amount. The next time you reconcile this account, Quicken displays an opening balance difference.

Changing the account from one type to another

See "Copying data from one account to another" on page 305.

You might want to turn a bank account into a credit card account. To change the type of the account, export the old account to a QIF file, set up a new account, and then import transactions from the QIF file into the new account. Note that investment transactions can only be exported to another investment account.

Deleting an account

Deleting a Quicken account permanently removes it from your file. Once you delete an account, there is no way to recover it.

Or press Ctrl+A

1 **From the Lists menu, choose Account.**

2 **Select the account you want to delete from the Account list.**

Or press Ctrl+D

3 **Click Delete.**

Quicken warns that you are about to permanently remove this account from your file. If Quicken deletes the account, it also deletes the account name from the Category field of any transfer transactions.

Windows Tip
You can press Enter instead of clicking OK. Or you can back out by pressing Esc instead of clicking Cancel.

4 **Type** YES **and click OK if you are certain you want to delete the account.**

Quicken permanently removes the account from your file.

Backing up your Quicken files

It's always a good idea to back up your work each time you use Quicken. Backing up is important because, if you accidentally lose data, you can use the copy of the file stored on the backup disk.

Backing up your files is the only safeguard against hard disk failure. If your hard disk fails, there is nothing you can do to recover your Quicken data. Your data is valuable—back it up regularly to a floppy disk.

You can put a Backup icon on the iconbar to make this task more convenient. See "Adding an icon to the iconbar" on page 294.

Quicken regularly prompts you to back up your current file before leaving Quicken. We recommend that you let Quicken back up your file.

Important: When you back up your work, *use a separate floppy disk,* even if you have plenty of space on your hard disk. Hard disks can fail. The first time you make a backup copy, you should have two sets of blank, formatted disks on hand before you begin. For subsequent backups, alternate between the two sets of backup disks.

Or press Ctrl+B

1 **From the File menu, choose Backup.**

2 **Insert your backup disk into the floppy drive.**

3 **Select the drive containing the backup disk from the Backup Drive drop-down list.**

4 **Select the file you want to back up from the File to Back Up box and click OK.**

Click this option to back up the file you are currently using. Then click OK and skip to step 6.

Click this option to select another file to back up.

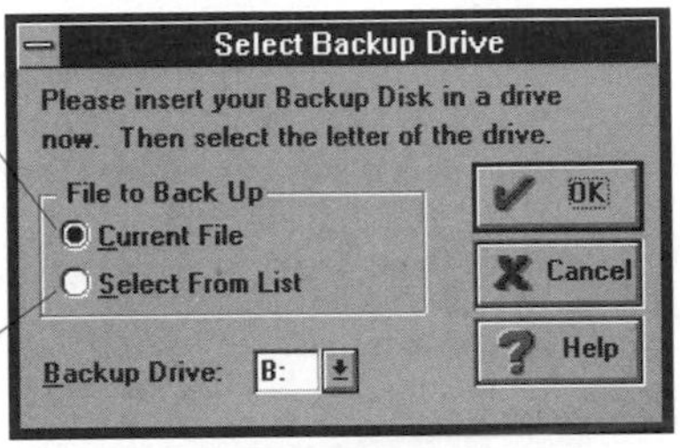

5 **(Optional) If you clicked the Select From List option in step 4, select the Quicken file you want to back up and click OK.**

Double-click the directory containing the Quicken file to be backed up. The line above the Directories list changes to show you the full pathname of the directory you have selected.

This list shows all Quicken files in the selected drive and directory. You probably have only one Quicken file. When you find it, select it so that it appears in the File Name box in the upper left corner.

Select the drive containing the Quicken file to be backed up from this drop-down list.

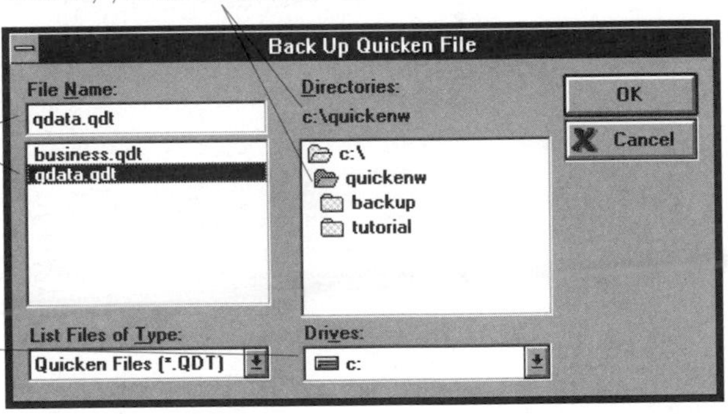

6 **If the file is larger than the space available on the backup disk, select the backup option you want, replace the backup disk with another disk, and then click OK.**

7 **When Quicken tells you that the backup is complete, click OK and remove the backup disk.**

Store the disk (or disks) in a safe place.

8 **Repeat steps 1 through 7 to make a second backup copy.**

Once you have made a backup copy of your file, you should update it at least once a month. Alternate between the two sets of backup disks each time you back up your work.

Restoring a Quicken file

If your hard disk ever accidentally loses data, you'll need to restore your files from your backup disk. In this event, first reinstall Quicken; then restore your files as described below. (See the *Getting Started Guide* for installation instructions.)

If you need to move a Quicken file from one computer to another (for example, from your home computer to your business computer), you can use Quicken's Restore command to restore files on one computer that you've backed up on another computer.

Restoring from a backup file replaces your current data.
When you restore from a backup file, Quicken overwrites your current Quicken file with the file stored on the backup disk. Be aware that you will lose any changes you have made to your file since the backup was made. To prevent this, rename one of the files.

---

1 **Insert the backup disk containing the file you want to restore.**

2 **From the File menu, choose Restore.**

3 **In the Restore Quicken File window, select the drive containing the backup disk from the Drives drop-down list.**

4 **Click on a filename to select the file you want to restore.**

Make sure the filename is shown in the File Name box.

This list shows all Quicken files in the selected drive and directory. Select the one you want to restore so that it appears in the File Name box in the top left corner.

If necessary, first double-click the directory containing the Quicken file to be restored in this list. The line above the Directories list changes to show you the full pathname of the directory you have selected.

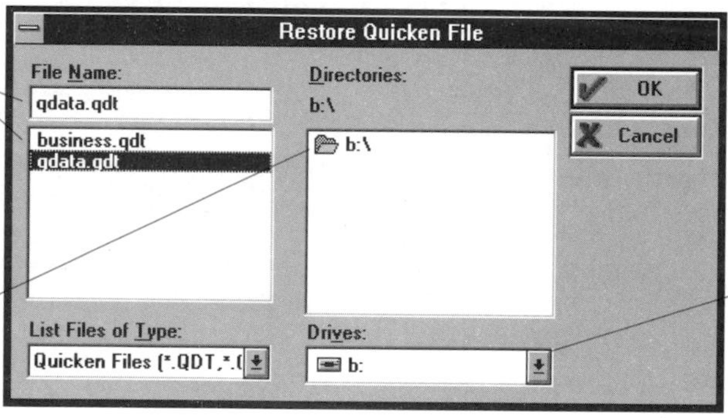

Select the drive containing the Quicken file to be restored from this drop-down list.

If the Quicken file to be restored is on a single disk, it has a .QDT extension. If the file spans multiple backup disks, it has a .QB1 extension.

Windows tip
You can double-click the file in the file list instead of selecting it and clicking OK.

5 **Click OK.**

6 **If you are restoring the current file, click OK to overwrite it.**

2 Setting up categories and classes

About categories

Quicken lets you identify your transactions according to a list of categories. For example, you can categorize a check you write to the supermarket as "groceries," your paycheck as "salary," and your gas and electric bills as "utilities." You can also *split* a transaction into multiple categories (see "Splitting transactions" on page 26).

Categories are divided into income (such as salary, dividends, and interest) and expense (such as dining, groceries, and telephone).

Categorizing your transactions allows you to easily create Quicken reports and graphs by category, and answer questions like:

- How much am I spending a month on groceries?
- How much do I receive each month in salary, dividends, or interest?

Categorizing your transactions also lets you:

- Generate Quicken's income- and expense-based reports and graphs to show where your money comes from and where it goes.
- Set up budget amounts for each category to compare your actual expenses with your budget amounts. You can also organize your categories by *supercategories* to simplify your budget.

See Chapter 21, *Creating a budget or savings goal,* on page 235.

See "Tax summary" on page 165.

- Prepare for your tax returns by printing a report that lists all tax-related income and expenses.*

See "Transferring Quicken data to tax preparation software" on page 220.

- Export your transaction data to tax software.

Setting up categories and subcategories

Quicken maintains a category list that includes the names of all the categories in the current Quicken file. Whenever you set up a new category, Quicken adds it to the list.

You can find the complete lists of Quicken home and business categories in online Help. In Quicken, press F1, click Search, type "home categories" or "business categories," and press Enter.

When you first start Quicken, you can choose to include Quicken's preset business categories as well as home categories. If you use the preset lists, Quicken gives you a head start with categorizing your income and expenses by providing a list of common home or business categories.

You can set up your category names before you enter transactions, or you can set them up as you enter transactions. Whenever you type a new category name in a transaction, Quicken sets up the new category and adds it to the list.

You can set up all your categories on one level or in a hierarchy with parent categories and subcategories. Subcategories offer an additional level of detail. You can choose to use one category called "Utilities" for all your utility transactions, or use subcategories under "Utilities" called "Gas and Electricity," "Trash," and "Water."

To see how Quicken uses categories in reports, graphs, and budgets, review the sample category report on page 164, the income and expense graph on page 203, and the budget on page 239.

The organization of your categories affects the organization of your budget and many reports and graphs. If you have many subcategories, they will appear in your budget and in reports, but they will be rolled up into the main categories in graphs.

Or press Ctrl+C

1 **From the Lists menu, choose Category & Transfer.**

Income categories appear first, followed by expense categories and transfers.

Subcategories are indented under their parent categories.

Account names are included in this list because if a register is open, you can double-click an account name to create an automatic transfer between the open account and the one you click. Quicken can't categorize a transfer transaction. See "Transferring money between accounts" on page 22 for more information.

Click Super to set up supercategories and assign categories to them. See "Using supercategories" on page 14 for details.

To print this list, press Ctrl+P.

The investment income and expense categories, which all begin with an underline (for example, _DivInc), appear on your category list automatically as soon as you add an investment account. See "Creating a regular investment account" on page 126.

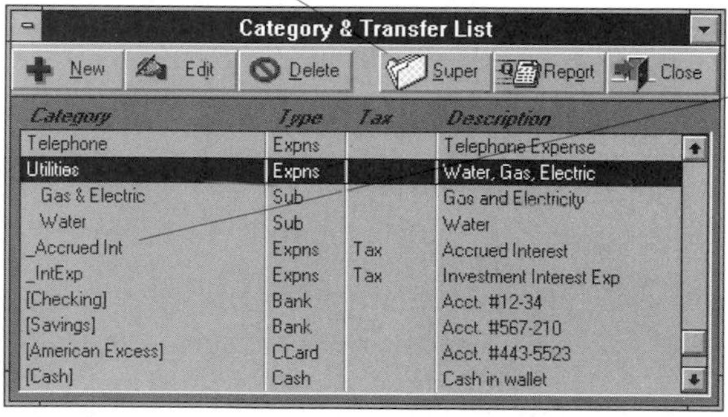

Category & Transfer List
New
Edit
Delete
Super
Report
Close
Category
Type
Tax
Description
Telephone
Expns
Telephone Expense
Utilities
Expns
Water, Gas, Electric
Gas & Electric
Sub
Gas and Electricity
Water
Sub
Water
_Accrued Int
Expns
Tax
Accrued Interest
_IntExp
Expns
Tax
Investment Interest Exp
[Checking]
Bank
Acct. #12-34
[Savings]
Bank
Acct. #567-210
[American Excess]
CCard
Acct. #443-5523
[Cash]
Cash
Cash in wallet

* Canadian users: The standard home category list includes GST and PST categories for tracking amounts you spend towards these taxes. To track these taxes as part of your business, set up liability accounts instead of using categories, as described in the separate booklet included in your package.

Or press Ctrl+N

2 **Click New.**

3 **Complete the Set Up Category window, and then click OK.**

Click a category type:

For a category, click income or expense.

For a subcategory, click Subcategory Of and enter the name of the subcategory in the Name box. Then enter the name of the parent category in the Subcategory of box. The subcategory takes on the income or expense type of its parent.

(Optional) Click here to use this category to track a particular type of tax information.

Enter a name for the new category or subcategory. You can use up to 15 characters.

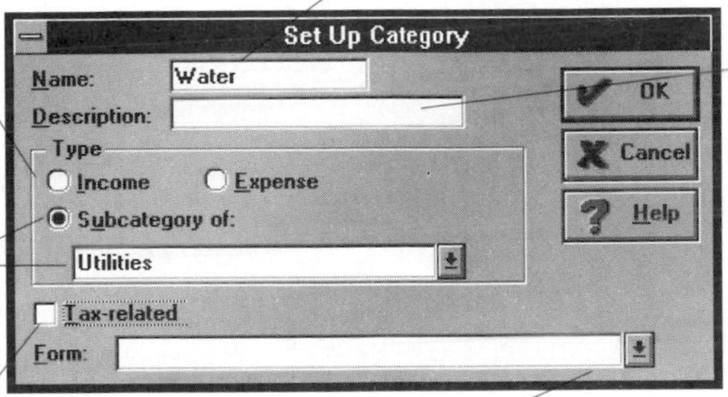

(Optional) Enter a description of the category or subcategory here. You can use up to 25 characters.

If you see the Form box, select a tax schedule line item for this tax category. (The Form drop-down list appears if the option for using tax schedules is turned on. See "Customizing other Quicken features" on page 297.)

Changing and deleting categories

When you change a category name, Quicken automatically changes all transactions categorized with the old name.

Changing categories

Or press Ctrl+C

1 **From the Lists menu, choose Category & Transfer.**

2 **Select the category you want to change.**

Or press Ctrl+E

3 **Click Edit.**

The Edit Category window appears.

Windows tip
Replace text in a box by holding the left mouse button down and dragging the insertion point through the text to be replaced. Then enter the new text.

4 **Make any changes you want to the category information.**

5 **Click OK.**

Deleting categories

Or press Ctrl+C

1 **From the Lists menu, choose Category & Transfer.**

2 **Select the category you want to delete.**

Or press Ctrl+D

3 **Click Delete, and then click OK.**

Quicken deletes the category from the list and erases it from the Category field of any transactions to which it has been assigned. Don't delete a category name as a step in changing it. See "Moving and merging categories in the list" on page 12 instead.

When you delete a subcategory, Quicken deletes it from the category list and reassigns its transactions to the parent category.

Quicken won't let you delete a category that has subcategories. You need to promote the subcategories to categories or move the subcategories under another category before you can delete the category.

Moving and merging categories in the list

After working with Quicken a while, you may want to move categories. You can change a category to a subcategory, change a subcategory to a category, or move a subcategory to another category.

When you change the name or level of a category, Quicken automatically changes the name in each of the transactions that you've categorized with the old name.

Changing (demoting) a category into a subcategory

1. **From the Lists menu, choose Category & Transfer.**

   Or press Ctrl+C

2. **Select the category you want to demote.**
3. **Click Edit.**

   Or press Ctrl+E

4. **Click Subcategory Of.**
5. **In the Subcategory Of list, select the name of the parent category.**

   Windows tip
   To pull down the list, click the underscored down arrow. Then click the Down Arrow in the scroll bar to move down the list. Click the parent category you want to use from the list.

6. **Click OK.**

Changing (promoting) a subcategory into a category

1. **From the Lists menu, choose Category & Transfer.**

   Or press Ctrl+C

2. **Select the subcategory you want to promote.**
3. **Click Edit.**

   Or press Ctrl+E

   The Edit Category window appears.
4. **Click Income or Expense.**
5. **Click OK.**

Moving a subcategory from one category to another

1. **From the Lists menu, choose Category & Transfer.**
2. **Select the subcategory you want to move.**
3. **Click Edit.**

   Or press Ctrl+E

   The Edit Category window appears.
4. **In the Subcategory Of list, select the name of the category or subcategory to which you want to assign the selected subcategory.**

   Windows tip
   To pull down the list, click the underscored Down Arrow. Then click the Down Arrow in the scroll bar to move down the list. Click the category or subcategory you want in the list.

5. **Click OK.**

Merging two categories

If you start off using two similar categories, and then later decide you only need one of them, don't just delete one. Instead, merge the categories.

For example, this Category & Transfer list has categories called "Home Repair" and "Household." To merge these categories into one category called "Household," first change "Home Repair" into a subcategory under "Household."

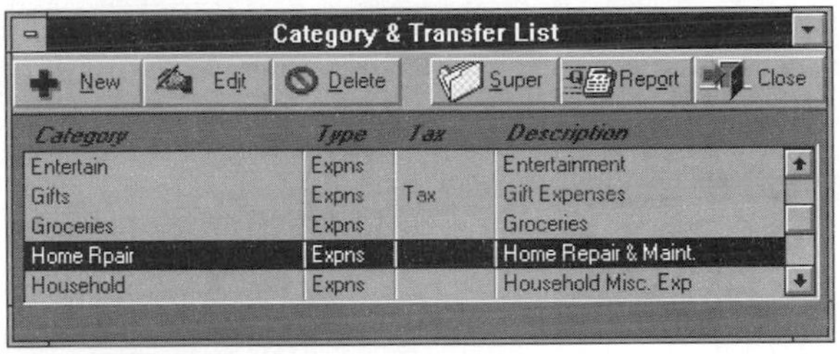

1 **Change the category you don't want into a subcategory of the category you want to keep.**

See "Changing (demoting) a category into a subcategory" on page 12.

Now "Home Repair" is a subcategory of "Household."

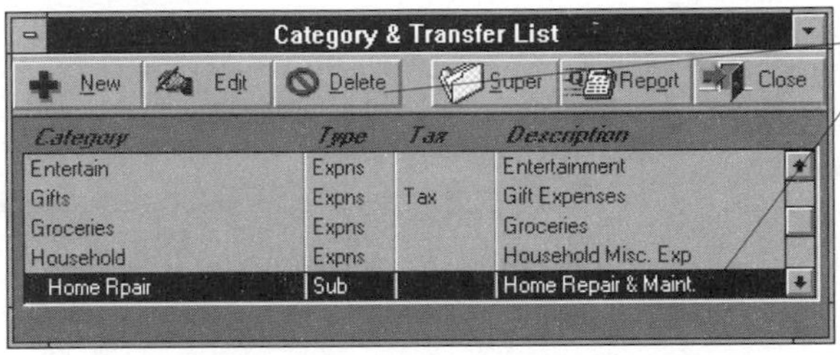

Next, delete the subcategory.

2 **Select the subcategory name and click Delete.**

3 **Click Yes to confirm the merge.**

Quicken deletes the subcategory name from the category list and reassigns its transactions to the parent category.

Reporting on transactions with a specific category

You can create a QuickReport that lists all transactions in the current file that use a single category. Use a QuickReport to:

- List your expenses in a certain area. You can see what you have spent on car maintenance this year, or what your mortgage interest payments amount to.
- Check whether you're using a category at all, to help you decide whether you should delete the category.

See "Creating a report" on page 183.

For a detailed report on your spending in all your categories, create an itemized category report instead. The Category QuickReport is a small section of an itemized category report, and it's quicker to create when you are interested in only one category.

Or press Ctrl+C

1 **Display the Category & Transfer list (from the Lists menu, choose Category & Transfer).**

2 **Select the category you want to report on.**

3 **Click Report.**

4 To close the report, click Close on the report button bar.

Initially, the report covers all transactions in your Quicken file, but you can limit the date range by customizing the report. To do this, click the Customize button, and see "Changing report settings" on page 185.

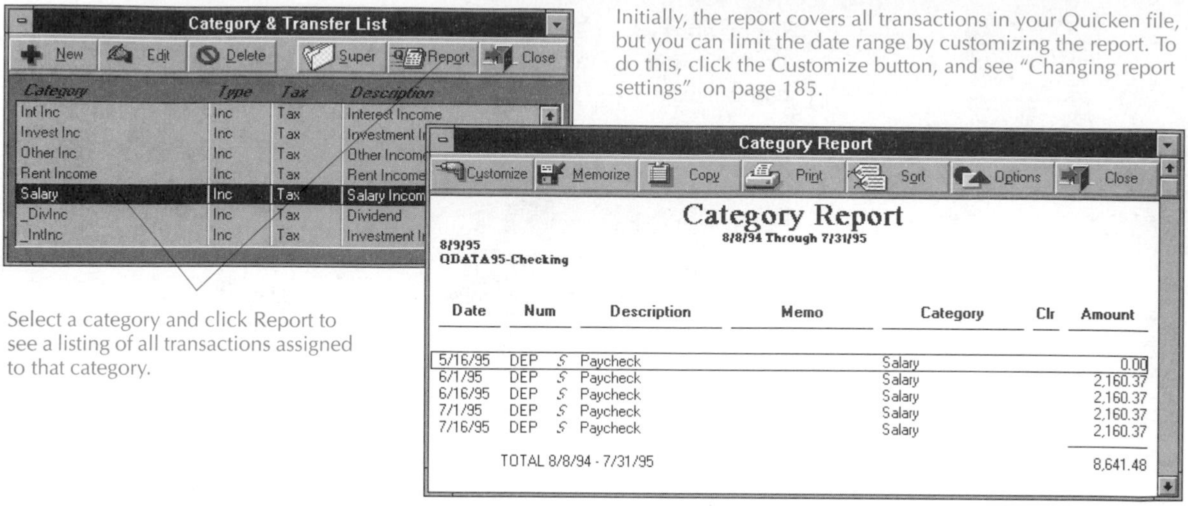

Select a category and click Report to see a listing of all transactions assigned to that category.

Using supercategories

See Chapter 21, *Creating a budget or savings goal,* on page 235.

Quicken lets you group categories together into supercategories which you can use in your budget, and in budget reports, to get a more simplified picture of your budget.

You can set up supercategories from the Category & Transfer list, or from Budgeting.

Setting up supercategories

Or press Ctrl+C

1 Display the Category & Transfer list (from the Lists menu, choose Category & Transfer).

2 Click Super.

To assign a category to a supercategory, select a category, select a supercategory, and then click Assign.

Click Print to print the list of categories and their supercategory assignments.

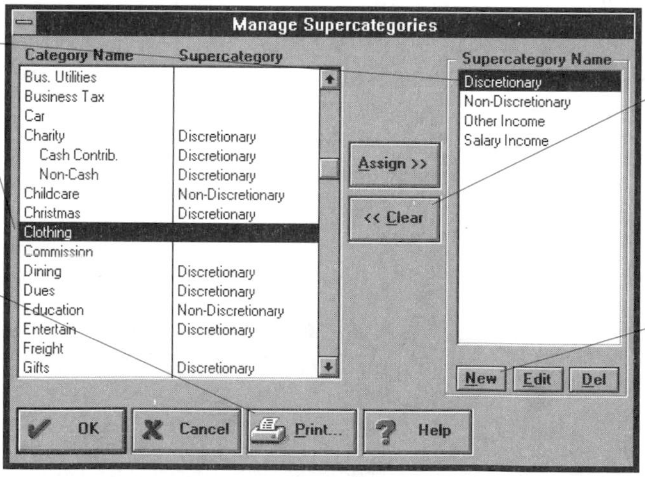

Click Clear to clear the supercategory assignment for the selected category.

Click New to create a new supercategory, click Edit to change the selected item, or click Del to delete the selected item.

3 Click New to set up a new supercategory.

Enter a name for the supercategory and then click OK.

4 **In the Manage Supercategories window, assign categories to supercategories.**

Select a category or categories in the left-hand list, select a supercategory in the right-hand list, and then click Assign to assign those categories to that supercategory.

5 **Click Done.**

Now you can use these supercategories in your budget and budget reports.

Using classes

You can use classes to specify where, to what, or to whom your transactions apply. Classes don't replace categories. Rather, classes complement categories by adding a second dimension to reports, graphs, and budgets.

You can classify transactions, categorize them, or both.

Use classes to:

- Use your personal checking account for business and personal expenses. Leave your personal transactions unclassified, but assign the class name Business to business transactions.
- Manage properties. You can identify transactions by property name or address. That way, six different utility bills could be marked clearly as utility expenses applying to six different properties.
- Work with multiple clients. You can identify transactions by client name. Then you could report separately on the income and expenses related to each client.

Use classes to specify	Examples
Who the transaction is for	Your clients Your salespeople (for tracking commissions) You or your spouse
Where the transaction applies	Sales regions: East vs. West Property names: Oak St. vs. North Ave.
What the transaction is for	Security names (in an asset account) Job or project names (for job costing) Business use (for tax reasons)

Using classes for your small business
If you have a small business, using classes can help you bill expenses to clients, track actual costs versus estimates, segregate income and expenses by rental property, and track expenses by job, project, or department. If you set up and use classes for each property, client, job, department, and so forth, you can create a report showing your income and expenses for each individual class. More information about using Quicken for small business finances is in the *Quicken Business User's Guide*.

Call Intuit to purchase this guide. See "Quicken Business User's Guide" on page 320.

Before you start using classes, think about what kind of reports you might need. There may be times when you want reports based on categories, other times when you want reports based on classes, and other times when you want a report that includes both category and class information. Because people use classes in so many different ways, Quicken doesn't provide a preset list of classes.

Setting up classes and subclasses

You can set up class names before you enter transactions, or as you enter them. When you type a new class name in a transaction, Quicken lets you set up the class "on the fly."

Quicken displays class names in the Class List, which is shared by all the accounts in the file. You can't change a class into a category, or vice versa.

Using subclasses lets you further refine your reports. To use subclasses, set up a class name for each item you want to function as a subclass. Then, when you are classifying a transaction in the register, enter a colon (:) to separate the main class from the subclass.

Or press Ctrl+L

1 **From the Lists menu, choose Class List.**

If this is the first time you're setting up classes, this list is empty. Click New to set up a new class.

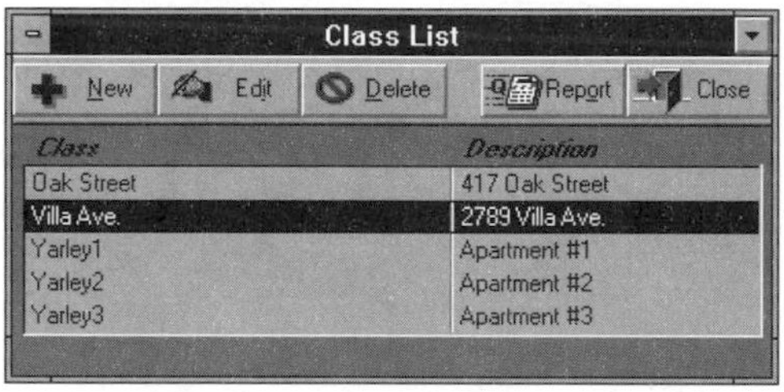

You can print the Class list. Open the list and then press Ctrl+P.

The property classes in this list make it possible to track rental income and expenses by property.

Or press Ctrl+N

2 **To set up a new class, click New.**

To view the information for an existing class, select it and click Edit.

Use up to 15 characters to enter a class name.

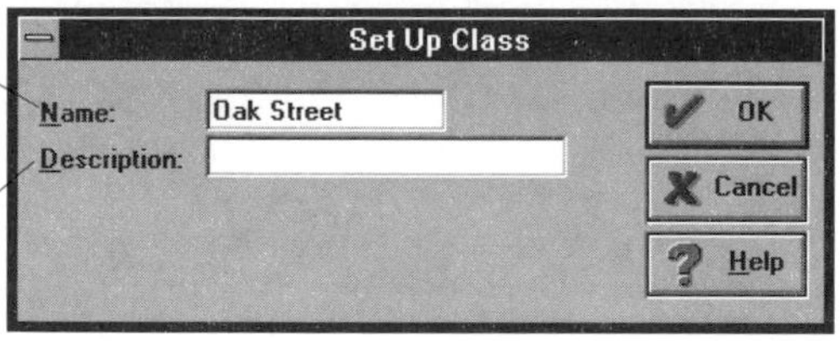

Use up to 25 characters to enter a description.

3 **Enter a name in the Class box.**

4 **(Optional) Enter a description of the class in the Description box.**

Windows tip
Place the insertion point in the Description box by clicking the box or by pressing Tab. Then start typing.

5 **Click OK.**

Reporting on transactions with a specific class

You can create a QuickReport on a specific class just as you can for a category. With the class selected in the Class list, click Report. Quicken creates a QuickReport that lists all transactions, in all accounts in the current file, that use the selected class.

3 Using the register

About the register

You're familiar with using a paper check register to record transactions in your checking account. Fill in Quicken's register much as you fill in a paper check register to keep a record of all activity that affects your bank account balance.

Each Quicken account has a register associated with it. This chapter describes using the check register for bank accounts. The basic steps for working in all Quicken registers are the same.

Adding transactions to the register

After you set up a Quicken bank account, you are in the Register window. Use the register to record all transactions, except checks you plan to print with Quicken.

If you plan to print checks with Quicken, enter them at the Write Checks window, not the Register window. When you create a check in the Write Checks window, Quicken automatically adds that transaction to your register. (See Chapter 6, *Writing and printing checks*, on page 63.)

Transactions are any items that affect the balance in your account:

- Checks written by hand
- ATM (automatic teller machine) or debit transactions
- Deposits
- Checking account fees and interest
- Bank service charges
- Electronic transactions

Registr

1 **From the Account list, select the bank account you want to work with and click Open.**

If you are already working with the account, choose Use Register from the Activities menu, or click the Register icon on the iconbar. Quicken opens the register for the account you used last and places the insertion point in an empty transaction at the end of the register.

2 **Enter information about the new transaction into each field.**

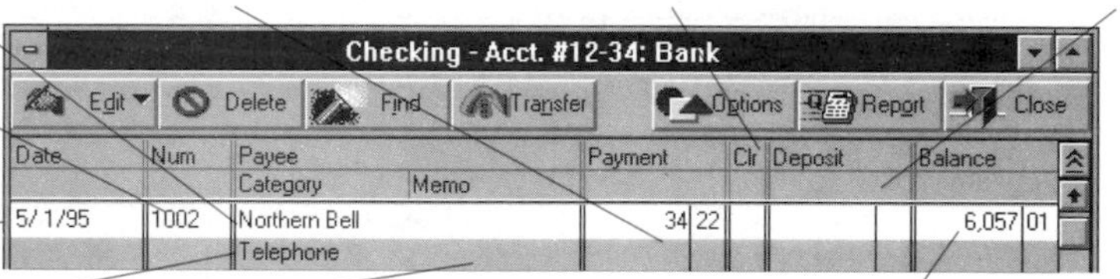
Person or institution to whom the payment is made.
Amount of the check or payment.
The Clr column indicates the cleared status of each transaction at the bank if you use Quicken to reconcile. Leave it blank for now.
Amount of a deposit.
Number of a printed check, handwritten check, or type of transaction.
The transaction date.
Checking - Acct. #12-34: Bank
Edit
Delete
Find
Transfer
Options
Report
Close
Date
Num
Payee
Category
Memo
Payment
Clr
Deposit
Balance
5/ 1/95
1002
Northern Bell
Telephone
34 22
6,057 01
Enter categories to track your income and expenses. See "Assigning categories to transactions" on page 21.
Enter a memo to record more information than the payee or category provides.
You can't edit the Balance column. Quicken automatically calculates your new balance each time you record a transaction.

To press Enter instead of Tab to move from field to field, see "Changing other register options" on page 40.

A *field* is a space for a particular item of information. *Enter* means type the information in a field and then press Tab. The insertion point moves forward to the next field.

Quicken offers shortcuts to make it easy to enter information. These shortcuts are described on page 19.

Help

Press F1 or click Help if you need more help entering information.

3 **Click Record to save the transaction as a permanent part of your records.**

The buttons in the register make it easy to enter transactions:

Insert, void, memorize, copy, or paste a transaction, or go to a transfer or to a specific date.

Delete the selected transaction.

Find a specific transaction or transactions. See page 31.

Transfer money between accounts. See page 22.

Change register options.

Report on the register. See page 33.

If you've entered postdated transactions, this bold line separates transactions dated on or before today from those that are dated after today.

Click one of these buttons to go to that account. To rearrange them, drag and drop with the mouse.

If you make a mistake while entering or editing a transaction, revert to the way it was before you started to change it.

Save a transaction.

Assign more than one category to a transaction. See "Splitting transactions" on page 26.

See more transactions in the register. See "Condensing the register" on page 30.

Hide or display the button bar.

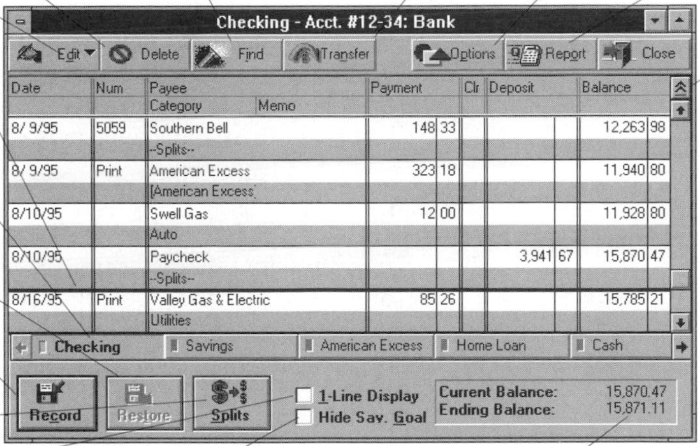

If you've set up a savings goal, display your actual bank balance by hiding transfers to savings goals.

The Ending Balance is the balance of all entered transactions. If you postdate transactions, Quicken also displays a Current Balance, which is based on all transactions entered through today only.

Each time you record a transaction, Quicken sorts it in the register first by date and then by check number and recalculates all subsequent balances. For example, suppose the date at the end of the check register is 5/27/94 and you want to enter an ATM withdrawal made on 5/10/94. When you enter the transaction at the end of the check register and click Record, Quicken automatically moves the transaction to where it belongs chronologically.

Using drop-down lists and QuickFill for fast entry

If the lists don't drop down automatically, click the drop-down button to see them. If you don't see the drop-down button, or to make the lists drop down automatically, see "Changing the way QuickFill works" on page 38 and select the Drop Down Lists Automatically checkbox.

Quicken provides two ways for you to enter transactions quickly:

Drop-down lists: When you tab to the Num, Payee, or Category field, a list drops down that you can select from. Click an item from the list to enter it in the register field.

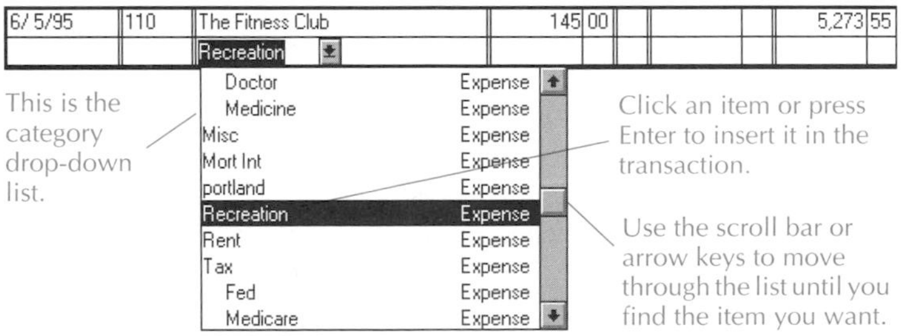

This is the category drop-down list.

Click an item or press Enter to insert it in the transaction.

Use the scroll bar or arrow keys to move through the list until you find the item you want.

If you don't want the lists to drop down automatically, you can turn off the feature.

Or press Alt+Down Arrow, or click the right mouse button

If a list isn't dropped down, you can still select an entry from the list by using the + and – keys on the numeric keypad (or Ctrl+Up Arrow or Ctrl+Down Arrow) to move through the list entries. Or, drop down the list manually by clicking the drop-down button. Click the button a second time to make the list disappear.

QuickFill: Begin typing the item's name. QuickFill completes the entire item as you type the beginning letters. Press Tab to accept it and move on to the next field. For example, if you type ch in the Category field, Quicken enters Charity.

If you type a category name that isn't in the category list, Quicken sets up a new category.

| 12/ 1/95 | 5061 | World Children | | 125 | 00 | | | Deposit | | | | |
| | | Charity | ± | Memo | | | | | | | | |

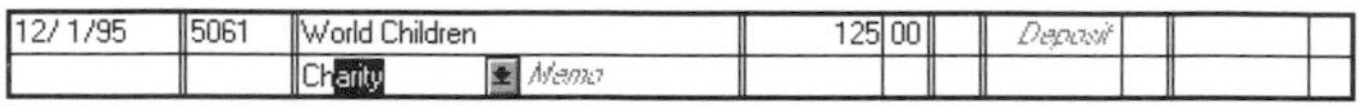

If the first few characters you type match the beginning of more than one category name, QuickFill enters the first category that begins with the letters you typed. Keep typing until QuickFill enters the correct category. Then press Tab to accept the entry.

QuickFill also fills in subcategory names or classes if you use these.

Typing the letter C after the colon makes QuickFill enter the subcategory name "Cable." Press Ctrl+Up Arrow or Ctrl+Down Arrow to move through the list of subcategories under Utilities.

| 6/15/95 | 113 | SouthVision Cable | | 18 | 55 | | | | 4,979 | 66 |
| | | Utilities:Cable | ± | | | | | | | |

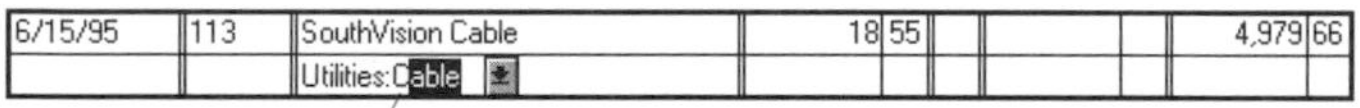

Using QuickFill in the Payee field

In the Payee field, QuickFill does even more for you. You'll notice that the payee drop-down list contains complete transaction details. As you type the name of a payee, QuickFill can complete the whole transaction. (You won't see this work until you already have a few transactions in the register.) For example, if you've just eaten at the Blue Sky Cafe for the second time this month, when you start to type "Blue..." in the Payee field, Quicken selects the previous transaction from the drop-down list. Press Tab to duplicate the whole transaction, and then change the amount if necessary.

Quicken displays the details from a previous similar transaction.

		Blue Sky Cafe	-25.00	Dining	With Denise		
8/ 7/95	Num	Blue Sky Cafe	±	Payment		Deposit	
		Category	Memo				

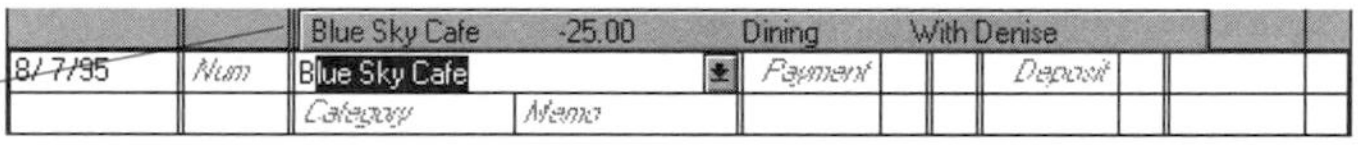

Press Tab to copy the details into the new transaction.

| 8/ 7/95 | Num | Blue Sky Cafe | | 25.00 ■ | | Deposit | |
| | | Dining | With Denise | | | | |

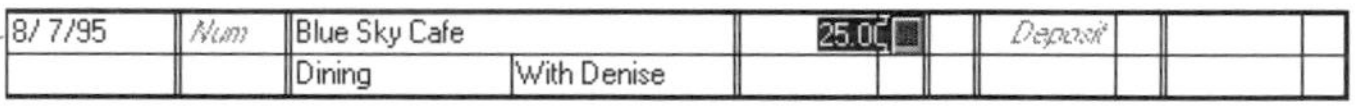

QuickFill also recalls information in the Num field. If the transaction is memorized with a check number, QuickFill recalls it with the next available check number. If the transaction is memorized with other information in the Num field, QuickFill recalls that information if it is appropriate to the account.

See "Setting up an account to use CheckFree" on page 278.

For example, if the transaction is memorized with XMIT in the Num field, and you recall the transaction in an account that is not enabled for CheckFree, QuickFill does not recall any information in the Num field.

Chapter 3

Managing the items in your drop-down lists

Payee field: The Payee drop-down list contains your memorized transactions.

See "Using the Memorized Transaction List" on page 44.

If the list of memorized transactions is too big, manage it from the Memorized Transactions list.

Num field: To add your own items to the Num drop-down list, click in the Num field with the right mouse button, and then click <New>. To delete an item you've added, click <Edit> and then Delete. You can't delete Quicken's default items.

Category field: To change your list of categories, choose Category& Transfer from the Lists menu, as described on page 10.

Special drop-down lists

The Date, Payment, and Deposit fields have special drop-down features. Just click the drop-down button to use them:

You can also press these keys:

+	next day
-	previous day
t	Today
m	beginning of the Month
h	end of the montH
y	beginning of the Year
r	end of the yeaR

Click on the date drop-down button to display a calendar. Select a date by clicking on it.

Click these arrows to display the previous or next month.

To calculate an amount, click on the Payment or Deposit drop-down button to display a calculator. You can add up several bills this way.

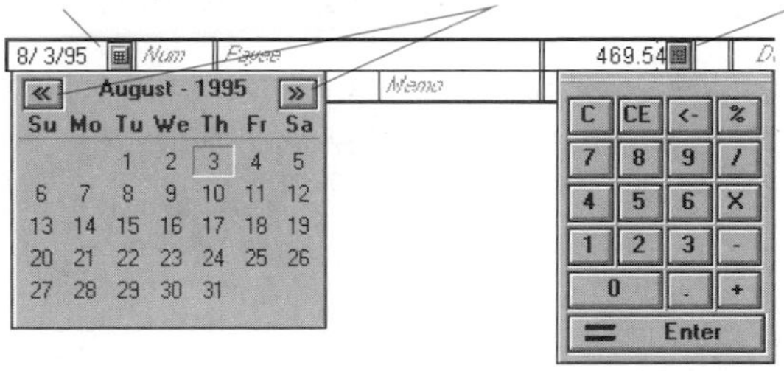

Click the calculator buttons or use the numeric part of your keyboard as usual to calculate an amount.

Assigning categories to transactions

Use categories to identify exactly where your income comes from and where your expenses go. When you categorize your transactions, Quicken can create reports and graphs about your income and expenses, sorted by category. (See "About categories" on page 9.)

See "Setting up categories and subcategories" on page 10.

Quicken provides standard home and business categories for you to use, but you can modify them or create your own in the Category & Transfer list.

To enter a category name in the Category field:

- Select it from the Category drop-down list in the register.
- Type it in the Category field. QuickFill completes the category name. If you type a category name that isn't in the category list, Quicken lets you set up a new category.
- Select it from the Category & Transfer List. From the Lists menu, choose Category & Transfer, and then double-click a category.

You can clear the Warn Before Recording Uncategorized Transactions checkbox as described in "Changing other register options" on page 40.

Quicken reminds you to enter a category whenever you attempt to record an uncategorized transaction. If you don't categorize transactions, Quicken labels these amounts "Other" in reports and "Uncategorized" in graphs. If you see "Other" in a report when you have assigned categories to all transactions, it could be because you sometimes add a subcategory for a particular category and sometimes don't.

See "Categorizing miscellaneous transactions" on page 36.

To find transactions that contain uncategorized amounts and assign categories to them, use Recategorize.

In addition to entering a category, you can use the Category field in the register for other types of entry:

Classes	With classes, you can define a transaction even more specifically than with a category alone. To decide whether classes can help you, see page 15.
Transfers	You can choose the name of another Quicken account from the Category & Transfer list to transfer money to that account. For example, you can withdraw money from your savings account and have Quicken automatically transfer the amount as a deposit to your checking account. Transfers are explained on this page.

Entering subcategories

To use subcategories to further break down the information in reports and graphs, enter the parent category, type a colon (:), and then enter the subcategory. For example, Utilities:Water.

Transferring money between accounts

Use transfers to record these and other common transactions:

- Movement of funds from a checking account to a savings account
- Cash advances from your credit card to your checking account
- Loan payments from a checking account into a liability account that tracks your loan balance

Recording a transfer transaction

You can enter transfer transactions in two ways: using the transfer form, or using the register.

To transfer money from one account to another, click the Transfer button from the register, complete the form, and then click OK.

Enter the amount of the transfer.

Enter an optional description.

Select the account you want to transfer money from.

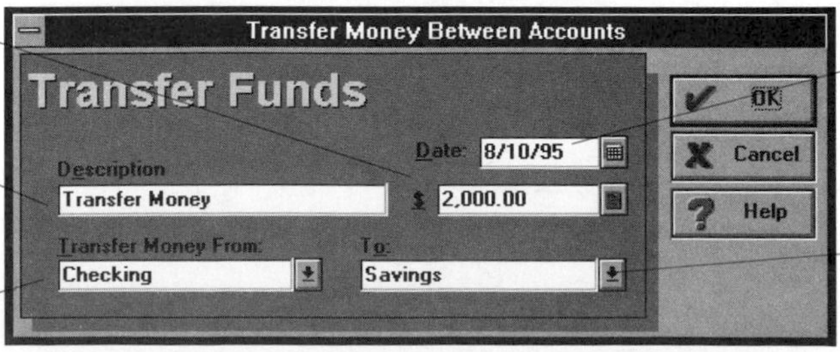

Enter the date of the transfer.

Select the account where you want the money to go.

Quicken enters the name of the transfer account in the Category field, and creates a parallel transaction in the other account.

For example, if you transfer $2000 from your checking account to your savings account, Quicken records this transaction in your checking account.

Note the square brackets around the transfer account name in the Category field.

Here's the corresponding transaction that Quicken records in Savings (the destination account).

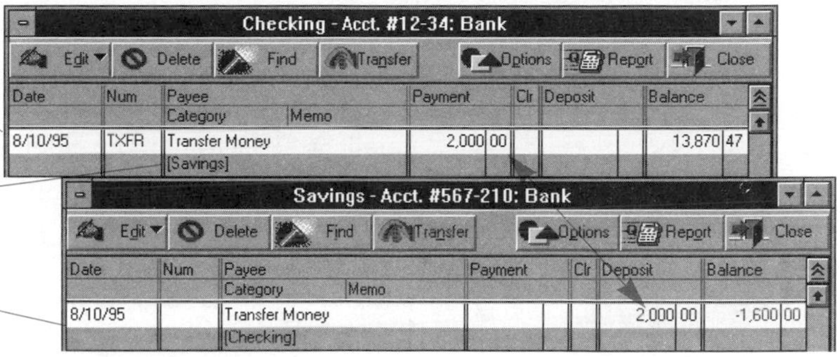

OR

To enter a transfer for part of the amount of a transaction, see page 24.

Record the transfer directly in the register:

1 **Start a new transaction in the Register or Write Checks window.**

Or select an existing transaction to change it into a transfer.

2 **Enter all the information for the transaction as usual, except in the Category field.**

3 **Go to the Category field. If you know the name of the account you want to transfer to, start typing it in the Category field.**

QuickFill enters the name of the account and puts brackets around it to show it's a transfer.

Or press Ctrl+C

If you're not sure of the name of the account you want to transfer to, click the drop-down button to display the list of categories. Scroll to the end of the list, where all account names are listed, and click the transfer account name to enter it in the Category field.

To enter a transfer, click the name of the destination account in the drop-down list to enter it in the Category field of the transaction.

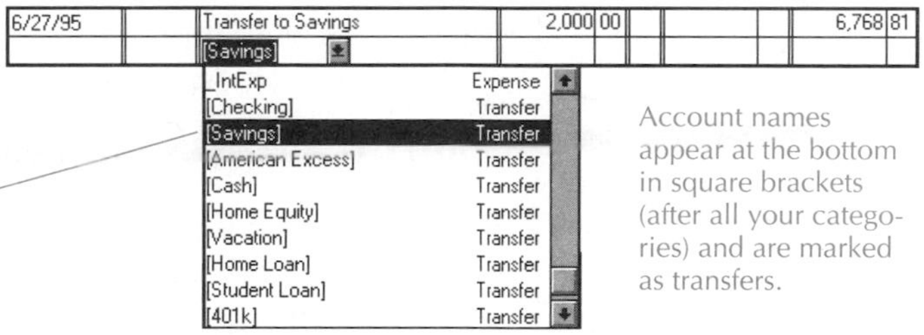

Account names appear at the bottom in square brackets (after all your categories) and are marked as transfers.

You can't include a transfer and a category in the same Category field. A transfer is simply a movement of funds between one account and another. For example, suppose you transfer $1,000 from your savings account to your checking account to cover household expenses. In the register of your savings account, you would enter [Checking] in the Category field.

You can, however, include class information with transfer information in the Category field. For example, if you pay for an antique table from a checking account and want to record the purchase in an asset account called Personal Assets, you would enter [Personal Assets]/Antiques in the Category field.

To read more about entering a mortgage payment, see Chapter 10, *Tracking loans and mortgages,* on page 105.

You can enter a transfer for part of the total amount of a transaction by using splits. For example, in a mortgage payment, the mortgage amount of the transaction is transferred to a liability account, and the mortgage interest is assigned to an expense category.

4 **Click Record to record the transfer transaction.**

Quicken records the check in your check register *and* creates a parallel transaction in the other account for that amount.

Transferring money to a savings goal

See "Creating a savings goal" on page 241 for more information.

You can set up savings goals to keep track of money you're saving for a particular purpose. Then, use transfers to contribute to goals from the register.

Click Transfer in the register. Then, select your savings goal in the To field, and enter the date and amount.

Changing a transaction that includes a transfer

When you change a transaction that includes a transfer, the transaction created by the transfer also changes:

- If you delete the transaction, Quicken deletes it from both accounts.
- If you change the date or amount of the transaction, the information changes in both accounts. But, if you change the transaction description, check number, memo, or cleared status, the information changes only in the current account.
- If you rename an account, Quicken updates every occurrence of the name in transfers.
- If a transfer was made in a split transaction, you can change it only from the original transaction. You can't change it from the account that received the transfer.

Going to a transfer transaction

If you are in a transaction that includes a transfer, you can go directly to the parallel transaction in another account. Use Go To Transfer to see the transaction created by a transfer. Use it also to make a change to a transfer that originated in a split transaction (you can change such transfers only in the split line item of the original transaction).

1 **In the Register window, select the transaction that includes the transfer information.**

(Or in the Write Checks window, display the check containing the transfer information.)

Or press Ctrl+X

2 **From the Edit menu, choose Go To Transfer.**

Quicken displays the register for the transfer account and selects the parallel transfer transaction.

If the transaction you are starting from is split and contains transfers to more than one account, you must click Splits first to open the split and click anywhere on the line containing the name of the transfer.

Assigning classes to transactions

In addition to using categories to organize your transactions, you can specify classes to further group the transactions. (See "Using classes" on page 15 for an introduction to classes.)

You can enter an existing class name in the Category field by choosing it from the Class list or by typing it after a category in the Category field. (You can also assign a class to a transaction without assigning a category to the transaction.)

Choosing a class from the Class list

1 **Click in the Category field of the transaction you want to classify. If you have already assigned a category to the transaction, click after the category name.**

Or press Ctrl+L

2 **From the Lists menu, choose Class.**

3 **Double-click the class name in the list to paste it after the category.**

Typing a class in the Category field

1 **Click in the Category field of the transaction you want to classify. If you have already assigned a category to the transaction, click after the category name.**

2 **Type a forward slash (/).**

3 **Begin typing the class name in the Category field and continue until QuickFill enters the correct class.**

As soon as you type a forward slash, Quicken recognizes that you are entering a class.

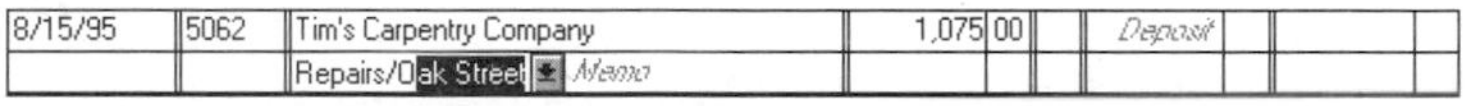

8/15/95
5062
Tim's Carpentry Company
1,075 00
Deposit
Repairs/Oak Street
Memo

In this example, the category is "Repairs" and the class is "Oak Street."

Entering subclasses

To use subclasses to further refine the information in reports, graphs, or budgets, enter a colon (:) after the class to separate the main class from the subclass: Repairs/Oak Street:Apt1.

Changing and deleting classes

See "Changing and deleting categories" on page 11.

Changing or deleting a class is the same as changing or deleting a category. The only difference is that you start by choosing Class from the Lists menu.

Splitting transactions

Sometimes you need to assign more than one category to a transaction. For example, a check to a department store might cover clothing, office supplies, and furnishings. This section describes how to "split" a transaction into different categories. You can also split a transaction with multiple transfers or multiple classes.

Entering a split transaction

1 **Select the transaction you want to split, or go to a new transaction.**

2 **Enter the total amount of the transaction in either the Payment or the Deposit field.**

If you don't know the total amount, leave the Amount field blank. Quicken totals the amount as you fill in the splits and displays it in the Splits Total field.

Or press Ctrl+S

3 **Click Splits.**

Quicken copies any information entered in the Category, Payment, or Deposit fields of the transaction to the first line of the split.

4 **If the first Category field of the split doesn't contain a category, enter a category.**

5 **(Optional) Enter a memo in the first Memo field.**

6 **In the first Amount field, enter the amount to be assigned to the first category.**

If an amount is already displayed, you can type right over it.

Quicken subtracts the amount entered from the total amount and displays the remainder in the next Amount field. In this way, Quicken helps keep track of the total amount of the transaction.

See "Setting up a split transaction using percentages" on page 46.

Instead of an amount, you can enter a percentage of the total amount that you entered in the register. For example, if you type 35% and press Tab, Quicken calculates 35% of the total and fills in the figure for you. (This works only if you entered an amount in the register before opening the Splits window.)

7 **Continue to add categories and amounts until you have added one categorized line for each part of the transaction.**

You can add up to 30 lines in one split transaction.

Use the Splits button bar to insert a line between two others, delete the selected line, or delete all lines.

Categorize each line of the split with any category you choose. As you enter amounts, Quicken prompts you to categorize any remainder by entering the remainder on the next free line.

The split transaction in this example is a mortgage payment, where part of the total is transferred to the liability account "Mortgage" and the rest is assigned to the Mortgage Interest expense category.

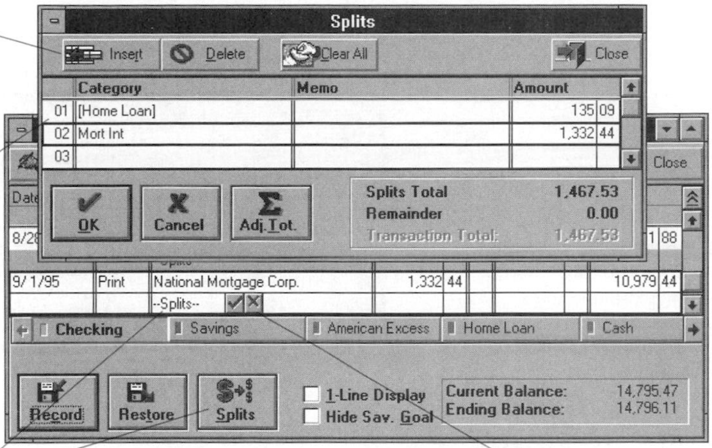

The word "Splits" in the Category field of the register indicates that more than one category is assigned to this transaction. Double-click the word "--Splits--" or click the Splits button to open the Splits window.

Click the checkmark to open the Splits window, or click the X to clear all splits.

8 **Click OK to close the Splits window.**

If you didn't enter an amount in the register (in the Payment or Deposit field) before opening the Splits window, Quicken asks if the total amount should be recorded as a payment or as a deposit.

Click Payment or Deposit and click OK.

The options depend on what type of account you are using. For example, in a credit card account you see the options Charge and Payment. In a cash account, you see Spend and Receive.

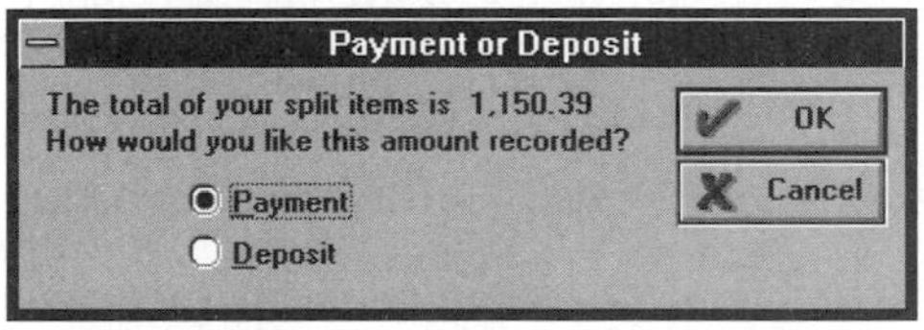

9 **Click Record to record the split transaction.**

If you entered an amount in the register before opening the Splits window, Quicken makes sure your split figures add up.

Making sure your split amounts add up

As you enter amounts in the Splits window, Quicken enters the remainder on the next free line. Sometimes the total of the amounts entered in the Splits window doesn't equal the figure entered in the register. For example, you might delete a Splits line, or change the total amount in the register. Quicken keeps a check on your figures at the bottom of the Splits window.

If your split amounts don't add up and you would prefer Quicken to change the total amount you entered in the register, click Adj Tot (Adjust Totals).

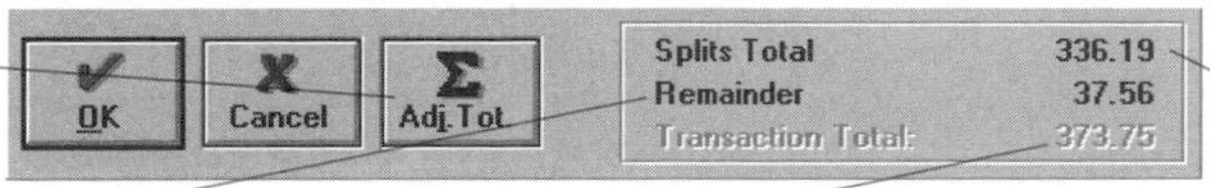

This is the total of the amounts you have entered in the Splits window.

This is the difference between what you have entered in the Splits window and what is entered in the register. You still have to account for this much.

The transaction total is what you entered in the register. You should enter split amounts that add up to this figure. (The figure is dimmed to show that it's a fixed amount.)

When your figures add up, the Remainder line shows 0.00.

If your split amounts don't add up to the register figure (the "transaction total") when you click OK, Quicken gives you two options:

If you see this window, choose one of the options by clicking it and click OK.

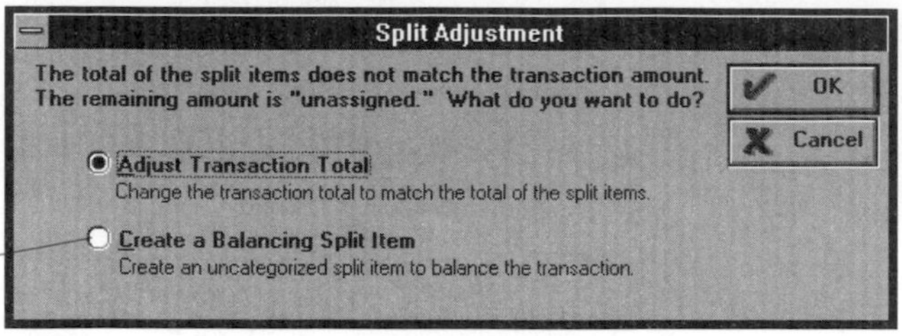

If you choose this option, you can reopen the Splits window later to categorize the extra amount.

Entering a paycheck deposit

You can use a split transaction to enter the details of your paycheck. Although you can just enter the net pay in the register if you prefer, entering your gross pay and all the deductions in the Splits window gives you more accurate reports and lets you see what taxes and other deductions you are paying. If you're going to import your Quicken data into a tax preparation program such as TurboTax for Windows, it helps to have the deductions already entered.

1 **In a blank transaction in your register, type** Paycheck **in the Payee field.**

2 **Click Splits.**

3 **Type** Salary **in the first Category field and enter the gross amount of the paycheck in the Amount field.**

The gross amount is your pay before any deductions are made.

4 **Enter the deductions from your pay on the following lines as negative amounts. Assign them to the expense categories Tax:Fed, Tax:State, and Tax:Soc Sec.**

Enter one deduction on each line. You may also have deductions for items such as 401(k) contributions, local withholding, medical insurance contributions, and state disability insurance. Set up new expense categories for these as needed.

See Chapter 11, *Tracking assets and liabilities,* on page 117.

See Chapter 12, *Tracking investments,* on page 121.

If you track your 401(k) in a separate asset or investment account, enter the account name instead of a category as shown in the next example. Quicken transfers the money to the other account, where it increases the account balance.

See "Editing account information" on page 5 for how to assign tax schedules to transfers.

See "Tax schedule" on page 166.

If you want Quicken to help you with your taxes, make sure you assign the tax schedule line item "W-2:Salary" to transfers into your 401(k) account. Then the tax schedule report will show the correct amount for your taxable income.

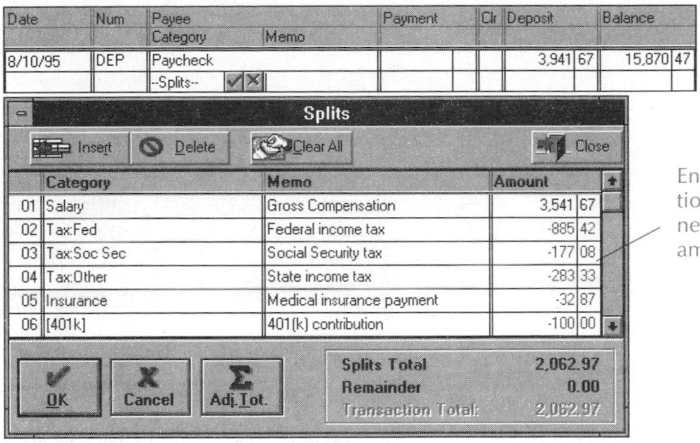

Enter deductions as negative amounts.

If your paycheck varies from one pay period to the next, you can set up the split without amounts, then memorize the transaction (as described in "Memorizing and recalling a transaction" on page 42). When you recall the transaction, open the split and fill in the amounts.

When you've entered all the deductions, check the amount in the Splits Total field at the bottom of the window. It should equal the net amount of your paycheck, which is the amount you actually receive.

5 **Click OK to close the split, and then click Record.**

See "Memorizing and recalling a transaction" on page 42.

6 **(Optional) Memorize your paycheck transaction and set it up as a scheduled transaction.**

Working with the register

You can review a register to find specific transactions at any time by scrolling through it. You can also condense the register to 1-Line display to view more transactions than you can see in 2-Line display.

Scrolling through the register

Use the scroll bar to move through the Register window and locate specific transactions quickly. When you drag the scroll box in the scroll bar, you'll see a date and check number appear and change as you scroll. These represent the date of the transaction, and its check number if appropriate, that will be at the top of the Register window when you release the scroll box.

Drag the scroll box in the scroll bar. The QuickScroll box appears and displays dates of specific transactions.

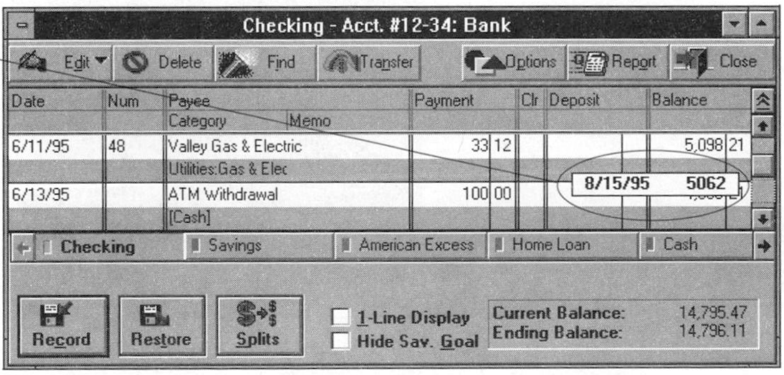

You can also use keyboard shortcuts to move around the register.

This keystroke	Moves to this part of the register
Up Arrow	Same field in the previous transaction
Down Arrow	Same field in the next transaction
Tab	Next field
Shift+Tab	Previous field
Home	Beginning of the field
Ctrl+Home	First transaction in the account
Home+Home	First field in the transaction
End	End of the field
Ctrl+End	Last transaction in the account
End+End	Last field in the transaction
Ctrl+Page Up	First transaction in the current month
Ctrl+Page Down	Last transaction in the current month
Page Up	Up one screen
Page Down	Down one screen

Condensing the register

When the register opens, it displays each transaction on two lines. You can double the number of transactions you can see at once in a window by clicking the 1-Line Display checkbox.

Use the normal 2-Line display when you're entering transactions. Then, click 1-Line Display to display and review more transactions in the same window.

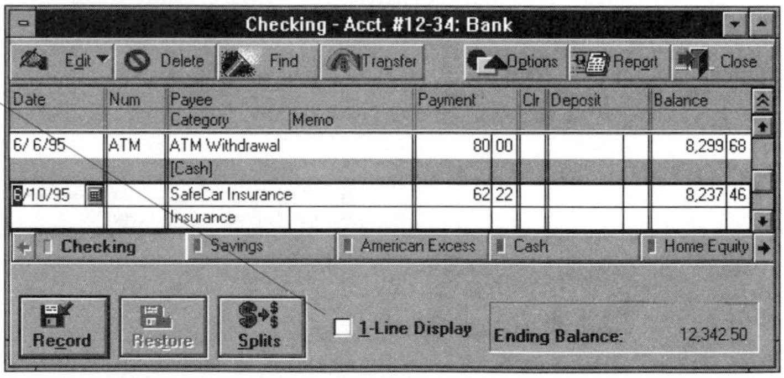

You can also enter a new transaction or edit existing transactions in 1-Line display.

Use 1-Line display when you want to scan many transactions quickly. Transactions in the register are condensed onto one line.

The active transaction remains selected when you switch the display.

The Memo field isn't displayed, so you can't enter (or see) any memos.

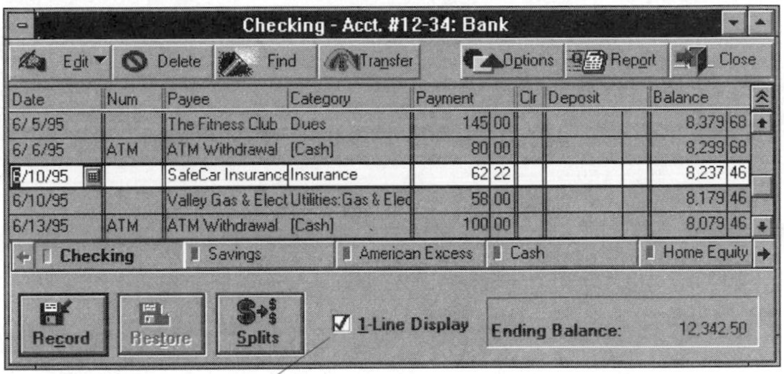

Clear 1-Line Display to display the transactions on two lines again.

Resizing the register

To resize a register to see more transactions, point to any corner of the Register window to change the mouse pointer into a two-headed arrow. Then drag the corner out to make the window larger.

To maximize a register (that is, to enlarge it to the maximum size that can be displayed), click the up button (▲) in the upper right corner of the Register window. To return it to its former size, click the double arrow button (⬍).

If you work with an account frequently, you can minimize it to an icon positioned at the bottom of the Quicken window. Click the down button (▼) in the upper right corner of the Register window. To display the register again, double-click the minimized icon.

Minimize accounts instead of closing them. The register remains open but is out of your way while you're working in another account.

Double-click minimized icons to restore the windows to their normal size.

Quicken remembers and opens the last ten registers from the last time you quit Quicken (whether the registers were minimized to icons or not).

Finding a specific transaction

Quicken's Find command locates specific transactions in the Register or Write Checks window. You can find a transaction even if you don't know all the information it contains.

You can find a check with a specific number or payee. In an investment account register, you can search for securities and actions.

1 **Click Find on the register button bar.**

Type some or all of the text or the exact amount to find here. (The text can be uppercase or lowercase and contain characters or numbers.) You can also use match characters, for example "B?A". See "Using matches to filter transactions" on page 192.

The field names in the Search drop-down list depend on the type of account you have open.

Click Find All to find all the transactions in all your accounts that match your criteria.

Select this checkbox to search backwards through the register. Otherwise, Quicken searches towards the end of the register.

2 **Type the word, phrase, or amount you want to find in the Find box.**

3 **(Optional) Choose a field name from the Search drop-down list.**

You can search all fields for the text or amount you want to find. If you know which field contains the text or amount, you can speed up the search by looking only in that field.

Press F1 for details about the choices in the Match If drop-down list.

4 **(Optional) Choose a search criterion from the Match If drop-down list.**

5 **(Optional) Clear the Search Backwards checkbox to search from the beginning of the register down instead of from the bottom up.**

6 **Click Find to begin the search.**

Quicken selects the first match it finds, or tells you it can't find one.

Or, click Find All to generate a list of all transactions from all your accounts that match.

Windows Tip
Close the window by double-clicking the Control-menu box in the upper left corner of the window.

7 **To continue finding items, continue to click Find.**

If you are finished with the search, close the Find window.

Quicken stops searching when it reaches the last transaction in the register (or the first transaction for backward searches) and asks whether you want to continue the search from the beginning of the register or from the end of the register. Click Yes or No.

Finding and replacing items

1 **From the Edit menu, choose Find/Replace.**

2 **Enter Find information and then click Find All.**

3 **Mark the transactions you want to replace.**

4 **Select a field from the Replace drop-down list and enter new information in the With field.**

5 **Click Replace to replace the field you chose with the new information in the marked transactions.**

To replace the Category or Amount field in a split transaction, you must first select Show Matches in Splits, and then select the matching split item.

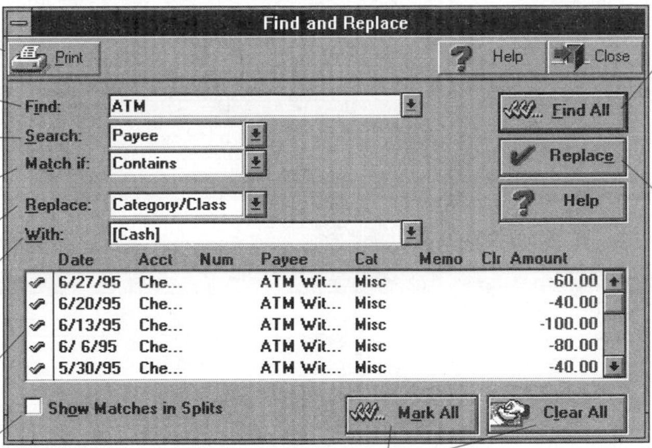

Click Print to print the list of found transactions.

Enter what you want to find here.

Select a field to search.

(Optional) Select a search criterion from the Match If drop-down list.

Select a field to replace.

Enter the new information here. (This field is not available until you click Find All.

Mark transactions by clicking on them.

Click this checkbox to show or hide splits.

Click Find All to search the registers again.

Click Replace to replace the Replace field in the marked transactions with the new information.

Use these buttons to mark or clear all the displayed transactions.

Reporting on a payee

Quicken can show a quick listing of all transactions in your register with a specific payee. For example, you can view all payments to a car repair station. Or you can check how much your phone bills are costing this year.

1 **Select a transaction containing the payee you want to report on.**

2 **Click Report on the register button bar.**

The report covers the current year up to today. To see transactions for past years, customize the report date range. Or select a transaction from the earlier year and click Report—the report then covers transactions from the start of the selected year up to today.

See "Changing report settings" on page 185.

(If you select a postdated transaction, the report covers transactions up to the end of the year.)

3 **To close the report and return to the register, click Close.**

Select any transaction with the payee to report on, and click Report.

The payee report lists all the transactions in your register containing the selected payee.

To go to a transaction listed in the report, double-click on the transaction. (This is called QuickZoom.)

The report spans the current year up to today. You can change the starting and ending dates or any other aspect of the report by customizing it. See "Changing report settings" on page 185.

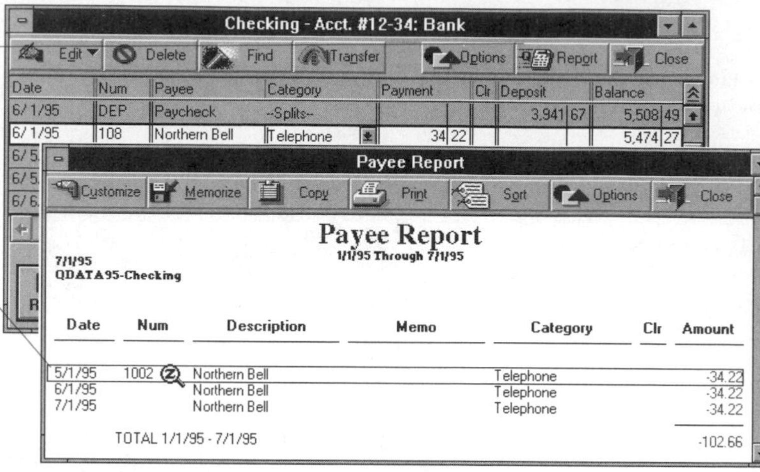

To get a report of the entire register (for all years), select the blank transaction at the end of the register and click Report.

See "Reporting on transactions with a specific category" on page 13.

You can also create a list of all transactions, in all your accounts, that use a specific category. To do this, select a category from the Category & Transfer list and click Report.

Revising transactions

This section explains how to correct mistakes, recategorize transactions, and void and delete transactions. When you finish recording changes to transactions, Quicken recalculates all subsequent balances if necessary.

Correcting mistakes

Or press Alt+Backspace

To correct a single mistake you make while you are editing a field, choose Undo from the Edit menu on the main menu bar.

To restore an entire transaction to the way it was before you started to change it, click Restore at the bottom of the window.

You can change this option: see "Changing other register options" on page 40.

When you leave a transaction, Quicken asks you to confirm any changes you made and then saves them.

See "Having Quicken adjust for differences" on page 90.

The only item in the register you can't edit is the Balance column. If you need to change the balance during reconciliation, you must add a payment or deposit as an adjustment in the register or have Quicken adjust the difference for you.

Changing a reconciled transaction affects future reconciliations. Quicken lets you know if you are about to change a reconciled transaction and asks you to confirm the change.

Your ability to change transactions after they are entered or even reconciled gives you complete control of your finances. However, if you want to protect your data from accidental or unauthorized changes, Quicken has two kinds of passwords:

See "Setting up a file password" on page 307.

- A file password requires a password before opening a file.

See "Setting up a transaction password" on page 308.

- A transaction password protects transactions prior to a certain date.

Voiding a transaction

Void a transaction instead of deleting it when you want to keep a complete record of each numbered check.

See "Stopping electronic payments" on page 289.

Caution if you use CheckFree:
Don't void an electronic payment. If you do, Quicken can't get the confirmation number it needs to stop the payment or transmit an inquiry about its status to CheckFree. Use Quicken's Stop Payment command instead.

When Quicken voids a transaction, it:

- Inserts the word *void* before the payee name.
- Marks the transaction as reconciled with an **x**, so it doesn't interfere with reconciling.
- Removes the dollar amount from the transaction and splits.

1 **Select the check or other transaction you want to void.**

If you wrote the check by hand and haven't yet entered it in the check register, enter the date and check number in a new transaction before selecting the transaction.

Or press Ctrl+V

2 **From the Edit menu, choose Void Transaction.**

3 **Click Record to record the transaction.**

Deleting a transaction

See "Setting up a transaction password" on page 308.

Once you delete a transaction and confirm the deletion, Quicken can't recover it. Be sure you really want to delete a transaction before doing so. To protect previous transactions from accidental change or deletion, assign a transaction password to them.

1 **Select the transaction you want to delete.**

Or press Ctrl+D

2 **Click Delete on the register button bar.**

Quicken asks "Delete the Current Transaction?"

3 **Click Yes to delete the transaction.**

Quicken removes the transaction from the register and recalculates all subsequent balances. If the transaction included a transfer, Quicken also deletes it from the other account.

Categorizing miscellaneous transactions

1 **From the Activities menu, choose Recategorize.**

2 **Leave the Search Category field blank and then click Find All.**

Quicken displays a list of uncategorized transactions.

Enter a replacement category for the selected transactions here.

Click on transactions to select them, or click Mark All or Clear All to mark or clear all transactions.

Click here to show or hide splits.

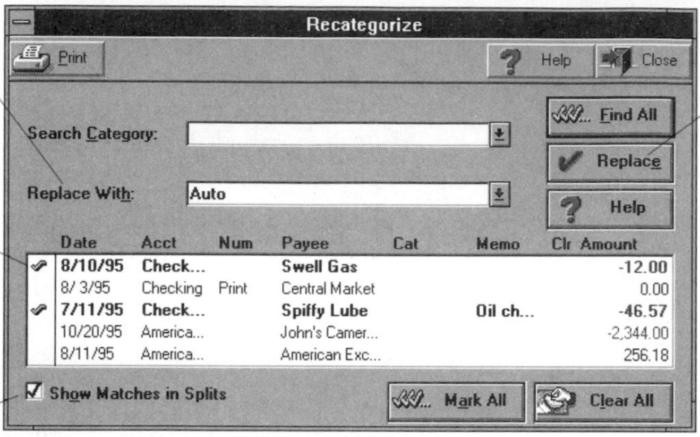

Click Replace to replace the category field of the selected transactions with the new category.

3 **Complete the Recategorize window and then click Replace.**

Printing the register

You can print all or some of the transactions in a register. You can specify a time period of a day, a week, a month, a year, or more so you will have a printed record of the period of time covered.

To change the fonts, see "Setting up your printer" on page 211.

The register is printed using the same fonts as for printed reports.

1 **Open the register you want to print.**

Or press Ctrl+P, or click Print

2 **From the File menu, choose Print Register.**

3 **Enter information in the Print Register window and click Print.**

(Optional) Change the range of dates to print. The preset range is for the year to date. Use the + or - key to increase or decrease the date in any Quicken date field.

Abbreviate each transaction to fit on one line. Quicken normally prints three lines per transaction.

Display all the lines in a split transaction.

This option appears only if you have created savings goals. See "Creating a savings goal" on page 241.

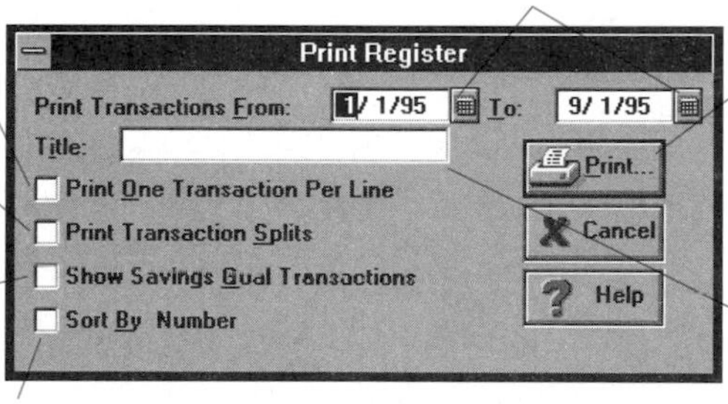

Click Print to continue.

(Optional) Enter a title for the register in the Title box.

Print in check number order instead of chronological order. When checks are sorted by number, Quicken doesn't print a running balance. The Balance column on your printout will be blank.

4 **Enter information in the Print Report window and click Print.**

Select the device you want to print to:

Your printer.

A file on disk that can be read into your word processor or other program.

A tab-delimited disk file that can be read by spreadsheets.

A comma-delimited disk file that you can read into Lotus 1-2-3 and other spreadsheets.

Select this if you have a color printer and want negative amounts to print in red.

Select draft mode for faster but less attractive printing.

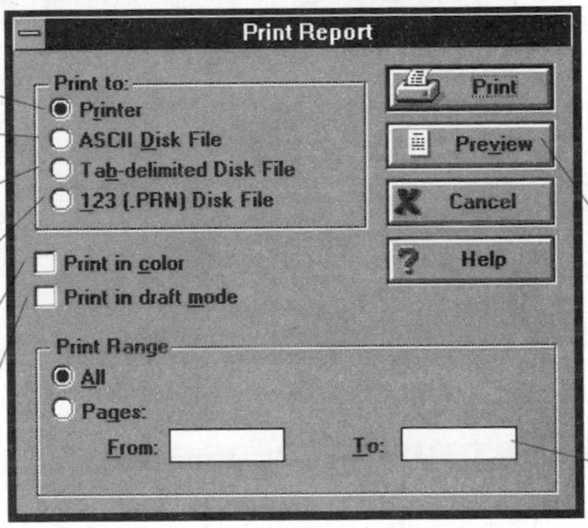

Select this to see a preview of the report before you print it.

Enter a page range if you don't want to print all pages.

Changing register options

Changing the register colors and font

Quicken offers a wide range of colors and fonts for displaying the registers. You can change them to your liking.

Changing the colors

1 **Click Options on the register button bar.**

2 **Click Colors.**

3 **Choose a color for each type of account, and then click OK.**

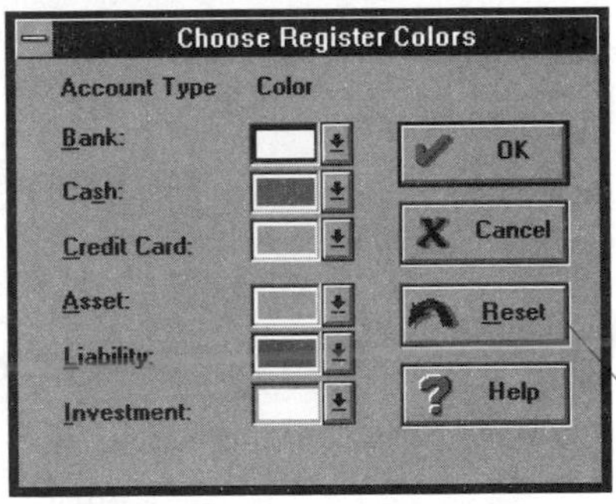

(If your registers never show any color, go to the Display tab in the Register Options window as described on page 39 and click the Color Shading in Register checkbox.)

To return *all* registers to Quicken's preset color settings, click Reset.

Changing the font

When you choose a different font, you'll see all registers and lists (for example, the Category & Transfer list) displayed in that font.

1 **Click Options on the register button bar.**

2 **Click Fonts.**

3 **Choose the font you want, and then click OK.**

All Quicken registers and lists are displayed in the same font.

Select a font and a type size.

You can see an example of the selected font.

Select Bold to see all fonts in bold.

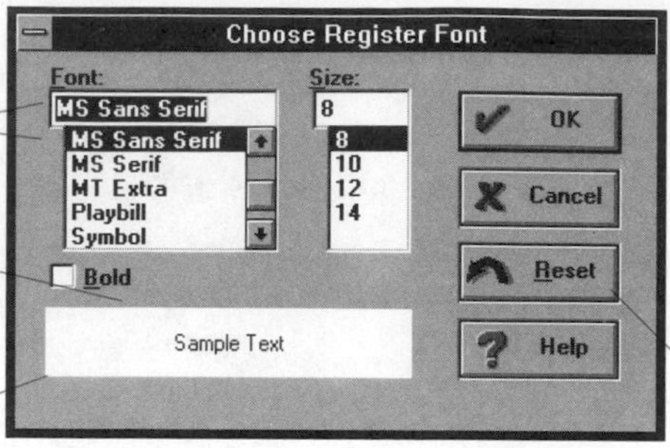

To return to Quicken's preset font setting, click Reset.

Changing the way QuickFill works

Quicken's automatic entry features are called "QuickFill." They work in the Register, Write Checks, and Splits windows. When you first install Quicken, all of the QuickFill features are turned on*, but you can turn QuickFill features on or off to work the way you like.

1 **Click Options on the register button bar.**

2 **Click the QuickFill tab.**

This illustration shows the options that Quicken selects at installation.*

To turn on an option, select a checkbox by clicking in it.

To turn off an option, clear the checkbox by clicking in it.

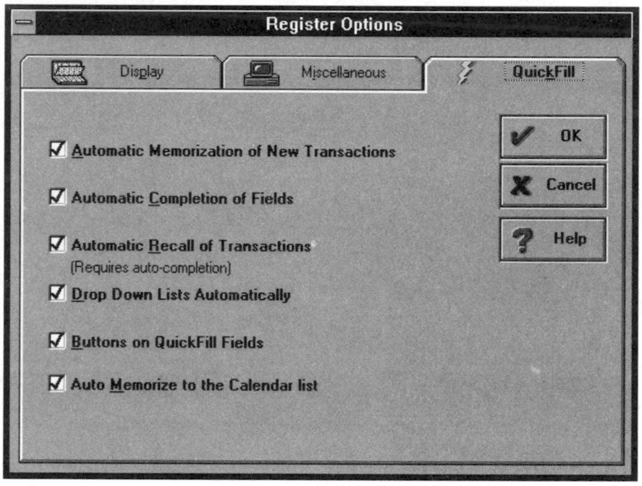

3 **Click the options you want to change, and then click OK.**

QuickFill options	**Quicken does this if the option is turned on**
Automatic Memorization Of New Transactions	Memorizes every new transaction you enter for a new payee (except investment transactions) and adds it to the Memorized Transaction list (see page 43).
Automatic Completion of Fields	Completes each field in a transaction as you type it. Works with check number (Num field in register), payee, category, subcategory, class, subclass, security names, investment action, and transfer account names.

* If you have upgraded from a previous version of Quicken, your settings may be different.

QuickFill options	Quicken does this if the option is turned on
Automatic Recall of Transactions	Recalls a memorized transaction when you press Tab to leave the Payee field.
Drop Down Lists Automatically	Displays the drop-down list when you move the cursor to a field. (If you like to see the drop-down list sometimes, but find it gets in your way when it appears in every transaction, try using "Buttons On QuickFill Fields" instead.)
Buttons on QuickFill Fields	Displays the drop-down buttons for fields with QuickFill. Click the button to drop down the list. If you have this option turned off, you can still display the list by clicking with the right mouse button.
Auto Memorize to the Calendar list	Memorizes every new transaction to the calendar list of memorized transactions. See "Displaying memorized transactions on the Calendar list" on page 44.

Changing display options

1 **Click Options on the register button bar.**

2 **Click the Display tab.**

This illustration shows the settings that are selected when Quicken is installed.

If a checkbox is selected, the option is turned on.

If a checkbox is cleared, the option is turned off.

Click in a checkbox to select or clear it.

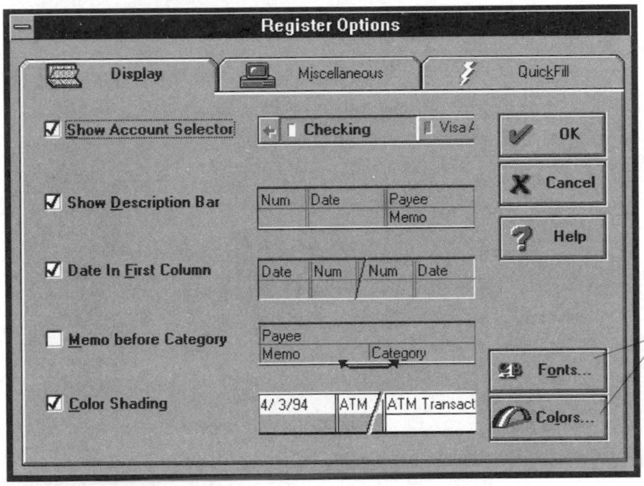

Click these buttons to change the fonts or colors. See "Changing the register colors and font" on page 37.

3 **Click the options you want to change, and then click OK.**

Display options	Quicken does this when the option is selected
Show Account Selector	Displays the account selector buttons at the bottom of the register window.
Show Description Bar	Displays the description bar with the names of the register fields at the top of the register.
Date In First Column	Displays the date column first and the Num column second. Clear this checkbox to display the Num column first.
Memo before Category	Displays the memo first and then the category. Clear this checkbox to display the category first.
Color Shading	Displays the Register window with color shading in each transaction. A different color is used for each account type. To change the colors, go to the Choose Register Colors window as described on page 37.

Display options	Quicken does this when the option is selected
Colors and Fonts	See "Changing the register colors and font" on page 37.

Changing other register options

You can change miscellaneous register settings from the Register Options window.

1 **Click Options on the register button bar.**

2 **Click the Miscellaneous tab.**

This illustration shows the settings that are selected when Quicken is installed.

If a checkbox is selected, the option is turned on.

If a checkbox is cleared, the option is turned off.

Click in a checkbox to select or clear it.

Canadian users: click DD/MM/YY to change the date format to the date style day/month/year.

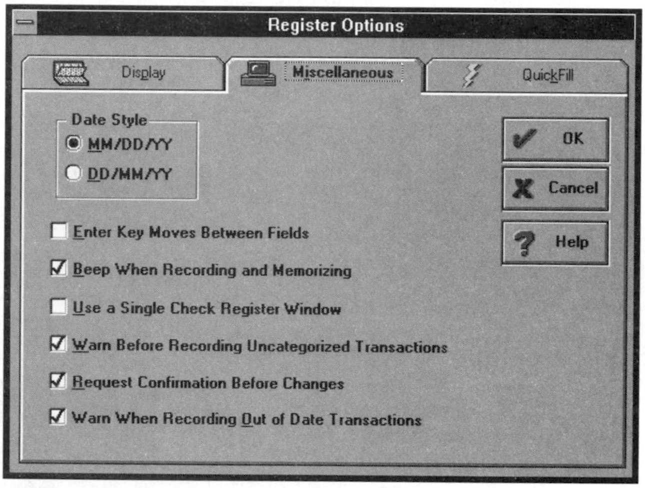

3 **Click the options you want to change, and then click OK.**

Miscellaneous options	Quicken does this when the option is selected
Date Style	Displays dates in a MM/DD/YY (month/day/year) format. Or, select DD/MM/YY to display the day first.
Enter Key Moves Between Fields	Uses the Enter key as well as the Tab key to move between fields in any account register and the Write Checks window. You'll probably want to turn this option on if you are accustomed to using Quicken for DOS.
Beep When Recording and Memorizing	Beeps after recording, deleting, or memorizing a transaction, or memorizing a report.
Use a Single Check Register window	Opens only one register window at a time. If you switch to another account, Quicken changes the open register window to that account.
Warn Before Recording Uncategorized Transactions	Prompts you to enter a category for the transaction that you are recording if you haven't already entered one. This helps you remember to categorize all your transactions for more complete reports, graphs, and budgets.
Request Confirmation Before Changes	Requires you to confirm any changes made to a transaction or list before going to a new transaction or a new window.
Warn When Recording Out of Date Transactions	Warns you if you attempt to record a transaction with a date for a different year.

4 Memorizing transactions

About memorized transactions

Memorizing a transaction lets you enter the details of a transaction once, so you can automatically recall it the next time you need to enter it. For example, enter the details of a $40 ATM withdrawal once, and the next time you make the withdrawal, Quicken automatically fills in the transaction details for you.

Other examples of when to use a memorized transaction:

- You often make more than one payment to the same payee. Just memorize several transactions with the same payee but with different payment details.
- You can memorize a transaction with the amount split according to percentages, so that, for example, several roommates contribute the same relative amounts to a bill.

See "Setting up a transaction group" on page 52.

- To set up transaction groups for fast entry of several transactions, you need to memorize the transactions first.

- You can assign an icon on the Quicken iconbar to enter a memorized transaction. For example, you can set up an icon for an ATM withdrawal so that when you can click the icon, Quicken instantly opens the checking account, inserts a $40 ATM cash withdrawal, fills out the rest of the transaction, and waits for you to click Record.

See "Assigning an icon to enter a transaction" on page 296.

See "Scheduling a transaction on the Financial Calendar" on page 56.

To memorize a transaction that is date-sensitive, such as a bill, paycheck deposit, or mortgage payment, set up a *scheduled* transaction. Quicken enters the transaction for you on the dates and at the frequency you specify.

Memorizing and recalling a transaction

QuickFill recalls any memorized transaction automatically as soon as you type the first letters of the payee's name. (QuickFill looks for the payee in the Memorized Transaction list.)

If you turn off automatic recall in your QuickFill options, you can still recall a memorized transaction in the Register or Write Checks window by selecting it from the Memorized Transaction list as described on page 43.

Memorizing a transaction that's already in your register

1 **Select the transaction in the register (or scroll to the transaction in the Write Checks window).**

Or press Ctrl+M

2 **From the Edit menu, choose Memorize Transaction.**

Quicken tells you the transaction is about to be memorized.

(If you didn't enter an amount in the register for the transaction, Quicken memorizes the transaction as a Payment type.)

3 **Click OK.**

Quicken memorizes all the information in the transaction except the date and the check number.

Memorizing a new transaction

Or press Ctrl+T

1 **From the Lists menu, choose Memorized Transaction.***

Or press Ctrl+N

2 **Click New.**

3 **From the Type drop-down list, select the type of transaction to memorize.**

Select Print Check if this is a check transaction you intend to print in Quicken.
Select Payment if this is a check you intend to write manually, or if it is some other type of withdrawal from the register.
Select Deposit if this transaction adds money to your account.
Select Elec Payment if you will be paying this through CheckFree.

Leave this new transaction uncleared.

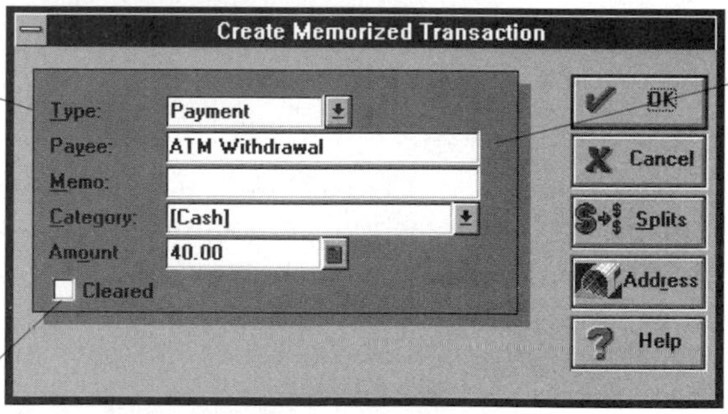

Enter information you want the memorized transaction to contain in each of these fields.

Windows Tip
To move to the next box in a window, click in the box or press Tab.

4 **Enter transaction information in each box as if you were entering the transaction in the register.**

5 **(Optional) Click Splits to enter a split transaction.**

6 **(Optional) Click Address if this is a check to be printed, and enter the address.**

---

* To set up a memorized investment transaction, choose Memorized Investment Trans.

7 **Click OK to add the new memorized transaction to the list.**

Automatically memorizing a transaction

See "Changing the way QuickFill works" on page 38.

You can automatically memorize every new transaction you enter in a register (except investment transactions). To do this, turn on the Automatic Memorization of New Transactions setting in your QuickFill options. This setting is on by default.

When you enter a new payee (who isn't already in the Memorized Transaction list), Quicken adds the payee to the list when you record the transaction.

After you have entered transactions for several months with automatic memorization turned on, you may want to turn it off. Most of your monthly transactions will be memorized by then.

The Memorized Transaction list can hold about 2,000 transactions. If the Memorized Transaction list becomes half-full, Quicken tells you it is turning off automatic memorization. Your list fills up like this if you don't usually make payments to the same payee more than once or twice. If this is the case, automatic memorization isn't much of a benefit to you anyway, so you should consider turning it off.

Recalling a memorized transaction manually

1 **Scroll to the bottom of the Register or Write Checks window to select a new transaction.**

Or, in the register, click Edit on the register button bar and select New Transaction.

(If you don't select a new transaction, Quicken overwrites the currently selected transaction.)

Or press Ctrl+T

2 **From the Lists menu, choose Memorized Transaction.***

3 **Double click the memorized transaction you want.**

4 **(Optional) Review the transaction and make any changes or additions you want.**

See page 44 for more information about locked transactions.

If the transaction is locked, any changes you make won't affect the transaction in the Memorized Transaction list unless you rememorize the transaction in the register.

5 **Click Record to record the transaction as usual.**

---

* For investment transactions, choose Memorized Investment Trans.

Using the Memorized Transaction List

From the Lists menu, choose Memorized Transaction.

After you've memorized a few transactions, your Memorized Transaction list may look like this.

To change the details of a memorized transaction, select the transaction and click Edit.

Click New to create a new memorized transaction.

You can group memorized transactions together for easier recall. See "Setting up a transaction group" on page 52.

You can print the Memorized Transaction list. Open the list. From the File menu, choose Print List (or press Ctrl+P).

Click here to view only locked transactions.

To remove a memorized transaction from the list, select the transaction and click Delete.

Click Report to see a listing of all entries of that memorized transaction.

Transactions marked in this column appear in the list of transactions on the Calendar. Click in this column to mark or unmark a transaction, or select it and then click the Calendar button.

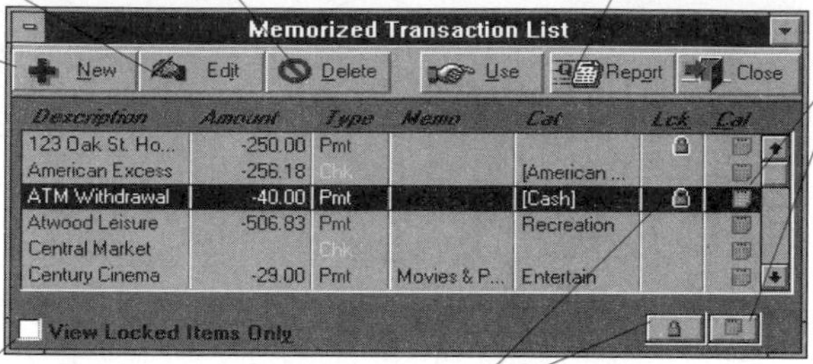

Transactions marked in the Lck column are locked. See below for more information on what this means. Click in this column to lock or unlock a transaction, or select the transaction and then click Lock.

Locking memorized transactions

Lock a memorized transactions to preserve all the information of a memorized transaction whenever you recall it.

For example, suppose you create a memorized transaction for a $40 ATM withdrawal. When you start typing ATM withdrawal in the register, QuickFill fills in the rest of the transaction. Instead of recording the transaction as is, you change the amount to $60 and then record it. If the memorized transaction is locked, the amount remains $40 the next time you recall that transaction. If the memorized transaction is unlocked, the amount changes to $60 the next time you recall that transaction.

Transactions that you memorize manually are locked by default. If you upgraded from an earlier version of Quicken, all your previously memorized transactions are also locked. Transactions that are memorized automatically are unlocked.

To change the locked status of any transaction, click in the Lck column.

Displaying memorized transactions on the Calendar list

Memorized transactions that are marked in the Cal column appear in the list of transactions on the Financial Calendar. To cut down the size of that list, unmark transactions in the Cal column by clicking in the Cal column.

Reporting on a memorized transaction

(Optional) To list each time a memorized transaction appears in all accounts in the current file, select the transaction in the list and click Report.

To customize this report, see Chapter 14, *Creating and customizing reports,* on page 183.

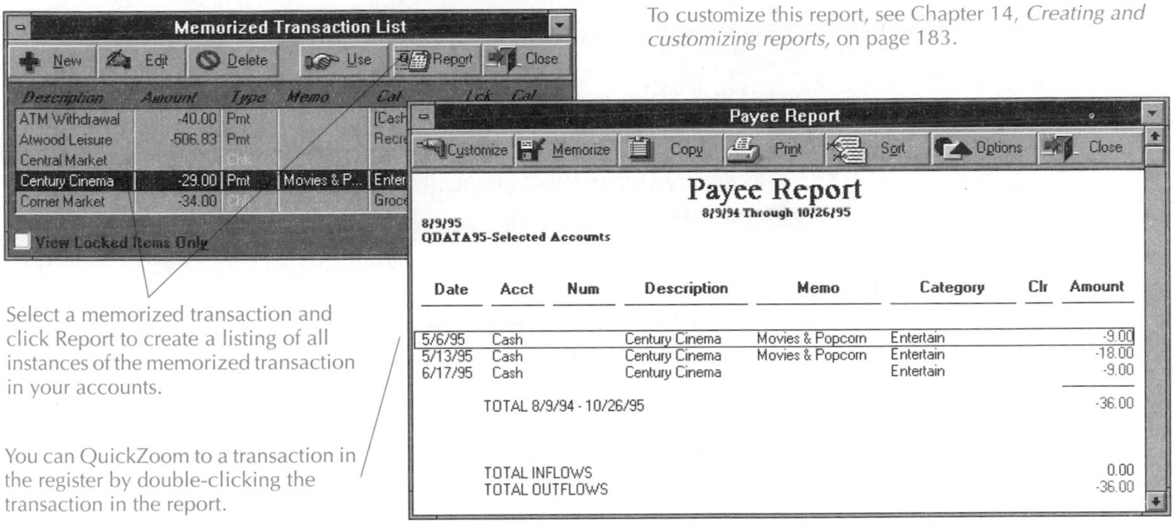

Select a memorized transaction and click Report to create a listing of all instances of the memorized transaction in your accounts.

You can QuickZoom to a transaction in the register by double-clicking the transaction in the report.

Changing a memorized transaction

You can change a locked memorized transaction in two ways:

- From the Memorized Transaction list. From the Lists menu, choose Memorized Transaction (or press Ctrl+T). Select the transaction you want to change and click Edit (or press Ctrl+E). The Edit Memorized Transaction window appears.

  If the transaction is an amortized payment that you memorized when setting up a loan, you see the Set Up Loan Payment window instead.

See "Setting up a loan" on page 106, for what to enter in that window.

- In the register. Recall the memorized transaction into the register, make the changes you want, and then press Ctrl+M to rememorize the transaction in the list.

To change an unlocked memorized transaction, recall it in the register and make the changes you want. The transaction will be automatically rememorized when you click Record.

Deleting a memorized transaction

From the Lists menu, choose Memorized Transaction. Select the transaction you want to delete and click Delete (or press Ctrl+D).

Memorizing a split transaction with percentages

You can memorize a transaction with the amount split in percentages, so that, for example, two roommates can always split their phone bill 60%/40%.

Setting up a split transaction using percentages

If you already have an existing transaction in your register that has the split amounts entered in the correct proportion, select it and go to step 5. Otherwise, set it up as follows.

1 **In the Register or the Write Checks window, enter the payee name and then enter the total transaction amount in the Payment or Deposit field.**

2 **Click Splits.**

3 **In the Splits window, enter the percentages in the Amount column.**

For example, type 60% on the first line and 40% on the second line.

In this example, $120 was entered in the register as the total amount of the bill.

When you type a percentage and then move to the next field, Quicken calculates the dollar amount.

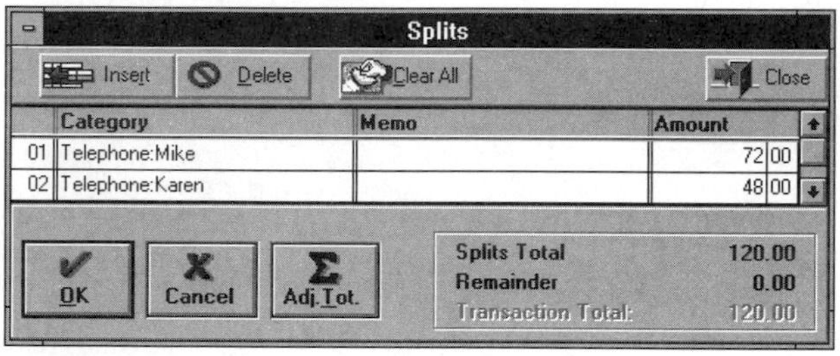

4 **Click OK to close the split.**

Or press Ctrl+M

5 **From the Edit menu, choose Memorize Transaction.**

Quicken asks if you want to memorize splits as percentages.

6 **Click Yes.**

7 **Click OK to memorize the transaction.**

8 **Click Record to record the transaction.**

In the memorized transaction list, Quicken shows %SPL in the Type column.

Recalling a memorized split transaction with percentages

1 **Start with a blank transaction in the register or display a blank check in the Write Checks window.**

2 **Start typing the payee name in the transaction and press Tab to recall the transaction from the list.**

Or press Ctrl+T

If QuickFill isn't turned on or you want to recall the transaction manually, choose Memorized Transaction from the Lists menu, and double-click the transaction.

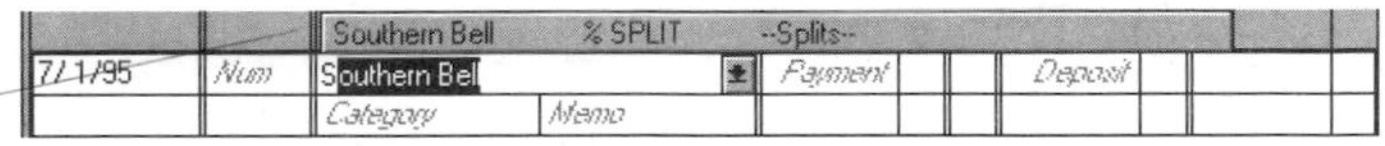

Use QuickFill to recall the transaction.

Quicken asks you to enter the total transaction amount.

3 **Enter the total dollar amount you want to divide into the percentages stored in the split transaction, and click OK.**

Quicken enters a transaction for the amount you specify, with the dollar amount split according to the percentages stored in the memorized transaction.

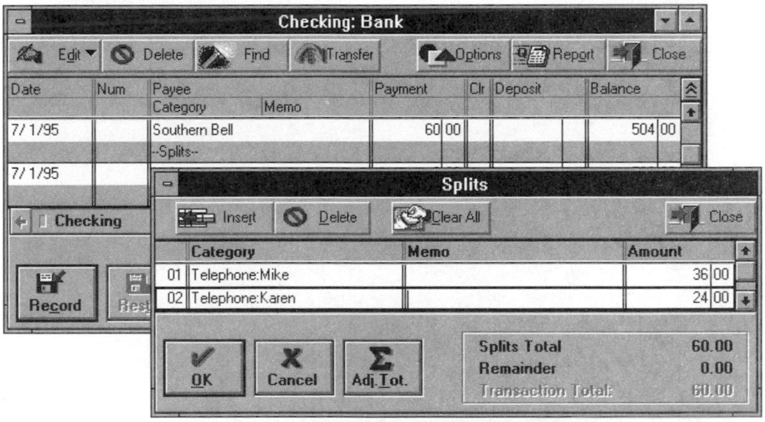

In this Splits window, Quicken calculates the dollar amounts on the basis of the percentages stored in the memorized transaction.

4 **Click Record to record the transaction.**

5 Using the Quicken Financial Calendar

How Quicken helps you schedule

Think of your expenses and deposits that come up on a regular basis. For instance, you may be paid every two weeks, pay rent once a month, and pay the gardener once a week.

You can use the Quicken Financial Calendar to keep track of all these transactions. It looks just like the calendar on your wall. On the Financial Calendar, you can mark one-time transactions such as a vacation, and recurring transactions like your rent and paycheck.

Enter recurring transactions only once, and Quicken then projects them forward as far as you want.

Enter a once-only transaction on the day you think it will happen.

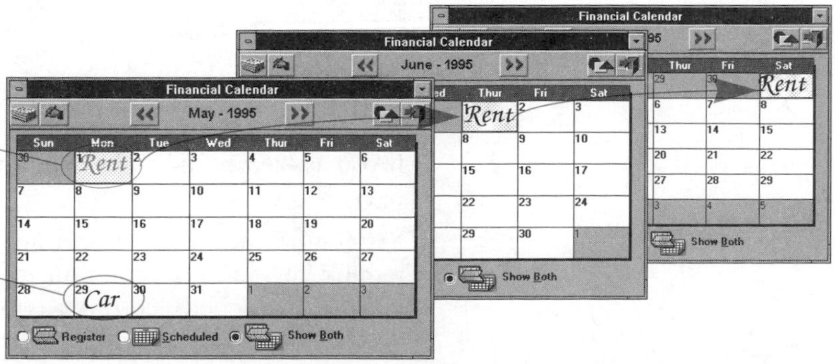

The Financial Calendar shows your upcoming bills, and enters them into your registers as they become due. For one-time bills, this serves as a useful reminder. For recurring bills, you've put your bill-paying on autopilot.

Setting up a scheduled transaction

Instead of entering a transaction on the day it's due, you can schedule transactions ahead of time. On the day the transaction becomes due, Quicken either reminds you, or automatically enters it for you in your register, whichever you prefer.

If you use automatic drafting to make amortized payments for a loan or mortgage, set these up through the View Loans window instead—see "Setting up a loan" on page 106.

If you define a scheduled transaction to be a recurring transaction, Quicken will automatically enter it in your register on the scheduled days, saving you time and, if it's a bill, reminding you to pay it. You can set up automatic drafting transactions in this way.

See "Scheduling a transaction on the Financial Calendar" on page 56.

There are two ways to schedule a transaction: from the Scheduled Transaction list, as described next, and from the Financial Calendar.

1 **From the Lists menu, choose Scheduled Transaction.**

2 **Click New.**

3 **Complete the Create Scheduled Transaction window.**

When you've finished making entries, your window may look something like the one shown below, which shows a recurring transaction to pay the rent.

Select the account into which the transaction should be entered. (To schedule investment transactions, memorize the transactions and include them in a scheduled transaction group as described on page 52.)

For recurring transactions, Quicken updates this date as it records each payment.

For more information on each field, press F1 in this window.

Select Payment, Deposit, Print Check, or Elec Payment. For example, for paychecks, select Deposit.

This part of the window contains the same fields as a transaction in your register. Whatever you enter here will be written into your register on the next payment date.

For a one-time transaction, select Only Once.

Quicken can enter the transaction in your register with or without asking you to confirm first.

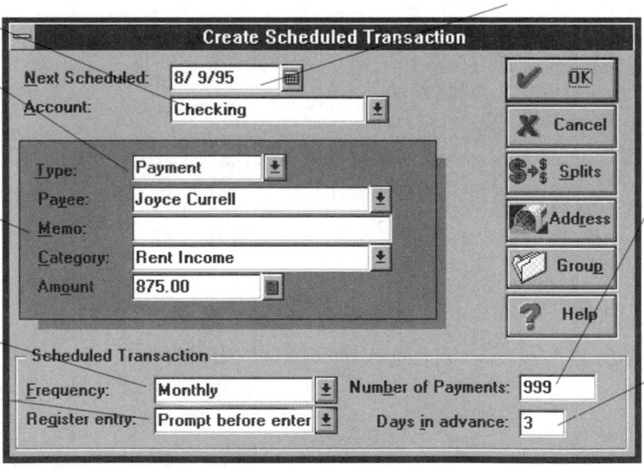

Leave this as 999 if you want Quicken to record transactions indefinitely.

Quicken can record the payments in your register ahead of time if you want. (Otherwise, enter 0 here.)

To break down the transaction into several parts, click Splits to open a split transaction, just as you do in the register.

If you are setting up a check payment, click Address to enter the payee's address.

You might want to enter transactions a few days in advance, to remind you and give you time to send the bills off. To do this, when you set up a scheduled transaction, enter a number in the Days in Advance field—Quicken enters the transaction in the register that many days before the next payment date. The transaction is then entered as a postdated transaction. Its transaction date doesn't change as a result of being entered in advance.

For example, the scheduled transaction example above is dated 8/9/95, but Quicken enters it in the register on August 6, because it was set up to be recorded three days in advance.

4 **Click OK, and then click OK again to confirm the transaction.**

The transaction is added to the Scheduled Transaction list. You can change the details of any scheduled transaction at any time by selecting that transaction in the list and clicking Edit. Remember that Quicken doesn't enter the transaction in the register until it becomes due. (However, you can pay a scheduled transaction ahead of time if you wish.)

See "Paying scheduled transactions ahead of time" on page 52.

When the due date for a scheduled transaction arrives, Quicken enters the transaction in the register of the selected account. This happens as soon as you start Quicken on or following the next scheduled date. (If the next scheduled date is today, exit Quicken and restart it to see the transaction entered.)

If you selected "Prompt before entering" from the Register Entry drop-down list in the Create Scheduled Transaction window, Quicken asks you to confirm that it should enter the transaction. If you selected "Automatically enter," then Quicken enters the transaction automatically. You will see the transaction in your register.

If you aren't sure which Register Entry option to use, select "Prompt before entering." This allows you to check the details of the transaction and change them if necessary before Quicken records the transaction in your register.

Viewing your Scheduled Transaction list

From the Lists menu, choose Scheduled Transaction.

Your Scheduled Transaction list shows all the future payments and deposits you have defined.

Click New to create a new scheduled transaction or transaction group.

Click Edit to change information for the selected transaction.

Click Delete to delete the selected transaction.

Click Pay to record the selected transaction now.

Press Ctrl+P to print the Scheduled Transactions list. The printed list includes the number of payments yet to be made for each item.

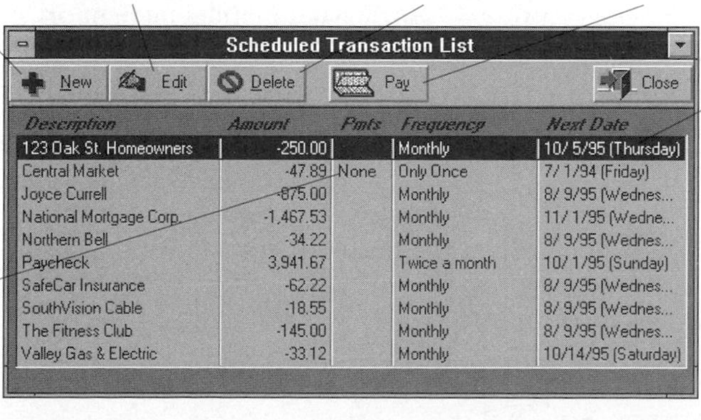

Scheduled Transaction List
New
Edit
Delete
Pay
Close
Description Amount Pmts Frequency Next Date
123 Oak St. Homeowners -250.00 Monthly 10/ 5/95 (Thursday)
Central Market -47.89 None Only Once 7/ 1/94 (Friday)
Joyce Currell -875.00 Monthly 8/ 9/95 (Wednes...
National Mortgage Corp. -1,467.53 Monthly 11/ 1/95 (Wedne...
Northern Bell -34.22 Monthly 8/ 9/95 (Wednes...
Paycheck 3,941.67 Twice a month 10/ 1/95 (Sunday)
SafeCar Insurance -62.22 Monthly 8/ 9/95 (Wednes...
SouthVision Cable -18.55 Monthly 8/ 9/95 (Wednes...
The Fitness Club -145.00 Monthly 8/ 9/95 (Wednes...
Valley Gas & Electric -33.12 Monthly 10/14/95 (Saturday)

This column shows the next payment date for each scheduled transaction.

If you left the number of payments as 999, this field is blank, meaning Quicken will continue entering transactions until you edit the scheduled transaction to stop it.

To temporarily disable a scheduled transaction that you will use later, edit the scheduled transaction and type 0 in the Number of Payments box. Quicken won't record any more transactions in your register until you enter a new number in this box, though the item remains in your Scheduled Transaction list.

Paying scheduled transactions ahead of time

You may want to record a scheduled transaction earlier than the date you originally scheduled. For example, you planned to have your car serviced next week but did it today instead.

On page 58 you can read how to pay scheduled transactions ahead of time using the Financial Calendar.

1 **From the Lists menu, choose Scheduled Transaction.**

2 **Select the scheduled transaction and click Pay.**

3 **The Edit Scheduled Transaction window appears. Check the details and click Record.**

Quicken enters the transaction in your register immediately, using the original Next Scheduled date unless you changed the date to today. For a one-time transaction, Quicken removes the transaction from the Scheduled Transaction list.

If you set up the scheduled transaction as a check to write in Quicken, you can print the check immediately.

When you become familiar with the Financial Calendar, described later in this chapter, you may prefer to use the Pay Now function through the Financial Calendar instead.

Setting up a transaction group

You may pay a group of bills regularly at the same time. For example, at the start of each month you pay your phone bill, electric bill, and car payment. Instead of setting up each payment separately as a recurring scheduled transaction, you can group them together into a recurring *transaction group*. This cleans up your Scheduled Transaction list, as the group appears as just one item in the list.

You can use any transaction groups you set up in a previous version of Quicken.

When a transaction group is due to be recorded, Quicken enters each transaction in the group into your register. If necessary, you can then go into the register and edit each transaction separately.

See "Memorizing a transaction that's already in your register" on page 42.

See page 44 for more information about locked transactions.

A transaction must be memorized before you can include it in a transaction group. If you include an unlocked transaction, Quicken will automatically lock it for you so that you won't overwrite it accidentally. However, you can unlock it later if you wish.

Set up a transaction group from the Scheduled Transaction list by assigning memorized transactions to it. You can have up to twelve transaction groups.

1 **From the Lists menu, choose Scheduled Transaction.**

2 **Click New.**

3 **Select an account from the Account drop-down list.**

All transactions in the group are entered into the same account.

4 **Click Group.**

To schedule investment transactions such as regular stock purchases or dividend income, memorize them first and then include them in a transaction group as described here. (You can't schedule investment transactions except as part of a group.) Note that investment transaction groups don't show on the Financial Calendar.

5 **Select whether this is a regular or investment transactions group.**

For all non-investment transactions, select Regular.

6 **Enter a group name.**

For example, type Utility bills or Monthly payments.

7 **Complete the other information in the Create Transaction Group window.**

Select a frequency and a register entry option.

8 **Click OK.**

The Assign Transactions to Group window appears. This window lists all your memorized transactions.

Click Mark to include the selected transaction in your group, or double-click the transaction.

Each transaction in this list can belong to only one group.

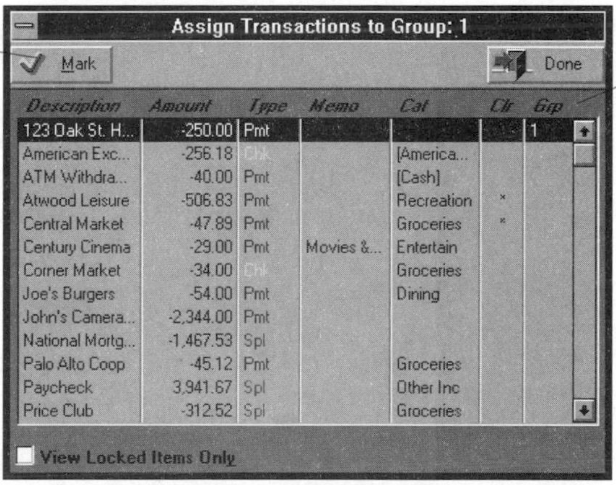

The number in the Grp column tells you to which group the transaction has already been assigned.

9 **Select the memorized transactions you want to include.**

To create printable checks by recalling a transaction group, be sure that Chk appears in the Type column for those memorized transactions when you are assigning them to a transaction group. Printable checks appear in the register with Print in the Num field. To change the type of a memorized transaction, edit the transaction in the Memorized Transaction list.

See "Changing a memorized transaction" on page 45.

10 **Click Done.**

The group is listed as a single item in your Scheduled Transaction list. The amount isn't shown, because there are several transactions in the group with different amounts.

To enter a group of transactions ahead of the scheduled time, select the group in the Scheduled Transaction list and click Pay.

Changing and deleting transaction groups

You can edit a transaction group at any time (by clicking Edit at the Scheduled Transaction list), to change the schedule details, assign new transactions, or remove transactions from the group. You can also display the Memorized Transaction list and edit a memorized transaction at any time, even if it belongs to a transaction group.

Caution: If you delete a memorized transaction from the Memorized Transaction list, Quicken automatically removes it from the transaction group.

If you delete a transaction group (by clicking Delete at the Scheduled Transaction list), the memorized transactions included in the group remain in the Memorized Transaction list.

Viewing your Financial Calendar

Quicken's Financial Calendar is a visual planning tool that shows you what lies ahead.

From the Activities menu, choose Financial Calendar, or click the Calendar icon on Quicken's iconbar.

Quicken shows transactions in the default font Small Fonts. (If you have deleted this font, Quicken chooses a similar font—install Small Fonts again to use it in the Financial Calendar.) If you prefer a larger font, open QUICKEN.INI in your WINDOWS directory and type CalendarFont=1 in the [Quicken] section. Then the usual register font is used in the Financial Calendar. Or type CalendarFont=–1 for a smaller font.

Click View to display the memorized transactions list and account balances graph.

To display other months, click Prev or Next, or click the date to enter a new date.

Click Options to change the settings for the Financial Calendar. You can hide or display the Memorized Transactions list or the account balances graph, and you can select the accounts to include.

Click Note to add a note to today's date.

Transactions you previously entered in your register are listed in black.

Today's date is shown in a different color (or shade).

Future transactions you have scheduled appear in blue on the date they are scheduled to be recorded in your register.

To see more information about the transactions, double-click on the date box.

Click these buttons to show only already recorded transactions or only scheduled transactions; click Both to show both register and scheduled transactions.

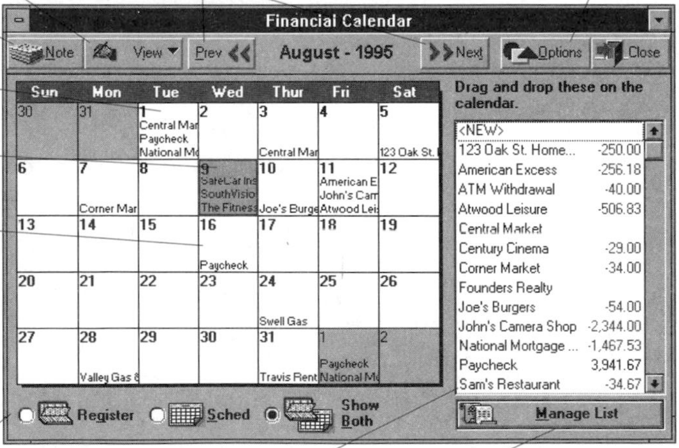

To print the calendar, press Ctrl+P.

To schedule a transaction, drag it from this list to a day in the Financial Calendar, or drag <NEW> to set up a new transaction.

Click Manage List to display the Memorized Transaction List.

The Financial Calendar displays all transactions for the selected accounts, which may be:

- Transactions already in your registers
- Single scheduled transactions you know are coming up soon (these are marked with "1x")
- Recurring scheduled transactions

Register transactions, displayed in black, are already in your register. Scheduled transactions are displayed in blue until they have been recorded. When you drag <NEW> to a day in the Calendar, you can create either a scheduled or a register transaction.

Entering recurring transactions also helps with the projections described in Chapter 22, *Creating a forecast,* on page 247.

You can enter scheduled transactions from the Scheduled Transaction list, as described previously in this chapter, or directly on the Financial Calendar, as described next. Enter one-time transactions as a reminder of upcoming bills. Also schedule all your recurring transactions (paycheck, mortgage, car payments, insurance, and so on) to save time entering transactions in your register.

Transactions scheduled on your Financial Calendar ahead of today *aren't yet entered in your register.* You can view them *only on the Financial Calendar* or in the Scheduled Transaction list. As they become due, Quicken enters them for you in the register and changes them from blue to black in the Financial Calendar.

Viewing the account balances graph

To display a graph of the balances of your selected accounts, click View and then select Show Account Graph.

Past balances are shown in yellow, the current date is in green, and future projected balances are in blue.

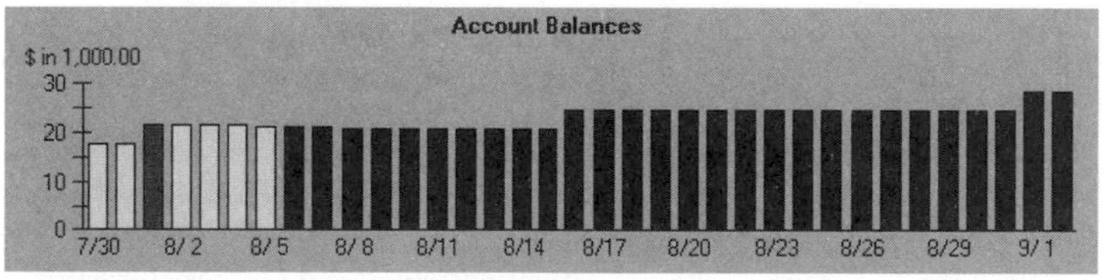

This graph shows actual account balances plus postdated and scheduled transactions. If you are upgrading from Quicken 3 for Windows, your forecast data and worksheet have been moved to Forecasting.

To create a forecast that also includes estimated amounts, see Chapter 22, *Creating a forecast,* on page 247.

Selecting accounts to view

You can't select investment accounts for viewing.

You can select which accounts to view. The Financial Calendar shows only transactions for the selected accounts.

To select accounts to include:

1. **Click Options in the Financial Calendar button bar.**
2. **Mark the accounts to include, and then click OK.**

   To mark or unmark an account, click it in the list, or click Mark All or Clear All to mark or clear all accounts.

Scheduling a transaction on the Financial Calendar

To the right of the Financial Calendar is a list of transactions, made up of the memorized transactions that are marked to be included in the calendar. If this list gets too big, you can hide any transaction by going to the Memorized Transaction list and clicking in the Cal column. For more information on how to manage this list, see “Using the Memorized Transaction List” on page 44.

1 **Select the correct month.**

Click the Prev or Next buttons to change the month.

2 **Move the mouse pointer over the list of transactions on the right.**

The pointer changes to a hand to show you are ready to pick up a transaction.

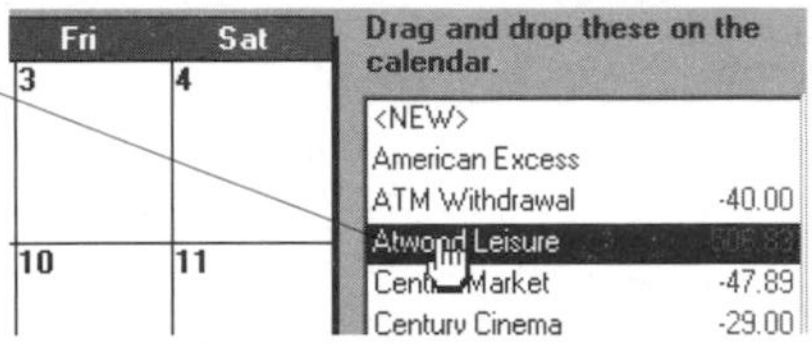

3 **Click on the transaction you want to schedule and hold down the left mouse button as you move the pointer to the Financial Calendar.**

To schedule a new transaction, click on <NEW> and drag it to the Financial Calendar instead. (Or double-click on the day and click New, as described in the next section.)

The pointer changes to a calendar to show that you can drop the transaction into a day. If you move the pointer over a date in the past, it changes to a register.

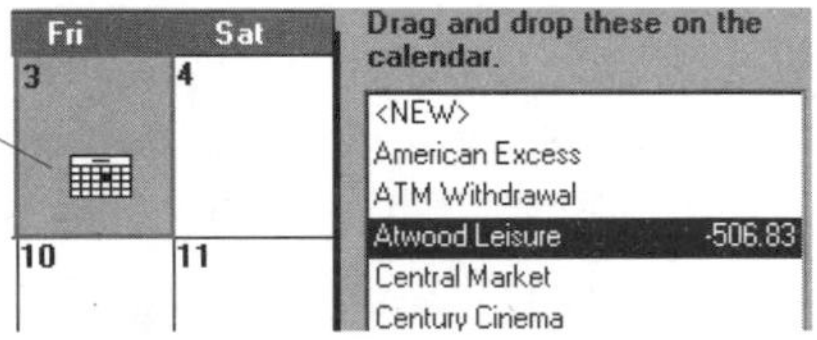

4 **With the pointer over the correct day, release the mouse button.**

5 **Complete the Drag and Drop Transaction window.**

Leave Scheduled Transaction selected to schedule a transaction for the future. To record a one-time transaction in your register now, click Register Transaction.

Make any changes to this information, or if this is a new transaction, complete these fields as described on page 50.

For example, you may want to set up this transaction as a recurring transaction by changing the frequency of payment.

Click Splits as usual to split the transaction.

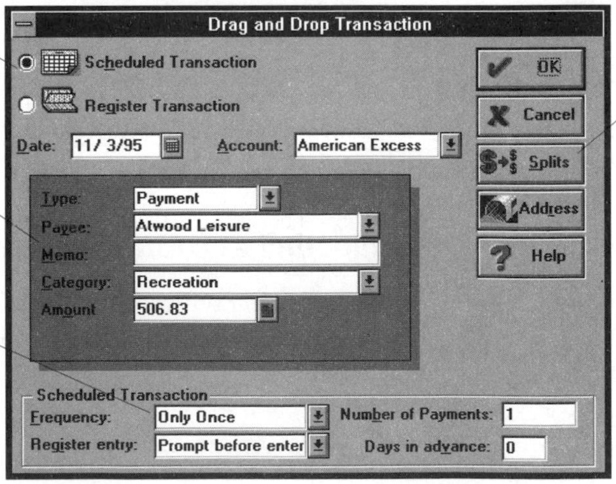

6 **Click OK.**

Quicken drops the transaction into the day you selected.

An Only Once payment is marked by a red 1x.
An Only Once deposit is marked by a green 1x.

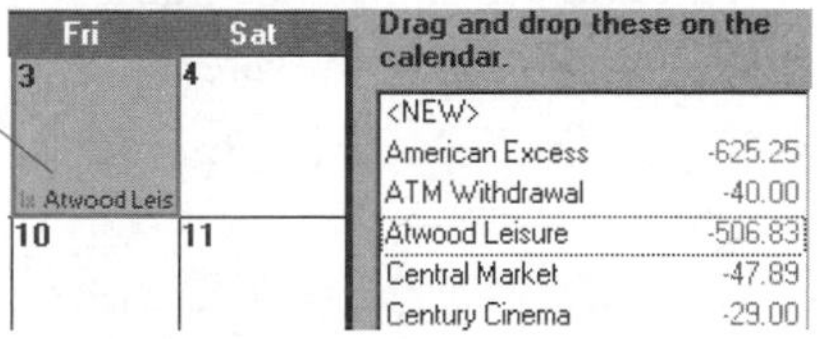

Each time you start Quicken, it checks for any transactions that are due that day. (This may be ahead of the actual scheduled date if you entered a number in the Days In Advance field.) For each transaction that is due, Quicken records the transaction in your register and changes its color in the Financial Calendar. If you specified Prompt Before Entering for the transaction, Quicken Reminders lists the transaction.

See page 50 for more information.

See "Using Quicken Reminders and Billminder" on page 60 for more information.

If you set up the transaction as a check to write in Quicken, you can now print the check.

Often, the transaction you scheduled on your Financial Calendar contains only an estimated amount. You may schedule estimated amounts to remind yourself of bills to pay, or to help you plan your finances ahead of time. In these cases, select Prompt Before Entering for the transaction, so that you can enter the actual amount before the transaction is recorded in your register.

Checking or changing your scheduled transactions

1 **To check the transactions for a particular day, double-click on that day (or click the right mouse button).**

The list window shows the transactions for the day you double-click.

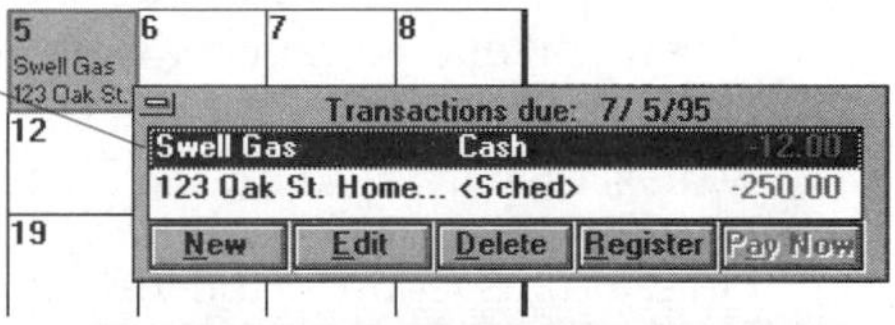

If you select a transaction that has already been recorded, the Register button takes you directly to the transaction in the register.

2 **Choose what you want to do.**

- To set up a new scheduled transaction for this day, click New.
- To check the details of a scheduled transaction, select the transaction and click Edit. At the Edit Scheduled Transaction window, you can change any of the details. To reschedule a transaction for a different date, for example, change the Next Scheduled field.

  If you are investigating transactions already in your register, you see the Edit Register Transaction window instead, which lets you edit the transaction details just as you would edit them in the register.
- To delete a scheduled transaction, select the transaction and click Delete. The transaction is removed from your Financial Calendar and from your Scheduled Transactions list. If the transaction was a recurring one, all future transactions are removed also.

See the Set Up Scheduled Transaction window shown on page 50.

- To go to a transaction already in your register, click Register. In this way, you are using the Financial Calendar as a place for viewing and editing your registers.

See "Paying scheduled transactions ahead of time" next.

- To pay the transaction immediately, click Pay Now.

Paying scheduled transactions ahead of time

You may want to record a scheduled transaction earlier than the date you originally scheduled. For example, you're going away for two weeks and want to pay some upcoming bills before you leave.

Or click the right mouse button.

1 **For each bill you want to pay ahead, double-click the date box to list the transactions scheduled for that day.**

2 **Select the transaction you want to pay and click Pay Now.**

3 **The Edit Scheduled Transaction window appears. Check the details and click Record to record the transaction.**

For an Only Once transaction, Quicken removes the transaction from the Scheduled Transaction list.

Quicken enters the transaction in your register immediately, with the transaction date you originally entered unless you changed it.

If you set up the scheduled transaction as a check to write in Quicken, you can now print the check.

Recording transactions in your register

Although the Financial Calendar is useful for scheduling upcoming transactions, you can also use it to enter transactions straight into your register. You can use the Calendar as your primary data entry method, instead of using the registers.

When you enter a register transaction in the Financial Calendar, Quicken immediately enters the transaction into your register as well as displaying it on the Financial Calendar.

Drag a transaction to the Calendar. Quicken opens the Drag and Drop Transaction window.

Click Register. If you want to enter a scheduled transaction instead, see "Scheduling a transaction on the Financial Calendar" on page 56.

Important: Check that the correct account is shown. Unless you select a different account, Quicken uses the same account as this transaction was last entered into.

Click Splits as usual to split the transaction.

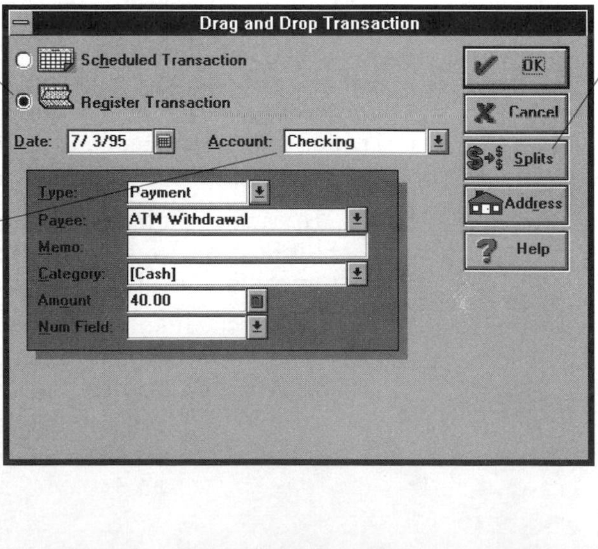

Adding notes to your Financial Calendar

In addition to scheduling transactions on your Financial Calendar, you can add notes like "Call tax accountant" or "Check price of XYZ stock." You can color-code the notes for extra usefulness.

1 **Select a day on your Financial Calendar by clicking the date box.**

2 **Click Note on the Financial Calendar button bar.**

A notepad appears.

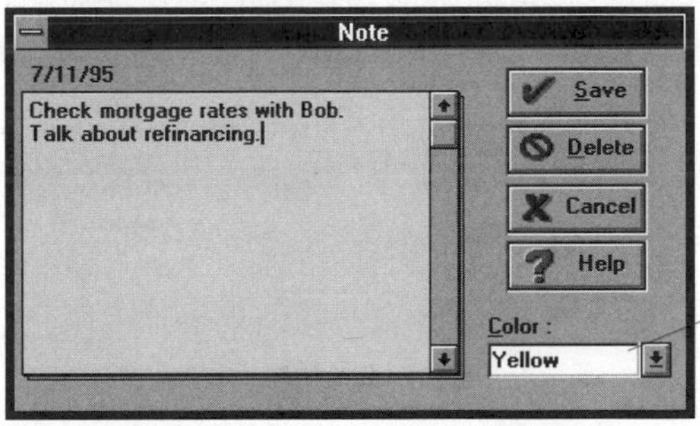

The note will be marked on your Financial Calendar in this color.

3 **Type your note and then click Save.**

The note is marked on your Financial Calendar by a little colored square in the date box.

This square tells you you've added a note to the Financial Calendar for this day.

To read the note, click on the little square.

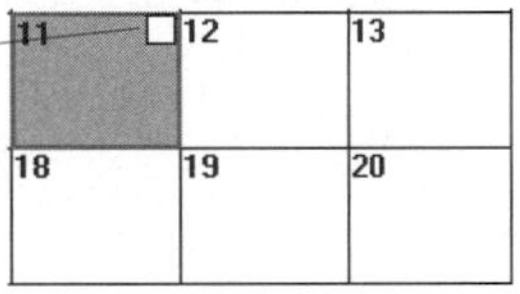

To delete the note, click on the little square and then click Delete.

A date box holds one note at a time.

You can use the colors to code your notes for importance, business subjects, financial vs. social, or any other system you want to use.

Quicken Reminders displays the notes for this week when you start Quicken. See the next section for more information.

Using Quicken Reminders and Billminder

The Financial Calendar gives you useful reminders to pay your bills when you start Quicken (and, if you have more than one Quicken file, open the appropriate file). Reminders and Billminder are two other features that can remind you even earlier. Billminder reminds you when you start your computer or when you start Windows, and Reminders appears when you start Quicken.

Quicken Reminders lets you know if you have:

- Checks or scheduled transactions in other files
- Investment reminders due
- An IntelliCharge statement to download
- Electronic payments to transmit

To turn off Billminder or Reminders, see "Changing Reminders options" on page 62.

If you have any calendar notes, checks to print, scheduled transactions that are due, investment reminders, or electronic payments to transmit, you'll see the Quicken Reminders window whether or not you are running Billminder.

Click here to select the period of calendar notes you want to display.

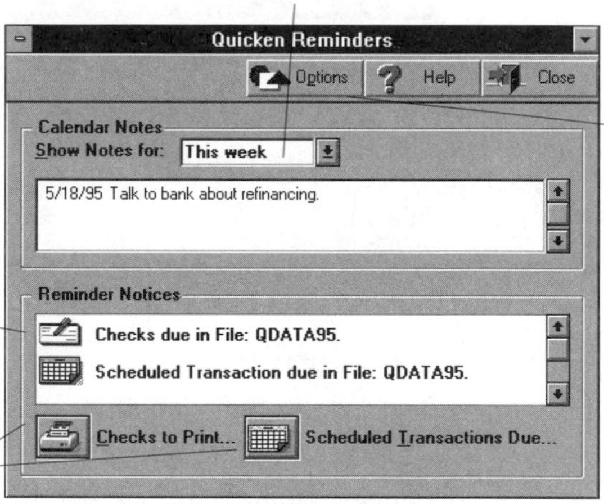

Click Options to change Reminders and Billminder settings.

Quicken Reminders also lets you know if you have checks or scheduled transactions due in other files.

Click these buttons to print checks or enter scheduled transactions.

If you chose to run Billminder "At Windows Startup" when you installed Quicken, Billminder displays messages when you run Windows and open the Billminder icon.

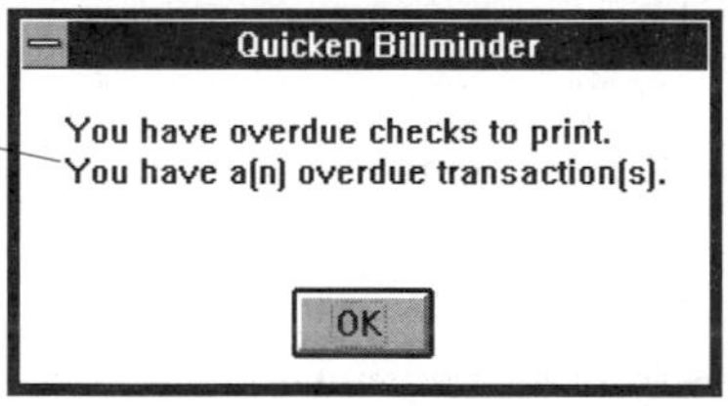

(You might have also chosen to run Billminder "From DOS At Boot Time.")

For Billminder to work, you must have selected the option to Install Billminder when you installed Quicken. (If you used Express Installation, Billminder is already installed to appear whenever you start Windows.) If you didn't install Billminder and want to install it now, insert these commands in your AUTOEXEC.BAT or your WIN.INI file:

- To see Billminder when you start your computer:
  In AUTOEXEC.BAT, type PATHNAME\BILLMNDW.EXE PATHNAME /P
  (For example, c:\quickenw\billmndw.exe c:\quickenw /p)

  /P means that Billminder messages remain displayed on the screen until you press Enter, before any other items in your AUTOEXEC.BAT file are executed.

- To see Billminder when you run Windows:
  In WIN.INI, type LOAD=PATHNAME\BILLMNDW.EXE
  (For example, load=c:\quickenw\billmndw.exe)

  If Billminder finds checks to print, scheduled transactions or transaction groups due, investment reminders due, or payments to transmit, it notifies you each time you start your computer.

When scheduled transactions are due

When you start Quicken or click Scheduled Transactions in the Quicken Reminders window, the Scheduled Transactions Due window appears:

Quicken displays the date, description, account, and amount of each scheduled transaction.

Select a transaction by clicking it. Use shift+click to select adjacent transactions, or use Ctrl+click to select multiple non-adjacent transactions.

Once you've marked transactions, click Record to record them. Once you record a transaction, Quicken removes it from the list and changes the payment date on the Scheduled Transaction list to the next scheduled date.

If you don't record a transaction, you will be reminded again the next time you start Quicken.

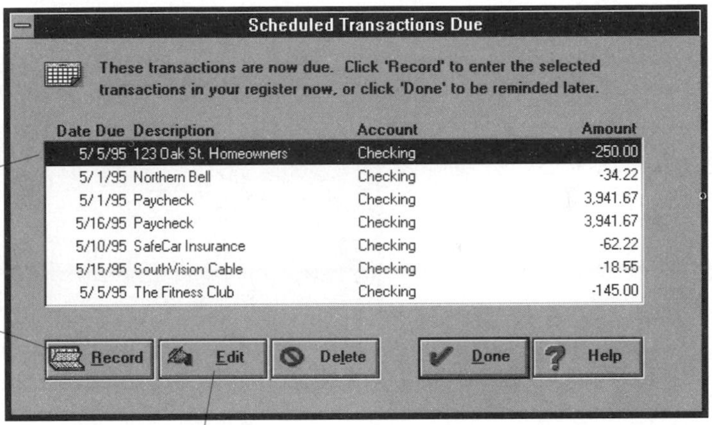

Select an item and click Edit or double-click an item to edit it.

Mark transactions and then:

- Click Record to record them in your register. If a transaction was set up as Only Once, Quicken removes it from the Scheduled Transaction list when you record it.

  OR

- Click Edit to edit the transaction information.

  OR

- Click Delete to skip the transaction for this occurrence only.

  OR

- Click Done if you don't want to record the transactions now. You will be reminded again if you click Scheduled Transactions Due in Quicken Reminders, or wait until the next time you start Quicken.

When you have checks to print

See Chapter 6, *Writing and printing checks,* on page 63, for details.

When you click Checks to Print in the Quicken Reminders window, the Print Checks window appears.

If you have more than one account with checks to print, Quicken first asks you to select the account to print from.

Changing Reminders options

1 **From the Activities menu, choose Reminders and then click Options.**

2 **Click the Turn on Billminder checkbox if it isn't already turned on.**

To turn off Billminder, clear this checkbox.

If you don't want to see Reminders messages every time you start Quicken, clear this checkbox.

Clear this checkbox if you don't want to see Calendar Notes in the Reminders window.

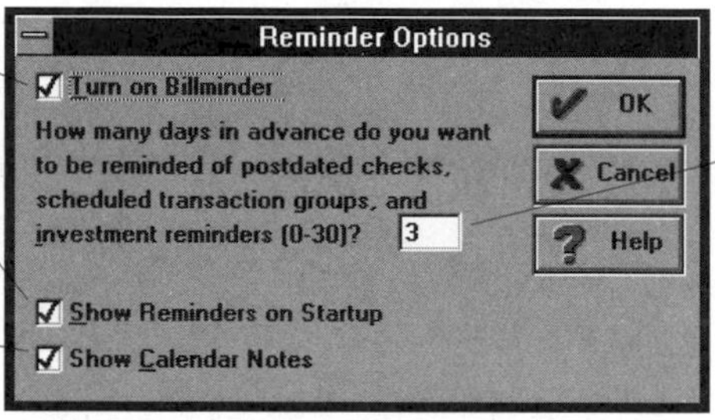

Enter a number of business days between 0 and 30.

3 **Enter the number of business days in advance that you want Quicken to remind you of upcoming bills, and then click OK.**

If you use Quicken:	Set business days in advance to:
Daily (except weekends)	0 days
At least every other day	1 day
At least once every three days	2 days
At least weekly	5 days
At least once every two weeks	10 days
At least once a month	30 days

6 Writing and printing checks

About Quicken checks

Having Quicken prepare your checks is a great convenience. If you print checks, you avoid the duplicate work of writing checks and then recording them in Quicken. You will save hours of valuable time, avoid clerical errors, and give your checks a very professional look.

For information about how to order different kind of Intuit checks, consult the check catalog in your Quicken package or see Appendix C, *Ordering Intuit software and supplies*, on page 313.

Filling out a check

Use the Write Checks window to enter checks that you plan to print with Quicken. Enter other transactions, such as checks that you've already written by hand, deposits, or bank fees in the check register. When you record a check in the Write Checks window, Quicken adds it automatically to the check register.

You can write checks in any Quicken bank account: checking, money market, or savings. You can write checks as bills arrive or at regular intervals: weekly, biweekly, or monthly.

Or press Ctrl+W, or click the Check icon on the iconbar

1 **From the Activities menu, choose Write Checks.**

2 **Complete the information in the Write Checks window. Press Tab or Shift+Tab to move between fields.**

If you plan to mail the check in an Intuit window envelope, enter the payee's name, address, city, state, and zip code. Press Enter to start a new line. Press the Quote key (') to automatically copy the payee name to the first address line.

Enter the payee name here (the person or organization to whom you are writing the check).

The date appears on the check when you print it. To change the date, enter your changes over the date shown.

To send a message to the payee or provide additional information for your own records, enter it as a memo, up to 31 characters long.

The memo may be visible when you mail the check in an Intuit window envelope. To ensure the information isn't visible, display a Message box and enter information there instead. See "Changing check options" on page 66.

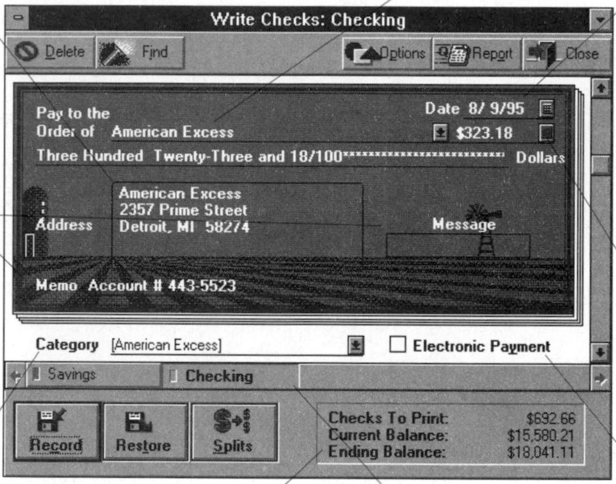

When you enter the dollar amount here, Quicken automatically spells out the amount on the next line.

Enter the category, class, or transfer information here. Click Splits to split a check just as you split transactions in the register. (See page 26.)

If you use Intuit voucher checks, Quicken prints up to 16 lines of split information on the voucher attachment. If you write a single check that covers 20 invoices, the first 16 invoice numbers and the amount to be applied to each invoice appears on the voucher attachment.

The Ending Balance is the balance in the account based on all entered transactions, including any postdated transactions.

Use these buttons to select the account you want to write checks from.

This option appears if you have set up the account to make electronic payments. See "Setting up an account to use CheckFree" on page 278.

When you fill out a check, QuickFill fills in the details for you if it recognizes the payee from an earlier transaction. You can use the drop-down calendar to modify the date and the drop-down field calculator to calculate the amount.

To print the checks you've entered, see "About printing checks" on page 67.

The Write Checks window doesn't display a check number. Intuit checks are prenumbered because most banks require prenumbered checks for stop payment purposes. Quicken inserts the correct check number in the register when it prints the check. Until then, Quicken displays Print in the Num field of the check register.

Reviewing checks you've written

Once you've written and recorded your checks, you can review them before printing by either scrolling through the Write Checks window or reviewing them in the register. After you've printed a check, you can't review it in the Write Checks window; you must review it in the register instead.

You can add to, change, delete, or void any check in the Write Checks window the same way you edit transactions in the register. When you finish changing a transaction, Quicken recalculates all subsequent balances if necessary.

Or press Ctrl+R

1 **From the Activities menu, choose Use Register.**

Or, from the Account list, select the account and click Open.

The Register window displays checks and other transactions by date, and it also shows the information written on the checks except for the Address and Message fields.

After you print a check, Quicken inserts the check number in the Num field.

Unprinted checks have Print in the Num field.

To view or edit splits (if any), select a split transaction and click Splits at the bottom of the register.

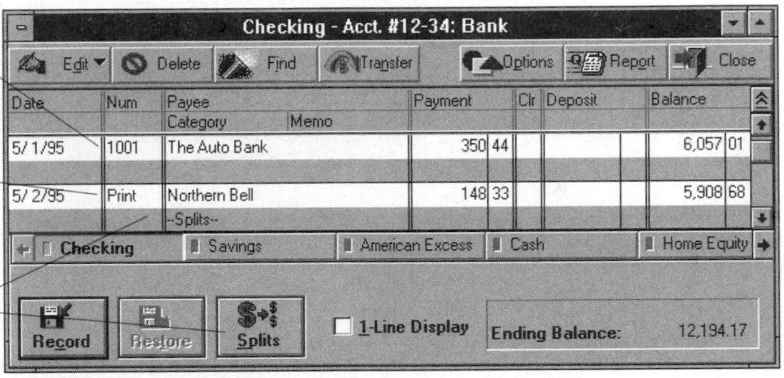

Windows Tip
A scroll bar appears along the right side of the Register window. To scroll the register, click the Up and Down Arrows in the scroll bar.

2 **Scroll through the register.**

You can also drag the scroll box to search by date, or use the Find command to locate the transaction you want. (See "Finding a specific transaction" on page 31.)

3 **As you review checks in the check register, you can delete or change them any way you like.**

For more information about changing transactions in the register, see "Revising transactions" on page 34.

Changes you make to an unprinted check will appear on the printed check.

Or press Ctrl+W

4 **Click the Write Checks window to return to it.**

Writing postdated checks

One way of scheduling checks for future payment is to postdate them. This method helps you forecast how much money you need in the coming weeks. Later, when you print checks, you can have Quicken print checks dated through a specific date. Except for changing the date, writing postdated checks is the same as writing regular checks with Quicken. (Caution: don't mail your postdated checks!)

You can also schedule transactions with the Quicken Financial Calendar. See Chapter 5, *Using the Quicken Financial Calendar,* on page 49.

1 **In the Write Checks window, change the current date to the date in the future when you want to print the check.**

2 **Complete the check as described on page 64.**

3 **Click Record to record the check.**

When you have postdated checks in your account, Quicken calculates a Current Balance and Ending Balance and displays them both at the bottom of the Write Checks window.

If this is a check you are printing, the Checks To Print amount shows the total amount of checks you have written, but not printed yet.

If this is a check you are paying electronically, the field is labeled "Checks to Xmit" and it shows the total amount of checks you have written, but not yet transmitted.

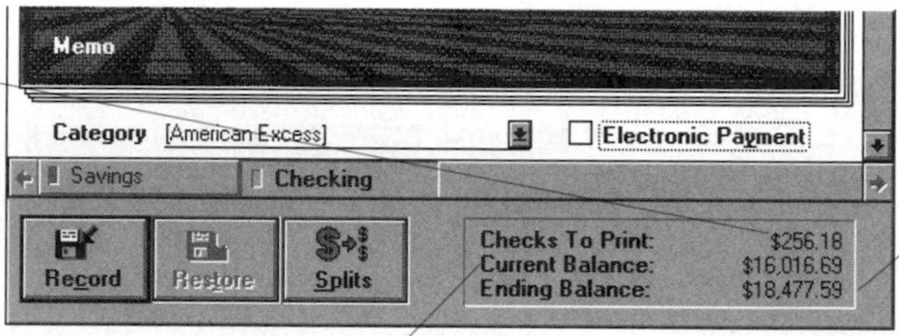

The Ending Balance amount shows the balance after all postdated transactions.

The Current Balance amount shows the balance in your account before any postdated transactions.

See "Using Quicken Reminders and Billminder" on page 60.

The Billminder and Reminders features can remind you to print postdated checks and other scheduled transactions up to 30 days before their scheduled dates. These reminders help you pay bills on time if you don't use Quicken every day.

Changing check options

You can change check, QuickFill, and miscellaneous options from the Write Checks window.

1 **Click Options in the Write Checks window.**

2 **Click the Checks tab.**

These are the default settings when Quicken is installed.

To turn on an option, select a checkbox by clicking in it.

To turn off an option, clear the checkbox by clicking in it.

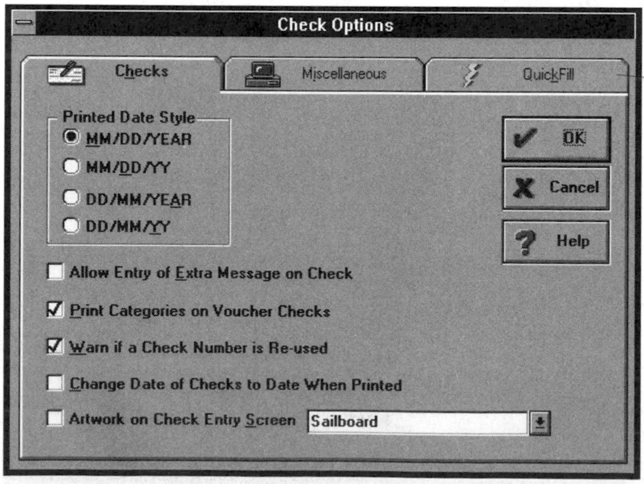

Click one of these tabs to change miscellaneous or QuickFill options.

3 **Click the options you want to change, and then click OK.**

Checks options	Quicken does this when the option is selected
Printed Date Style	Displays dates in a MM/DD/YY (month/day/year) or MM/DD/YEAR format. If you prefer the Canadian and European date style, select DD/MM/YY or DD/MM/YEAR.
Allow Entry of Extra Message on Check	Adds an extra Message box on the check that isn't visible when you mail the check in an Intuit window envelope, so you can use it for confidential information such as a credit card number. See page 64. If you turn off this off, Quicken saves any information entered into this box and redisplays it when you turn it on.
Print Categories on Voucher Checks	Prints categories from a split transaction on the perforated attachment to voucher checks. (See "Splitting transactions" on page 26 for more information.)
Warn if a Check Number is Re-used	Warns you if you enter a check number that has already been used.
Change Date of Checks to Date When Printed	Changes the date on checks to today's date when you print them.
Artwork on Check Entry Screen	Displays artwork in the Write Checks window. Select an artwork choice from the drop-down list. This artwork will not show up when you print.

About printing checks

When you print checks with Quicken, you use special personalized checks from Intuit, designed to work with Quicken. Intuit makes checks for page-oriented and continuous-feed printers.

You can print checks as soon as you've written them, or you can wait and print them at another time. For example, you can enter checks in the Write Checks window at various times throughout the month, but wait and print them only once or twice each month. (If you haven't entered the check details yet, see "Filling out a check" on page 64.)

See "Using Quicken Reminders and Billminder" on page 60.

You can print checks from the register, as described in the following sections, or you can click Checks to Print in Quicken Reminders when you start Quicken.

See "Changing check options" on page 66.

To reprint checks that you have already printed, see "Reprinting checks" on page 81. You can also set your own options for how checks are displayed onscreen and printed.

See Appendix C, *Ordering Intuit software and supplies,* on page 313.

When you order personalized Intuit checks, Intuit prints your name, address, account number, bank name, check numbers, and all the information required by financial institutions on your checks.

Printing checks on page-oriented printers

This section explains how to print checks on a laser, inkjet, postscript, or other *page-oriented* printer (including a dot matrix printer that has a paper tray). If you have a continuous-feed (also known as tractor-feed or dot matrix) printer, turn to page 74.

The basic steps for printing checks are:

- **Set up your check printer.**
  See "Setting up page-oriented printers" on this page.
- **Load the checks in your page-oriented printer just as you would any letterhead paper.**
  Refer to the manual that came with your printer for information on using letterhead with your printer. You need to know how to orient checks when you insert them in your printer. If your first page of checks is partial (has only one or two checks left on it), the instructions are a little different.
- **If this is the first time you've printed an Intuit check, print a sample check to make sure the alignment is correct.**
- **Print your checks.**
  See "Printing checks from your account" on page 70.
- **Examine the checks to make sure they've all printed correctly.**

Setting up page-oriented printers

1 **From the File menu, choose Printer Setup and then choose Check Printer Setup.**

Click the drop-down button to display the Printer drop-down list.

Quicken can automatically detect whether your printer is continuous-feed or page-oriented.

There are three types of Intuit check styles:
- Standard checks
- Voucher checks
- Wallet checks

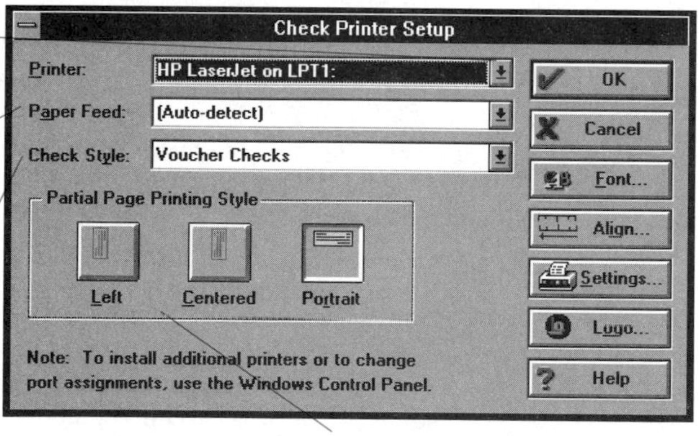

These icons represent three possible orientations for when you need to print a partial page of checks. See "Printing a partial first page of checks" on page 72.

2 **Select the printer you want to use from the Printer drop-down list.**

If the printer you want to use isn't listed, use the Windows Control Panel to install the printer driver for your printer.

See your *Microsoft Windows User's Guide* for instructions on installing a printer driver.

3 **Select Auto-detect from the Paper Feed drop-down list.**

Quicken automatically detects if your printer is continuous-feed or page-oriented. (If you want, you can force Quicken to use one or the other by selecting it here.)

4 **Select the style of check you will be printing from the Check Style drop-down list.**

5 **(Optional) Click Font to select a different font type, style, or size for the printing on your checks and click OK.**

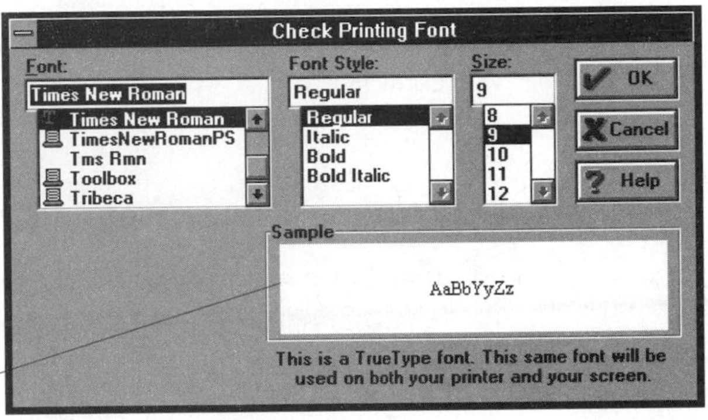

The Sample box shows the currently selected font style and size.

See page 82 for more details of the settings you can choose.

6 **(Optional) Click Settings to change the paper source and click OK.**

7 **(Optional) Click Logo to include artwork on your printed checks.**

You can include your own logo on your checks by specifying an art file stored on disk (standard or voucher checks only). The artwork must be a bitmap (.BMP) file. You can create bitmaps in applications such as Paintbrush. The logo is printed in the upper left corner of each check. (You can choose whether or not to include the logo on the check each time you print checks.)

Now you are ready to print a sample check. Your Quicken package includes sample checks for continuous-feed printers. To practice printing with them in your page-oriented printer, separate the checks into pages of three checks each. Remove the tractor strips at the sides from each page of three checks.

8 **Insert one full page of three checks in the paper tray of your printer.**

9 **Make sure your printer is turned on and online.**

10 **Click Align, and then click Test to print a sample check.**

Quicken prints a sample check.

If you see a message that your printer isn't set up for the form size Quicken requires, click OK. You need to change your printer setup before printing any other checks.

See "Changing the settings for your printer driver" on page 82.

11 **Look at the sample check.**

Check the horizontal alignment. Does the text appear too far to the left or right? Check the vertical alignment. If the check is aligned correctly, the type rests just above the lines on the check.

- If the sample check printed correctly, click Done in the Check Printer Alignment window to save your setup, and see "Printing checks from your account" next.
- If the sample check *didn't* print correctly, see "Correcting the alignment of your checks" on page 75 before printing checks.

Saving sample check stock
If you have trouble getting your checks to print at first, don't continue to use the sample checks that came with Quicken. Instead, print sample checks on blank paper. After printing a sample check, place the paper on top of the sample checks and hold them both up to the light to see if the text printed correctly.

Printing checks from your account

To print a partial first page of checks instead of a full page, see "Printing a partial first page of checks" on page 72.

1 **Insert one full page of checks in the paper tray of your printer.**

A partial page means that the last time you printed standard or wallet checks, you may have printed only one or two checks instead of all three checks on the final page, and now you are starting to print with that leftover page. (Voucher checks only come one to a page.)

2 **Make sure your printer is turned on and online.**

3 **Open the account you want to print checks from.**

To open an account, select it and click Open.

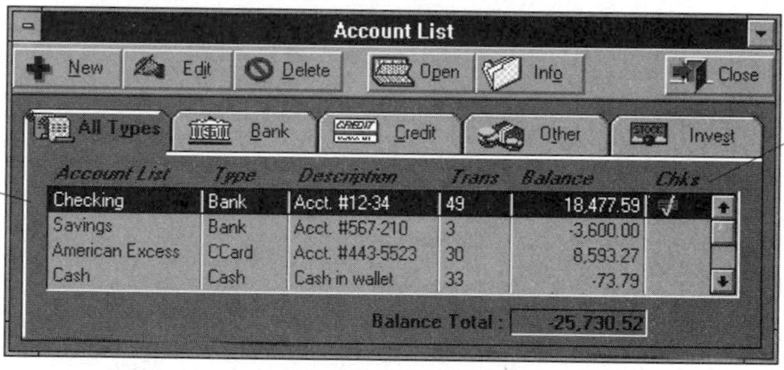

Quicken displays a checkmark in the Chks column when you have checks to print in an account.

4 **From the File menu, choose Print Checks.**

This number should be the same as the number on the first check in the printer.

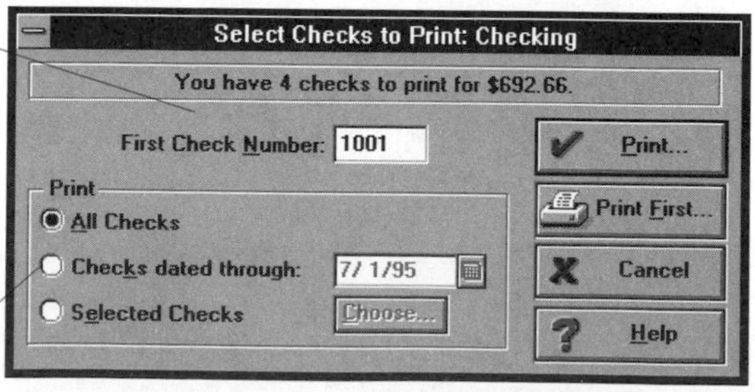

Choose this option to select checks in a different date range to be printed.

5 **In the First Check Number box, type the number of the first check in your printer.**

6 **Select the checks you want to print from the Print box:**

- Click All Checks to print all unprinted checks, including postdated checks.
- Click Checks Dated Through to change the date range of the checks to be printed; usually, the date is the current date. Specify a date later than today to print postdated checks.
- Click Selected Checks and then click Choose to print only specified checks.

7 **If you chose Selected Checks, mark each check you want to print, and then click Done.**

To mark a check to be printed, select that check and press the spacebar, or click the transaction. If you accidentally mark a check that you don't want to print, mark the check again.

Quicken lists all the checks you've written and not yet printed in chronological order.

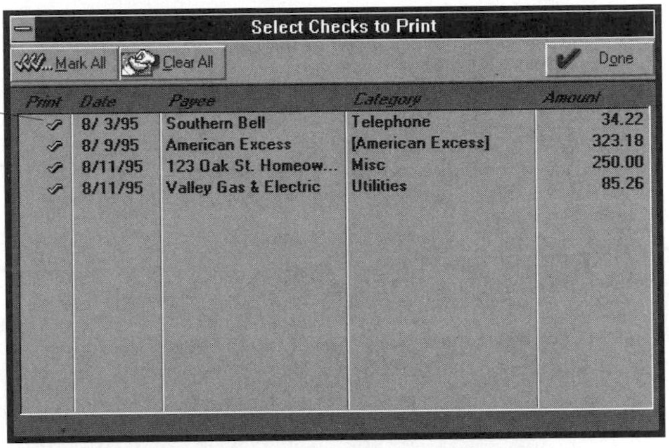

8 **Click Print in the Select Checks to Print window.**

If you need to print less than a full page of three checks, see "Printing a partial first page of checks" on page 72.

To include your logo artwork on the printed checks, select this checkbox. (Standard and voucher checks only.) You must have already specified the artwork while setting up, as described earlier in this chapter.

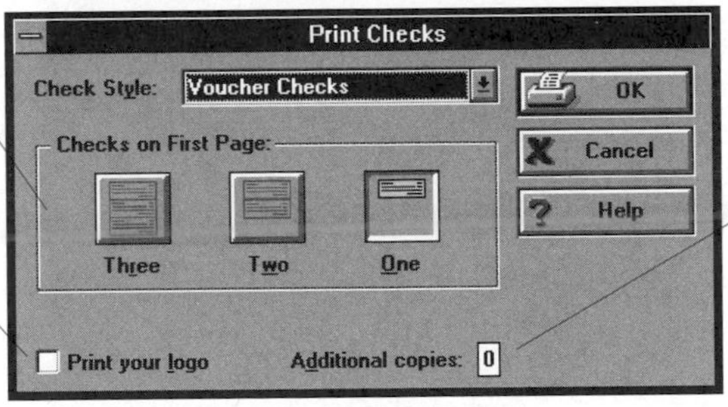

Voucher checks only: If you would like to print more than one copy of each voucher check, enter the required number of additional copies here.

9 **Select the correct check style.**

10 **Choose the number of checks that are on the first page of checks.**

Three (a full page) is the usual setting. If your first page has only one or two of the original three checks left on it, see page 72 for information about printing a partial first page of checks. If you are printing on voucher checks, you don't need to select an icon.

11 **Click OK.**

Quicken asks if your checks printed OK.

If any of the checks didn't print correctly, enter the check number of the first incorrectly printed check and then click OK.

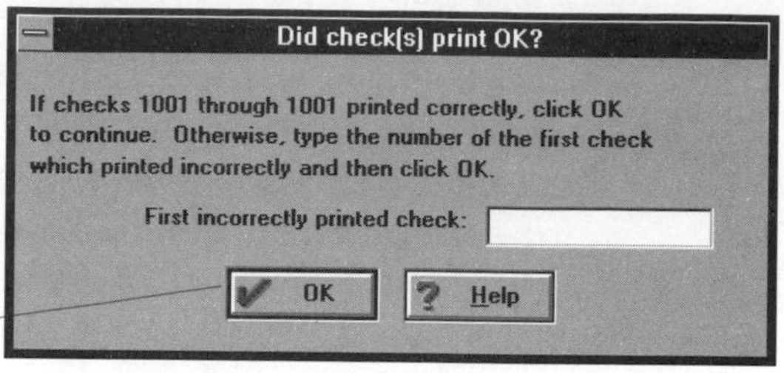

If the checks printed correctly, click OK.

12 **If the checks printed correctly, click OK.**

Otherwise, type the number of the first check that didn't print correctly and click OK. Quicken makes them available for printing again. Examine your printer to see if the checks jammed or the printer ran out of checks. If the text on the checks in your printer isn't aligned correctly, you may need to adjust the check printing settings.

See "Correcting the alignment of your checks" on page 75.

If only one check in the middle of a series of checks didn't print properly, and the rest printed properly, don't enter a number but click OK. Then reprint the check that didn't print properly.

See "Reprinting checks" on page 81.

Printing a partial first page of checks

InkJet printers can't print partial page checks.

If you use standard or wallet checks in your page-oriented printer, you'll sometimes find that a *partial page* of one or two blank checks remains after you have finished printing. You can easily use that partial first page the next time you print checks.

You can print partial pages of standard or wallet checks, but not voucher checks, which come one to a page only.

1 **Turn on your printer, but don't load your checks yet.**

2 **From the File menu, choose Printer Setup and then choose Check Printer Setup.**

3 **Click one of the Partial Page Printing Style icons to show how you insert envelopes (and partial pages of checks) into your printer and click OK.**

Before you insert your checks into the envelope feeder, you need to know:

- The type of envelope feeder your printer has (Left, Centered, or Portrait).
- If you should insert the check face up or face down.

- If you should insert the left edge, right edge, top, or bottom of the check into the printer first.

The direction of the arrow is toward the printer.

Positioned on the left side of the envelope feeder, with the right or the left edge of the check feeding into the printer.

Centered in the envelope feeder, with the right or the left edge of the check feeding into the printer.

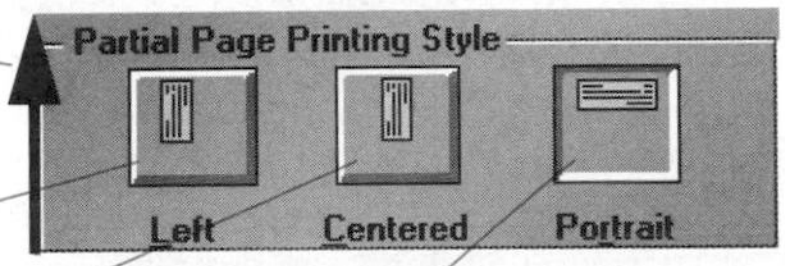

Centered in the envelope feeder, with the top or the bottom edge of the check feeding into the printer.

Feed partial pages of checks into your printer the same way you feed envelopes. Consult your printer manual to find out which of these three basic positions the printer manufacturer recommends for loading envelopes.

If your checks print upside down or on the wrong side, reverse the way you load the checks into the feeder.

4 **From the File menu, choose Print Checks.**

5 **Be sure the displayed first check number is the same as the first check on your partial page of checks.**

6 **Select the checks you want to print in the Print box.**

7 **Click Print.**

8 **In the Print Checks window, click one of the Checks on First Page icons:**

Three, which is initially selected, represents a complete page of three checks.

Choose the icon that represents the number of checks you will be printing. (Depending on the printer you use to print checks, the orientation of the check icons on the buttons may be vertical instead of horizontal as shown here.)

9 **Load the one or two checks in your envelope feeder or cassette as pictured in the partial-page icon you selected.**

If your printer requires that you load letterhead face down (as the HP LaserJet IIP printer does), load your checks that way. Look in your printer manual if you aren't sure.

Preventing wasted checks:
You may need to use Intuit Forms Leaders to prevent wasted checks if your page-oriented printer doesn't have an envelope feeder, *and* you are using standard three-to-a page checks, *and* you want to print checks on partial pages. See "Intuit Supplies" on page 320 for the phone number to order Forms Leaders.

---

10 **Click OK.**

If your printer uses the Centered type of envelope feeder, Quicken asks whether or not you have removed the tear-off strip at the side of the page. This information affects the positioning of the checks.

Quicken asks if your checks printed OK.

11 **If your checks printed correctly, click OK.**

Otherwise, see "Correcting the alignment of your checks" on page 75, and then reprint your checks.

Printing checks on continuous-feed printers

This section explains how to print checks on continuous-feed (also known as tractor-feed or dot matrix) printers. If you have a laser, inkjet, postscript, or other *page-oriented* printer (including a dot matrix printer that has a paper tray), go to page 68.

The basic steps for printing checks are:

- **Set up your check printer.**
  See "Setting up continuous-feed printers" on this page.
- **Load the checks in your continuous-feed printer just as you would any printer paper.**
- **If this is the first time you've printed an Intuit check, print a sample check to make sure the alignment is correct.**
- **Print your checks.**
  See "Printing checks from your account" on page 78.
- **Examine the checks to make sure they've all printed correctly.**

Setting up continuous-feed printers

1 **From the File menu, choose Printer Setup and then choose Check Printer Setup.**

Click the drop-down button to display the Printer drop-down list.

Quicken can automatically detect whether your printer is continuous-feed or page-oriented.

There are three types of Intuit check styles:
- Standard checks
- Voucher checks
- Wallet checks

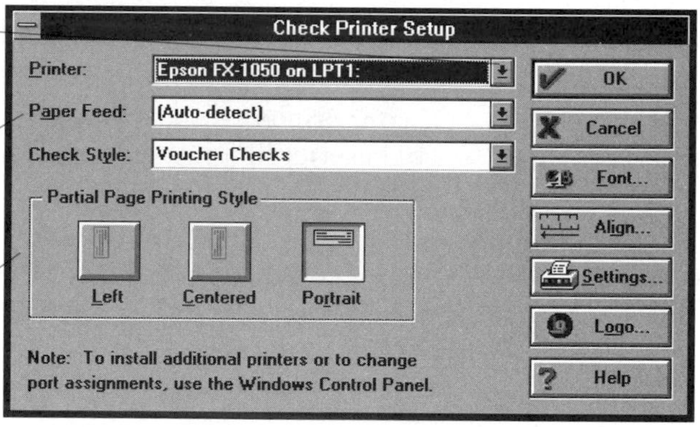

2 **Select the printer you want to use from the Printer drop-down list.**

See your *Microsoft Windows User's Guide* for instructions on installing a printer.

If the printer you want to use isn't listed, use the Windows Control Panel to install the printer driver for your printer.

3 **Select Auto-detect from the Paper Feed drop-down list.**

Quicken automatically detects if your printer is continuous-feed or page-oriented. However, you can force Quicken to use one or the other by selecting that option here.

4 **Select the style of check you will be printing from the Check Style drop-down list.**

5 **(Optional) Click Font to select a different font type, style, or size for the printed type on your checks and click OK.**

See page 82 for more details of the settings you can choose.

6 **(Optional) Click Settings to change the paper source and click OK.**

Now you are ready to print a sample check. Your Quicken package includes sample checks for continuous-feed printers, and Quicken helps you line up the checks correctly in your printer.

7 **Insert the checks in your printer.**

See "Intuit Supplies" on page 320 for the phone number to order Forms Leaders.

Preventing wasted checks:
You may need to use Intuit Forms Leaders to prevent wasted checks if your continuous-feed printer has a tractor feed mechanism above the print head and you can't print on the first check.

8 **Make sure your printer is turned on and online.**

9 **Click Align.**

The Alignment For Continuous Printer window appears.

10 **Prints a sample check. Either:**

- Click Coarse and then click OK.
- Click Fine, make any adjustments necessary, and then click Done.

11 **Without moving the check in the printer, look at the sample check.**

Check the horizontal alignment. Does the text appear too far to the left or right? Check the vertical alignment. If the check is aligned correctly, the type rests just above the lines on the check.

- If the sample check printed correctly, click Done in the Check Printer Alignment window to save your setup, and see "Printing checks from your account" on page 78.
- If the sample check *didn't* print correctly, see "Correcting the alignment of your checks" next.

Correcting the alignment of your checks

If your checks didn't print correctly, adjust the alignment. You can do this either while setting up your printer or while printing checks.

For page-oriented printers, you see the Check Printer Alignment window—continue as described on page 76.

1 **At the Check Printer Setup window, click Align.**

2 **For continuous-feed printers, make an approximate side-to-side positioning adjustment by hand, moving the paper clamps on the printer as necessary.**

The Intuit Printer Library window offers two methods of check alignment:

- Coarse vertical alignment. Click Coarse to make up and down adjustments using Quicken's patented pointer-line method (see below). If only a horizontal adjustment is needed, click Fine instead. If you use this method, note the position of the paper in your printer, as Quicken does not memorize it.

See "Fine alignment with the Check Printer Alignment window" on this page.

- Fine vertical or horizontal alignment. Click Fine for fine-tuning in any direction.

Coarse alignment with the pointer-line method

Follow the onscreen instructions to print a sample check and to tell Quicken where the pointer line appears on the sample check. Tell Quicken which number the pointer line points to. In this example, the line points to number 26. Quicken automatically compensates when it prints further checks.

Tell Quicken which number at the edge of the sample check the pointer line is pointing to.

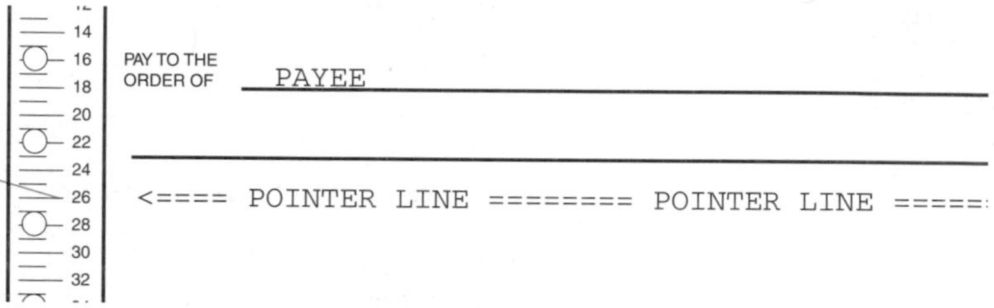

Fine alignment with the Check Printer Alignment window

The Check Printer Alignment window shows how text should be aligned on your check.

If you move the arrow cursor over the check illustrated in this window, an alignment cursor appears. The alignment cursor allows you to move the text on the screen to show Quicken how the text on your checks is actually aligned.

Your printed check may not look exactly like the check illustrated here, but you can still show Quicken how the text is actually aligned by using the name of the payee and the "Pay to the Order of" line as your guide.

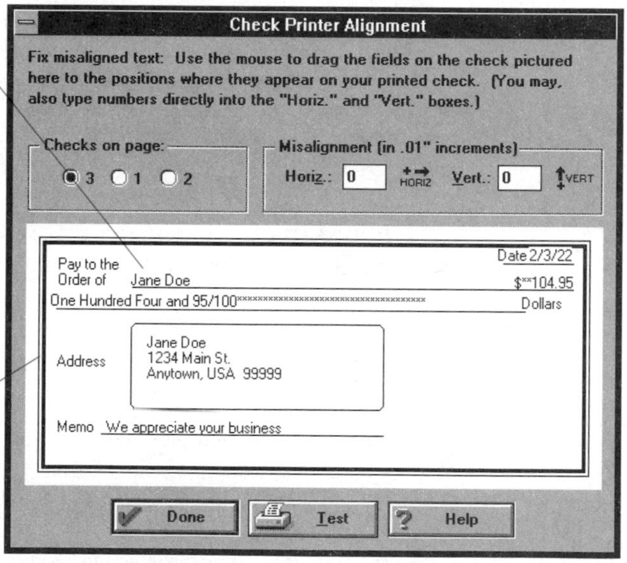

This window initially shows how text *should be aligned* on your check. Use the alignment cursor to show how text is *actually aligned* on your check. Quicken takes the alignment you indicate and transposes it into the correct alignment on the next sample check you print.

1 **Move the arrow cursor over the check in the Check Printer Alignment window to see the alignment cursor.**

2 **Using the printed sample check as your guide, show how your check is aligned incorrectly.**

- Hold down the left mouse button and move the text around until it looks the same as your printed sample check.

Use the alignment cursor to move the text in the check on the screen. In this example, the payee printed too far to the right and too low on the printed check.

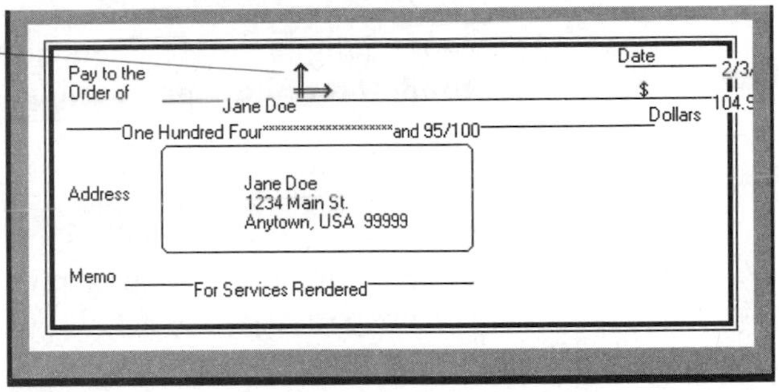

OR

- Enter numbers in the Horiz box or Vert box.

This method works well if the printing on the check needs just a small nudge to correct the horizontal or vertical alignment of the printed text.

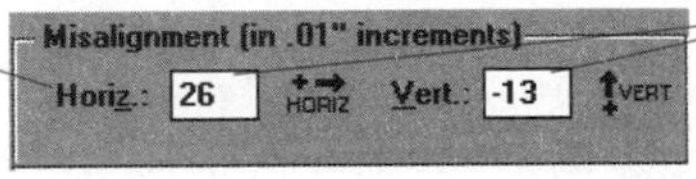

The numbers you enter here are in 1/100s inches.

Use the values from the following table to determine what to enter

If the text prints	Type a
Too high	Positive number in the Vertical field. For example, if the text is printing 1/4″ too high, type 25.
Too low	Negative number in the Vertical field. For example, if the text is printing 1/4″ too low, type -25.
Too far to the left	Negative number in the Horizontal field. For example, if the text is printing 1/4″ too far to the left, type -25.
Too far to the right	Positive number in the Horizontal field. For example, if the text is printing 1/4″ too far to the right, type 25.

3 **Click Test to print another sample check with the new settings.**

Quicken aligns the check vertically or horizontally in the printer before printing the next check.

4 **Look at the second sample check.**

- If the second check printed correctly, continue to the next step.
- If the text is misaligned by a noticeable amount, repeat the steps above until a sample check prints correctly. If the text is misaligned by a tiny amount, use the Horizontal or Vertical boxes to nudge the alignment very slightly.

5 **If you change check styles often, note the correct horizontal and vertical alignment numbers in the Check Printer Alignment window for future positioning.**

For example, you may print voucher checks for your small business and standard or wallet checks for your personal finances.

Page-oriented printers only: Quicken saves the horizontal and vertical numbers according to the numbers of checks on a page. If you use partial pages of wallet or standard checks, you may have to adjust the alignment for each of the three options.

To print a partial page of checks, you may need to change the horizontal and vertical numbers for each of these options.

Once you have determined the correct alignment for each of these conditions, Quicken remembers the correct settings until you use a different check style or select a different printer to print checks.

6 **Continuous-feed printers only: Note the correct check position in the printer for future positioning.**

Visually line up part of your printer, such as the sprocket cover or print head, with one of the position numbers at the edge of the check.

7 **Save your check printer setup.**

Page-oriented printers: click Done and then click OK to save your check printer setup. Continuous-feed printers: click Done, click Cancel, and then click OK.

You are now ready to print your checks.

Printing checks from your account

1 **Insert the checks in your printer.**

2 **Make sure your printer is turned on and online.**

3 **Open the account you want to print checks from.**

To open an account, select it and click Open.

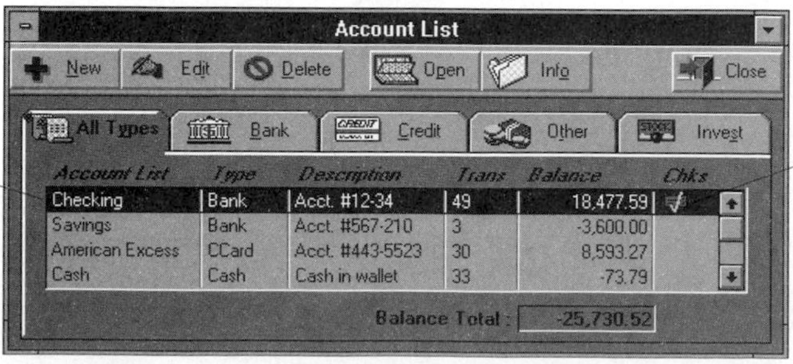

Quicken displays a check-mark in the Chks column when you have checks to print in an account.

4 **From the File menu, choose Print Checks.**

Enter here the number shown on the first check positioned in the printer.

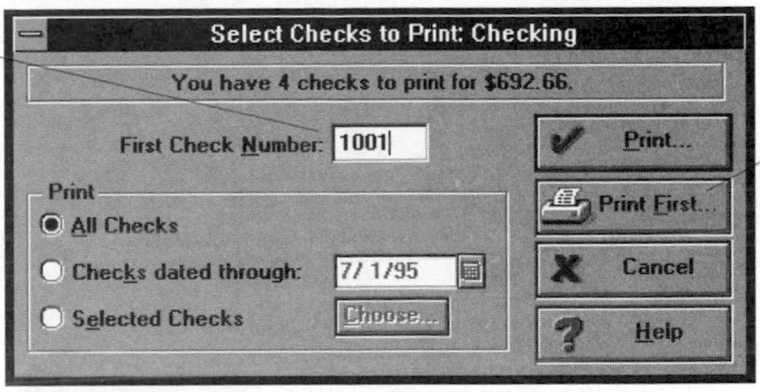

Click here to print only the first check in the series of checks you intend to print. Use this option instead of Test when you're fairly sure that everything is aligned correctly and ready to print. That way, you can sign and use the printed check.

5 **Type the number of the first check in your printer.**

6 **Select the checks you want to print from the Print box:**

- Click All Checks to print all unprinted checks, including postdated checks.
- Click Checks Dated Through to change the date range of the checks to be printed; usually, the date is the current date. Specify a date later than today to print postdated checks.
- Click Selected Checks and then click Choose to print only specified checks.

7 **If you chose Selected Checks, mark each check you want to print, and then click Done.**

To mark a check to be printed, select that check and press the spacebar, or click the transaction. If you accidentally mark a check that you don't want to print, mark the check again.

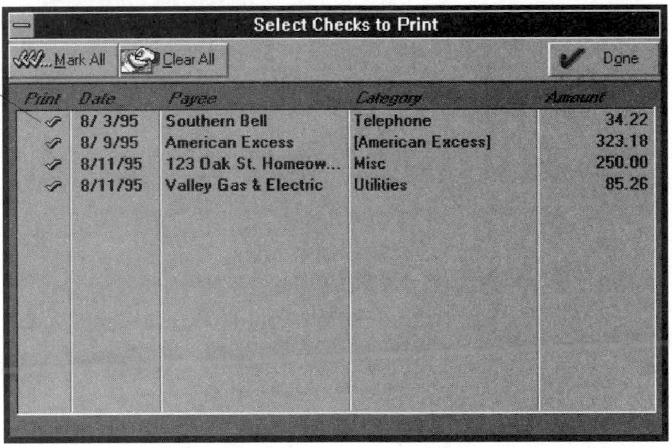

Select Checks to Print
Mark All
Clear All
Done
Print Date Payee Category Amount
8/ 3/95 Southern Bell Telephone 34.22
8/ 9/95 American Excess [American Excess] 323.18
8/11/95 123 Oak St. Homeow... Misc 250.00
8/11/95 Valley Gas & Electric Utilities 85.26

Quicken lists all the checks you've written and not yet printed in chronological order.

8 Click Print in the Select Checks to Print window.

To print less than a full page of three checks, see "Printing a partial first page of checks" on page 72.

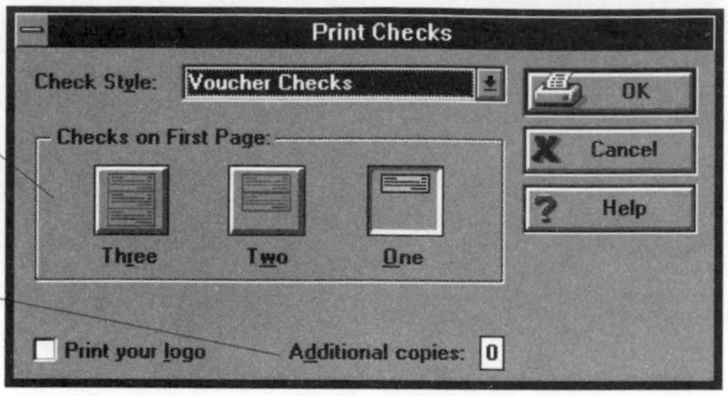

Voucher checks only: If you would like to print more than one copy of each voucher check, enter the required number of additional copies here.

9 Select the correct check style from the Check Style drop-down list.

10 Click OK.

Quicken asks if your checks printed OK.

If any of the checks didn't print correctly, enter the check number of the first incorrectly printed check and then click OK.

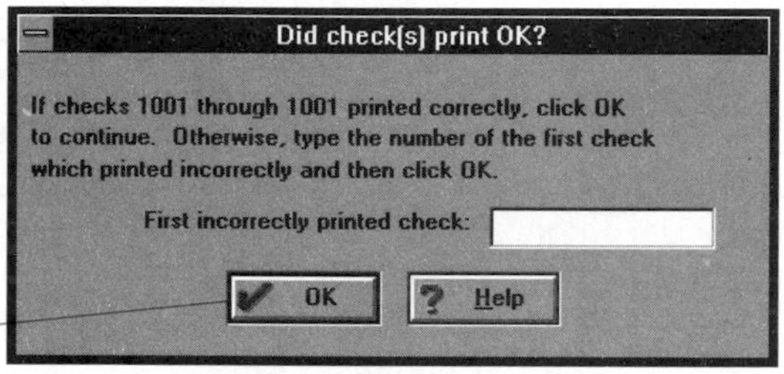

If the checks printed correctly, click OK. Your check printing is finished!

11 If the checks printed correctly, click OK.

Otherwise, type the number of the first check that didn't print correctly and click OK. Quicken makes them available for printing again. Check if the checks jammed or the printer ran out of checks. If the text on the checks in your printer isn't aligned correctly, you may need to adjust the check printing settings.

See "Correcting the alignment of your checks" on page 75.

If only the first check of a series of checks didn't print properly, and the rest printed properly, don't enter a number but click OK. Then reprint the check that didn't print properly.

See "Reprinting checks" on page 81.

Reprinting checks

You can easily reprint any check at any time. You can also enter any number of copies in the Print Checks window to print multiple copies of checks.

1 **In the register, select the transaction for the check you want to reprint.**

2 **Select the check number and type** Print **over the check number.**

(If you have QuickFill turned on, all you have to type is P.)

Quicken replaces the check number with Print in the Num field and considers the check unprinted.

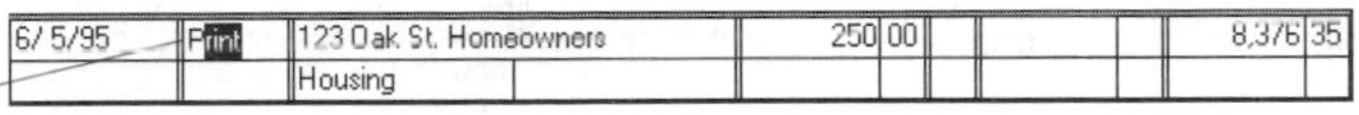

Typing Print in the Num field turns a check that has already been printed into a check that you can print again.

3 **Click Record.**

4 **Print the check as usual, taking note to enter the correct first check number.**

Check printing problems and solutions

This section describes some common check printing problems and their solutions. If you continue to have problems, see your printer manual or call Quicken Technical Support. (See "Quicken Technical Support" on page 319 for the phone number.)

Problem	Solution
Printer doesn't print.	Check your equipment: • Make sure your printer is turned on and online, and that the cable connection between the printer and the computer is secure. • From the File menu, choose Printer Setup and then Check Printer Setup. Make sure that the correct printer is selected. • Try to print a Windows Write document. Look for Write in the Accessories Program Group. Open it and type a few words. Then, from Write's File menu, choose Print. If the document prints OK, the problem probably lies with your check printer setup.
Text prints too high, too low, too far left, or too far right on checks.	Adjust the Horizontal or Vertical setting in the Check Printer Alignment window. See "Correcting the alignment of your checks" on page 75.
Text is left-aligned correctly, but right-aligned incorrectly.	If this is a wallet check, choose 10-point Courier as the font. See the font settings on page 69. If you have an early version of a printer driver for your printer, you may be able to change the printer driver settings. See "Changing the settings for your printer driver" on page 82.

Changing the settings for your printer driver

1 **From the File menu, choose Printer Setup and then choose Check Printer Setup.**

2 **Select the printer you want to use from the Printer drop-down list.**

3 **Click the Settings button.**

Windows displays the printer driver window for your printer. The options you see on your screen may be different from the settings illustrated here, depending on the type of printer you are using.

These are the settings for the printer driver of a continuous-feed printer.

The Resolution setting doesn't affect check printing.

Select User Defined Size from the Paper Size drop-down list to set up the correct size for the check style you are using. If the User Defined Size option isn't available, set the Paper Size at Letter 8 1/2 x 11 inches.

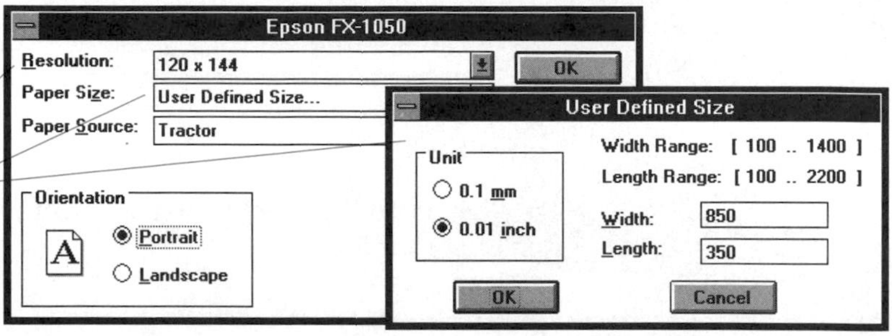

These are the settings for the printer driver of a page-oriented printer.

Select User Defined Size from the Paper Size drop-down list to set up the correct size for the check style you are using. If the User Defined Size option isn't available, set the Paper Size at Letter 8 1/2 x 11 inches.

Select portrait.

Set the rest of the options according to your printer's user manual.

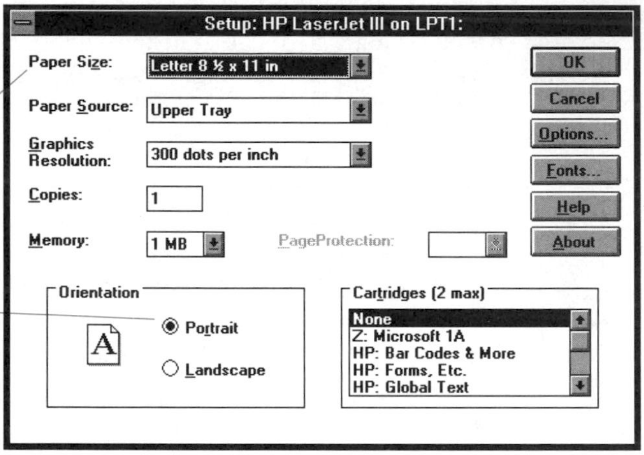

4 **In the printer driver window, set the correct paper size for the style of checks you are using.**

In the Paper Size drop-down list, select the User Defined Size option, then enter the paper size according to the following table. If there isn't a User Defined Size option in this list, select Letter 8 1/2 x 11 inches and click OK.

Check style	Standard checks	Wallet checks	Voucher checks
Paper size (unit .01 inch)	Width: 850 Length: 350	Width: 850 Length: 284	Width: 850 Length: 700

5 **Click OK to close the printer driver window.**

7 Balancing your checkbook

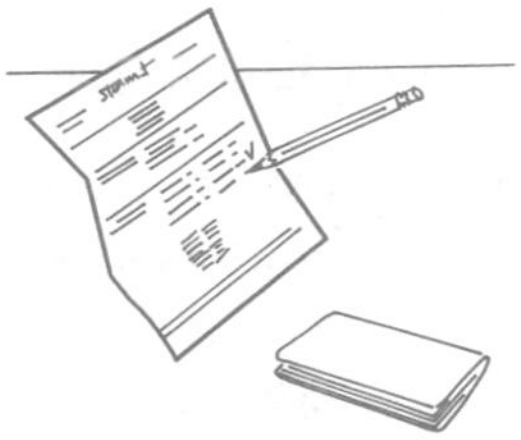

How Quicken helps you balance your account

When your bank statement arrives, use Quicken to balance, or reconcile, your checkbook.

The overall goal of reconciliation is to bring your Quicken records into balance with your bank records.

Quicken lets you reconcile to the degree of accuracy that works for you. You can track down every cent if you prefer, but Quicken doesn't require you to balance every penny.

When your bank statement arrives, follow the steps below to reconcile your account. Quicken reconciles one statement at a time. If you have two or more statements that need reconciling, start with the earliest statement and reconcile each one individually.

- **If this is the first time you've reconciled the bank account:**
  See "Balancing your account for the first time" on page 84.
- **Start reconciling by entering information from your current bank statement.**
  See "Starting reconciliation" on page 85.
- **Mark the transactions that have cleared your bank account in the Reconcile window.**
  See "Marking cleared transactions" on page 86.
- **Compare the totals of cleared items in the Reconcile window with those on your bank statement.**
  See "Completing reconciliation" on page 87.
- **(Optional) Create and print a reconciliation report.**
  See "Completing reconciliation" on page 87.

Balancing your account for the first time

The first time you balance your account may take some extra time. After you find the point where Quicken and the bank agree on the amount of money in your account, reconciling your account each month should be easier. Before you can reconcile your accounts accurately, you need to do two things:

1. **Enter *all* uncleared transactions in your account.**

   For bank accounts, these are all transactions that haven't cleared the bank or shown up on previous bank statements.

   In most cases, you'll be reminded to enter all uncleared transactions because the transactions appear on the bank statement when you're trying to reconcile. You can also enter these transactions in the register as you find them during reconciliation.

2. **Update the Opening Balance transaction to reflect the amount that was actually in your account when you began using Quicken with that account.**

   You can correct the amount of the Opening Balance transaction in your check register to match the ending balance from the last bank statement you received before you started Quicken. Or Quicken can create an opening balance adjustment at the end of your first reconciliation.

Your opening balance . . .

Suppose the ending balance on the bank statement for your checking account was $200.52 on December 31, 1994. You start using Quicken on January 12, 1995. You use the ending balance from your December statement as the balance for your Quicken checking account.

Then you enter transactions from your paper check register from January 1 to 12 into Quicken. From January 12 on, you enter all transactions into Quicken as they occur.

and checks that were outstanding when you started with Quicken

In February, you receive your January 31, 1995 bank statement. You see two checks (totaling $80) that you wrote in December 1994 and that had not yet cleared the bank in December. Now they have cleared the bank, so they appear on the January bank statement. You didn't enter those checks in Quicken at the time you set up the checking account because they occurred before January 1.

Even though those two checks were written before the date of the first transaction in Quicken, you need to enter them into Quicken's register. (You wouldn't enter any other checks that you wrote in December if they had already cleared the bank in December.) If you don't enter these uncleared transactions, Quicken will create an opening balance adjustment for $80 when you have finished reconciling.

Where the balances go

Quicken uses the opening balance from the account for the opening balance in the Reconcile Bank Statement window.

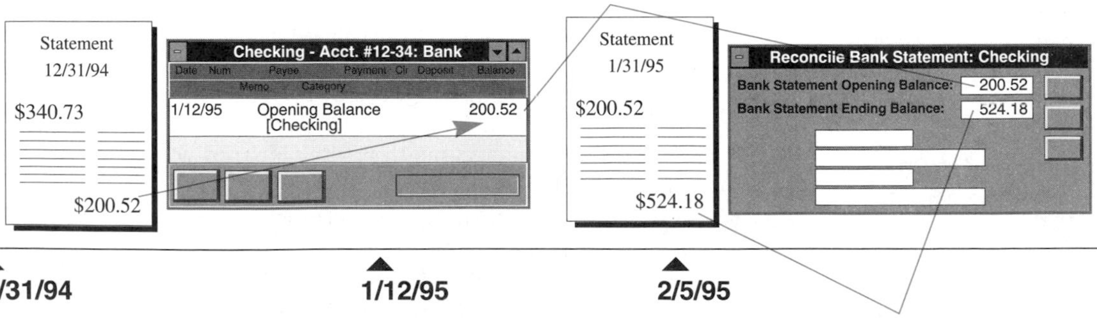

Enter the ending balance from your most recent bank statement as the opening balance in your Quicken account.

When your next bank statement arrives, enter the ending balance from it in the Reconcile Bank Statement window.

Starting reconciliation

If the balance shown on your bank statement is different from Quicken's balance for the account, don't assume that the bank balance is current. You've probably entered transactions into Quicken after the bank prepared your statement. You may also have checks or other transactions from earlier months that haven't yet cleared the bank. Be sure to enter these transactions in the register now if you haven't already done so.

1 **Select the account you want to reconcile.**

2 **From the Activities menu, choose Reconcile.**

If this is your first time to reconcile this account, this number is taken from the ending balance of your previous bank statement.

If this isn't your first time to reconcile this account, this number equals the total of all reconciled transactions in the check register. In the register, all reconciled transactions are marked with an **x** in the Clr (Cleared) column, just like your Opening Balance transaction.

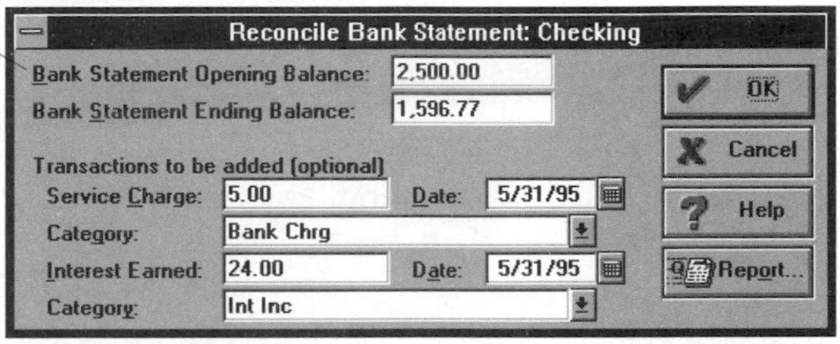

For example, if you started using Quicken in January 1995 and your latest bank statement was dated December 31, 1994, the ending balance amount from the December statement is the same amount in the Opening Balance transaction in your Quicken register. Quicken enters that number here.

3 **Compare the opening balance amount shown on your bank statement with the amount shown in the Bank Statement Opening Balance box in the Reconcile Bank Statement window.**

Your bank statement might call this the *beginning* or *previous* balance.

See "Updating your previously reconciled balance" on page 91.

The amount in Quicken's Bank Statement Opening Balance box should be the same as the previous balance on your statement. If this is the first time you've reconciled your account, or if you haven't reconciled in quite some time, the amounts may differ.

4 **If the amount in the Bank Statement Opening Balance box doesn't match the opening balance shown on your bank statement for this account, correct the Quicken amount by entering the opening balance from the bank statement.**

See "Having Quicken adjust for differences" on page 90.

Quicken creates an opening balance difference that you will need to resolve later.

5 **Find the ending balance on your bank statement and enter it in the Bank Statement Ending Balance box in the Reconcile Bank Statement window.**

Your bank statement might call this the *current* or *new* balance.

6 **If any service charges are listed on your bank statement and you haven't already entered them in your Quicken register, enter the total amount in the Service Charge box, and then enter the date of the service charge in the Date box.**

7 **Enter a category for the Service Charge amount.**

Quicken remembers the category you use (such as Bank Chrg) and inserts it in this Category field the next time you reconcile.

8 **If your statement shows interest earned for your bank account and you haven't entered it in your Quicken register, enter the amount in the Interest Earned box, and then enter the date when the interest was earned in the Date box.**

9 **Enter a category for the Interest Earned amount.**

Quicken remembers the category you use (such as Int Inc) and inserts it in this Category field the next time you reconcile.

10 **Click OK.**

The Reconcile Bank Statement window appears, described in the next section.

Marking cleared transactions

Your next step in reconciling is to mark all cleared transactions. This involves matching each transaction on your bank statement with the corresponding entry in Quicken, and marking it as cleared.

1 **Match each transaction on your bank statement with the corresponding transaction in the Reconcile Bank Statement window, and mark the transaction as cleared.**

Click the transaction to mark it. Once you've marked a transaction as cleared, a checkmark appears in the Clr (Cleared) column. To unmark a marked transaction, click the transaction again.

As you check off cleared transactions, Quicken displays their total as the Cleared Balance in the lower right corner.

To sort transactions by date instead of check number, click this checkbox.

To edit an existing transaction, highlight it and then click Edit. To enter a missing transaction in your check register, click New.

To mark or clear a transaction:
- click it, or
- select it and click Mark or press the spacebar, or
- drag the mouse pointer across a range of transactions.

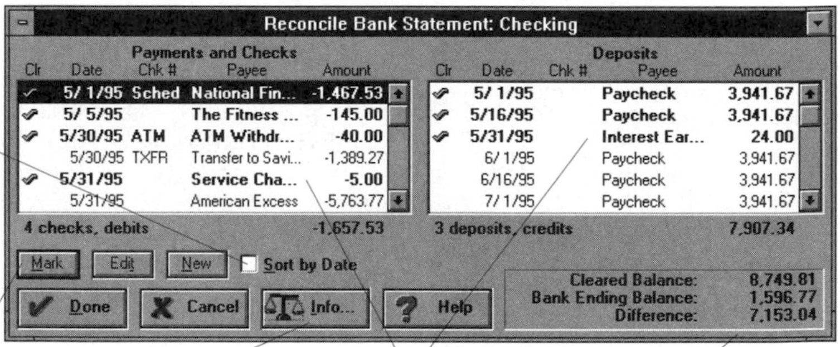

To edit reconciliation information (see the window on page 85), click Info.

This shows the interest and/or service charges you entered in the window on the previous page.

Quicken compares the total items marked cleared and the total items shown on the bank statement.

2 **If a transaction on your bank statement doesn't appear in the list of uncleared transactions, enter it now in the check register.**

- Click New to move to the blank transaction at the end of the register.
- Enter information for the transaction, then click Record.
- Click Close to return to the Reconcile Bank Statement window.
- Mark the transaction as cleared.

3 **If a transaction contains an incorrect amount or other error, correct it now in the check register.**

Or double-click the transaction

- Select the transaction in the Reconcile Bank Statement window.
- Click Edit to display the transaction in the register.
- Correct the error in the register, then click Record.
- Click Close to return to the Reconcile Bank Statement window.
- Mark the transaction as cleared.

Completing reconciliation

When you've finished checking off cleared transactions, look at the Difference amount in the Reconcile Bank Statement window. Compare it to the following three results:

- The Difference amount is zero and there is no Opening Balance Difference (see below)
- The Difference amount isn't zero (see page 88)
- The Difference amount is zero and there is an Opening Balance Difference (see page 88)

Result 1: If the Difference amount is zero *and* there is no Opening Balance Difference amount displayed above the Cleared Balance, you've reconciled the current bank statement successfully.

Click Done to complete reconciliation. The account register shows an X in the Clr (Cleared) field next to each reconciled transaction.

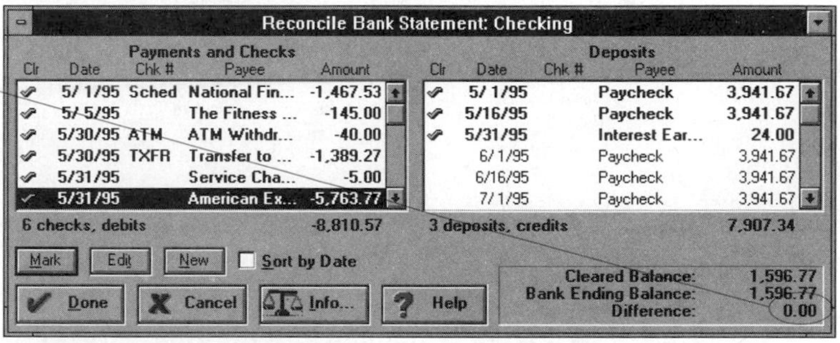

When you successfully complete balancing your account, Quicken asks if you would like to create a reconciliation report. (To create a reconciliation report at any time, choose Reconcile from the Activities menu, and then click Report.)

(Optional) Change the date if you want the report to state your reconciled balance as of a different date than today. For example, you might want a reconciliation report that ends on the last day of your accounting period, even if your bank statements arrive mid-month.

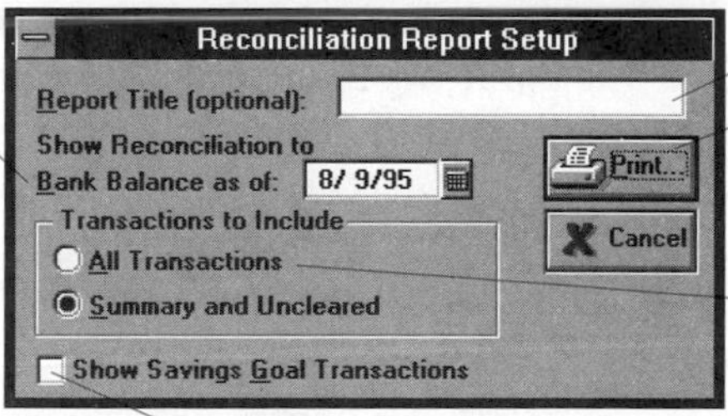

(Optional) Change the report title.

Click Print to print the report. (You see the Print Report window shown on page 213.)

(Optional) Click here to see detail for every reconciled transaction in addition to summary information.

Click here to show savings goal transactions. (See "Creating a savings goal" on page 241 for more information.)

Result 2: If the Difference amount isn't zero, you haven't finished balancing your account.

The Difference amount compares the total items marked cleared and the total items shown on the bank statement. In this example, there's a $40 difference between the check register and the bank statement.

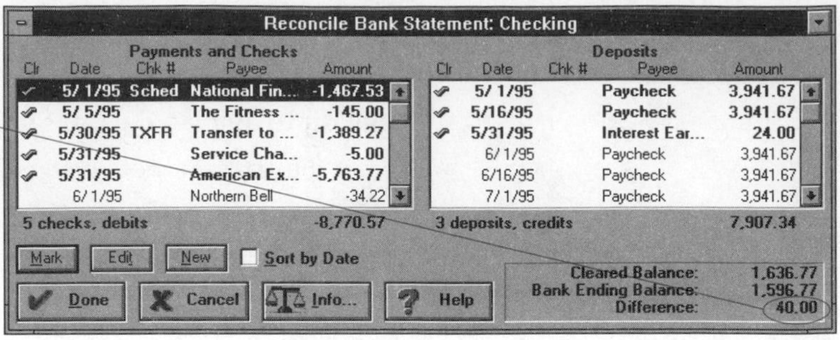

You have two options when your account doesn't balance:
Find the difference between your check register and the bank statement and correct it. See "Correcting differences" on this page.

OR

Have Quicken modify your Quicken balance to agree with the bank's by recording an adjustment transaction. See "Having Quicken adjust for differences" on page 90.

Result 3: If the Difference amount is zero, but an Opening Balance Difference amount is shown, you need to resolve the difference. See "Updating your previously reconciled balance" on page 91.

The Opening Balance Difference is the difference between the total of the previously reconciled items in the register and the opening balance shown in the current bank statement.

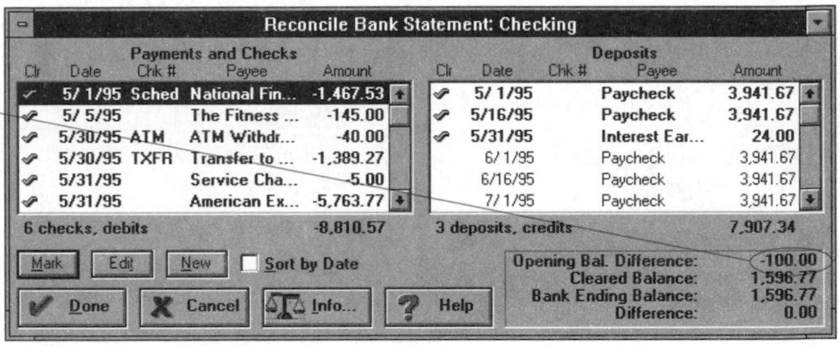

Correcting differences

You can find the differences between your Quicken account and the bank statement in a systematic way.

Finding a problem with the number of items

Compare the number of debit items on your bank statement with the number of "checks, debits" items you've marked in the Reconcile Bank Statement window. Compare the number of credit items listed on your bank statement with the total number of "deposits, credits" items checked off in the Reconcile Bank Statement window.

Check here for the total number and dollar amount of items that you have checked off.

Debits include checks, transfers out of the account, ATM withdrawals, service charges and fees, and automatic payments.

Credits include direct deposits, transfers into the account, ATM deposits, and interest earned.

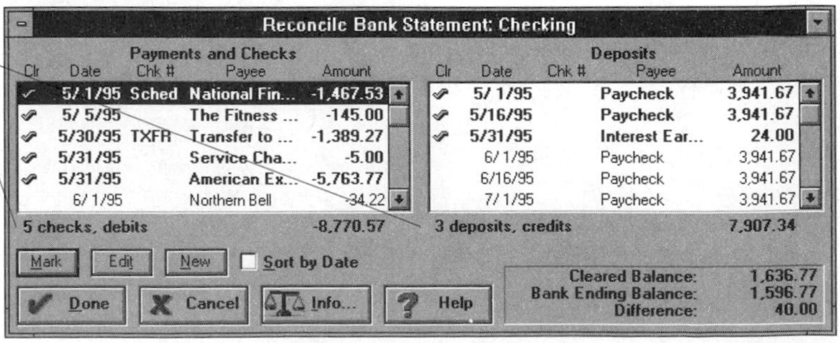

Check to see if you:

- Missed recording an item in the check register.
- Missed marking an item as cleared.
- Mistakenly marked an item as cleared.
- Entered any transactions twice.
- Entered a deposit as a payment or a payment as a deposit.

Caution: The bank may summarize transactions that you've listed separately in your register. For example, if you made several deposits on a single day, the bank might indicate the total sum of deposits for that day rather than listing each deposit separately. Similarly, you may summarize transactions in your register, such as bank charges, that the bank itemizes. Some statements count the number of credits for you; others list interest earned and ATM deposits separately. Some statements count the number of debits for you; others list service charges and ATM withdrawals separately.

Finding a problem with the dollar amount of items

Compare the dollar amount of the "checks, debits" total in the Reconcile Bank Statement window with the dollar amount of debits shown on your bank statement. Compare the dollar amount of the "deposits, credits" total in the Reconcile Bank Statement window with the dollar amount of credits shown on your bank statement.

If the dollar amounts don't agree, check to see if:

You recorded a transaction with the wrong amount. If you find an incorrect amount, return to the transaction in the Register window (click Edit), correct the amount, then return to the Reconcile Bank Statement window.

The bank recorded a transaction with the wrong amount. Adjust the balance by entering a transaction (or let Quicken make the adjustment for you as described in "Having Quicken adjust for differences" on page 90). Then contact your bank. The bank will make an adjustment that will appear on your next statement. Because this adjustment will appear as an already cleared item in the check register, your account will be off by the same amount at the end of the next reconciliation. Have Quicken make another adjustment when you finish reconciling the next statement.

Having Quicken adjust for differences

You can ignore the difference between your check register and the bank statement if the amount is small and you feel it isn't worth your time to track it down. If you ignore the difference, you'll want to have Quicken enter a balance adjustment for the amount of the difference. That way, you'll be starting with accurate totals the next time you reconcile your account.

1 **Click Done in the Reconcile Bank Statement window.**

If there is an Opening Balance Difference amount to resolve, Quicken asks "Would you like Quicken to create an adjustment of this amount to make your totals agree with the bank statement?"

- Click Yes if you want Quicken to enter an adjustment transaction and resolve the discrepancy for you.

OR

- Click No to complete reconciliation without adjusting for the Opening Balance Difference. Do this if you want to resolve the discrepancy yourself.

OR

- Click Cancel to return to reconciliation.

2 **Adjust the balance or continue to resolve the differences.**

If there is a Difference amount to resolve (resulting from transactions in the current statement period), Quicken tells you the amount of the discrepancy.

- Click Adjust Balance to record an adjustment transaction in the check register equal to the difference between your cleared items and the bank statement. You can delete the adjustment transaction later if you find the error that resulted in the difference.

OR

- Click Cancel to return to the Reconcile Bank Statement window and track down the difference.

Updating your previously reconciled balance

If the opening balance from your bank statement is different from the amount Quicken expected as your previously reconciled balance, you need to account for the difference so that Quicken can reconcile your account accurately.

The previously reconciled balance might differ because:

You are balancing your Quicken account for the first time.
Quicken uses the amount of the Opening Balance transaction in your check register as the Bank Statement Opening Balance in the Reconcile Bank Statement window (page 85). When you set up the Quicken account, you may have entered a balance that was different from the actual amount in your bank account. There are probably transactions missing from your Quicken account that affect the balance.

See "Balancing your account for the first time" on page 84.

OR

You were using Quicken and reconciling your bank account, and then you started recording earlier transactions in Quicken.
For example, say it's July. You started recording transactions in May and subsequently reconciled your account for May and June. Then you went back and recorded transactions starting in January so that you could create reports based on the full year's transactions. After entering these earlier items, you noticed that the ending balance in the check register was incorrect. So you updated the date and amount of the original Opening Balance transaction that Quicken recorded in the register when you set up your account in May.

In this case, see "Adding earlier transactions to Quicken" on page 93.

OR

You have started reconciling with a current bank statement, but you didn't reconcile each of the previous months' statements.
You should reconcile one month at a time, starting with the earliest month.

If you have skipped several months and don't want to balance each bank statement, see "Reconciling more than one month at a time" on page 92.

OR

You inadvertently changed or deleted a previously reconciled transaction.
Quicken always asks to confirm a change to a previously reconciled transaction. If you have already ruled out other possible errors, you probably should continue with reconciliation and have Quicken record an adjustment transaction when reconciliation is complete.

See "Correcting differences" on page 88.

Reconciling more than one month at a time

If you have used Quicken for a number of months and have just decided that you want to reconcile, you might not want to go back and reconcile your Quicken account against the bank statements for each of the previous months. In this case, you can approach reconciliation in two ways—the recommended best way, and the second-best way.

For example, if you are starting to reconcile with your June bank statement after entering transactions in Quicken since January of the same year:

The best way to catch up

Balance each month separately, starting with your earliest (January) statement and continue through your most recent (June) statement. Follow the steps in "Starting reconciliation" on page 85, continue with the steps in "Marking cleared transactions" on page 86, and then in "Completing reconciliation" on page 87 for each month before reconciling the statement for the next month.

The second-best way to catch up

Balance all the unreconciled bank statements at the same time. Your records may not be as accurate as they would be if you reconciled each month separately. The second best method follows.

1 **From the Activities menu, choose Reconcile.**

2 **In the Bank Statement Ending Balance box of the Reconcile Bank Statement window, enter the ending balance from the most current bank statement and click OK.**

The ending balance from the current bank statement is June in this example.

See "Marking cleared transactions" on page 86.

3 **In the main Reconcile window, mark the transactions shown on all the bank statements for the period covered by your Quicken check register.**

See "Completing reconciliation" on page 87.

4 **Finish reconciling.**

If there is a Difference amount, you or your bank may have made an error at an earlier date. If the difference is fairly small, you can have Quicken enter an adjustment transaction when it completes the reconciliation. Then your records will match the next time you reconcile your account. If the difference is large and you can't account for it, you may want to ask your bank to determine which balance is accurate.

Adding earlier transactions to Quicken

If you've used Quicken to record and reconcile transactions, you may want to add earlier transactions to your Quicken bank account so you can create more comprehensive reports, graphs, and budgets.

In the following example, we assume that you started entering transactions in June. When you set up the Quicken bank account, you used the ending balance from your May statement as the opening balance for the Quicken account. You've already reconciled your June bank statement. Now you want to go back and add earlier transactions starting on January 1.

1 **Make a note of the ending balance in your Quicken register before you begin to enter earlier transactions.**

2 **Change the date and amount of the Opening Balance transaction in the Quicken register to reflect the opening balance on the first date for which you are about to enter transactions.**

For best results, enter the beginning balance from the first bank statement you want to reconcile.

Suppose your opening balance transaction is now dated June 1 and is in the amount of $450. Your January bank statement, which covers the period from December 14 to January 15, shows a beginning balance of $210. So, change the date of the Opening Balance transaction in the check register to December 14 and the amount to $210.

3 **Enter all the earlier transactions starting January 1 in your check register, just as you would enter any current transaction.**

Don't worry about any transactions that occurred in the period between the beginning date of the January bank statement (December 14) and the first date for which you entered transactions (January 1). You'll take care of those transactions when you update the reconciled balance in step 5.

4 **When you have finished entering transactions, the ending balance in the register should be the same as it was when you started.**

If the balance isn't the same, you have made an error. You'll fix any errors in the next step.

5 **Reconcile all the transactions that you entered for previous months (January to May).**

Balance each month separately, starting with your earliest (January) statement. Follow the steps in "Starting reconciliation" on page 85, continue the steps in "Marking cleared transactions" on page 86, and then in "Completing reconciliation" on page 87 for each month before starting to reconcile the statement for the next month.

6 **Now you can go on and reconcile for the current month (June).**

The total of reconciled transactions in your register now includes all the transactions that appeared on your bank statements from January to June.

8 Tracking credit card transactions

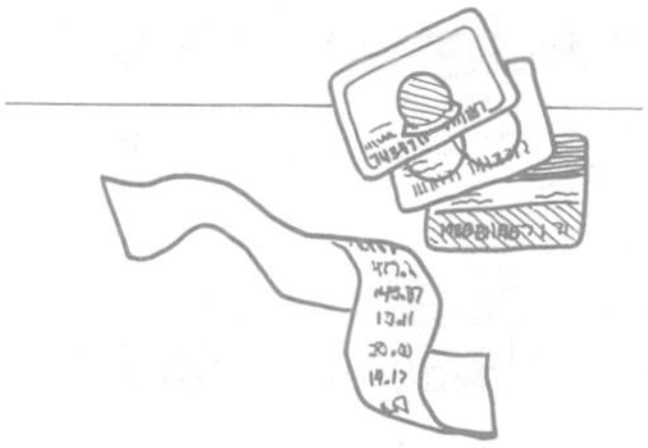

Choosing the best account to track your credit card

Use the following table to determine the best account to track your credit card transactions and payments.

Credit habits	Account to use	Actions to take
You pay your credit card bills in full and keep records of only a few individual credit card transactions.	Checking account	Record the check that pays the bill in your Quicken checking account. Split the transaction to categorize particular credit card charges or groups of charges. See "Tracking credit card transactions in a checking account" on page 96. This method doesn't track your outstanding credit card balance.
You pay your credit card bills over time, and keep records of some (but not all) credit card transactions.	Credit card account	In each credit card account, enter only those transactions you want to keep a record of. (Use your charge slips or your monthly credit card statement.) Create one transaction covering all the charges you don't want to take the time to enter. This lets you keep detailed records of selected transactions without entering every credit card transaction.
You want to keep a record of every credit card transaction *and* know your outstanding credit card balance at all times.	Credit card account	Enter each credit card transaction in the account from your charge slips as you make purchases throughout the month. The credit card register shows your card balance and the available credit remaining on the card. Use Quicken to update your credit card statement and pay your bill. See "Reconciling your credit card account" on page 98.
You want to keep a record of every credit card transaction, but don't want to take the time to enter transactions in the account. You don't need to know what your outstanding credit card balance is more often than once a month.	Credit card account with IntelliCharge	Use IntelliCharge to update your credit card account *automatically* every month. See Chapter 24, *Tracking credit card transactions online,* on page 261.

Tracking credit card transactions in a checking account

This section explains how to track credit card expenses in a Quicken bank account. With this method, you keep track of some or all of your credit card purchases by entering multiple categories in a split transaction when you write a check to pay your bill.

Suppose your credit card statement shows five clothing purchases, two gift purchases, and a finance charge.

1 **Enter the payment in either the Write Checks or Register window.**

Fill in everything but the category information.

2 **Click Splits.**

The total amount of the check appears in the first line of the split.

See "Assigning categories to transactions" on page 21.

3 **Categorize the first line with the category Gifts, press Tab twice, and type the amount you spent on gifts.**

4 **Press Tab, categorize the second line with the category Clothing, press Tab twice, and enter the amount you spent on clothing.**

5 **Press Tab, categorize the third line as Finance Charges, press Tab twice, and enter the amount.**

See "Setting up categories and subcategories" on page 10.

You may need to set up the category Finance Charge.

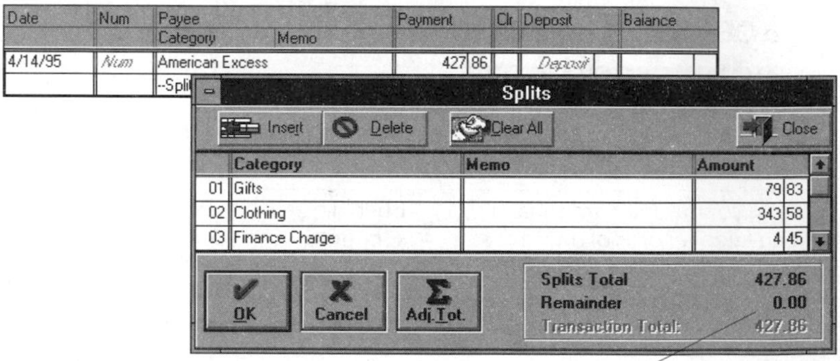

If your figures add up correctly, there should be no remainder.

For more information about classes, see "Using classes" on page 15.

You can classify credit card transactions with classes as well as categorize them with income and expense categories. For example, if you use a credit card for both business and personal expenses, you can use a class called Business to identify business-related charges.

6 **Click OK to close the split transaction, then click Record to record the transaction.**

If the total in the Splits window differs from the amount you entered in step 1, click Adj. Tot. and then click OK to use the splits total.

Tracking credit card transactions in a credit card account

The steps to use a credit card account are:

- **Set up the account.**
  See "Setting up additional Quicken accounts" on page 1 to set up a credit card account for each card you use.
- **Enter your credit card transactions.**
  See "Entering credit card transactions" on this page.
- **Update your account with the credit card statement.**
  See "Updating a credit card account" on page 98.
- **Pay your credit card bill.**
  See "Paying your credit card bill" on page 100.

Entering credit card transactions

To enter transactions in the credit card register you can:

- Save your transaction slips when you charge items and enter the transactions as they occur throughout the month.

  This method provides you with your current credit card balance at all times. It also lets you double-check your charges against those listed on your credit card statement.

  OR

- Wait until you receive your monthly statement and enter the transactions from the statement.

  Use this method if you don't need to know your balance throughout the month. You can also enter some or all of the transactions.

  OR

- Create transfers between the credit card account and other Quicken accounts. You use transfers to track the movement of money from your bank account to your credit card account (bill payments, for example), or from your credit card account to your bank account (overdraft protection through your credit card account, for example).

To keep a record of every credit card transaction without having to enter all the transactions yourself, consider using IntelliCharge. IntelliCharge updates your credit card account *automatically* every month. See "About IntelliCharge" on page 261.

To open the register for a credit card account, open the Account list and double-click the account name.

The credit card register has a Ref column that you can use to track transaction numbers.

This shows you made a credit card transfer payment from an account called Checking. To pay the credit card bill, see page 100.

Instead of Payment and Deposit columns, the credit card register has Charge and Payment columns. Use the Charge column for amounts you have charged, finance charges, and other fees. Use the Payment column to record bill payments or a credit to your account.

The Clr (Cleared) column shows an X for transactions you have already reconciled with previous credit card statements.

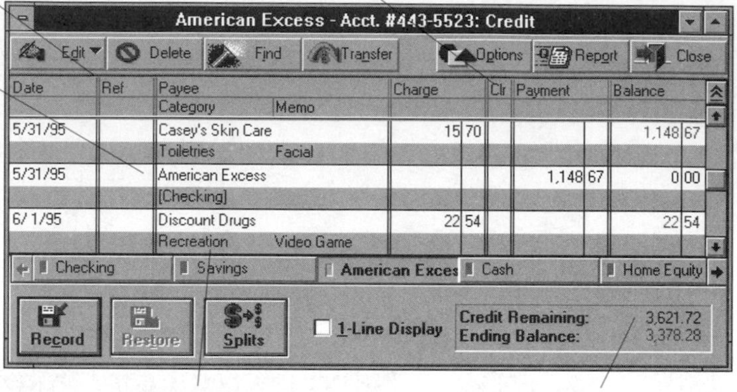

Categorize your credit card charges to see credit card expenses categorized in income and expense reports and graphs.

The credit limit for this account is $7,000. Credit Remaining is your credit limit for the account less the balance of the account. Ending Balance is your outstanding balance.

Updating a credit card account

There are two steps to updating a credit card account. First, reconcile your credit card statement like you reconcile your bank account against your bank statement. You mark transactions as cleared, and enter any missing transactions you want to keep a record of. Reconcile one monthly statement at a time, starting with the oldest statement first. The second step is to then pay your bill.

Reconciling your credit card account

Reconcile your credit card account each month with your credit card statement. This lets you:

- Record a single adjustment transaction that covers all the charges that you don't want to record individually.
- Record a transaction for any finance charges to your credit card account.
- Record any credit card payment.

1 **Open the credit card account.**

2 **From the Activities menu, choose Pay Credit Card Bill.**

3 **Complete the information in the Credit Card Statement Information window.**

Enter the total amount of payments and credits and the new balance for your card, as shown on your statement.

Enter any finance charges shown on your statement. You can select a different category to assign to the transaction. Quicken adds a Finance Charge transaction to your credit card register.

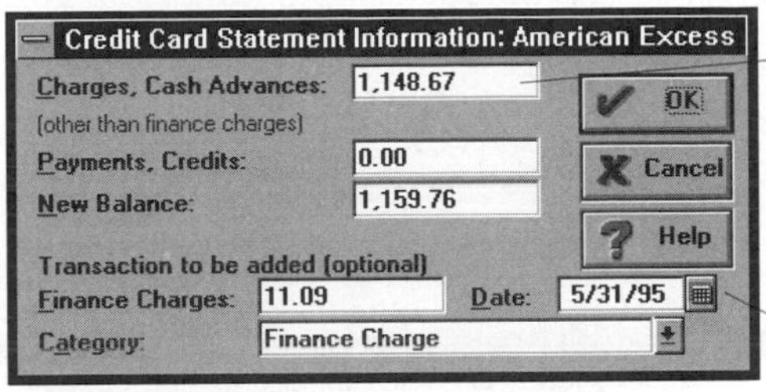

Enter the total amount of charges and advances shown on your statement. Don't include interest or service charges.

Quicken uses the current date unless you change it.

4 **Click OK.**

5 **Reconcile your credit card statement in the same way that you reconcile a bank statement for a Quicken bank account.**

As you check off cleared transactions, Quicken displays their total as the cleared balance.

To edit an existing transaction, highlight it and then click Edit. To enter a missing transaction, click New.

To mark or clear a transaction:
- click it, or
- select it and click Mark or press the spacebar, or
- drag the mouse pointer across a range of transactions.

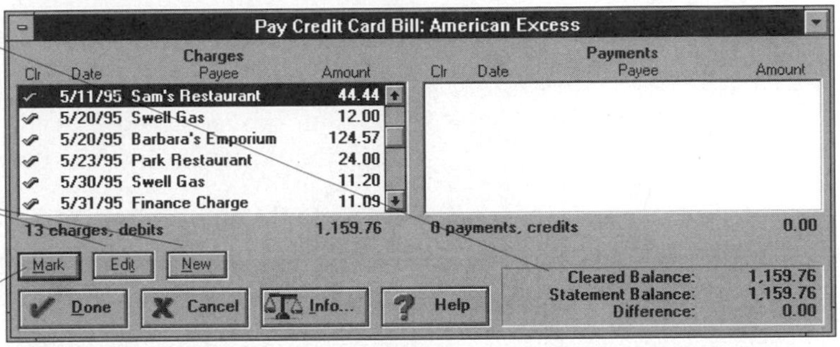

To edit reconciliation information you entered in step 3 above, click Info.

Quicken compares the total items marked cleared and the total items shown on the credit card statement.

6 **If you find transactions listed on your statement that are missing from the list of uncleared items, enter them now in the register.**

Click New to enter the missing transactions in the register. (Or lump these new charges into a single adjustment transaction when you finish reconciling your statement.)

7 **Check the Difference amount.**

If the Difference amount isn't zero, see "Completing reconciliation" on page 87.

If the Difference amount is zero, click Done and make the credit card payment. See "Paying your credit card bill" on page 100.

Paying your credit card bill

As the final step in updating your credit card account, Quicken can write a check to print with Quicken or record a handwritten check in the check register.

1 **Complete the Make Credit Card Payment window.**

Select the name of the checking account you plan to write the check from. Quicken records the payment in the checking account as a transfer to the credit card account.

Select Hand Written to enter the payment in the Register window instead of the Write Checks window.

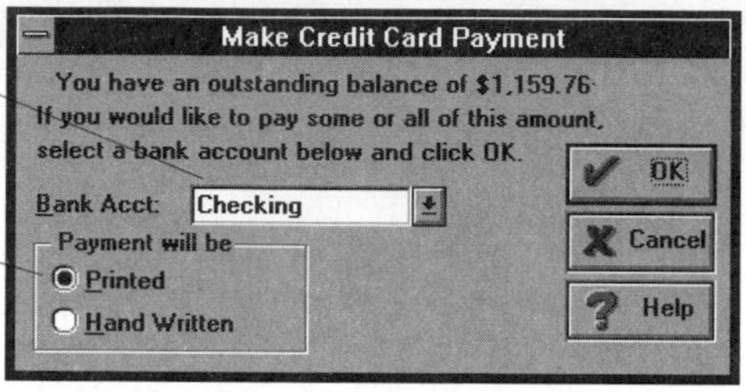

2 **Click OK to enter the payment and the transfer information in the Write Checks or Register window.**

After Quicken records the payment, it selects the payment transaction in the Write Checks window or the check register.

3 **Complete the transaction and click Record.**

Quicken remembers the payment information and uses it the next time you make a payment on this credit card.

9 Tracking cash transactions

Choosing the best account to track your cash

Use a cash account to keep detailed records of what you spend your cash on. Save your cash receipts and enter them in the register for your cash account. Cash accounts are useful if you are often paid in cash. Businesses can use cash accounts to track petty cash.

On the other hand, to track only a few cash transactions, treating the rest as miscellaneous expenses, enter the information in your checking account, as explained in the next section. Neither method requires you to account for every penny.

Tracking cash in a checking account

Record each cash withdrawal (check or ATM) in your checking account with a category such as Cash Withdrawal. Then to record a cash withdrawal with greater detail, split it.

Splitting a cash withdrawal

Categorize cash expenses in your bank account so you can show them in summary and budget reports and graphs.

Suppose you give $100 in cash to a charity, and spend $45 in cash for dinner in a restaurant. You want to categorize the first amount as Charity and the second as Dining.

1. **Open your checking account.**
2. **Enter a cash withdrawal transaction.**

   Or press Ctrl+N
3. **Click Splits.**
4. **Categorize the first line as Charity, press Tab twice, and type the amount 100.**

5 **Press Tab, categorize the second line as Dining, press Tab twice, and type the amount 45.**

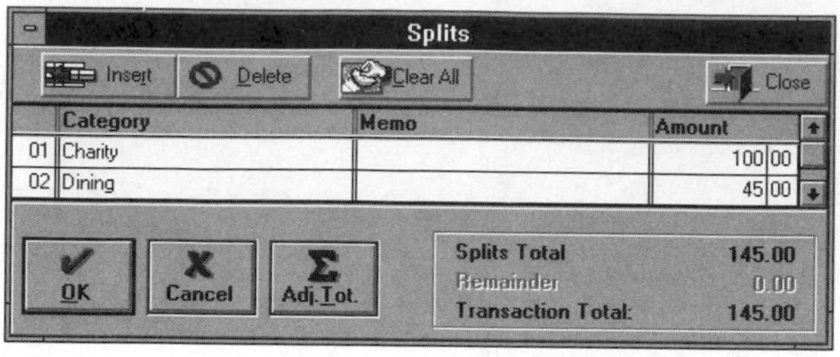

6 **Click OK to close the Splits window, then click Record to record the transaction.**

Entering a deposit with "cash back"

Let's say you receive a $500 bonus check. You want to deposit $400 of it in your checking account and get $100 cash back. You don't want to track how you spend the $100.

1 **Open your checking account.**

2 **Go to a blank transaction.**

Or press Ctrl+N

3 **In the Deposit column, enter $400.**

4 **Click Splits.**

5 **Categorize the first line with the income category Bonus, and type the bonus amount ($500) over the amount in the first line ($400).**

See "Assigning categories to transactions" on page 21.

Quicken shows the remainder ($100) at the bottom of the window.

6 **Press Tab, then categorize the second line as a cash withdrawal expense and enter the remainder amount (negative).**

Make sure there is no remainder (lower right corner of the Splits window) after you have entered your split lines.

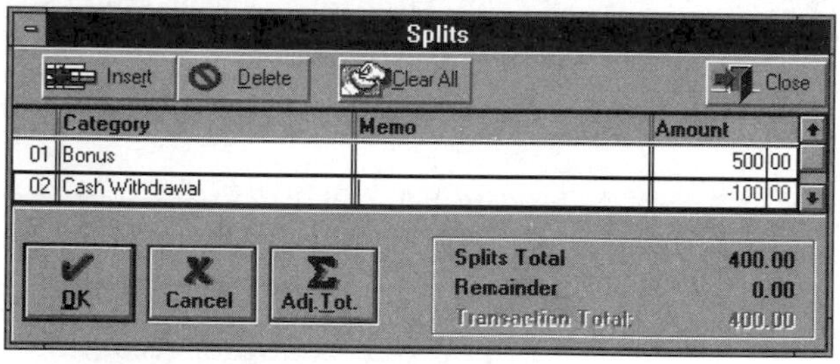

7 **Click OK to close the Splits window, then click Record to record the transaction.**

Tracking cash in a cash account

Use a cash account to keep records of most or all of the cash transactions you make. To keep records of only a few cash expenditures, see "Tracking cash in a checking account" on page 101.

- **Set up a cash account.**
  See "Setting up additional Quicken accounts" on page 1 to set up a new account.
- **Open the account.**
  Select the account from the Account list.
- **Enter transactions in the cash account.**
  See "Entering transactions in a cash account" next.
- **From time to time, update the value of the account.**
  See "Updating your cash balance" on page 104.

Entering transactions in a cash account

Save the cash receipts and other records of your cash transactions and enter each one as a separate transaction. If one receipt covers several items that you want to keep track of individually, split the transaction. Also enter transactions for cash received when you're paid in cash or given cash, or when you cash a check without depositing it in another account.

To review entering transactions in a register, see page 17.

If you enter transactions for most or all of the cash you spend, add icons to the iconbar that are assigned to recording your most common transactions.

See "Assigning an icon to enter a transaction" on page 296.

Create transfer transactions when you withdraw cash or make a deposit less cash from a bank account.

See "Transferring money between accounts" on page 22 for more information.

You don't have to enter transactions for the cash you've spent. However, you should have transactions that show all the cash you've received, either directly or by recording transfer transactions for cash withdrawals or advances from your other accounts.

Instead of Payment and Deposit columns, the cash account register has Spend and Receive columns. Use the Spend column for purchases made with cash; use the Receive column to record increases in the amount of cash on hand.

The cash account register has a Ref column, which you can use to track ATM transaction codes, for example.

The cash account received cash as a transfer when an ATM withdrawal was recorded in a checking account. The name of the checking account is in the Category field.

The Payee field specifies the restaurant where this cash purchase was made.

Categorize all cash transactions so they'll be included in income and expense reports and graphs.

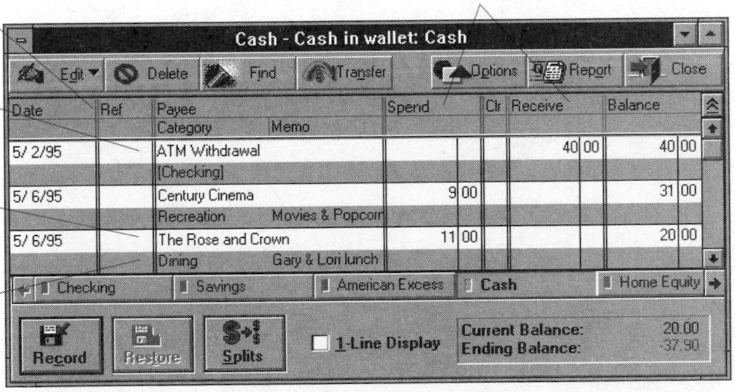

Updating your cash balance

Use the Update Account Balance window instead of entering every cash transaction.

Enter only those cash transactions you want to track in the register; then when you update your cash balance, update your cash balance with one adjustment transaction for the remaining amount of miscellaneous cash expenses.

1 **Open the cash account by choosing it from the Account list.**

2 **From the Activities menu, choose Update Balances and then choose Update Cash Balance.**

3 **Complete the Update Account Balance window.**

If your current cash balance is $20 and you enter $18.50 here, Quicken adds a Balance Adjustment of $1.50 in the Spend column of your cash account register.

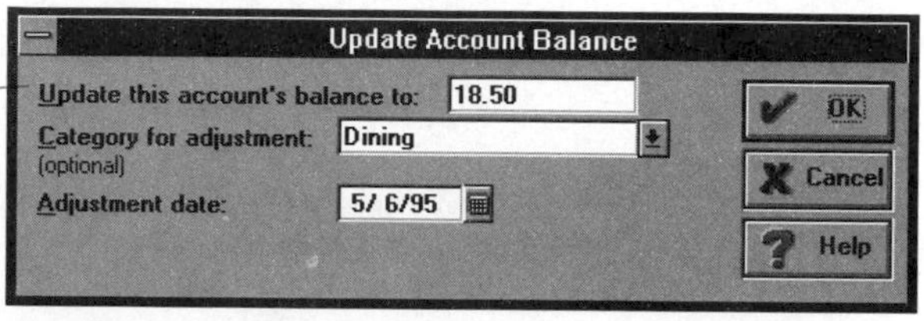

4 **Enter the amount of cash you currently have on hand.**

Quicken compares this amount with the current balance in the account. Don't enter the amount of the adjustment here, but the ending balance of your cash account.

5 **Enter a category if you want to categorize the adjustment transaction. Then click OK.**

Quicken creates the balance adjustment transaction in the register.

10 Tracking loans and mortgages

Tracking loan amortization

Amortization is the gradual reduction of a loan by periodically paying off the principal as well as the interest. Although your total payment each time is the same, the split between principal and interest is always changing.

For example, if you make a steady payment of $1,000 each month, you will pay a little less interest with each payment:

Payment	Principal	Interest	Total
1	$671.21	$328.79	$1000.00
2	$675.69	$324.31	$1000.00
3	$680.19	$319.81	$1000.00
etc.	etc.	etc.	etc.

Eventually, the interest part of the payments falls towards zero, and your loan is paid off.

For each loan, Quicken calculates a schedule of payments like the one above, including the principal/interest split. If the interest rate changes, or you prepay part of the principal, or you refinance your mortgage, Quicken recalculates the schedule.

For information on CheckFree, see Chapter 26, *Paying bills online,* on page 277.

With your loan set up, Quicken can automate the entry of payment transactions—just set up your loan payments as a memorized transaction or a scheduled transaction (or as a CheckFree fixed payment if you use CheckFree). When you enter a loan payment in your checking account register, Quicken fills in the principal and interest automatically, and updates your payment schedule.

Setting up a loan

When you set up a loan, Quicken creates a liability or asset account (depending on whether you are borrowing or lending) to track the principal remaining on the loan.

Upgraders: Quicken sets up an account for you.
If you used the amortization feature in a previous version of Quicken but didn't use an account for tracking principal, you may notice that Quicken 4 for Windows sets up the account for you. Quicken enters the correct opening balance and current balance according to the amortized state of your loan. The loan is in your loan list.

The example below shows how to set up an account for a simple house mortgage. See "Handling different types of loans" on page 110 for information on other types of loans.

1 **From the Activities menu, choose Loans.**

The View Loans window appears. This is your main information window for all your loans. It is described later in this chapter.

See page 109.

2 **Click the New button.**

Click New.

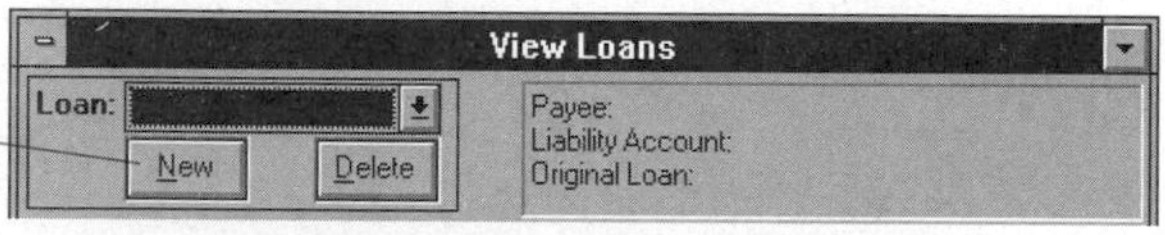

3 **Complete the Set Up Loan Account window and click OK.**

If this is a loan you have taken out, click Borrow Money.

If this is a loan you have made to someone else, click Lend Money.

Enter a new account name or select an existing account. Quicken will use this account to track the principal remaining on the loan. The account name also becomes the loan name in your loan list.

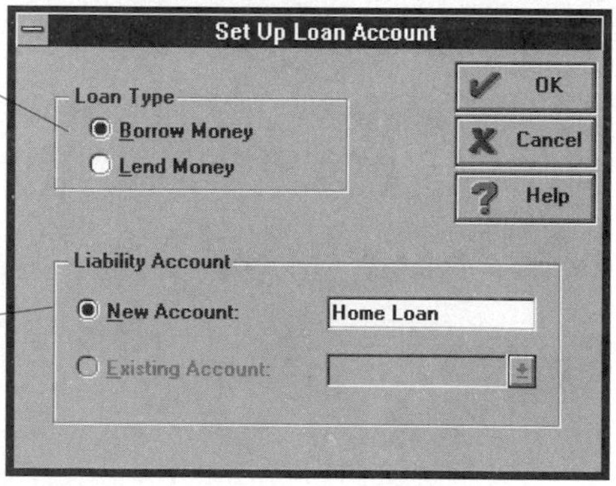

Using an existing principal account:
If you have been manually tracking a loan in Quicken (that is, you've been entering payments for the loan by copying the principal and interest amounts from your loan statement into the split transaction of the payment, and tracking the principal in a liability or asset account), you can use your existing principal account in the loan setup. Quicken will use the ending balance of your principal account as the current loan balance on which it bases its amortization calculations. Be sure that, in your principal account register, the ending balance and the date of the last transaction correctly reflect your most recent payment.

4 Complete the Set Up Loan window and click OK.

This example shows a 30-year mortgage for $200,000 that was taken out on 5/1/95.

If you make monthly payments, enter 12 here.

Enter today's balance (the amount of principal remaining). If you are setting up a brand-new loan, leave the Current Balance blank.

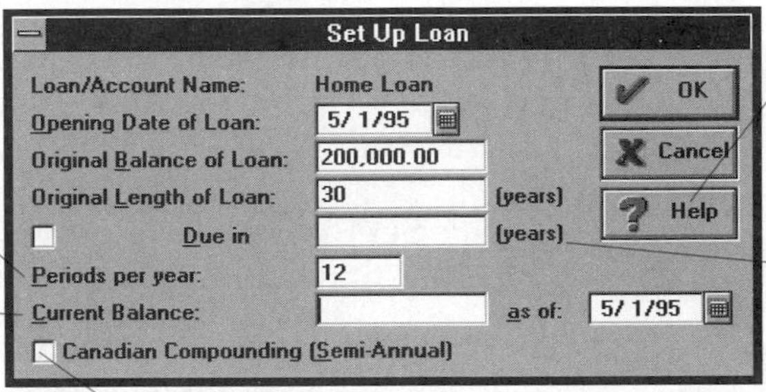

For more information on what to enter in each box, click Help.

If your loan includes a balloon payment, click the Due in checkbox and enter the total number of years in which the loan must be paid off (that is, counting from the beginning of the loan). See page 111.

Canadian users: Make sure Canadian Compounding is selected, so that Quicken calculates interest on the basis of semi-annual compounding as used in Canada.

To set up a(n):

- New bank loan: enter the loan amount in the Original Balance box, and leave the Current Balance blank. Quicken inserts today's date as the opening date of the loan, but you can change it if necessary.
- Existing bank loan, without entering all previous loan payments into Quicken: enter the Original Balance of the loan and the Opening Date on which you first took out the loan. Also enter the amount of principal remaining today in the Current Balance box.
- Existing bank loan and keep a complete record of all previous payments: complete this loan setup procedure, and then enter all previous payments in your checking account. We don't recommend such a detailed setup, as Quicken's payment schedule works perfectly well without historic data.

For more information on what to enter in each box, click Help.

Enter today's interest rate.

Quicken uses the interest rate to calculate the regular payment amount (principal plus interest).

Select Chk to write checks with Quicken for the loan payments, or Pmt if you don't. Select Epmt if you use CheckFree to make payments. If you collect payments, the Type is set to Deposit.

If you select Chk, enter the payee's address by clicking the Address button (far right).

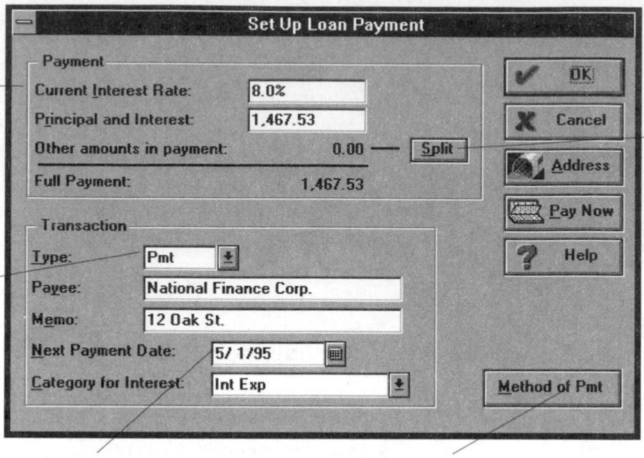

To include impound items like insurance and property tax in your regular payments, click Split. For more information about splits, see "Splitting transactions" on page 26.

Enter the date of the next payment.

Quicken sets up the payment as a memorized transaction unless you specify otherwise.

5 In the Set Up Loan Payment window, enter the current interest rate and transaction information.

See page 110.

If your loan has an adjustable (variable) interest rate, enter the current rate. You can change the rate at any time.

You can change the actual payment amount each time you enter a payment in your register (page 113).

Quicken calculates your regular payments (principal plus interest). You can change the regular payment amount in this window: if you increase the payment amount, the number of scheduled payments is reduced, but interest is still calculated based on the original length of the loan; if you decrease the payment amount, the last scheduled payment is increased to make up the remaining balance. (Adjusting it a few cents up or down shouldn't make a difference to the length of the loan.)

6 (Optional) Click Method of Pmt to specify how Quicken should enter the payment transaction in your register.

For a scheduled transaction, Quicken can enter the transaction in your register with or without asking you to confirm first.

Select the account into which the transaction should be entered.

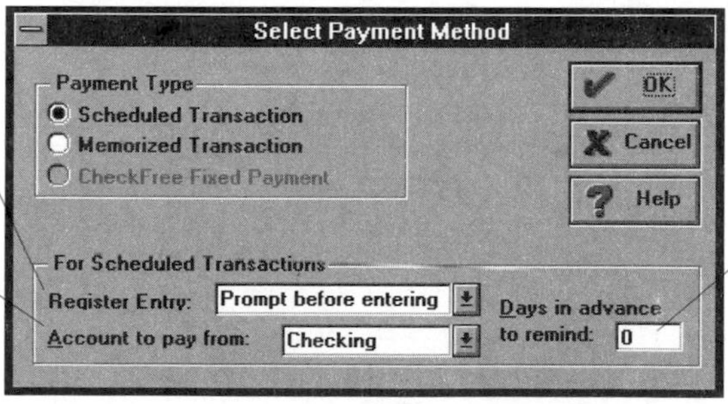

Quicken can record the payments in your register ahead of time if you want. (Otherwise, enter 0 here.)

See "Setting up a scheduled transaction" on page 50.

- Click Scheduled Transaction so Quicken automatically enters the payment transaction in your register (or in the Write Checks window if you entered Chk as the transaction Type). Quicken uses the Next Payment Date and the Periods Per Year that you've already entered. This is useful if you make your loan payments through automatic drafting set up at your bank.

  Fill in the lower part of the window too for a scheduled transaction.

See Chapter 4, *Memorizing transactions,* on page 41.

- Click Memorized Transaction so you can manually recall the transaction and enter it in your register (or in the Write Checks window) whenever you make the payment.

See "Amortizing a fixed payment" on page 282.

- If you use CheckFree to make your payments, you must click CheckFree Fixed Payment so you can set up the payment transaction as a fixed (recurring) payment. Select a payee from the drop-down Fixed Payee list that appears.

7 **Click OK to return to the Set Up Loan Payment window.**

8 **Click OK to return to the View Loans window.**

Your loan is set up. Your View Loans window should look something like this:

This example shows a loan named "Home Loan." Display the payment details of any loan by selecting it from the drop-down list.

The upper payment window shows the payments already made on this loan. (Quicken gets this information from the transactions in your principal account.)

The lower payment window shows the payments to be made next.

Click Show Running Totals to see the accumulated principal and interest payments.

To change the loan details, click Loan.

To change the payment details, click Payment.

To change the interest rate, click Rates.

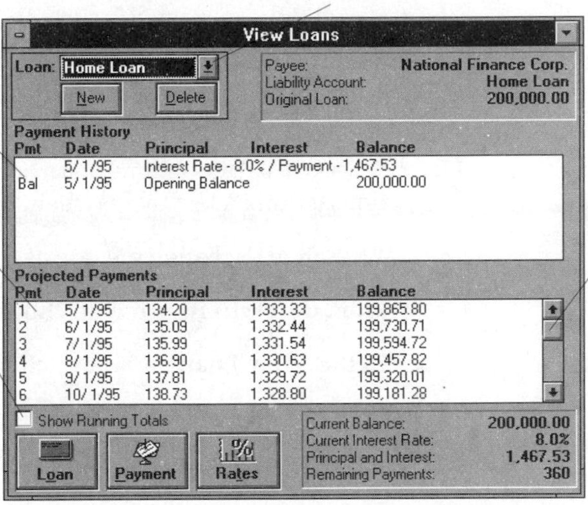

Scroll the payment window to show the rest of the payment schedule.

Scroll to the end and you will see the balance fall to zero, unless your loan is a balloon payment type.

Each time you make a loan payment (or deposit) in your checking account register, Quicken updates the past and future payment schedules shown in the two payment windows. You can also change the details of any loan at any time from this window.

To work out "what if" scenarios with your loan, use the Loan Planner or Refinance Planner. See page 230.

To enter the first payment in your register now, click Payment in the View Loans window, then click Pay Now.

Handling different types of loans

This section provides guidelines for setting up several different types of loans. Refer to these guidelines as you follow the procedure in "Setting up a loan" (starting on page 106). If your loan involves several different features (for example, an adjustable-rate loan with negative amortization), follow all the guidelines that apply.

Adjustable-rate loans

An adjustable-rate loan has a variable interest rate. When the rate changes, the scheduled payment amount also changes. When you set up your loan in Quicken, enter the current interest rate. Whenever the rate changes, change the rate in Quicken. You can do this in two ways. If the rate change is effective today, before your next payment date enter a new Current Interest Rate in the Set Up Loan Payment window. You can access this window from the:

- View Loans window by clicking Payment.
- Memorized Transaction list if you set up the payment as a memorized transaction (select the payment transaction and click Edit).
- Scheduled Transaction list if you set up the payment as a scheduled transaction (select the payment transaction and click Edit).

You can also change the rate as follows:

1 **From the Activities menu, choose Loans.**

2 **In the View Loans window, click Rates.**

3 **In the Loan Rate Changes window, click New.**

4 **Enter the new interest rate and the effective date, and click OK.**

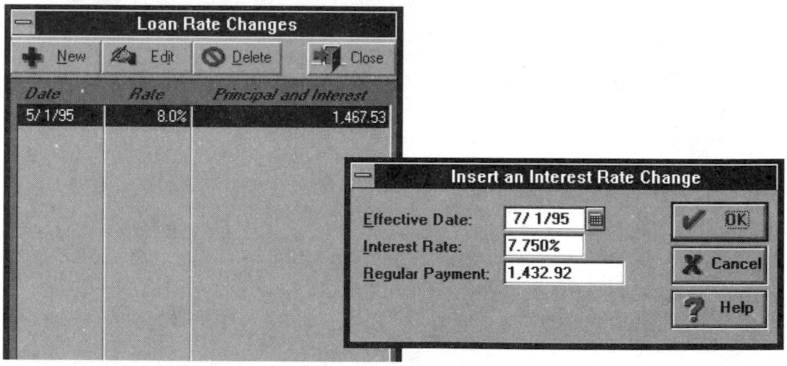

The Loan Rate Changes window lists the history of your interest rates as they change up or down.

5 **Click Done in the Loan Rate Changes window.**

Quicken uses the new rate to calculate the new regular payment amount. Quicken keeps the length of the loan constant.

However, if you increase the Regular Payment amount, Quicken reduces the length of the loan accordingly. If you decrease the Regular Payment amount, Quicken doesn't change the length of the loan but adds the extra remaining principal to the last payment.

Quicken indicates the interest rate change in the Payment History section of the View Loans window, and adjusts the principal and interest amounts in the projected payment schedule to match.

You can see when the interest rate changed.

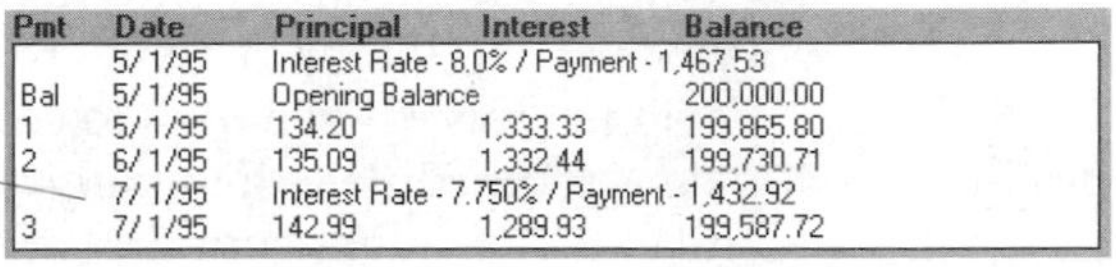

Pmt	Date	Principal	Interest	Balance
	5/ 1/95	Interest Rate - 8.0% / Payment - 1,467.53		
Bal	5/ 1/95	Opening Balance		200,000.00
1	5/ 1/95	134.20	1,333.33	199,865.80
2	6/ 1/95	135.09	1,332.44	199,730.71
	7/ 1/95	Interest Rate - 7.750% / Payment - 1,432.92		
3	7/ 1/95	142.99	1,289.93	199,587.72

You can also enter an interest rate change effective on some future date in the Loan Rate Change window; Quicken then recalculates the projected payments shown in the View Loans window. You can enter future rate changes to create "what-if" scenarios that estimate your future payments.

Balloon payments and nonamortized loans

In a loan with a balloon payment, the principal isn't fully repaid when the regular payments stop, so the balance of the loan (the "balloon payment") is due at the end of the payment period. In this case, the loan is amortized over a longer period than the period of payments. For example, if you have a "30 due in 7" loan, your payment is amortized over 30 years. But at the end of seven years, you must either pay off the balance or refinance the loan.

In the Set Up Loan window, click the Due in checkbox and enter the period of regular payments in years.

Enter the period over which the loan is amortized.

Enter the period over which loan payments will be made.

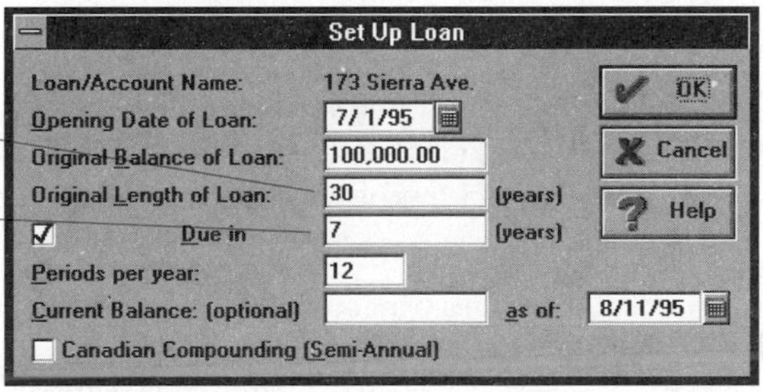

In some balloon payment loans, each payment covers only the accrued interest (no principal), and the original loan amount is due at the end of the repayment period. For such a nonamortized, or "interest-only" loan, don't use Quicken's loan tracking feature. Instead, create a regular memorized transaction for the payment and categorize the entire payment amount as interest.

See "Memorizing and recalling a transaction" on page 42 to create a regular memorized transaction.

Negative amortization

Negative amortization happens when your payment is less than the interest on the loan. Not only is no principal paid off, but the unpaid part of the interest is added to the loan balance, increasing the principal. Often, this is an agreed and temporary arrangement, usually for the first part of the loan only.

When you set up the loan in Quicken, enter the length of the loan (the period over which you are making payments) as the Original Length of Loan in the Set Up Loan window. In the Set Up Loan Payment window, after entering the interest rate, modify the Principal and Interest amount to be the amount you are actually paying. If this isn't enough to cover the interest on the loan, the payment schedule will initially show you that you owe more at the end of the payment period than the original amount of the loan.

You can also adjust the repayment amount on a one-time basis in the Confirm Principal and Interest window when entering a payment in your register, as described in step 3 on page 113.

If you know when your repayment amount is due to increase, enter this change through the Loan Rate Change window. From the View Loans window, click Rates and then click New to enter a new Regular Payment amount and effective date. The payment schedule now shows a reduced, or zero, ending balance on your loan.

Zero-interest loans

If you have a zero-interest loan, you don't have any interest expenses. Your entire payment (excluding other charges such as impound payments) is principal.

In Quicken, enter an interest rate of zero while setting up the loan. In the View Loans window, click Payment and clear the Category for Interest box, so that zero amounts don't show up on reports.

Loans for which you receive payments

If you hold a loan note and receive payments on a loan, you can set up your loan for amortization in Quicken. Quicken creates a memorized loan deposit (instead of a payment) and uses an asset account (instead of a liability account) as the principal account for tracking how much the borrower still owes you.

In this window	And in this box	Enter this
Set Up Loan Account	Loan Type	Lend Money
Set Up Loan Payment	Type	Dep
	Payee	Name of the borrower
	Category for interest	Name of an income category

Making a loan payment

If you set up your loan payment as a memorized transaction, you can recall it to record a payment in your checking account register. If you set up the loan payment as a scheduled transaction or as a CheckFree fixed payment, the entry is made automatically; for a scheduled transaction, if you specified Prompt Before Entering, you will be prompted for the payment amount when you start Quicken.

When you enter the payment, Quicken updates the loan balance in the View Loans window.

Recalling a memorized loan payment

1 **Open the register or the Write Checks window of the bank account from which you will make the loan payment.**

2 **Start typing the Payee name. When QuickFill completes the full name, press Tab to recall the memorized payment.**

If QuickFill is turned off, click the drop-down payee list and select the memorized loan payment. Or choose Memorized Transaction from the Lists menu, select the memorized loan payment, and click Use.

Quicken asks to confirm the principal and interest amounts, and gives you a chance to modify them.

Any impound items (such as escrow and insurance fees) that you set up will be recorded in addition to the principal and interest amounts shown.

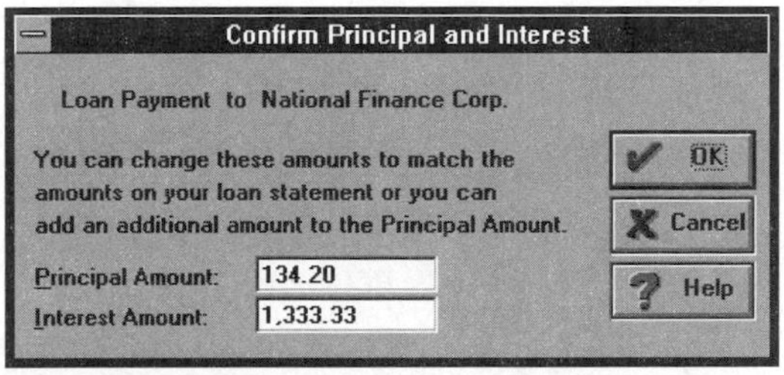

3 **Change either figure if necessary and click OK.**

If you change the amount of principal or interest, you are changing the figure for this one payment only. (To change the amount for all future payments, edit the transaction in the Memorized Transaction list or in the Set Up Loan Payment window, as described on page 110.)

- If you increase the amount of principal, you are making an additional payment of principal. Quicken recalculates the payment schedule in the View Loans window accordingly, which may shorten the term of the loan.
- If you decrease the amount of principal, you aren't fully paying what is due on the loan. Quicken keeps the length of the loan fixed, which means you may have an extra balance to pay off at the end of the repayment period.

4 **Click Record.**

If you open the split for this transaction, you will notice that Quicken has included any impound items you set up.

The first line of the split is a transfer of the principal amount to the liability (or asset) account that tracks the principal.

The second line is your interest payment.

Below the second line are any impound items you set up.

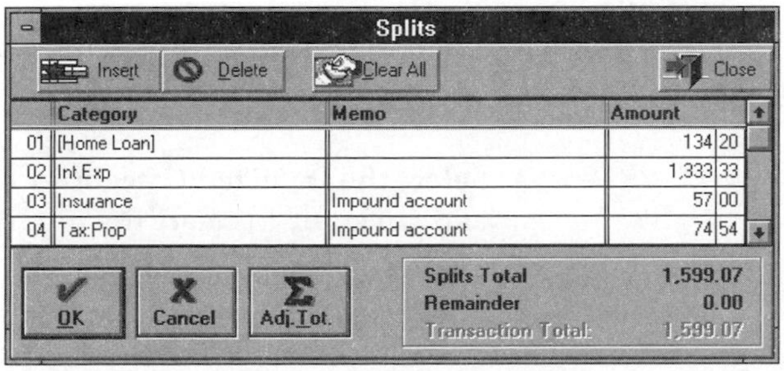

Each time you record an amortized loan payment, Quicken updates the payment schedule in the View Loans window to show the new state of your balance. The transfer to the liability (or asset) account on line 1 of the split reduces the remaining balance on your loan and keeps your net worth up to date in reports and graphs.

Additional prepayments of principal

By making prepayments, you pay off the loan balance sooner and pay less in interest than if you pay only the scheduled payment amount.

- To include an additional prepayment of principal with your regular payment, adjust the principal amount in the Confirm Principal and Interest window, as described in step 3 on page 113.
- To make a separate prepayment of principal, don't recall the memorized payment transaction. Instead, enter a separate payment (or deposit) transaction in your checking account register. In the category field, enter a transfer to the liability (or asset) account that tracks the principal:

Enter the name of the principal account in the Category field.

Date	Num	Payee / Category	Memo	Payment	Clr	Deposit	Balance
6/1/95	5057	National Finance Corp.		1,000 00		Deposit	
		[Home Loan]	Prepayment				

When you make an additional prepayment of principal, Quicken recalculates the payment schedule, and the term of the loan may be shortened. You can see the new schedule in the View Loans window.

Undoing a mistaken loan payment

If you accidentally record an extra loan payment in your register, simply delete it from the register, and reset the Next Payment Date in the Set Up Loan Payment window. Quicken removes the payment from the View Loans window. Similarly, if you edit the principal or interest amounts in the split, Quicken reflects your changes in the View Loans window.

Reporting on your year-to-date loan interest

For tax purposes, you can create an itemized category report to see how much interest you've paid on the loan since the beginning of the year.

1 **Click the Reports icon on the iconbar.**

2 **Confirm that the date range is from January 1 through today.**

3 **Select the Itemized Categories report in the Home report family and click OK to create the report.**

The report contains the interest figures under EXPENSES-Interest Expense, but you can narrow down the report further.

4 **Click the Customize button and then click Accounts.**

Or double-click the header line in the report that tells you which accounts are selected.

5 **Select only the account from which you make loan payments.**

6 **Click Categories/Classes and select only the Int Exp category.**

If you used some other category for your loan interest payments, for example Mort Int, select that category instead.

7 **Click OK to create the report again.**

The total for Interest Expense shows you how much interest you have paid so far this year.

Click Memorize to memorize the report.

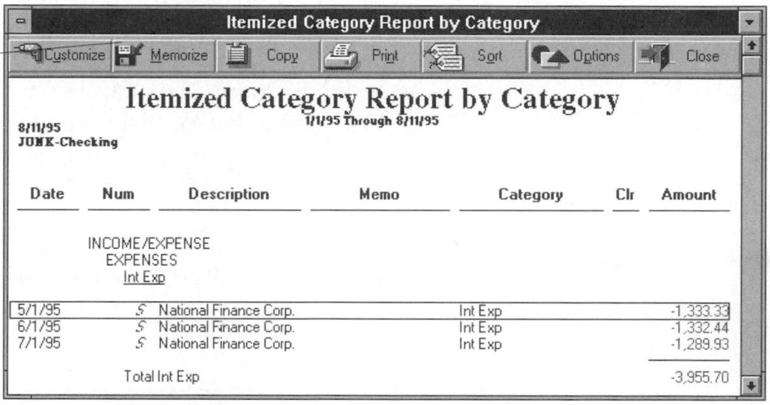

Forecasting interest payments for the entire year

You can forecast how much interest you will pay for the entire year by clicking Show Running Totals in the View Loans window.

For example, at the start of the year, you had paid a total of $ 10,391.36 in interest.

By the end of the year, you will have paid a total of $ 25,738.18 in interest.

Total interest for the year is $ 25,738.18
– $ 10,391.36
= $ 15,346.82

Click Show Running Totals to show the cumulative principal and interest.

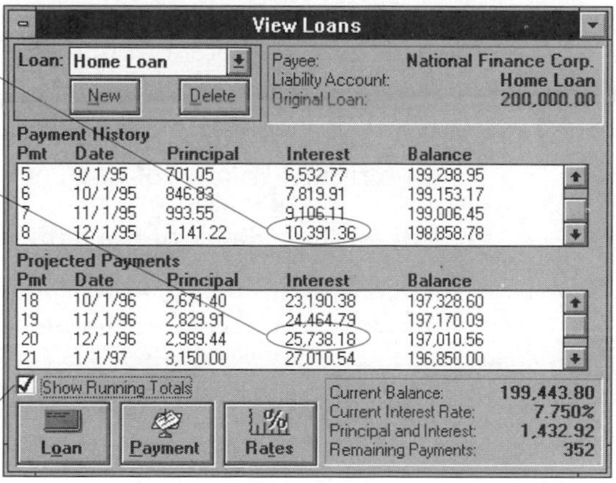

Changing the details of a loan

You can edit any of the loan setup information at any time. To change the interest rate, see "Adjustable-rate loans" on page 110. To change the name of the principal account, see "Editing account information" on page 5.

See the instructions for filling in the loan windows in "Setting up a loan" on page 106.

- To change loan setup information, display the View Loans window and click Loan, Payment, or Rate/Amt.
- To change payment information, you can also select the payment transaction in the Memorized Transaction list or the Scheduled Transaction list and click Edit.

Deleting a loan

Delete a loan from the View Loans window when you have finished paying off the loan. When you delete the loan, Quicken removes it from the loan list in the View Loans window, the Memorized Transaction list (and any transaction groups that contain it), Scheduled Transaction list, or Electronic Payee list.

1 **In the View Loans window, select the loan and click Delete.**

2 **Click OK to confirm the deletion.**

To delete the account, see "Deleting an account" on page 6.

Quicken doesn't delete the loan's principal account, as you may want to keep the account for your records.

Refinancing a loan

If you refinance a loan that you've been tracking in Quicken, follow this procedure to set up the new loan and "pay off" the old loan. (To help you determine whether you should refinance, see "Calculating the cost of refinancing a loan" on page 231.)

1 **Set up your new loan.**

See "Setting up a loan" on page 106 for a complete description.

- Set Up Loan Account window: Create a new liability account with a name that's different from the one for the old loan.
- Set Up Loan window: Enter the total term of the new loan in the Original Length of Loan box. Enter the amount of the new loan in the Original Balance of Loan box.

2 **Adjust the balance of the liability account for the old loan to zero.**

Open the liability account. Choose Update Balances from the Activities menu, and choose Update Cash Balance. Enter an amount of 0.

See "Deleting a loan" on this page.

3 **(Optional) In the View Loans window, delete the old loan from the drop-down loan list.**

11 Tracking assets and liabilities

Choosing the best account to track assets and liabilities

With Quicken's asset and liability accounts, you can track such things as loan balances, lines of credit, capital equipment, 401(k) retirement plans, and the tax basis of your home. Quicken then provides a home net worth report and a business balance sheet that each combine the balances from all your accounts for a complete financial picture.

If you have a small business, you can use a Quicken asset account to track accounts receivable and a liability account to track accounts payable. More information about using Quicken for small business finances is in the *Quicken Business User's Guide*. To purchase this guide from Intuit, see "Quicken Business User's Guide" on page 320.

Assets show what you own and *liabilities* show what you owe. The difference between your assets and your liabilities is your *net worth*. The balances in your bank and cash accounts show your assets. The balances due on your credit cards show your liabilities. But they may not give a total picture of your finances.

To track	Use this type of account	To
Home tax basis	Asset	Track your home improvements over the years. Use your purchase price as the opening balance and record each improvement in the register as you make it. When you sell your home, accurate records will allow you to justify a higher tax basis and reduce your taxes.
Capital equipment	Asset	Track the value of all capital equipment as it is acquired and depreciation as it occurs.
Accounts receivable	Asset	Keep up-to-date A/R records.
Loan balances	Liability	Track loans, such as car loans and lines of credit. When you write a check to make a loan payment, transfer the amount of the principal payment to your loan liability account, so you can see your up-to-date loan balance at any time. If you use Quicken's amortization feature to track your mortgage, Quicken automatically tracks your remaining principal in a liability account.
Accrued liabilities	Liability	Track accrued liabilities, such as payroll taxes and income taxes payable. When you do your company's payroll, as part of the split transaction detail, transfer the payroll taxes portion of each check to a payroll liability account. This technique makes it easy for you to keep track of how much is due for payroll taxes.
Accounts payable	Liability	Keep up-to-date A/P records.
Stocks, mutual funds, and IRAs	Investment	See Chapter 12, *Tracking investments,* on page 121.

Using an asset or liability account

Follow these steps:

- **Set up an asset or liability account.**
  See "Setting up additional Quicken accounts" on page 1.
- **Enter transactions in the asset or liability account.**
  See "Using the liability account register" on page 119.
- **From time to time, close inactive items in the account or update the value of the account.**
  See "Updating the value of an asset or liability account" on page 120.

Important!
To set up a liability account to track an amortized loan such as a house mortgage, see Chapter 10, *Tracking loans and mortgages,* on page 105, first. That chapter explains how Quicken sets up a liability account for you as part of setting up the loan.

Using the liability account register

The Opening Balance shows the balance of the loan at the time you set up the liability account.

These transactions show monthly car payments as transfers from a checking account to the loan account. The amounts appear in the Decrease column because they decrease the total amount owed.

The Ending Balance amount is the outstanding balance of the loan (principal only).

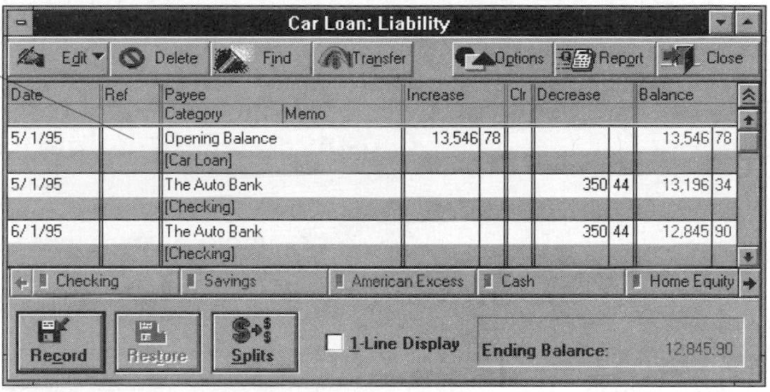

This example shows a liability account set up for one car loan. To set up a single liability account for a group of related liabilities, use classes to identify specific items. Then you can track both transfers and classes in the Category field. For example, if you have one liability account to track three loans, set up a class name for each loan: Car Loan, Boat Loan, and Equity Loan. When you use classes in this way, you can create summary reports subtotaled by class. (See "Summary" on page 180.)

Using the asset account register

These purchases of new capital equipment were recorded as transfers from a checking account to the Cap Equipment asset account. The amounts appear in the Increase column because they increase the total value of the account. Set up a single asset account for a group of related assets.

Instead of Payment and Deposit columns, the asset account register has Decrease and Increase columns. Use the Decrease column to record amounts that decrease the value of your asset; use the Increase column to record amounts that increase the value of your asset.

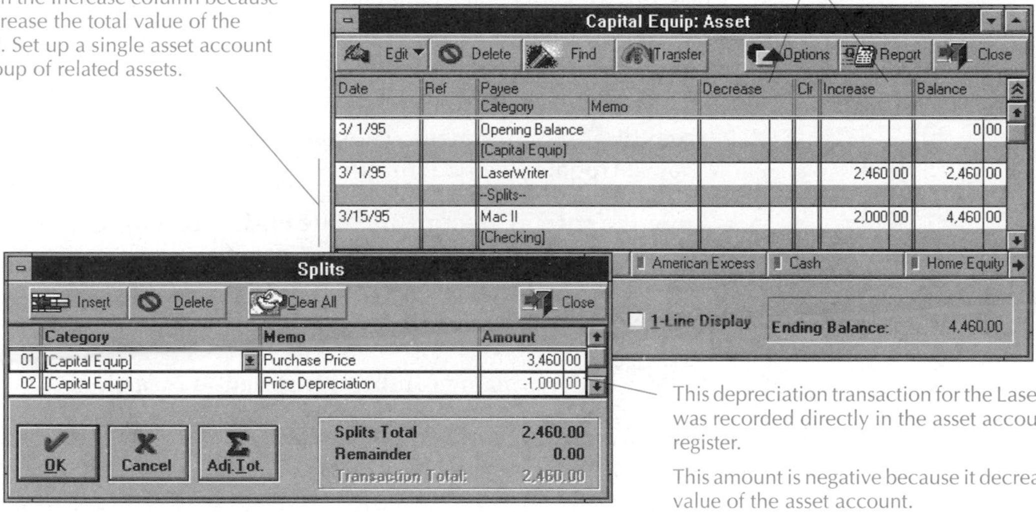

This depreciation transaction for the LaserWriter was recorded directly in the asset account register.

This amount is negative because it decreases the value of the asset account.

Updating the value of an asset or liability account

In asset and liability accounts, you don't have to reconcile the account in the same way you reconcile a checking account. Instead you can mark transactions that are closed or update the values of those that are open.

Closing assets or liabilities

Closed items are those that are no longer active as assets or liabilities. For example, if you sell an asset listed in an asset account, such as an antique, or you pay off a loan listed in a liability account, those items are no longer part of your net worth. However, you don't want to delete them from your account, either. (In the event of an audit, you might want to produce a report that includes them.)

The solution is to mark closed items as cleared. Then you can filter your report to uncleared items only. Open the asset or liability account and mark as cleared both the transaction for the purchase and for the sale of an item. Click twice in the Clr (Cleared) column of a transaction (an X appears), then click Record. Use Find to locate related transactions.

Updating the account balance

You can make an adjustment to the account balance to update the current value of the account. For example, if you have an asset account for some real estate you own, you can enter a transaction to update the current value of the property.

1. **Open the account.**
2. **From the Activities menu, choose Update Balances and then choose Update Cash Balance.**
3. **Enter the current amount and date of the account.**

   For example, if your property is worth $15,000, enter that amount. Quicken compares this amount with the current balance in the account and creates an adjustment transaction for the difference.
4. **Enter a category name for the adjustment transaction.**
5. **Click Record to record the balance adjustment transaction in the register.**

12 Tracking investments

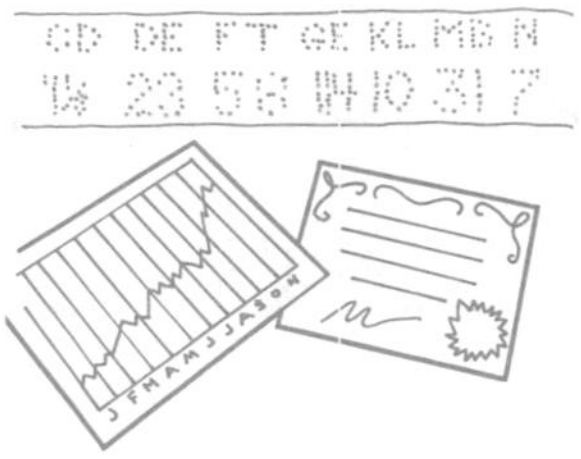

How Quicken helps you with investments

A Quicken investment account has a register just like any other account in which you record your transactions, such as buying and selling shares, reinvesting dividends, recording interest income and capital gains distributions, and so on.

In addition, you can use the Portfolio View to show the current market value, return on investment, price changes, and other essential data of all your securities.

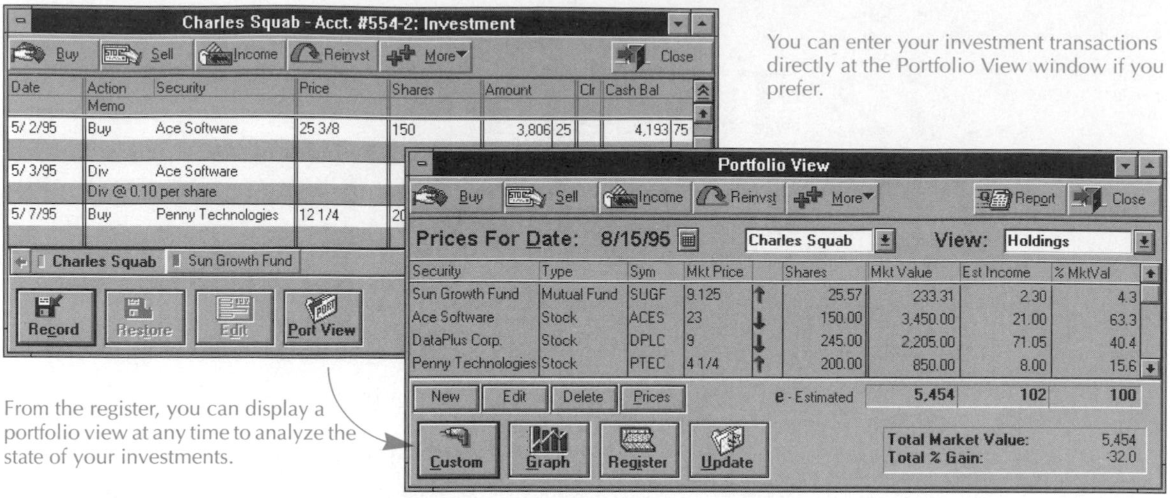

You can enter your investment transactions directly at the Portfolio View window if you prefer.

From the register, you can display a portfolio view at any time to analyze the state of your investments.

Quicken investment reports and graphs complete the information you need to analyze your investment portfolio. Quicken's reports distinguish between taxable investment income and tax-deferred accounts such as an IRA or a 401(k) account.

For more information, see Chapter 25, *Updating your portfolio prices online,* on page 267.

You can update security prices at the Portfolio View window, either manually or automatically via modem with Portfolio Price Update.

While Quicken provides tax reports, it doesn't keep track of changes in tax laws. Also, Quicken doesn't track sophisticated transactions such as commodities trading, strike prices of options, or expiration dates.

Choosing the best account to track investments

The following table suggests what type of Quicken account to use with different types of investments.

It's simpler to use an asset account if an investment has a constant share price or no share price and isn't in a brokerage account with investments that do fluctuate. (See Chapter 11, *Tracking assets and liabilities,* on page 117.) However, you may want to use an investment account to take advantage of Quicken's ability to calculate return on investment.

Use this type of account	If you invest in
Investment	One or more securities (stocks, bonds, or mutual funds) for which you want to track a cash balance in addition to the securities (for example, a collection of investments in a brokerage account). Real estate investment trusts (REITs) or partnerships. Unit trusts. IRA or Keogh accounts. Variable annuities.
Investment (single mutual fund type)	A single mutual fund account that has no cash balance.

Use this type of account	If you invest in
Checking for checking part of account Investment for everything else (use transfers for purchases, dividends, and so on)	Cash management accounts (CMAs).
Money market	Money market funds.
Investment or asset	CDs or Treasury bills. Fixed annuities. Collectibles and precious metals. Employer retirement plans (401(k), 403(b), pension). For more information on tracking a 401(k), press F1 in Quicken, click Search, type "401," and press Enter.
Asset	Securities for which you don't know the share price and dollar amount of each purchase or sales transaction. Real estate.

How to arrange your investment accounts

Quicken has two types of investment accounts: the regular investment account and the mutual fund investment account. When you set up an investment account, you designate the type.

Regular investment account Designed for one or more than one security.	May have a cash balance, as in a brokerage account, or no cash balance. Its register displays the cash balance after every transaction and the current market value of the account. It doesn't display the share balance (total number of shares) of individual securities within the account. (Quicken displays share balances of individual securities in the Portfolio View window, which you access directly from the register.) The advantage of a regular investment account is flexibility. You can change the securities in it and leave cash in it.
Mutual fund investment account Designed for a single mutual fund. (You shouldn't have two or more mutual funds in the same mutual fund account.)	It has no cash in it, only shares of the security. Its register displays the share balance (total number of shares) of the single security and the current market value of the security. The name of the security and the most recent price, if you enter no new price, appear automatically in the register when you enter a new transaction. The advantage of a mutual fund investment account is that certain procedures are streamlined. For example, when you write a check from your Quicken checking account to the mutual fund account, the transaction automatically appears in the investment register as a purchase of shares. The disadvantage is that you can't record interest income.

Regular investment accounts and mutual fund investment accounts give you the same information about your investments. The main difference is that a cash balance appears in the register for a regular account, and a share balance appears for the mutual fund account. You can track income, capital gains, and performance of individual securities in either type of account.

If you wish, you can track several mutual funds in one regular investment account.

Once a regular account, always a regular account.
Once you have set up an account as a regular investment account, you can't change it to be a mutual fund account. However, you can change a mutual fund account to a regular investment account.

Arranging your securities within investment accounts

Here are some recommendations for grouping your securities within one or more Quicken investment accounts:

Security type	Recommendation
Brokerage accounts	Use a separate, regular investment account for each actual brokerage account or other managed account you have. If you have a cash management account (CMA) with a broker, set up the checking part as a Quicken bank account. (You'll be able to print checks, track check numbers, and reconcile easily.) Set up a regular investment account for the rest of the investments in the brokerage account. You transfer money between the two Quicken accounts when you buy and sell investments or receive investment income.
IRAs	Use separate (regular) investment accounts for your IRA and for your spouse's IRA. (Even if you don't now have securities with fluctuating prices in your IRA, set up your IRA as an investment account, as you may want to change the investments later.) This applies to other retirement plans that you manage directly, such as a Keogh plan. If you have more than one security in your IRA, put them in the same (regular) investment account, even if the securities are managed by different mutual fund managers. If you transfer an IRA security from one manager to another, you can still track the performance of your IRA as a whole.
Securities you hold directly	If you have a few individual securities you hold directly, you may wish to set each one up as a separate (regular) investment account. Then you can easily reconcile each account with its statement. On the other hand, you may prefer to lump the securities in a single (regular) investment account, especially if you have other investment accounts. Then you can subtotal these securities by account on reports and track them as a group.

Choosing how much detail to set up

When you set up a new investment account, you have three options for creating your opening balance, depending on how much historical data you want to include, as shown on the next page. We recommend the first option.

<table>
<tr><th>Options</th><th>Advantages</th><th>Disadvantages</th></tr>
<tr><td>Option 1: Enter all historical data.
For each security in the account, enter the initial purchase and all subsequent transactions:
• Name and type of security
• Date, amount invested, and number of shares bought (or price per share) for initial purchase
• All subsequent acquisitions (including reinvestments), sales and gifts, stock splits, and return of capital
• All dividends, interest, and capital gains distributions for the current year
• (Optional) All nonreinvested dividends, interest, and capital gains distributions from prior years (this data gives you a more accurate IRR of your security for past years but doesn't affect Quicken's value for the cost basis)
• Price per share at the end of last year (and prior years, if available) and today</td><td>All Quicken reports are complete and accurate.
If you sell a security, the capital gains report displays the purchase dates, amounts invested, and the realized gain, so you can use this report to prepare Schedule D tax information.
All your investment records are in one convenient place, making it easier for you to analyze your investments and produce data for tax and other purposes.</td><td>You have to locate data for transactions that occurred in the past.
You must spend time entering all prior transactions.</td></tr>
<tr><td>Option 2: Set up for this year.
Enter your investment holdings as of the end of last year. Then enter all investment transactions for each security since the beginning of this year.
For each security in the account, enter:
• Name and type of security
• Number of shares owned at the end of last year
• Price per share at the end of last year and today
• All transactions (purchases, sales, dividends, reinvestments, and so on) for the current year
• Total cost basis</td><td>The information you need to gather goes back only to the end of last year and is probably easy for you to find.
Data for the year is complete, so you can use the investment income report to prepare Schedule B tax information.
Quicken produces accurate reports on performance, income, and changes in unrealized gain for time periods starting with the beginning of this year.</td><td>Because you are starting as of the end of last year, Quicken can't give you an accurate value for all quantities that depend on cost basis for a security: average cost per share, percent gain, total unrealized gain.
If you sell the security, the capital gains report doesn't display an accurate purchase date. Also, because the cost basis dates back only to the beginning of the year, the realized gain isn't subtotaled short vs. long term.</td></tr>
<tr><td>Option 3: Set up fast.
Enter your current investment holdings.
For each security in the account, enter:
• Name and type of security
• Number of shares you own
• Current price per share
• Total cost basis</td><td>You can get started with the minimum amount of information to gather.
You can start using the account right away to see whether you think it's worthwhile to gather and enter more information. (If you set up quickly using this option, you can go back later and enter historical data, as described in "Entering prior history for investments" on page 158.)
Quicken produces accurate reports on income and changes in unrealized gain for time periods starting now.</td><td>Data for this year is incomplete, so you can't use the investment income report to prepare Schedule B tax information.
You may have to wait a few months before your investment data is in the range where you can display a valid investment performance report.
Because you are starting from today, Quicken can't give you an accurate value for all quantities that depend on cost basis: average cost per share, percent gain, total unrealized gain. If you sell the security, the capital gains report doesn't display an accurate purchase date. Also, the realized gain isn't subtotaled short vs. long term.</td></tr>
</table>

Setting up a regular investment account

A regular investment account is designed to track more than one security. There are three steps:

- **Create a regular investment account (below).**
- **Set up all the securities in the account (page 127).**
- **Set up the opening share balance (the number and value of shares you own) for each security in the account (page 129).**

Creating a regular investment account

To set up a mutual fund investment account, see "Setting up a mutual fund investment account" on page 132.

1 **From the Activities menu, choose Create New Account.**

The Select Account Type window appears (shown on page 2).

2 **Choose Investment and click OK.**

Make sure this checkbox is clear.

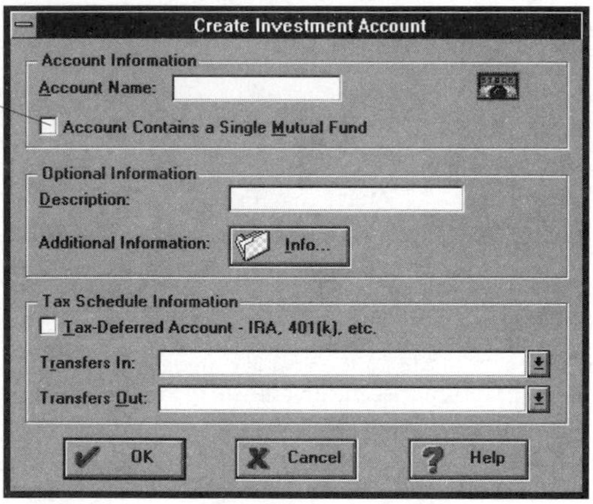

3 **Enter a name for the investment account in the Account Name box.**

Use up to 15 letters, numbers, or spaces.

For example, type the broker's name or "Sally's IRA."

4 **Clear the Account Contains a Single Mutual Fund checkbox.**

This lets you track a variety of securities, including mutual funds, in a regular account. You may also have a cash balance.

(After setting up a regular investment account, you can't later change it to be a mutual fund account.)

Use up to 21 letters, numbers, or spaces.

5 **(Optional) Enter a description of the account.**

6 **(Optional) Click Info to enter additional information about the account for your own benefit.**

Examples of tax-deferred accounts: IRAs, 401(k) plans and 403(b) plans, annuities, and Series EE and HH U.S. Savings Bonds.

7 **If the earnings from this account are tax-free until you take possession of them, select the Tax-Deferred Account checkbox.**

8 **Select the tax schedules to be assigned to transfers into and out of this account.**

9 **Click OK.**

See Appendix A, *Customizing Quicken,* on page 293.

If this is the first investment account you have set up, Quicken asks if you would like to add an icon to the iconbar to give more direct access to the Portfolio View window. If you click Yes, you can always delete the icon later if you want. Or you can click No and add the icon later.

You *can* change their descriptions; see "Changing report options" on page 196.

The investment categories, which all begin with an underline (for example, _DivInc), automatically appear on your category list, whether or not you selected standard categories, as soon as you add an investment account. You can't delete these categories or edit their names while you have investment accounts in your Quicken file.

You're ready to set up each security in the account.

Setting up securities for a regular investment account

Before you can enter transactions for your securities, you must set up the securities to give Quicken some information about them. You can set up new securities at any time, either in advance or "on the fly" as you enter transactions for them. All investment accounts in the same Quicken file share the same Security list, so the same security can appear in more than one account.

Or press Ctrl+Y

To edit or delete an existing security, select the security and click Edit or Delete. You can delete a security only if you have no transactions for it.

1 **From the Lists menu, choose Security.**

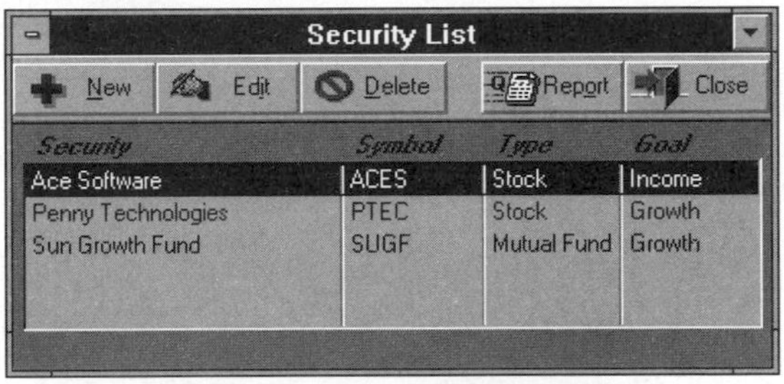

Or press Ctrl+N

2 **Click New to create a new security.**

Select a Type and Goal from the drop-down lists. If none is appropriate, you can set up new ones. (However, you can't set them up "on the fly." See steps 5 and 6 below.)

Check here if this is a tax-free security. These are filtered out of capital gains reports.

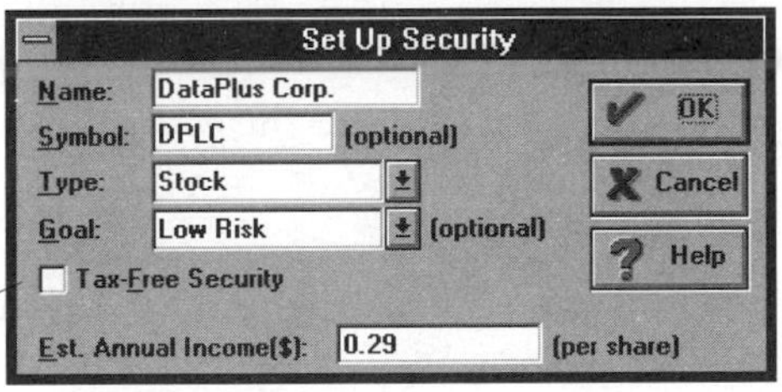

3 **Enter the name of the security in the Name box.**

For more information about using symbols, see "Importing prices from an ASCII file" on page 160.

4 **(Optional) Enter a symbol in the Symbol box if you plan to import price data from a file.**

5 **From the Type drop-down list, select the security type.**

The securities appear in the Portfolio View window alphabetically within security type, making it convenient for you to enter prices from the newspaper. You can also use types for sorting and subtotaling in investment reports and graphs.

The preset list of security types is:
Bond
CD
Mutual Fund
Stock

You can customize the list of security types. For example, you can add Money Fund, T-Bill, Tax-Free Bond, Option, REIT, Unit Trust, NYSE, NASDAQ, or AMEX. To customize the Security Type List:

- Click Cancel to temporarily leave the Set Up Security window.
- From the Lists menu, choose Security Type.

Or press Ctrl+N

- To set up a new security type (up to a maximum of 15), click New.
- After customizing the Security Type list, return to this procedure to set up your securities.

At the Edit Security Type window, specify whether prices for that security type should be displayed in decimals or fractions (multiples of 1/16).

6 **(Optional) From the Goal drop-down list, select the investment goal.**

Investment goals give an idea of what you hope the investment will achieve for you. When you create reports, you can sort and subtotal by investment goal. Using goals lets you group investments within the same account or within different accounts.

The preset list of investment goals is:
College Fund
Growth
High Risk
Income
Low Risk

As with security types, you can customize the Investment Goal list by adding new goals, deleting unused goals, or modifying existing goals. You can add Retirement, Down Payment, Remodeling, Growth & Income, or Medium Risk to this list of goals. Or you can use goals to label investments for your children or grandchildren, distinguish taxable income from tax-free income within the same account, or distinguish different industry groups, such as energy and computer. To customize the Investment Goal List:

- Click Cancel to leave the Set Up Security window.
- From the Lists menu, choose Investment Goal.

Or press Ctrl+N

- To set up a new goal (up to a maximum of 15), click New.
- After customizing the Investment Goal list, return to this procedure to set up your securities.

7 **(Optional) Enter the estimated annual income per share for this security.**

Often, when you buy a security you will be provided with this information. Entering the figure into Quicken can help give you a more complete picture. (It's used for calculating yield.)

8 **Click OK to record the new security.**

9 **Repeat steps 1 through 8 to set up each security in the account.**

You are now ready to enter transaction information about your securities in your new investment account, as described next.

Setting up the opening balance of each security

Before entering transaction information, see "Choosing how much detail to set up" on page 124. We recommend that you record a complete transaction history for each security in the account, starting with your initial purchase or acquisition of the security. If you don't enter a complete transaction history, Quicken can't report accurate unrealized or realized gains.

This is discussed in more detail on page 158.

You can enter the security opening balances in either the investment Register window or in the Portfolio View window. The following steps refer to the register, but they apply to the Portfolio View window as well.

The Register window and the Portfolio View window have the same button bar for entering investment transactions. The Portfolio View window also has a Report button.

1 **Open the register for your new investment account (select it from the Account list and click Open) and go to a new transaction.**

2 **Click the More button in the button bar and then click Add Shares to Acct.**

You can type information directly into the register fields if you want, but these steps describe investment forms that make transaction entry much easier.

The Add Shares To Account investment form appears. How you fill in the form depends on which of the three setup options described on page 125 you chose. We recommend that you use option 1 to enter a complete transaction history for each of your securities.

If your investments date back to before you started using Quicken, you need to record an Add Shares transaction for each security in the account. Add Shares to Account lets you:

- Add shares you already own to a Quicken account.
- Enter a purchase of shares for a date prior to when you started using Quicken, without deducting the money from a Quicken account.

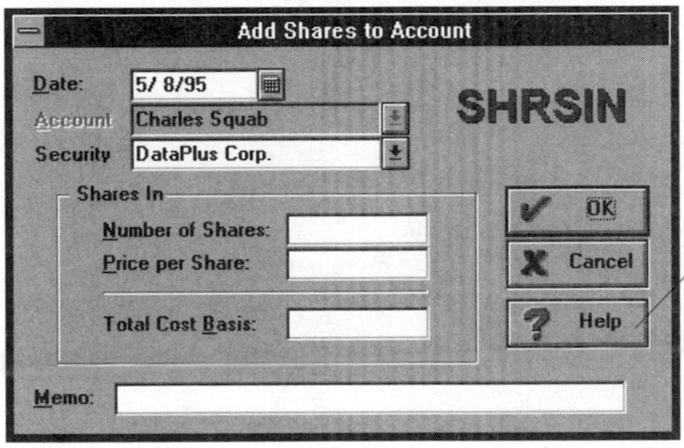

For specific information about completing any of the fields in these forms, click Help.

If you opened your real-world investment account *after* you started using Quicken, you might start by transferring money from your Quicken bank account to your Quicken investment account. Use the Transfer Cash In form (click More in the button bar and choose Transfer cash in) to record the opening cash balance of the investment account as a transfer from your bank account. Then use the Buy form instead of the Add Shares to Account form to record the initial purchase of a security.

3 **Enter the date appropriate for the setup option you have chosen.**

- For option 1, enter the date of your initial purchase or acquisition of the security.
- For option 2, enter 12/31 of last year.

- For option 3 enter today's date.

4 **Enter the name of the security.**

See the description on page 127.

If you haven't yet set up this security, do so now.

5 **Enter the number of shares (up to four decimal places) you owned on the date you entered in the Date box.**

Security type	Number of shares to enter
Stock or mutual fund	Actual number of shares.
Bonds	Ten times the actual number of bonds (to match the way prices are quoted). Or, enter one hundredth of the total face value of the bonds. For example, if you have two bonds with a total face value of $2,000, enter 20 in the Shares field.
Money market fund or CD	The total value.
Collectible	One (1).
Precious metal	The number of ounces.

6 **In the Price per Share box, enter a share price in fractions or decimals.**

- For option 1, enter your actual initial cost per share (including commission, fees, and load) or (if you prefer to enter the total cost) leave the Price box blank.
- For options 2 and 3, enter the cost per share (including commission, fees, and load) if you purchased the security all at one time, or leave the Price box blank.

Security type	Price to enter
Stock or mutual fund	Actual price per share.
Bonds	One-tenth of the actual market value of each bond (to match the way prices are quoted).
Money market fund or CD	One dollar.
Collectible	Total value.
Precious metal	Price per ounce.

To enter a share price as a whole number plus a fraction, leave a space after the whole dollar amount, and use a slash (/) between the numerator and denominator. For example, type 36 3/8. If a price for a stock or bond isn't an exact multiple of 1/16, Quicken displays it as a decimal.

If you leave the Price per Share box blank but complete the Total Cost Basis box, Quicken calculates and fills in the price per share.

7 **In the Total Cost Basis field, enter a dollar amount, including commission, fees, and load, if you didn't enter a price per share.**

8 **(Optional) In the Memo field, enter any notes to yourself about this transaction.**

9 **Click OK to record the transaction.**

10 **Repeat steps 2 through 9 for each security in the account.**

Now that you have set up the opening balances for your securities, you are ready to bring your investment account up to date. If you chose setup option 3, it is already up to date—skip to step 12.

See "Recording your investment transactions" on page 135 for more information.

11 **For options 1 and 2, use the buttons in the button bar to enter all subsequent transactions for each security (purchases, sales, dividends, reinvestments, and so on).**

Temporarily ignore amounts that appear in the Cash Bal field.

Quicken normally displays prices for stocks and bonds as whole numbers plus fractions (multiples of 1/16) and all other prices in decimals. You can change this format by editing the Security Type.

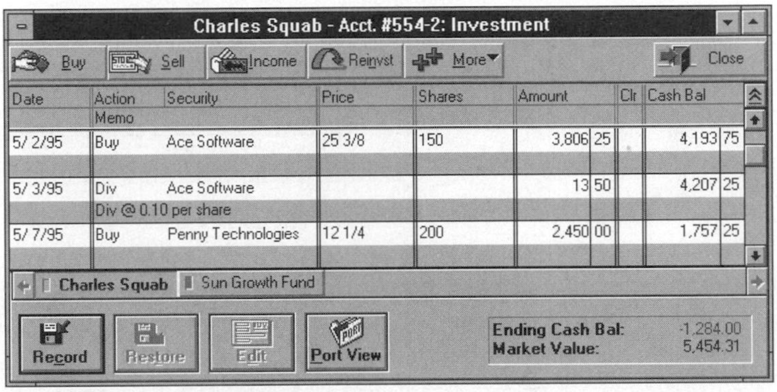

12 **When you have finished entering historical transactions for all the securities in this account, determine whether or not the ending cash balance in this account is correct.**

In the Register window, look at the Ending Cash Balance at the lower right corner. In the Portfolio View window, the cash balance is shown on the last line (make sure the correct account is selected in the account box).

See "Updating the prices of your securities" on page 153 to continue.

- If the final amount displayed for the cash balance in this account is correct, your investment account is now set up.
- If the final amount displayed for the cash balance in this account isn't correct, continue with the next section.

Entering the beginning cash balance for a regular investment account

You might have a cash balance in your regular investment account if, for example, you have transferred some funds from a bank account, sold some securities, or received a cash dividend or interest.

1 **From the Activities menu, choose Update Balances and then choose Update Cash Balance.**

In the Portfolio View window, you must select a single account before you can choose the Update Balances option.

2 **Enter the current cash balance and date for this account.**

Quicken adds an adjustment that corrects your cash balance.

Your regular investment account is now set up. The market value of your account appears in the lower right corner of the investment register, based on the latest prices you have supplied.

For a regular investment account, this column displays the cash balance for the account. When you record a transaction, Quicken calculates the correct cash balance. If you have no cash in the account, the column displays zeros.

If Quicken displays a row of asterisks (*****) in a register column, the number is too large for Quicken to display. Quicken displays dollar amounts between -$999,999.99 and $9,999,999.99. Outside that range, Quicken tracks the amount but doesn't display it.

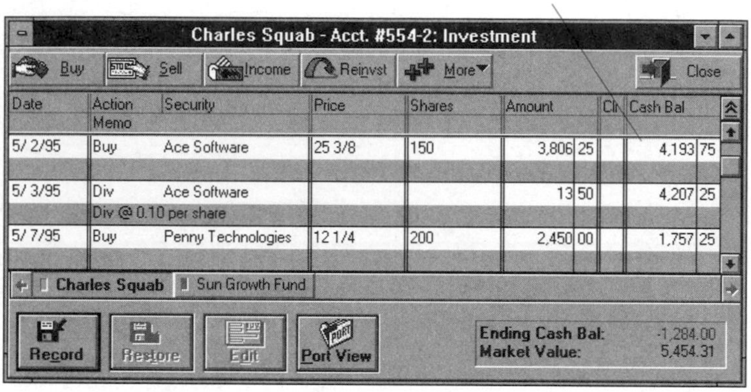

See "Updating the prices of your securities" on page 153.

3 **Update the security prices in the Portfolio View window.**

- For options 1 or 2, enter prices for the end of last year as well as for today. Then you can track unrealized (paper) gains or losses and performance for the current year.
- For option 3, enter current prices for your securities.

Setting up a mutual fund investment account

A mutual fund investment account is designed to track a single mutual fund with no cash balance. To set up a mutual fund investment account, follow these steps:

- ◆ **Create a mutual fund investment account.**
- ◆ **Set up the opening share balance—the number and value of shares you own.**

Creating a mutual fund investment account

1 **From the Activities menu, choose Create New Account.**

2 **In the Create New Account window (shown on page 2), choose Investment and click OK.**

Use up to 15 letters, numbers, or spaces.

3 **Enter a name for the account in the Account Name box.**

You probably want to use the name of the mutual fund.

4 **Select the Account Contains a Single Mutual Fund checkbox.**

Make sure this checkbox is selected. ——— ☑ Account Contains a Single Mutual Fund

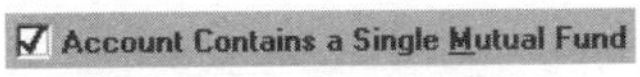

Changing the account type

If you set up a mutual fund account and then want to include another security or a cash balance, edit the account information and clear the Account Contains a Single Mutual Fund checkbox to change to a regular investment account. (You can't change the account back to a mutual fund account.)

5 **If the earnings from this account are free from taxation until you take possession of them, select the Tax-Deferred Account checkbox.**

Examples of tax-deferred accounts are IRAs, 401(k) plans and 403(b) plans, annuities, and Series EE and HH U.S. Savings Bonds.

Use up to 21 letters, numbers, or spaces.

6 **(Optional) Enter a description of the account.**

7 **(Optional) Click Info to enter additional information about the account for your own benefit.**

8 **Click OK.**

The Set Up Mutual Fund Security window appears. In a mutual fund investment account, you set up the security when you set up the account.

Although the name for the security is filled in with the account name, you can change it.

(Optional) Enter a symbol in the Symbol box if you plan to export or import price data from a file.

For more information, see "Importing prices from an ASCII file" on page 160.

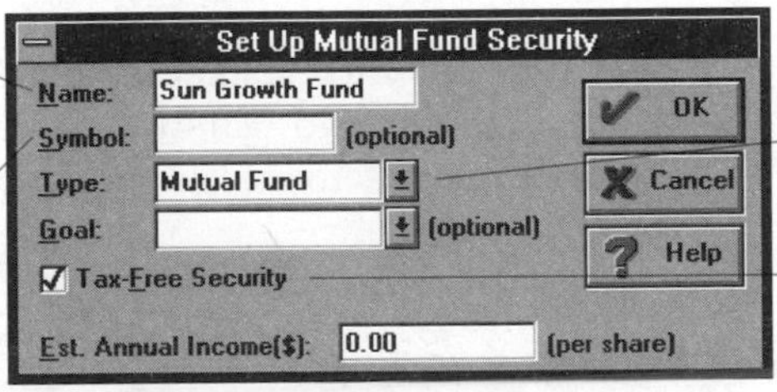

Unless you decide to customize the Security Type list to your own needs, leave the type as Mutual Fund.

Check here if this is a tax-free security. These are filtered out of capital gains reports.

Set Up Mutual Fund Security	
Name:	Sun Growth Fund
Symbol:	[optional]
Type:	Mutual Fund
Goal:	[optional]
☑ Tax-Free Security	
Est. Annual Income($):	0.00 (per share)

(Buttons: ✓ OK, ✗ Cancel, ? Help)

9 **Enter information in the Set Up Mutual Fund Security window and click OK to set up the investment account.**

Quicken adds the account to your Account list. The investment categories, which all begin with an underline (for example, _DivInc, _IntInc), automatically appear on your category list (whether or not you selected standard categories) as soon as you add an investment account. You can't delete these categories nor edit their names.

If you'd like reports to show the categories' descriptions instead of the names, see "Changing report options" on page 196.

10 **Open the new mutual fund account (select it from the Account list and click Open).**

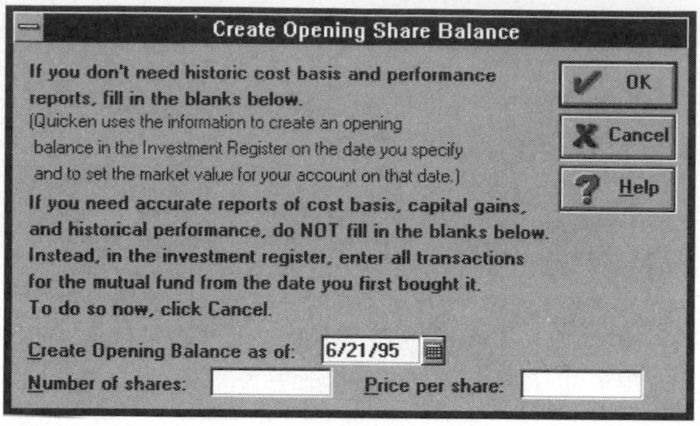

Before entering an opening balance, see "Choosing how much detail to set up" on page 124. We recommend that you record a complete transaction history for the mutual fund, starting with your initial purchase or acquisition. If you don't enter a complete transaction history, Quicken can't report accurate unrealized or realized gains.

11 **To enter historical data under option 1, click Cancel and continue with "Setting up the opening balance of each security" on page 129.**

- For option 2, enter the date 12/31 of last year, the number of shares you owned then, and the price per share. Click OK and continue with step 12.
- For option 3, enter today's date, the number of shares you now own, and today's price per share. Click OK. Your mutual fund account is now set up.

The investment register appears with your opening balance filled in. In the Action field, ShrsIn ("shares in") shows that you added existing shares to this new Quicken account.

This column displays the number of shares you hold (to two decimal places, although Quicken calculates to four decimal places). When you record a transaction, Quicken calculates the correct total number of shares of the security you hold in the account.

Quicken displays the market value, based on the price per share you entered.

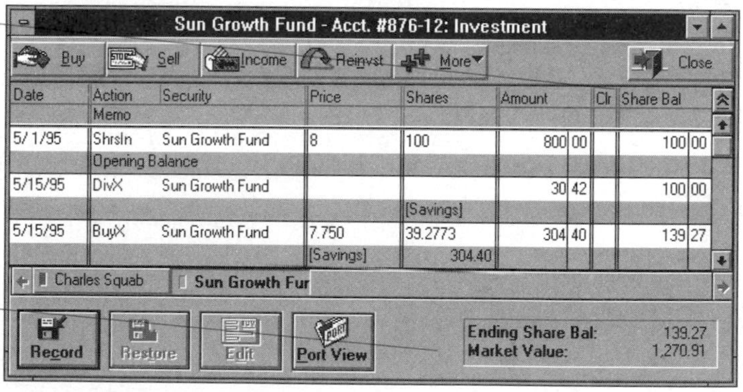

See "Entering investment transactions" on page 135.

12 **Enter transactions for this year.**

13 **Update the market value of your account to reflect today's share price.**

See "Updating the prices of your securities" on page 153. (For more information on the Portfolio View, see page 147.)

Recording your investment transactions

When you have set up your investment account or accounts, you can begin entering transactions. Record a transaction any time a security or money enters or leaves one of your accounts, for example when you buy or sell shares, reinvest a dividend, receive interest, or transfer money into a broker account.

Changes in the prices of your securities *don't* constitute transactions. Record price changes as described in "Updating the values of your investments," on page 153.

Entering investment transactions

Enter investment transactions either in the account register or in the Portfolio View window. Both windows have an investment button bar that you use to enter transactions.

If you prefer to enter the details directly in a blank transaction in the register, see page 138.

Click More to choose from a menu of transactions that are used less frequently.

1 **Click a button on the investment button bar.**

See the table on the next page for the kinds of transactions you can enter.

Quicken displays an easy-entry investment form in which you enter the details of the transaction. For example:

Quicken displays a different form for each type of transaction.

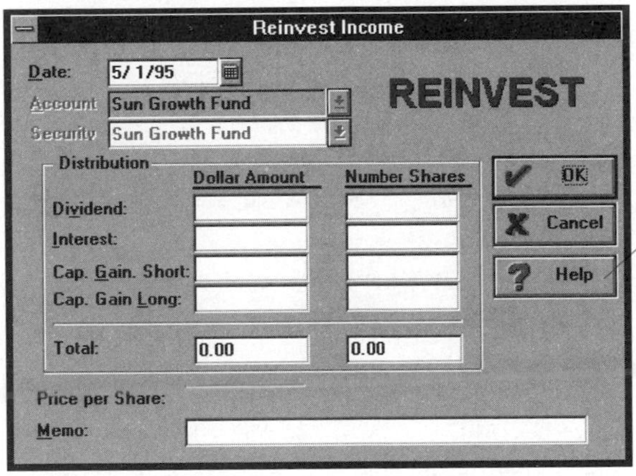

Click Help for more information on how to fill in a form.

2 **Complete the form and click OK.**

To avoid errors, have Quicken confirm your entries before you leave the form (see page 150).

Quicken writes your entries into a transaction in the investment register. (Quicken may create more than one transaction if you entered several transactions on the same form.)

If you're entering transactions in the Portfolio View window, click Register to see the transactions listed.

The header bar tells you what information is in each field.

The Action field tells you what type of transaction this is. To see an alphabetic listing of Action codes with descriptions, click the drop-down button when the cursor is in the Action field.

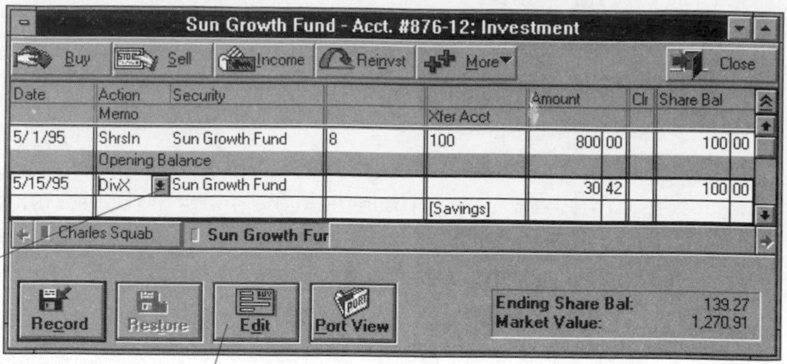

To change a transaction's details, either click Edit to display the investment form or edit the entries directly in the register.

The next table summarizes the types of transactions you can enter.

To enter this type of transaction	Click this button
Buy a security, or shares in a security (see page 138). (For example, buy shares, bonds, or a CD.)	**Buy**
Sell a security, or shares in a security (page 139).	**Sell**
Receive money from dividends, interest, or capital gains distributions (page 140). Also any miscellaneous income.	**Income**
Reinvest earnings from dividends, interest, or capital gains distributions (page 141). Also stock dividends (page 143).	**Reinvst**
Increase the balance of shares in the account without a monetary transaction. Use this to set up the opening share balance (page 129).	**More** ➤ Add shares to account
Adjust the share balance downwards, with no money involved (page 159).	**More** ➤ Remove shares from account [a]
Pay interest on a margin loan (page 143).	**More** ➤ Margin interest expense [b]
Any type of expense associated with a security, for example, portfolio management fees.	**More** ➤ Miscellaneous expense [b]
A reminder note to yourself (page 146).	**More** ➤ Reminder transaction
Return of capital or principal (page 145).	**More** ➤ Return of capital [b]
Receive additional shares from a stock split (page 143).	**More** ➤ Stock split
Transfer cash into the investment account from another account (page 141). (For example, transfer cash into your broker account.)	**More** ➤ Transfer cash in [b]
Transfer cash out of your investment account (page 141).	**More** ➤ Transfer cash out [b]

a. In the SHRSOUT form, you can specify which portion, or lot, of shares to remove. It is similar to the form for selling lots, on page 140.

b. This option isn't available for mutual fund investment accounts, as it adds cash to or removes cash from the account.

Understanding what each transaction does

Depending on what you enter in the investment form, Quicken enters it in the Action field of the investment register. The action identifies the type of transaction.

The category isn't displayed in the register.

Each action has a category associated with it, so you can create reports and graphs sorted by category.

The following table matches actions to categories, and shows what effect each investment transaction has on your portfolio. (Quicken takes care of all these details for you.) The cost basis is the total cost of all shares of a security.

			Effect on						
Transaction	**Action** [a]	**Category**	**Average cost**	**Gain/Loss %**	**Number of shares**	**Cost basis**	**IRR by security**	**Market value**	**Cash balance**
Buy security	Buy BuyX	—	Either	Either	Increase	Increase	Either	Increase	Decrease
Sell security	Sell SellX	_RlzdGain	Either	Either	Decrease	Decrease	Increase	Decrease	Increase
Receive dividend	Div DivX	_DivInc	—	—	—	—	Increase	—	Increase
Receive interest	IntInc	_IntInc	—	—	—	—	Increase	—	Increase
Receive short-term capital gains distribution	CGShort CGShortX	_ST CapGnDst	—	—	—	—	Increase	—	Increase
Receive long-term capital gains distribution	CGLong CGLongX	_LT CapGnDst	—	—	—	—	Increase	—	Increase
Receive miscellaneous income	MiscInc	Choose from list	—	—	—	—	Increase	—	Increase
Reinvest dividend	ReinvDiv	_DivInc	Either	Either	Increase	Increase	Increase	Increase	—
Reinvest interest	ReinvInt	_IntInc	Either	Either	Increase	Increase	Increase	Increase	—
Reinvest short-term capital gains distribution	ReinvSh	_ST CapGnDst	Either	Either	Increase	Increase	Increase	Increase	—
Reinvest long-term capital gains distribution	ReinvLg	_LT CapGnDst	Either	Either	Increase	Increase	Increase	Increase	—
Add shares to account	ShrsIn	—	Either	Either	Increase	Increase	Either	Increase	—
Remove shares from account	ShrsOut[b]	—	Either	Either	Decrease	Decrease	Either	Decrease	—
Margin interest expense	MargInt	_IntExp	—	—	—	—	Decrease	—	Decrease
Miscellaneous expense	MiscExp	Choose from list	—	—	—	—	Decrease	—	Decrease
Reminder	Reminder	—	—	—	—	—	—	—	—
Return of capital	RtrnCap	—	Decrease	Increase	—	Decrease	Increase	See note c	Increase
Stock split 2 for 1 1 for 2	StkSplit	—	 Decrease Increase	 Increase [c] Decrease[c]	 Increase Decrease	 — —	 Increase Decrease	 See note c See note c	 — —
Transfer cash in	XIn	[Account name]	—	—	—	—	—	—	Increase
Transfer cash out	XOut	[Account name]	—	—	—	—	—	—	Decrease

a. An X in the action name (for example, BuyX) indicates that the money for or from the transaction is transferred from or to another Quicken account, and so doesn't affect the cash balance of the investment account.

b. When you click the More button in the investment register or Portfolio View window, and then choose ShrsOut, you can specify which portion, or lot, of shares to remove. It is similar to the form for selling lots, on page 140.

c. You must update the share price.

Entering transactions directly in the register

You don't have to use the investment forms for entering transactions. If you prefer, you can complete the fields of the register directly, as in other Quicken registers.

When you QuickZoom from an investment report, you are taken to an investment form to edit the transaction. To show the register transaction instead, choose Options from the Edit menu (or click the Options icon on the Quicken iconbar), click Reports, and then clear the QuickZoom to Investment Forms checkbox (page 196).

See "Memorizing and recalling a transaction" on page 42.

You can memorize a recurring transaction (such as a quarterly dividend) and recall it for quick entry.

Entering numbers in investment transactions

Quicken knows that share price, number of shares, and dollar amount are related. If you fill in only two of the three quantities, it will calculate the third quantity from the relationship:

Number of Shares × Price = Total Amount

Rounding of these amounts varies by field.

Field	Rounding rules
Shares	The number of shares appears to four decimal places. It displays exact integers without decimals. It doesn't display zeros after the decimal point unless they are followed by nonzero digits. If there are more than four decimal places, Quicken cuts off the additional places. For example, Quicken truncates the number of shares 8.21678 to 8.2167.
Price	Quicken keeps internal track of decimal prices to the nearest 0.0005 and normally displays them to the nearest 0.001. It displays exact integers without decimals. If the fourth decimal place is a 5, Quicken displays it; otherwise it rounds to three decimal places. For example, Quicken displays 8.2175 but rounds the price 8.2177 upward to 8.218.
Total Amount	Quicken displays total amounts in dollars and whole cents. When it calculates the amount from the price and number of shares, it rounds to the nearest cent. For example, if you enter 40.3 shares at $8.26, Quicken rounds the total amount upward to $332.88.

See "Adjusting the cash or share balance" on page 159.

At the end of each year, you may wish to adjust for the effects of rounding, to make the register match your statements. You can adjust the cash balance or the share balances of individual securities.

Buying securities

Click the Buy button.

- If you're buying securities with cash in the same account, Quicken subtracts the purchase amount from the cash balance in the account.

See also "Transferring money to and from other accounts" on page 141. It describes situations in which it may be more convenient to record the transaction from the source account.

- If you're buying securities with cash you transfer in from another account, enter the source account in the Transfer Acct box in the investment form. (Quicken enters BuyX in the Action field.) Quicken automatically subtracts the purchase amount from the cash balance in the source account.

Commissions and fees. If an explicit commission or fee is added to the purchase, enter it in the Commission/Fee field. (If the Total of Sale amount doesn't equal the price times the number of shares, Quicken enters the difference in the Commission/Fee field.)

See "Updating the values of your investments" on page 153.

Loads. A *load* (sometimes called a *front-end load*) is a commission built into the purchase price of a mutual fund or other security. A load fund has two share prices: a *buy* or *offer* price, and a *sell* or *net asset value* (NAV) price. Enter the purchase of a load fund at the buy price with no additional commission.

The true market value of your investment is based on the sell or NAV price. To correct the market value, update the price of the fund using the NAV price. The difference between the market value and what you paid is the load.

A *back-end load* is a commission built into the selling price. Funds with these loads have a net asset value (share price) greater than the selling price. Enter the sale of such a fund using the actual selling price.

Accrued interest. When you buy a bond after its original date of issue, you usually have to pay *accrued interest* to the previous owner. Accrued interest is interest the bond has already earned but not yet paid out.

Use the Buy form to enter the bond purchase transaction without including accrued interest.

Enter the payment of accrued interest as a separate transaction. Click More and choose Miscellaneous expense. Enter the security name in the Security box, the dollar amount in the Price box, and the expense category _Accrued Int in the Category box. (Quicken adds this category at the end of your expense categories when you set up your first investment account.)

If you paid the accrued interest out of another Quicken account, enter a third transaction to show a cash transfer equal to the accrued interest. Click More and choose Transfer cash in. Enter the other account name in the Transfer Acct box.

Selling securities

Click the Sell button.

- If you're keeping cash from a sale in the same account, Quicken adds the sale proceeds to the cash balance in the account.
- If you're transferring cash from a sale to another account, enter the destination account in the Transfer Acct box. Quicken automatically adds the sale proceeds to the cash balance in the receiving account.

Commissions and fees. If an explicit commission or fee is subtracted from the sale proceeds, enter it in the Commission/Fee field. (If the Total of Sale amount doesn't equal the price times the number of shares, Quicken enters the difference in the Commission/Fee field.)

Specifying which lot you're selling. If you have bought shares in the same security more than once, and now want to sell only a portion of your shares, you can specify which shares you're selling. If you don't specify which shares you're selling, Quicken assumes you're selling the ones you bought first (a rule known as First In, First Out, or FIFO).

In the Sell form, enter the name of the security and the number of shares to sell. Then click Lots.

Your previous purchases of the security are listed as different lots.

As you select all or part of a particular lot, Quicken keeps a count of the total number of shares selected. This must match the total number of shares to sell that you entered.

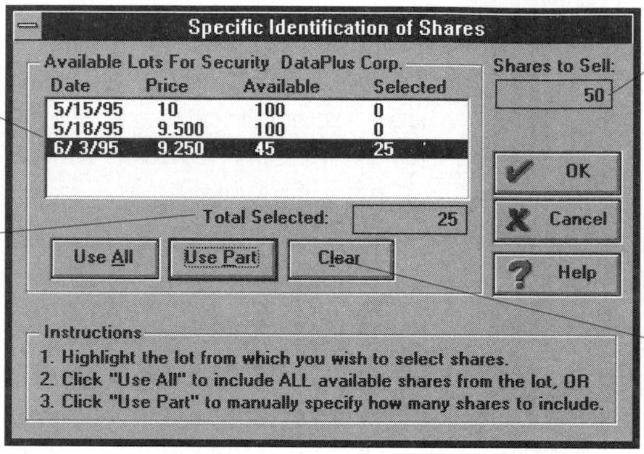

This is the number you entered in the Sell form.

Click Clear to begin selecting again.

To sell all the shares in a particular lot (up to the total number you are selling), select the lot and click Use All. To sell just some of the shares, select the lot and click Use Part, and then specify the number to sell from that lot. When you have finished, the Total Selected should equal the Shares to Sell. Click OK.

Entering income (dividends, interest, and capital gains distributions)

Click Income to enter the receipt of cash from dividends, interest, or capital gains distributions.

You can't transfer interest or miscellaneous income to another account.

If the cash is being transferred out of the investment account, enter the receiving account's name in the Destination of Funds box. Quicken automatically adds the income to the cash balance in the receiving account.

- For dividend income from a money market fund that is the cash balance of a brokerage account, enter the name of the money market fund as the security name.
- An *income distribution* is money a mutual fund pays you as a result of dividends and interest it receives from the securities within the fund. Treat it like a dividend in Quicken.
- A *capital gains distribution* is money paid to you by a mutual fund as a result of capital gains the fund earns by selling securities within

the fund. The fund usually informs you whether the distribution is for *short-term* or *long-term* capital gains. (You may receive both at the same time. If the fund doesn't tell you whether a capital gains distribution is short-term or long-term, assume it's long-term.)

For reinvested dividends, interest, or capital gains distributions, including interest that stays in a CD or dividends that stay in a money market fund, click Reinvst instead of Income—see "Entering reinvestments" next.

Entering reinvestments

A *reinvestment* is the purchase of additional shares of a security with money paid to you by that security as dividend or interest income or capital gains distribution. (For a CD or money market fund, you are buying new shares at a share price of one dollar.)

Reinvestments work like an Income and a Buy transaction combined. Reinvestments increase your cost basis and your Return On Investment (ROI).

Click Reinvst. Enter the dollar amount (in the appropriate box) and the number of new shares you are receiving. Quicken calculates the price per share. If a mutual fund doesn't tell you whether a capital gains distribution is short-term or long-term, assume it's long-term.

Redeeming shares for IRA custodial fees

In a mutual fund account set up as an IRA or other retirement account, the fund custodian may redeem shares as a custodial fee.

For redemption of shares as a custodial fee, select Sell in the Action column of the register. Enter the share price and the total amount, so that Quicken calculates the number of shares. Now enter the same dollar amount of the fee in the Commission/Fee column, to make the net amount of the transaction zero. Enter the name of the investment account itself in the Category column.

Transferring money to and from other accounts

If you have never created a transfer before, see "Transferring money between accounts" on page 22.

When you complete the Transfer Acct box in an investment form, for example when buying shares, Quicken creates a cash transfer between the investment account and the other account. For regular investment accounts, the transfer amount need not be the same as the total transaction amount—the difference is added to or subtracted from the cash balance of the investment account. (For mutual fund accounts, you can't do this because the account doesn't have a cash balance.)

Examples of when you would use a transfer:

- If you write checks by hand to pay for a security in a regular investment account, complete a Buy form in the investment account, and then fill in the check number on the bank account side of the transfer.
- If you're buying a security in a mutual fund account, Quicken knows that you have only one security. When you write a check or enter the transaction in your checking account register, Quicken records the transaction in the investment register with the security name, and enters the number of shares on the basis of the most recent price known to Quicken. Thus, you'll probably choose to record the transaction from your checking account.
- If you record a check at the Write Checks window or in the check register to pay for a security in a *regular* investment account, enter the transaction as a cash transfer to the investment account that contains the security you're buying. The action for the transaction in the investment register is XIn. Then go to the investment register, change the XIn action to BuyX, click Edit, and fill in the Buy form.
- If you're transferring cash out of an investment account, start at the investment register. You can enter more information about the transaction in this register.

The action for any investment transaction involving a transfer has an X in the name, for example, BuyX or DivX.

Giving and receiving securities

- To give shares that are now in a Quicken account, click More and choose Remove shares from account. Enter the number of shares. Quicken reduces your number of shares and records a sale with a capital gain of zero, without adding cash to any account.

  To transfer the shares to another Quicken account, enter a separate transaction for receipt of the shares in the register of the second account. In the second account, click More and choose Add shares to account.
- To receive shares, click More and choose Add shares to account. This form increases your number of shares without subtracting cash from any account. Enter the number of shares received and the actual initial cost per share (including commission, fees, and load). The cost depends on whether you're receiving the shares as a gift or as an inheritance:

  Inherited shares. The cost basis of inherited shares is generally the value of the shares on the date that the deceased died or alternative valuation date. When you receive the inherited shares, record the cost per share on that date.

  Gift shares. The cost basis of shares you received as a gift depends on the value of the shares on the date of the gift and the price that the giver paid for the shares, as well as your sale price if you sell the shares. When you receive the gift shares, record the cost per share when the giver originally purchased the shares.

Consult your tax advisor about any additional rules that may apply to determining your gain or loss.

Entering stock splits and stock dividends

Stock splits. When a security declares a *stock split*, you are given additional shares. Each share is now worth less than it was before the split, but the total market value of all your shares is unchanged. (In a *reverse split*, you receive fewer shares than you have now.)

For a stock split, click More and choose Stock split. In the New Shares and Old Shares boxes, use numerals to enter the ratio of new shares to old. For example, if you receive one additional share for every three old shares, you now have four for every three you had before, so enter 4 in the New Shares field and 3 in the Old Shares field. Also enter the new price per share, after the split.

If you have more than one transaction for the security on the same day, Quicken places the stock split ahead of the other transactions. For example, if you had 100 shares before a two-for-one split, and you sell 100 shares on the day of the split, Quicken knows you still have 100 shares remaining.

When you record a stock split, Quicken recalculates your average cost per share. (Quicken doesn't change any transactions previously recorded in the register.)

Stock dividends. A *stock dividend*, which is rare, is a dividend in the form of additional shares *instead of cash*. Most stock dividends are nontaxable. The company issuing the stock dividend will inform you whether it is taxable.

A stock dividend isn't the same as a cash (normal) dividend issued by a company nor is it the same as a reinvested cash dividend.

- Enter a nontaxable stock dividend as a stock split (click More and choose Stock split). For the ratio of new shares to old shares, add 1 to the number of dividend shares given per existing share. For example, if you receive 0.05 share per existing share, enter 1.05 to 1 as the ratio of new shares to old shares.
- Enter a taxable stock dividend as a reinvested dividend (click Reinvst).

Buying on margin

A *margin loan* is money you borrow from a broker to pay for a security you're buying.

You don't have to tell Quicken you have a margin loan. (If you buy a security and don't have enough cash for it in your account, Quicken displays a negative cash balance.) Alternatively, you may want to set up a liability account for the loan.

- To record interest you pay on the margin loan, click More and choose Margin interest expense.

- If you have set up a liability account for the loan, click More and choose Transfer cash in. Enter the amount you are borrowing and the name of the liability account in the Transfer Acct box. (Click More and choose Transfer cash out when you pay off the loan.)

Buying and redeeming U.S. Savings Bonds

The U.S. government issues Series EE bonds in various face value denominations. You buy a Series EE bond at a discount from its face value. Interest is paid only when a bond is redeemed. The interest from a Series EE bond is exempt from state and local taxes, and no federal tax is due until the bond is redeemed.

- When you buy a Series EE bond, click Buy and set up the form like this:

In this example, the buyer purchased one Series EE bond with a face value of $1,000.

(To match the way bond prices are quoted, divide the price by 10 and multiply the number of shares by 10.)

The purchase price was $500 because it was purchased at half face value. The security name is

US $1000 6% 1/23

This means "face value $1000, Series EE Bond, maturity date 1/2023."

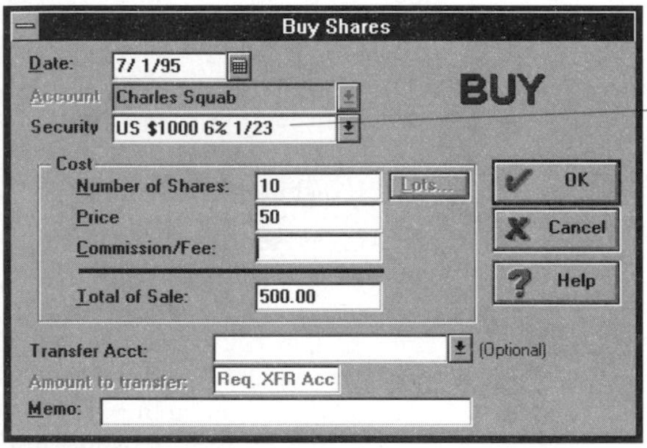

Important: If you have more than one U.S. savings bond, you must give each one a unique security name.

- When you redeem the savings bond (at or before maturity), enter the purchase price as the sales price in the Sell transaction. The difference between the purchase price and the redemption price is taxable interest. Use the Record Income form to record the remainder of the proceeds as interest income.

  If you use the cash method of accounting, as most individual taxpayers do, you generally report the interest on U. S. savings bonds when you receive it. If you use the accrual method of accounting, you must report interest on U. S. savings bonds each year as it accrues.

To record the annual accrual of interest, see "Recording zero-coupon bonds" on page 145.

Redeeming Treasury bills (T-bills)

When you buy a T-bill, you buy it at a discount from its face value. When you sell it, part of the sale proceeds is interest you've earned while you've held the bill or bond.

- To record interest received when you sell, use the Record Income form.
- Subtract the interest received from the total you receive. Enter the difference as the dollar amount for the sale transaction (using the Sell form).

Entering a return of capital or principal

A *return of capital* is money paid to you as total or partial repayment of the money you invested. Return of capital differs from a sale in that you aren't the one who initiates the return of capital. For example, a mortgage-backed security (such as a Ginnie Mae) returns capital when the underlying mortgages pay off principal, which is passed on to you. A unit trust returns capital as it sells the bonds within the trust. Note that return of capital, which isn't a taxable event, is different from a capital gains distribution.

- For a return of capital or principal, click More and choose Return of capital.

  Quicken reduces the cost basis of the security by the amount of the return of capital. If you have purchased shares of the security on different dates, Quicken reduces the cost basis of each set of shares in proportion to the number of shares in each set. If you enter a *negative* amount in the Return of Capital form, you *raise* the cost basis and decrease the cash balance in your account.

Recording zero-coupon bonds

You buy a zero-coupon bond at a discount. While you hold it, its value increases because of the interest it earns. Even though you don't receive this interest until you sell, it is reported to you every year on a Form 1099-OID as taxable interest.

- To record interest shown on a Form 1099-OID, click Income and enter it in the Interest box.
- To record the subsequent increase in value of the bond, use the Return of Capital form to record a second transaction. Enter a dollar amount equal to the *negative* of the interest. (The negative return of capital increases your cost basis. It thus reduces unrealized gain if you sell the bond or update to the current market price of the bond.) Your cash balance is increased by the interest income and then decreased by the return of capital. It should be unchanged after the two transactions.

Selling short

A *short sale* is the sale of a security you don't own. You deliver to the purchaser shares you borrow from your broker. You hope to buy the security later at a lower price to pay back your broker.

- For a short sale, click Sell and enter the details of the sale. Before it records the transaction, Quicken warns you that this transaction is a short sale, in case you have entered it in error.
- When you buy the security later, use the Buy form. Quicken calculates your gain or loss on the entire process at that time. The gains from short sales appear on Quicken capital gains reports and investment income reports.

When you buy a security, Quicken always closes a short sale before opening a new position on the security. For example, if you sell 100 shares short, then later buy 150 shares, Quicken closes the short sale and records a purchase of 50 new shares.

See the description of specifying lots on page 140.

If you record two short sales in the same security before buying the security, when you buy the security you can specify which lot you are closing.

In investment performance reports, the average annual total return for short sales is displayed as a negative value.

Entering options (puts and calls)

Treat an option as a security but give it a distinctive name (such as "XYZ put Aug 40"). For example, you might buy a $40 call for $5 (use the Buy form). When you exercise the call, close your position with a Sell transaction for the amount of the call ($5, in this case). When entering the purchase of the underlying security, include the cost of the call as a fee paid (to correct the cost basis). In this case, you would enter a purchase (Buy) of $40 plus $5 commission.

If you sell an option you don't already own, Quicken treats it like a short sale. If an option you bought or sold expires worthless, enter the opposite transaction (Sell or Buy) for the option at a price of zero to close your position. Quicken then records a realized gain or loss.

Using reminder memos

If you haven't installed Quicken's Billminder, see "Using Quicken Reminders and Billminder" on page 60.

You can enter a reminder memo in the investment register. For example, you may want to remind yourself that a CD is maturing next month. If you have installed Billminder, every time you turn on your computer or start running Windows, you see a message that you have a reminder.

Click More and choose Reminder Transaction. Fill in the Description and Memo boxes. Enter a reminder date. (You'll see the reminder message anyway, whatever date you enter here.)

To turn off a reminder memo, double-click the Clr (Cleared) field of the transaction in the register and click Record.

Viewing your portfolio

The Portfolio View window shows a complete picture of your investments. The window lists your securities alphabetically within each security type (Bond, CD, Mutual Fund, Stock) and gives analytical information about each security, such as the number of shares you own, the current price, market value, and return on investment.

Definitions of all the terms used in the Portfolio View window are listed on page 151.

The Portfolio View also lets you:

See page 153 for details.

- Update security prices.
- Record all your investment transactions, such as buying and selling securities, receiving interest, reinvesting dividend income, and so on.
- Create reports listing all transactions involving a security.
- Create graphs showing a security's price history.

Or press Ctrl+U

From the Activities menu, choose Portfolio View OR click the Port View button in the investment register window.

To print the Portfolio View, press Ctrl+P.

Use the button bar to enter your investment transactions (see "Recording your investment transactions" on page 135).

Click here to list six different ways to view your investments.

Choose which accounts to include in the Portfolio View.

Click these buttons to add a new security, edit or delete an existing security, or list a security's price history.

Graph the security's price history (see page 155).

Customize the view (see page 149).

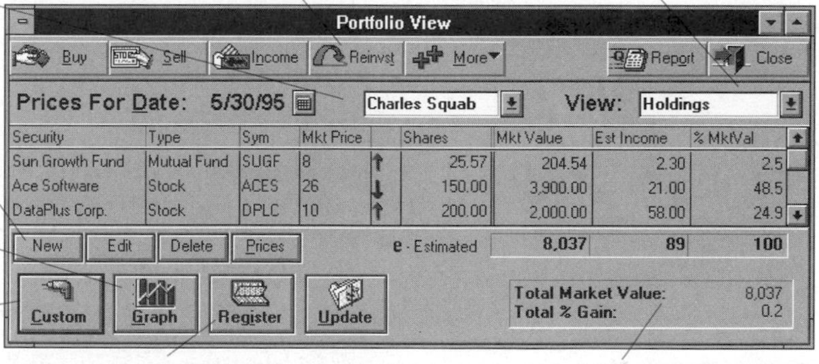

Go to the register (only when a single account is selected).

The window summarizes your portfolio by showing totals.

Change the viewing date: The Portfolio View window shows the state of your securities on a certain date. To change the viewing date, click the button next to the date and select a date in the pop-up calendar, or click the date itself to enter a new date. Quicken ignores any transactions that happened after the viewing date. Also, if you sold all your shares in a security on a date before the viewing date, you won't see the security any more in the Portfolio View window. (You can display securities you don't hold any more—see page 152.)

Select one or several accounts: The Portfolio View window normally lists only those securities that are currently held in the account shown near the top of the window. To list the securities of a different account, click the drop-down button and select an account from the drop-down list. Or select All Accounts or Selected Accounts.

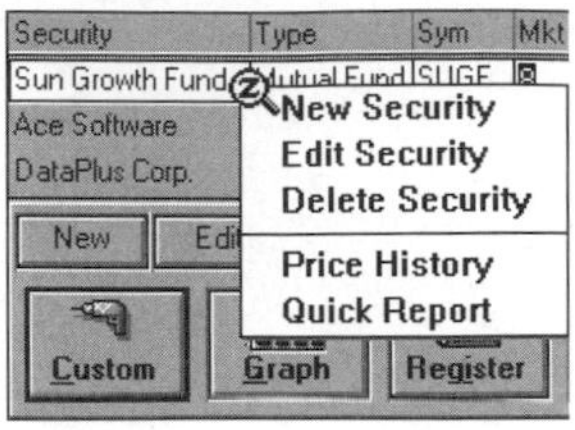

Edit the securities: You can edit or delete securities, or set up new ones. Move the mouse pointer over one of the securities and in the left part of the window (for example, in the Security column) until the cursor changes to a QuickZoom magnifying glass ( ). Now click the right mouse button to display a menu of options for editing that security. You can also use the New, Edit, and Delete buttons in the Portfolio View. (The QuickReport option is described on this page.) You can't delete a security if you have transactions for it in any of your accounts.

Go to the register: To go to the register of the selected investment account, click the Register button at the bottom of the window. You can click this button only when a single account is selected.

Shortcut icons: You can put a Portfolio View icon on the iconbar to take you straight to the Portfolio View window. See "Adding an icon to the iconbar" on page 294. You can also add a Use Account icon to open a specific investment account with the Portfolio View window displayed—this is useful if you frequently update security prices for a certain account. See "Assigning an icon to open an account" on page 295.

Reporting on a security's transactions

At the Portfolio View window, select the security and click the Report button.

The security report lists all transactions in the selected account(s) involving the one security.

You can QuickZoom to the investment form to edit any transaction by double-clicking the transaction in this report.

(If you would prefer to QuickZoom to the transaction in the register, select Options from the Edit menu, then click Reports and clear the QuickZoom to Investment Forms checkbox.)

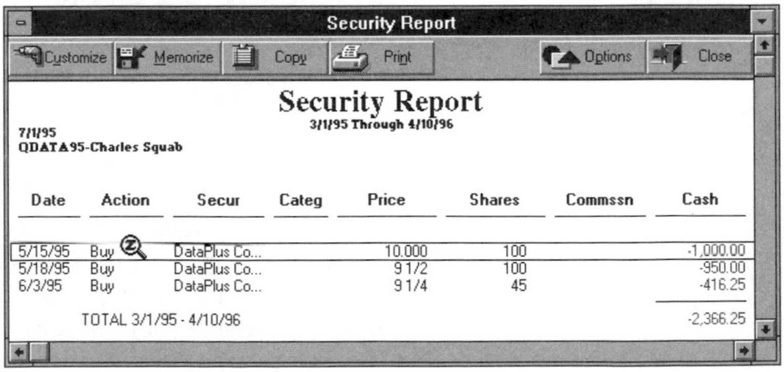

Changing the view

The Portfolio View window can actually show you up to six different views of your investments, each view containing different information about your securities. The three right-most columns in the window change according to the view you choose.

To change the view, click the button next to the View box and select a view from the drop-down list. Here is what each view shows you:

Choose this view	To
Holdings	Assess the total value of your investments and see their relative values (as a percentage of the total market value of all investments).
Performance	Compare how well each of your investments is performing, shown by the ROI (Return on investment) percentage.
Valuation	See how much an investment is worth compared to how much it has cost you.
Price Update	Enter current prices for your securities and see price trends. See "Updating the prices of your securities" on page 153 for details.
Custom 1 and 2	Compose your own custom views to give other facts about your investments. See "Customizing your portfolio views" on this page for details.

For a detailed explanation of what the column headings in each view mean, see the table on page 151.

Customizing your portfolio views

1 **In the Portfolio View window, click Custom.**

These tabs describe the areas you can customize.

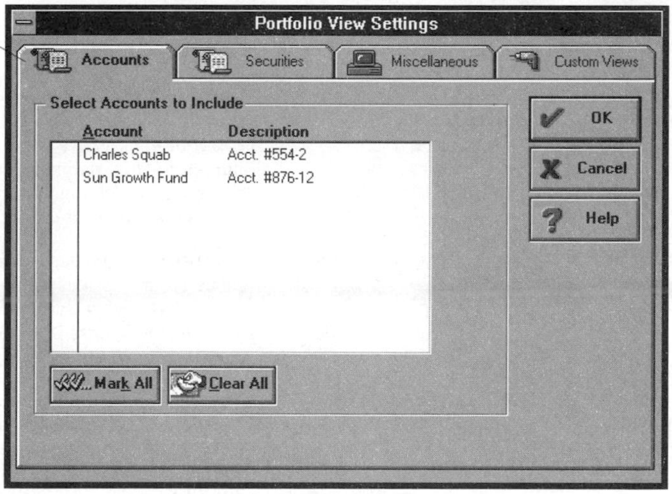

2 **Click the Accounts, Securities, Miscellaneous, or Custom Views tab.**

3 **Modify the settings and click OK.**

The table on the next page describes the customize options.

Customize area	What you can change	Options	Results
Accounts	Select the accounts to display when you choose Selected Accounts in the Portfolio View window. (All other accounts are still offered for selection in the Portfolio View window.)	Mark All	Select all accounts to be displayed.
		Clear All	Select no accounts to be displayed.
Securities	Select the securities to display. The initial (or default) status is to display a security in the selected account(s), whether you own shares in it or not. See "Choosing which securities to display" on page 152 for more information.	Show Always	Always show the security.
		Hide Always	Always hide the security.
		Default, with the Hide Securities You Do Not Own checkbox *cleared*	Display securities labeled Default whether you own shares in those securities or not in the selected account(s).
		Default, with the Hide Securities You Do Not Own checkbox *selected*	Display securities labeled Default *only if you own shares* in those securities in the selected account(s).
Return Calculations (click the Miscellaneous tab)	Choose the period over which Quicken should calculate the returns on investments. All options calculate returns up to and including the date displayed in the Portfolio View window ("Set Prices For:").	Entire History	Use all transactions entered in Quicken.
		This Year	Calculate returns from this year only.
		Last 365 Days	Calculate returns over the preceding year.
		From (specify date)	Calculate returns since the entered date.
Layout (click the Miscellaneous tab)	Normally, the Portfolio View window lists each security's name, security type, and symbol. You can hide the type and symbol columns if you want, to give more space to the other columns.	Name/Type/Symbol Name/Symbol Name/Type Name Only	If you hide the security type or symbol column, or both, they are removed from all views.
Copy Price Updates to All Securities with the Same Symbol (click the Miscellaneous tab)		You may want to separate two different trades in the same security. For example, you and your spouse invest in the same security but want to keep your transactions separate. You can do this by using two slightly different security names but the same symbol. When this checkbox is selected, if you change the price of one security, Quicken copies the price to the other security with the same symbol.	
Copy Price History to DOS Format on Exit (click the Miscellaneous tab)		If you use both Quicken for DOS and Quicken for Windows, you can update security prices for the same file in either program. Your price updates in Quicken for DOS are visible in Quicken for Windows. However, the reverse isn't normally true. To see Quicken for Windows price updates in Quicken for DOS, select this checkbox.	
Confirm Investment Transactions from Forms (click the Miscellaneous tab)		When you fill in an investment form, Quicken asks you to confirm your entries before leaving the form.	
Custom Views		You can set up your own arrangements of column headings in the Custom Views. See "Setting up your own portfolio views" next.	

Setting up your own portfolio views

Quicken comes with four preset portfolio views: Holdings, Performance, Valuation, and Price Update. You can set up your own views with different column headings.

1 **In the Portfolio View window, click Custom.**

2 **Click the Custom View tab.**

3 **For the Custom 1 view, select a Column 1 heading from the drop-down list. Do the same for Columns 2 and 3.**

Quicken offers column headings not included in the four preset views.

The column headings are explained in the table below.

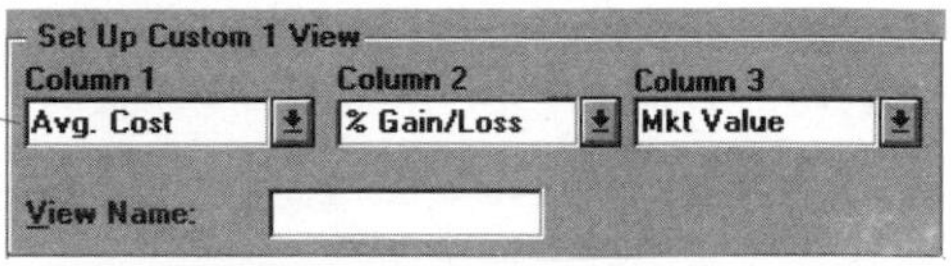

4 **In the View Name box, type a name for your view.**

5 **To customize a second view, repeat steps 3-4 for the Custom 2 view.**

6 **Click OK.**

Now you can select your custom view from the View drop-down list in the Portfolio View window. Instead of "Custom 1" or "Custom 2," it has the name you gave it.

This table shows what the column headings mean.

Column heading	Description
Avg. Cost	(Average cost) The average cost of each share of the security. This is equal to the total cost of all currently-held shares of a security (the cost basis) divided by the number of shares currently held.
Cost basis	The total cost of all currently-held shares of a security, including income reinvested in the security.
Est Income	The estimated annual income from each security's interest, dividends, and distributions. This is the per share estimate you entered when setting up the security multiplied by the number of shares.
Gain/Loss	The gain or loss (in $) of all currently-held shares of the security. This is the market value of the shares minus the cost basis.
Inv. Yield	The yield on investment is the estimated income (as you specified when setting up the security) divided by the dollar amount invested (see $ Invested in this table).
Last Price	The market price before the most recent price was entered.
Mkt Price	The most recent price entered for this security. (If today's price has not been entered, Quicken puts an "e" for Estimated next to the price.)
Mkt Value	The market value of your holdings in each security, equal to the market price per share multiplied by the number of shares you hold.
MktVal Chg	The increase or decrease in the market value as a result of the latest price change.
ROI	Return on investment, defined as $ Return divided by $ Invested. This is an indication of how well a security has performed. It is the total profit you could make from a security if you sold your shares in it today, expressed as a percentage of the amount you invested in the security. ROI takes account of the current market price and includes previous sales of the security and income received from the security. For example, let's say you bought shares for $100, have received $5 in dividends, and today the shares are worth $120. The $ Invested is $100, and the $ Return is $25 ($5 dividends plus the increase in market value). The ROI is 25/100 = 0.25, displayed as 25%. ROI is a *guide* to performance and not a precise analysis. For example, it doesn't take timing of purchases and sales into account. To see a more exact calculation of performance, generate an investment performance report to find the average annual total return, or IRR (see page 156).
Sym	The security's symbol, which is used for importing prices. See "Importing prices from an ASCII file" on page 160.
Total Market Value	The total market value of all the securities you hold in the selected account(s).
Total % Gain	The percentage increase in the total market value of the selected account(s). To be specific, this is the current market value less the cost basis of all currently-held securities, divided by the cost basis. A negative value indicates a loss.

Column heading	Description
Type	The security type, as you specified when setting up the security.
% Cost	The cost basis of a security, expressed as a percentage of the total cost basis of all displayed securities.
% Gain/Loss	The gain or loss of all currently-held shares of the security (the market value minus the cost basis) divided by the cost basis.
% Income	The total dollar amount of income received from a security (interest, dividends, capital gains distributions, not including reinvested income) divided by the cost basis.
% Invested	The amount you have invested in a security (excluding reinvestments) expressed as a percentage of what you have invested in all displayed securities.
% MktVal	The market value of a security expressed as a percentage of the total market value of all displayed securities.
% Yield	The estimated income per share divided by the current market price per share.
$ Income	The total income received from a security (including reinvested income), in dollars.
$ Invested	The actual dollar amount that you have invested in a security to date, including any expenses for that security (but *excluding* reinvestments). Note that, when you change the period over which Quicken calculates returns (see page 150), Quicken calculates $ Invested to be the market value of the security at the starting date plus the dollar amount you have invested in the security since that date (excluding reinvestments). In this way, $ Invested indicates the total cost of the security to you since the starting date.
$ Return	The total return (or profit) from a security since you invested in it. This is the current market value plus the income taken out as cash plus cash received from sales of shares, minus the amount invested. For example, let's say you bought 100 shares for $5 each ($500 total). You later sold 50 shares for $6 each ($300 total), and now the market price of your 50 remaining shares is $7 each ($350 total). The $ Return is $350 (current market value) plus $300 (sales), minus the $500 you invested = $150 total return. (Note that reinvestments aren't explicitly added to $ Return, because they contribute to the market value, which is a part of $ Return.)

Choosing which securities to display

The Portfolio View window initially displays securities in the selected account(s), whether they are *open* or not. Open means to hold the security or to have a short position in it as of the date shown at the top of the Portfolio View window.

To show all securities in all accounts, only if they are open: click Custom in the Portfolio View window, click the Accounts tab, and click Mark All. Then click the Securities tab, select each security and click Default, and *select* the Hide Securities You Do Not Own checkbox.

To show all securities in all accounts, whether they are open or not: do the same as above, except *clear* the Hide Securities You Do Not Own checkbox.

To hide a security: click Custom in the Portfolio View window, click the Securities tab, highlight the security you want to hide, and click Hide Always.

Updating the values of your investments

Quicken makes it easy for you to update the prices of your securities from the newspaper. In the Portfolio View window, Quicken lists your securities alphabetically within each security type, just as the newspaper does. Quicken uses the prices you enter in the window to recalculate the market value of each investment account.

If you have a modem, you can update prices with Portfolio Price Update. See Chapter 25, *Updating your portfolio prices online,* on page 267.

Updating the prices of your securities

Or press Ctrl+U

If you often update prices for a specific account, add a Use Account icon to the iconbar. Specify the account's name, and that it should be opened directly at the Portfolio View window. See "Assigning an icon to open an account" on page 295 for more details.

1 **From the Activities menu, choose Portfolio View.**

2 **In the View box, select Price Update.**

You can update the prices at any of the portfolio views, but the Price Update view gives the most relevant information. The market prices are the only values you can edit directly in this window.

3 **Make sure the window is displaying the investment account or accounts you want (shown in the Account box).**

Select an account, or all accounts, by clicking the drop-down button and choosing an account from the list.

See "Viewing your portfolio" on page 147 for a detailed explanation of this window.

Make sure the date displayed is the date for which your price updates are valid. Quicken displays today's date. But if, for example, you are entering prices from last week's newspaper, you might want to change the date for greater correctness.

An up arrow (↑) means the price has gone up since the previous price entered. A down arrow (↓) means it has gone down.

The window lists only the securities in the account shown here.

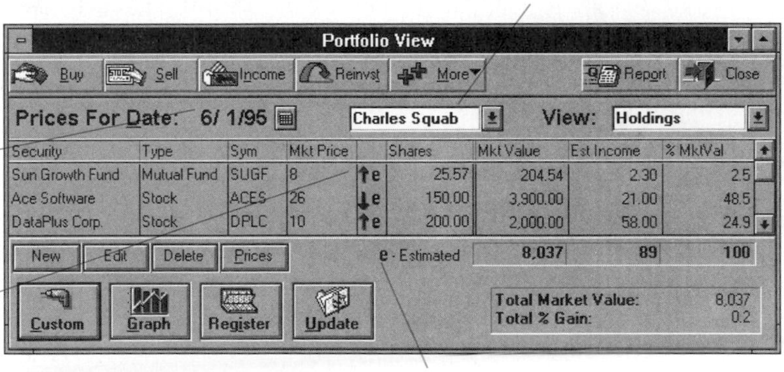

"e" is for "estimated," meaning not today's price, but the most recently entered price.

For more about entering prices of different kinds of securities, see page 130.

4 **Use the Up Arrow or Down Arrow key to select a security, and enter the latest market price.**

Use this key	To do this
+ or –	Change the price to the next 1/8 (or 0.125).
* (Asterisk)	When a price is unchanged, press the asterisk key (*) to indicate that the price is correct for the current date. (The "e" now displayed disappears.) If you make a mistake changing a price and want to return to the estimated price previously displayed, press the asterisk key (*).

5 **Repeat for each security.**

Quicken records the price when you leave the Market Price field. (You don't need to click Record or confirm the price change.)

Quicken recalculates the market value as you change the price, and shows you the change in market value.

Or press Ctrl+P

6 **(Optional) From the File menu, choose Print Summary to print the contents of the window.**

Entering security market prices for other dates

To build up a price history for a security, see "Listing a security's price history" next. To enter prices for just one date, follow these steps.

1 **At the Portfolio View window, click on the button next to the date and click a date in the pop-up calendar.**

Select the date for which you wish to enter market prices.

Or press Ctrl+G

Or click the date itself in the Portfolio View window and then, in the Go To Date window, enter a date and click OK.

The market prices and market values appear for that date (or the most recent prices you have entered before that date).

2 **Enter prices for the chosen date just as you would a current price.**

Listing a security's price history

Quicken stores a price history for each security as you update the prices at the Portfolio View window. Also, whenever you enter a buy or sell transaction, Quicken adds the new security price to the price history (and updates the calculations in the Portfolio View window).

Or press Ctrl+E

To display a list of a security's price history, select the security and click Prices.

The most recent prices are at the top of the list.

You can add new prices to the price history by clicking New.

To change or delete an existing price in the price history, click Edit or Delete.

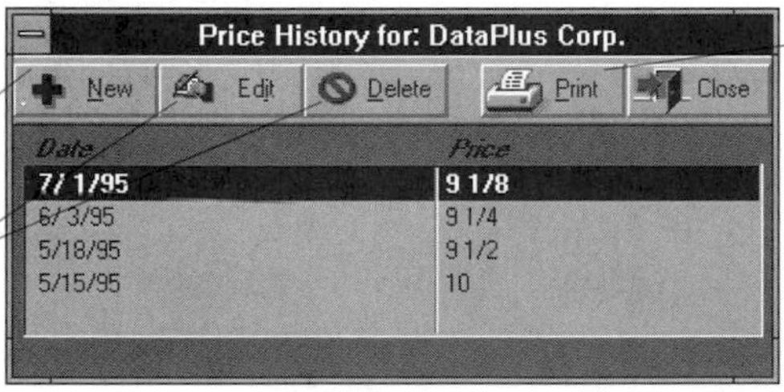

To print the price history, click Print.

Graphing a security's price history and market value

Select the security in the Portfolio View window and click the Graph icon. The Portfolio View window expands, displaying a graph of the security's price history.

Click here to display or hide the security's market value.

Click here to display the graph below.

You won't see this graph in VGA; instead, you'll see the graph below.

Click here to close the graph.

Click the start or end date to change the date range.

Click here to adjust the graph for splits.

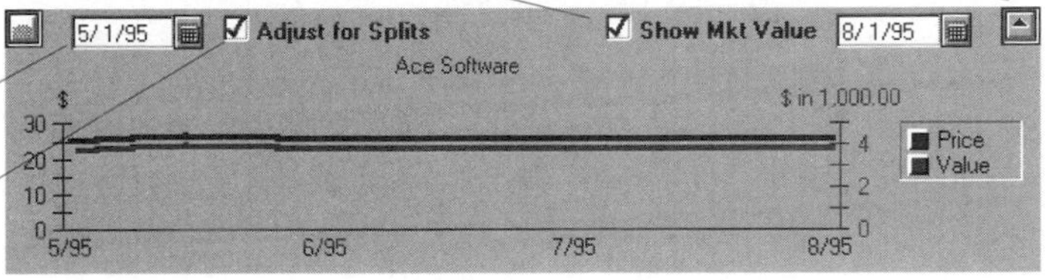

As with all Quicken graphs, whenever you see the QuickZoom magnifying glass you can hold down the right mouse button to show the actual price in the graph.

Click the start or end date to change them.

Click here to adjust the graph for splits.

This line shows the change in price over time for this security.

This line shows the change in market value over time for this security.

Click here to display or hide the security's market value.

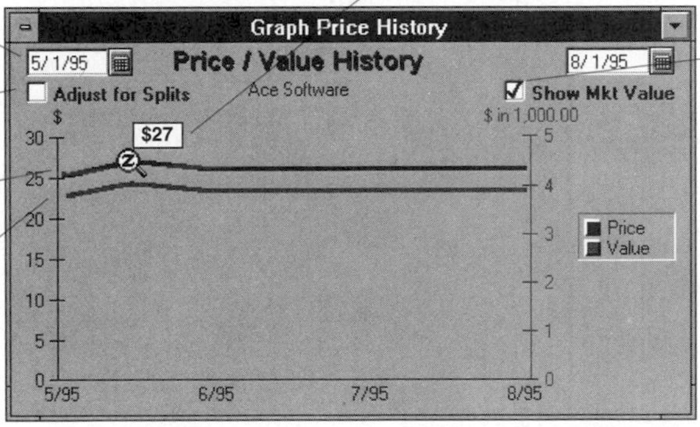

Creating reports and graphs

Quicken's investment registers and portfolio view show you almost everything you need to know about your investments. Creating investment reports and graphs can summarize the information more clearly and help you analyze your portfolio.

- Quicken offers five types of preset investment reports. For examples, see "Investment reports," on page 169. Full details of how to create reports are given in Chapter 14, *Creating and customizing reports*, on page 183.

  In addition, you can create transaction reports on each security from the Portfolio View window (see page 148).

- You can create two types of investment graphs. The investment performance graph, described on page 206, shows your portfolio value and the average annual total return of your investments. In addition, you can create a price history graph to show the price trend of any security, as shown on this page.

Here are explanations of some of the terms used in Quicken's reports and in this *User's Guide*.

Term	Description
Average annual total return (or IRR, internal rate of return)	The *average annual total return* is a percentage equal to the interest rate on a bank account that would give you the same total return on your investment. It takes into account money earned by the investment (interest, dividends, capital gains distributions) as well as changes in share price. Since it's an annual rate, it acts like a bank interest rate that compounds annually. • For example, if you invest \$10,000 and get an average annual total return of 12.0% over two years, you'd have \$12,544 (an increase of \$2,544, or 25.4%) at the end of the two years. Average annual total return depends on the date range you have set for the report. If the return seems surprisingly high, it could be because you have set a short date range. Average annual total return isn't the same as ROI (return on investment), which is displayed in the Performance portfolio view. Average annual total return depends on the amount of time it takes for the investment to grow to its value at the end of the time period. An investment that earns no income and doubles in five years has a higher average annual total return than one that doubles in ten years. ROI, on the other hand, is 100% in both cases. The average annual total return appears in the investment performance report. A negative value indicates a loss, which can be either paper or real.
Average cost per share	The average cost per share of a security equals the cost basis divided by the number of shares. $\textbf{avg. cost per share} = \dfrac{\textbf{cost basis}}{\textbf{number of shares}}$ (This value won't be accurate unless you entered all historical purchases and sales of this security. See "Entering prior history for investments" on page 158 if you want to give Quicken data to calculate the correct average cost per share.)
Cost basis	The cost basis is the total cost of all shares of a security.
Market value	The market value for each security equals the market price times the number of shares. $\textbf{market value} = \textbf{market price per share} \times \textbf{number of shares}$ Quicken can't display a market value greater than \$9,999,999. Quicken displays a row of asterisks (*******) when the market value is greater than that amount.
Realized gain/loss	The realized gain or loss is the difference between the selling price of a security and the cost basis. If you sell it for more than you paid, there is a (real) gain; if you sell it for less, there is a (real) loss. Quicken displays realized gains or losses in the capital gains report.
Unrealized gain/loss	The unrealized gain or loss is the difference between the current market value of a security and the cost basis. If the current market value is greater, there is a (paper) gain; if the cost basis is greater, there is a (paper) loss. • For example, if your 525 shares have a cost basis of \$1,250 but they're now worth \$2,100, you have an unrealized (paper) gain of \$850. Quicken displays unrealized gain or loss in the portfolio value report under the heading Gain/Loss. A negative value indicates a (paper) loss. If Quicken doesn't have the data to calculate the average cost per share, it displays "NA" (not available) in reports for the gain.
%Gain/loss	The percent unrealized (paper) gain (or loss) equals the market price per share minus the average cost per share, divided by the average cost per share, expressed in percent. $\textbf{\% gain} = \dfrac{\textbf{market price per share} - \textbf{avg. cost per share}}{\textbf{avg. cost per share}} \times \textbf{100\%}$ A negative value is a (paper) loss.

Tracking indexes and securities you don't own

You may want one or more of the popular stock indexes, such as the Dow Jones Industrial Average or Standard & Poor's 500-stock index, to appear in the Portfolio View window. Or, perhaps you'd like to follow the price of a security you don't own. By creating a special account to hold the security or index (treated as a security), you can track its price and performance.

1 **Set up a new regular investment account.**

See "Creating a regular investment account" on page 126 for full details of setting up an investment account.

You can call the account "Index" or "Other Securities."

You can track mutual funds in a regular investment account too.

2 **Add the index or security to your Securities list.**

See "Setting up securities for a regular investment account," on page 127. For an index, you may wish to set up a security type called "Index."

You can set up as many securities or indexes as you want to track, and track them all in the one account.

3 **In the new investment register, click More and choose Add Shares To Account.**

4 **Enter the date from which you are beginning to track.**

5 **Enter the name of the index or unowned security in the Security box.**

6 **Enter** 1 **in the Number of Shares box.**

7 **Enter the index value or security price in the Price per Share box and record the transaction.**

In the Portfolio View window, choose the Index or Other Securities account to track the price and performance.

If you watch the price of a mutual fund you don't own, be aware that the price may drop because of income or capital gains distributions. When a fund makes a distribution, the share price is reduced by an equal amount (in addition to any changes caused by changes in market value of the underlying securities in the fund).

Entering prior history for investments

You may have set up a new investment account by entering a rough estimate of what you paid for the securities. You may have omitted dividends or capital gains distributions that you received since buying the securities.

To get accurate	Enter in Quicken
Market values for a specified date	• Price and number of shares of securities owned on that date
Average annual total return for a specified time period	• Price and number of shares on the *day before* the beginning of the period and on the last day of the period • All transactions during the period
Capital gains summary (realized short-term and long-term gain or loss) for a specified time period	• Number of shares and cost basis on date at least one year before beginning of period for all securities you have sold • All purchases and sales (including stock splits, reinvestments, and return of capital) from that date to the end of the period
Income and expense summary for a specified time period	• All transactions during the period • Number of shares owned and price per share at the beginning and end of the period (if you're including unrealized gains)

If you decide to go back and enter a complete transaction history for your securities, the first step is to revise the Add Shares to Account transactions that you first entered for each security.

Revising the initial ShrsIn transaction for a security

1 **In the investment register, select the initial transaction for the security (look for ShrsIn in the Action field), and click Edit.**

2 **(Optional) Revise the date to the initial date of acquisition.**

3 **Revise the number of shares.**

4 **Delete the price in the Price field to leave it blank.**

5 **Revise the total cost basis.**

Enter the amount paid, including commission, fees, and load, or, if you acquired the shares from someone, your cost basis for the shares.

6 **Click Record to record the revised transaction.**

The revised transaction appears in the register in the correct sequence for the new date.

Entering transactions for dates in the past

Enter additional transactions as described in "Recording your investment transactions," on page 135. Make sure you enter the correct date for each transaction. Each transaction moves up and appears in the register chronologically.

If a transaction involves a transfer of cash out of the account (for example, a dividend paid directly to you), enter the name of the investment account itself in the Destination of Funds box. Use this procedure for both types of investment accounts. It has no effect on the cash balance in a regular account.

See "Adjusting the cash or share balance" on this page.

After you've entered the transactions from the past, your cash balance for the whole account or your share balance for any security may be incorrect. Adjust it by choosing Update Balance from the Activities menu.

Reconciling the investment register

When you get a statement from your broker or other financial adviser, you can reconcile your account with the statement.

See "Starting reconciliation" on page 85 for more information.

Reconciling an investment account is similar to reconciling other Quicken accounts.

Reconcile regular investment and mutual fund investment accounts the same way, except that you reconcile a cash balance in one and a share balance in the other.

- After you've reconciled the cash balance for a regular investment account, Quicken can take you to the Portfolio View window. If you haven't already entered the share prices from the statement, you have a chance to do so now.
- After you've reconciled the share balance for a mutual fund account, Quicken displays your new market value in the Share Balance Reconciled window. Quicken automatically adds the latest price to the price history for the security.

Adjusting the cash or share balance

If you don't want to use the Reconcile command, you can adjust the cash or share balance to match what appears on your statement. Start in the investment register.

1. **From the Activities menu, choose Update Balances and then choose Update Cash Balance or Update Share Balance.**
2. **Enter the date for the adjustment, the correct value for the balance, and the security name (if requested).**

   In the Security to Adjust box, press Ctrl+Y to view and choose from the Security list.

   The adjustment appears in the register with the action MiscExp or MiscInc for cash balance adjustments, and with the action ShrsIn or ShrsOut for share balance adjustments. The memo for the adjustment is "Balance Adjustment."

Updating security prices

If you have a modem, the easiest way to update security prices is with Portfolio Price Update. See Chapter 25, *Updating your portfolio prices online,* on page 267. Otherwise, see the sections below.

Importing prices from an ASCII file

You can import security price data from an ASCII file. For example, the Prodigy Quote Track feature can export stock prices to a Quicken-compatible ASCII file (see below). The data to import must be in standard ASCII format with one symbol/price/date per line, delimited by either commas or double spaces (using only one type of delimiter per line).

These import formats are all acceptable:

ABC, 123.456
ABC, 123.456, 12/31/95
ABC 123.456 12/31/95
"ABC", 123.456, "12/31/95"
"ABC", "123.456", "12/31/95"

If your import file doesn't include quotation marks, it must have double spaces between items.

1 **From the Activities menu, choose Portfolio View.**

2 **From the File menu, choose Import Prices.**

3 **Enter the name of the ASCII file that contains the price data.**

Specify the full DOS path for the location of the file to be imported (for example, C:\STOCKS.CSV).

4 **Change the date in the window, if necessary, then click OK.**

Saving security prices from Prodigy's Quote Track feature to a file that Quicken can import

Follow these steps before you start Quicken.

For more information about using Prodigy quotes, open the Prodigy ABOUT menu and select the appropriate topic.

1 **In Prodigy, [Jump]:** QUOTE TRACK **and follow the onscreen instructions for creating or viewing a Quote Track list.**

2 **From the Quote Track screen, choose Download.**

3 **Set your report options:**

File Name:	C:\STOCKS.CSV
Write Mode:	Replace File
Data:	Closing Prices
Format:	Quicken.CSV No Headings

4 **Select COMPLETE to save your options, and then select PRINT to save your changes to the file you specified.**

If the file already exists, Prodigy asks whether you want to write over it or add these quotes to it.

5 **If you have more Quote Track lists, you can view them and print them to the same file without resetting your print options.**

13 Sample reports

Home reports

To create a report, see "Creating a report" on page 183.

This section describes each of Quicken's home reports. To see the home reports available, click the Reports icon on the iconbar and select the Home report family.

Cash Flow	Summarize income and expense by category
Monthly Budget	Compare actual income/expense to budget
Itemized Categories	List transactions and subtotal by category
Tax Summary	List tax-related transactions
Net Worth	Calculate net worth based on account balances
Tax Schedule	List transactions and subtotal by tax line item
Missing Checks	List transactions in order and highlight missing checks
Comparison	Compare two transaction periods by category (or other item)

Cash flow

A cash flow report summarizes income and expenses by category.

Quicken groups income categories with any transfers *from* accounts not included in the report.

If you have an "Inflows - Other" or "Outflows - Other" amounts, it is because you recorded a transaction without a category, or you recorded a transaction with a category that you sometimes use subcategories with, and sometimes don't.

Quicken groups expense categories with any transfers *to* accounts not included in the report.

```
                              Cash Flow Report
                          5/1/95 Through 8/31/95
8/31/95
QDATA95-Bank,Cash,CC Accounts                                       Page 1
                                                       5/1/95-
        Category Description                           8/31/95
        ----------------------  ------------------
        INFLOWS
        Other Inc                                    15,500.00
          Salary                  8,641.48
          _LT CapGnDst              -85.40
                                                     ---------
        TOTAL INFLOWS                                24,056.08

        OUTFLOWS
          Auto:
            Fuel                     24.34
            Service                  81.57
                                                     ---------
          Total Auto                                    105.91
          Charity                                         9.99
          Clothing                                      200.72
          Dining                                        360.41
          Entertain                                      97.14
          Groceries                                     502.52
          Household                                   1,710.79
          Insurance                                     221.17
          Misc                                        6,103.92
          Recreation                                    532.68
          Tax:
            Fed                   4,427.10
            Other                 1,416.65
            Tax - Other             200.43
                                                     ---------
          Total Tax                                   6,044.18
          Telephone                                     102.66
          Utilities:
            Gas & Electric          149.12
                                                     ---------
          Total Utilities                               149.12
          _IntExp                                       164.35
          Outflows - Other                              518.55
          TO Home Loan                                  544.37
          TO Charles Squab                              218.02
                                                     ---------
        TOTAL OUTFLOWS                               17,586.50

                                                     ---------
        OVERALL TOTAL                                 6,469.58
                                                   ===========
```

Initial settings for this report (a type of summary report)	
Row headings:	Category
Column headings:	Don't subtotal
Organization:	Cash flow basis
Accounts to report on:	Bank, cash, credit card
Transfers:	Exclude internal

These are transfers to asset, liability, and investment accounts from bank, cash, and credit card accounts.

A cash flow report initially excludes transfer transactions that occur between the accounts included in the report (that is, between bank, cash, and credit card accounts). For example, Quicken doesn't include a transfer of funds from checking to savings. To change the Transfers setting, see "Changing report settings" on page 185.

Monthly budget

The monthly budget report compares actual income and expenses against budgeted income and expenses by month.

Before creating a budget report, set up budget amounts as described on page 241.

If your budget is organized by supercategories, then the monthly budget report is also. Otherwise, it is organized like a cash flow report: income categories are shown at the top under INFLOWS and expense categories are shown below them under OUTFLOWS.

Initial settings for this report (a type of budget report)	
Column headings:	Month
Organization:	Supercategory
Accounts to report on:	Bank, cash, credit card
Include unrealized gains:	No
Transfers:	Exclude internal
Categories:	Budgeted categories only

The Actual column contains the amounts for categories used in transactions that fall within the date range for the report column.

The Budget column contains the amounts you entered in the Budget window.

The Diff column is the difference between what you budgeted and what you actually spent or received.

Monthly Budget Report
6/1/95 Through 6/30/95

6/30/95
QDATA95-Bank,Cash,CC Accounts — Page 1

Category Description	6/1/95 Actual	- Budget	6/30/95 Diff
INFLOWS			
Other Income			
Income - Other	0.00	0.00	0.00
Other Inc	6,000.00	2,214.00	3,786.00
Salary	4,320.74	2,000.00	2,320.74
_IntInc	0.00	447.00	-447.00
Total Other Income	10,320.74	4,661.00	5,659.74
TOTAL INFLOWS	10,320.74	4,661.00	5,659.74
OUTFLOWS			
Discretionary			
Discretionary - Other	0.00	0.00	0.00
Clothing	76.15	29.00	-47.15
Dining	58.43	51.00	-7.43
Entertain	70.14	14.00	-56.14
Misc	2,785.45	2,664.00	-121.45
Recreation	532.68	76.00	-456.68
Telephone - Other	34.22	15.00	-19.22
Total Discretionary	3,557.07	2,849.00	-708.07
Irregular Spending			
Irregular Spending - Other	0.00	0.00	0.00
Auto:Service	0.00	12.00	12.00
Total Irregular Spending	0.00	12.00	12.00
Monthly Spending			
Monthly Spending - Other	0.00	0.00	0.00
Insurance	118.80	32.00	-86.80
Tax - Other	0.00	29.00	29.00
Tax:Fed	1,770.84	632.00	-1,138.84
Tax:Other	566.66	202.00	-364.66
Utilities:Gas & Electric	33.12	21.00	-12.12
Total Monthly Spending	2,489.42	916.00	-1,573.42
Unassigned			
Unassigned - Other	0.00	0.00	0.00
Auto:Fuel	12.34	3.00	-9.34
Charity - Other	9.99	1.00	-8.99
Groceries	133.99	69.00	-64.99
Home Rpair	97.87	15.00	-82.87
Household	1,687.02	244.00	-1,443.02
TO Home Loan	272.17	78.00	194.17
FROM Home Loan	0.00	0.00	0.00
Total Unassigned	2,213.38	410.00	-1,803.38
TOTAL OUTFLOWS	8,259.87	4,187.00	-4,072.87
OVERALL TOTAL	2,060.87	474.00	1,586.87

Unfavorable amounts are negative and are displayed in red.

A negative value under INFLOWS means your Actual income amount was less than your Budget income amount.

A negative value under OUTFLOWS means your Actual expense amount was more than your Budget expense amount.

The OVERALL TOTAL at the bottom of the Actual column is your net savings for the month. If the number is positive, you earned more than you spent. If the number is negative, you spent more than you earned. The OVERALL TOTAL difference shows how well you've done compared to your budget.

Itemized categories

An itemized category report lists transactions from all your accounts, grouped and subtotaled by category.

Quicken lists income transactions first, unless no income transactions occurred during the report date range.

Quicken lists expense transactions after income transactions, followed by transfers between accounts and balances forward.

Initial settings for this report (a type of transaction report)	
Subtotal by:	Category
Sort transactions by:	None
Organization:	Income and expense
Accounts to report on:	All accounts
Include unrealized gains:	No
Transfers:	Include all

```
                              Itemized Category Report
                              6/1/95 Through 6/30/95
7/1/95
 QDATA95-All Accounts                                                        Page 1

Date      Acct         Num    Description       Memo   Category    Clr   Amount
------    ------       ----   ------------      -----  ---------   ---   ------
          INCOME/EXPENSE
             EXPENSES
                Entertain

6/12/95   American Excess     Valley Springs           Entertain             -43.00
6/15/95   American Excess     Starry Sky Cafe          Entertain             -18.14
6/17/95   Cash                Century Cinema           Entertain              -9.00
                                                                           -------
                Total Entertain                                              -70.14

               Tax:

               Fed

6/1/95    Checking    DEP     Paycheck                 Tax:Fed              -885.42
6/16/95   Checking    DEP     Paycheck                 Tax:Fed              -885.42
                                                                           -------
                 Total Fed                                               -1,770.84

               Other

6/1/95    Checking    DEP     Paycheck                 Tax:Other            -283.33
6/16/95   Checking    DEP     Paycheck                 Tax:Other            -283.33
                                                                           -------
                 Total Other                                                -566.66
                                                                           -------
               Total Tax                                                 -2,337.50
                                                                           -------
             TOTAL EXPENSES                                              -2,407.64
                                                                           -------
          TOTAL INCOME/EXPENSE                                           -2,407.64

          TRANSFERS
          American Excess

6/30/95   Checking    114     American Excess          [American Excess]-2,304.85
                                                                           -------
             Total TO American Excess                                    -2,304.85

          Cash

6/6/95    Checking    ATM     ATM Withdrawal           [Cash]                -80.00
6/13/95   Checking    ATM     ATM Withdrawal           [Cash]               -100.00
                                                                           -------
             Total TO Cash                                                  -180.00

          Home Loan

6/1/95    Checking    Sched   National Mortgage Corp.[Home Loan]            -137.08
6/1/95    Checking    Sched   National Mortgage Corp.[Home Loan]            -135.09
                                                                           -------
             Total TO Home Loan                                             -272.17

          Checking

6/30/95   American Excess     American Excess          [Checking]          2,304.85
6/6/95    Cash                ATM Withdrawal           [Checking]             80.00
6/13/95   Cash                ATM Withdrawal           [Checking]            100.00
6/1/95    Home Loan           National Mortgage Corp.[Checking]             137.08
6/1/95    Home Loan           National Mortgage Corp.[Checking]             135.09
                                                                           -------
             Total FROM Checking                                           2,757.02
                                                                           -------
           TOTAL TRANSFERS                                                    0.00
                                                                           -------
          OVERALL TOTAL                                                  -2,407.64
                                                                          ========
```

Tax summary

A tax summary report lists tax-related transactions from all your accounts except tax-deferred accounts (such as IRAs or 401(k) accounts), grouped and subtotaled by category.

If you set up a file with Quicken's standard home category list, tax-related categories are already marked in the list. If you have set up your own categories, mark the ones that are related to the tax forms you want to fill out. See "Setting up categories and subcategories" on page 10.

Quicken lists expense transactions after income transactions, followed by transfers between accounts and balances forward.

Tax Summary Report
6/1/95 Through 6/30/95

7/1/95
All Accounts Page 1

Date	Acct	Num	Description	Memo	Category	Clr	Amount
	INCOME/EXPENSE						
	INCOME						
	Salary						
6/1/95	Checking	DEP	Paycheck		Salary		2,160.37
6/16/95	Checking	DEP	Paycheck		Salary		2,160.37
	Total Salary						4,320.74
	_LT CapGnDst						
6/1/95	Checking	DEP	Paycheck		_LT CapGnDst		-17.08
6/16/95	Checking	DEP	Paycheck		_LT CapGnDst		-17.08
	Total _LT CapGnDst						-34.16
	TOTAL INCOME						4,286.58
	EXPENSES						
	Tax:						
	Fed						
6/1/95	Checking	DEP	Paycheck		Tax:Fed		-885.42
6/16/95	Checking	DEP	Paycheck		Tax:Fed		-885.42
	Total Fed						-1,770.84
	Other						
6/1/95	Checking	DEP	Paycheck		Tax:Other		-283.33
6/16/95	Checking	DEP	Paycheck		Tax:Other		-283.33
	Total Other						-566.66
	Total Tax						-2,337.50
	TOTAL EXPENSES						-2,337.50
	TOTAL INCOME/EXPENSE						1,949.08

Initial settings for this report (a type of transaction report)

Subtotal by:	Category
Sort transactions by:	None
Organization:	Income and expense
Accounts to report on:	All accounts except tax-deferred accounts
Tax-related transactions only:	Yes
Transfers:	Include all

Net worth

A net worth report calculates your net worth on the basis of all accounts in the current Quicken file. Net worth is the difference between your assets and your liabilities.

Initial settings for this report (a type of account balances report)	
Report at intervals of:	None
Organization:	Net worth format
Accounts to report on:	All accounts
Include unrealized gains:	Yes
Tax-related transactions only:	No

Net Worth Report
As of 7/29/95

7/29/95
All Accounts

Page 1

Acct		7/29/95 Balance
ASSETS		
Cash and Bank Accounts		
Cash		102.10
Checking		
Ending Balance	11,581.04	
plus: Checks Payable	625.25	
Total Checking		12,206.29
Savings		8,526.02
Total Cash and Bank Accounts		20,834.41
Other Assets		
Home Equity		350,000.00
Total Other Assets		350,000.00
Investments		
Charles Squab		12,894.52
Sun Growth Fund		2,089.16
Total Investments		14,983.68
TOTAL ASSETS		385,818.09
LIABILITIES		
Checks Payable		625.25
Credit Cards		
American Excess		2,764.12
Total Credit Cards		2,764.12
Other Liabilities		
Home Loan		198,594.72
Total Other Liabilities		198,594.72
TOTAL LIABILITIES		201,984.09
OVERALL TOTAL		183,834.00

If your bank accounts include any unprinted or postdated checks, Quicken adds them to your bank balance and also lists them as a liability.

You can see subtotals by class in an account (or by security if it's an investment account).

Create the report, and then click Customize. Click Report Layout under "Customize." Select the Account Detail checkbox under "Show." (For more information, see "Changing the report layout" on page 186.)

The OVERALL TOTAL shows your net worth.

If you have set up investment accounts, the net worth report shows the market value of your investments based on the most recent prices you entered prior to the report date.

Tax schedule

To define an account to be tax-deferred when setting up the account, see "Setting up additional Quicken accounts," on page 1.

A tax schedule report lists those transactions with categories assigned to tax schedule line items, grouped and subtotaled by tax form name and line item. The initial report excludes tax-deferred accounts (you can customize the report to include them).

See "Setting up categories with tax time in mind" on page 217 for information about assigning categories to a tax form and line item.

Before you can assign categories to tax forms, turn on the option. From the Edit menu, choose Options and click the General icon. Then select the Use Tax Schedules With Categories checkbox.

Initial settings for this report (a type of transaction report)	
Subtotal by:	Tax schedule
Sort transactions by:	None
Organization:	Income and expense
Accounts to report on:	All accounts except tax-deferred accounts
Tax-related transactions only	No
Transfers:	Include all

Tax Schedule Report
6/1/95 Through 6/30/95

7/1/95
All Accounts — Page 1

Date	Acct	Num	Description	Memo	Category	Clr	Amount
	Schedule B						
	Div inc., capital gain distr						
6/1/95	Checking	DEP	Paycheck		_LT CapGnDst		-17.08
6/16/95	Checking	DEP	Paycheck		_LT CapGnDst		-17.08
	Total Div inc., capital gain distr						-34.16
	Form 4952						
	Investment interest						
6/1/95	Checking	DEP	Paycheck		_IntExp		-32.87
6/16/95	Checking	DEP	Paycheck		_IntExp		-32.87
	Total Investment interest						-65.74
	W-2						
	Salary						
6/1/95	Checking	DEP	Paycheck		Salary		2,160.37
6/16/95	Checking	DEP	Paycheck		Salary		2,160.37
	Total Salary						4,320.74
	Federal Withholding						
6/1/95	Checking	DEP	Paycheck		Tax:Fed		-885.42
6/16/95	Checking	DEP	Paycheck		Tax:Fed		-885.42
	Total Federal Withholding						-1,770.84

After creating this report, you can export the report to a file to use in tax preparation software. See "Creating tax schedule reports" on page 218.

Missing checks

The missing checks report lists payments in the current account by check number and highlights any breaks in the check number sequence. It shows both missing and duplicate check numbers. This report is based on the transaction report (see page 179).

Initial settings for this report (a type of transaction report)	
Organization:	Income and expense
Accounts to report on:	Current account
Transfers:	Include all

Missing Check Report
6/1/95 Through 6/31/95

7/1/95
QDATA95-Joint Account — Page 1

Date	Num	Description	Memo	Category	Clr	Amount
Checking						
6/11/95	48	Valley Gas & Electric		Utilities:Gas & Electric		-33.12
		*** Missing Check(s) 49 to 107 ***				
6/1/95	108	Northern Bell		Telephone		-34.22
6/5/95	109	123 Oak St. Homeowners				-250.00
6/10/95	110	Sam's Restaurant		Dining		-26.13
		*** Duplicate Check 110 ***				
6/5/95	110	The Fitness Club		Recreation		-145.00
6/10/95	111	SafeCar Insurance		Insurance		-62.22
		*** Missing Check(s) 112 ***				
6/15/95	113	SouthVision Cable				-18.55
	Total Checking					-569.24

If a check number is missing in the sequence, Quicken lists it as a "Missing Check" item.

If a check number is duplicated in the sequence, Quicken lists it as a "Duplicate Check" item.

Comparison

A comparison report compares your income and spending for two different periods. For example, you can see if, and in which areas, you are spending more or earning more than a year ago. The report shows a breakdown of your finances by category, and lets you define two different periods to display side by side.

You can display the difference between the two periods in dollars, or as a percentage of the first figure, or both.

Initial settings for this report (a type of summary report)

Comparison dates:	Year-to-date and Prior Year Period
Row headings:	Category
Subtotal by:	Don't subtotal
Organization:	Cash flow basis
Show difference as %:	No
Show difference in $:	Yes
Accounts to report on:	Bank, cash, credit card
Transfers:	Exclude internal

Comparison Report
6/1/95 Through 8/31/96
8/31/95
QDATA95-Bank,Cash,CC Accounts
Page 1

Category Description	6/1/95- 8/31/95	6/1/96- 8/31/96	$ Difference
INFLOWS			
Bonus	0.00	3,000.00	3,000.00
Interest Income	0.42	0.42	0.00
Salary	18,508.35	11,025.01	-7,483.34
Inflows - Other	162.19	0.00	-162.19
TOTAL INFLOWS	18,670.96	14,025.43	-4,645.53
OUTFLOWS			
Auto:			
Fuel	190.31	150.00	40.31
Maintenance	262.00	0.00	262.00
Total Auto	452.31	150.00	302.31
Books, Music	0.00	129.76	-129.76
Childcare	400.00	400.00	0.00
Clothing	1,226.63	189.69	1,036.94
Computer	145.01	0.00	145.01
Entertain	276.50	290.91	-14.41
Groceries	319.54	449.43	-129.89
Int Exp	79.12	77.72	1.40
Mort Int	1,417.48	0.00	1,417.48
Recreation:			
Hiking	319.51	0.00	319.51
Skiing	506.83	0.00	506.83
Total Recreation	826.34	0.00	826.34
Taxes:			
Fed	4,127.10	2,456.26	1,670.84
FICA	1,097.90	637.49	460.41
SDI	65.74	32.87	32.87
State	1,204.15	743.74	460.41
Total Taxes	6,494.89	3,870.36	2,624.53
Telephone	187.52	198.27	-10.75
Utilities:			
Electricity	64.97	62.35	2.62
Garbage	0.00	15.50	-15.50
Water	0.00	28.75	-28.75
Total Utilities	64.97	127.83	-62.86
Vacation	0.00	1,332.31	-1332.31
Outflows - Other	177.97	515.85	-337.88
TO Home Loan	1,210.63	1,212.03	-1.40
TO Savings	5,116.43	5,312.90	-196.47
TO American Excess	100.00	0.00	100.00
TOTAL OUTFLOWS	18,495.34	14,257.06	4,238.28
OVERALL TOTAL	175.62	-231.63	-407.25

The $ Difference column shows how much you are earning or spending in each category compared with an earlier period. Unfavorable comparisons—when you are earning less or spending more—are shown by negative figures and are displayed in red.

(For INFLOWS, the differences are the second column amounts minus the first column amounts. For OUTFLOWS, the differences are the first column amounts minus the second column amounts.)

If you customize the report, you can display another column which shows the percentage change from the first period to the second. (If you see INF in the % Difference column, meaning Infinity, it's because the first amount is zero.)

The overall difference shown in the lower right corner of the report indicates that this person has saved $407.25 less this year than in the same period last year.

Investment reports

This section briefly describes each of Quicken's investment reports. To see the investment reports available, click the Reports icon on the iconbar and select the Investment report family.

You can't run investment reports unless you have set up investment accounts. See Chapter 12, *Tracking investments,* on page 121. The basic procedure to create a report is in "Creating a report" on page 183.

Portfolio Value	Calculate value of securities in investment accounts
Investment Performance	Calculate investment returns (internal rate of return)
Capital Gains	List realized gains on securities sold
Investment Income	Summarize investment income and expenses by category
Investment Transactions	List investment transactions

Portfolio value

A portfolio value report shows the value of each of your securities on a specified date. It shows unrealized gain in dollars (instead of as a percentage) and has options for subtotaling by account, security type, or investment goal.

Initial settings for this report (a type of account balances report)	
Subtotal by:	Don't subtotal
Investment accounts to report on:	Current
Tax-related transactions only:	No
Select to include	All securities, security types, and investment goals

Most recent price per share. Estimated prices are marked with an asterisk (*). (Quicken estimates the price if you haven't updated the price for the date of the report.)

Your cost basis for the security. Quicken displays 0.00 if you didn't enter the cost basis of the security.

Unrealized (paper) gain or loss in dollars.

Market value on the date of the report.

Portfolio Value Report
As of 8/31/95

8/31/95
QDATA95-Charles Squab
Page 1

* Estimated Prices

Security	Shares	Curr Price	Cost Basis	Gain/Loss	Balance
Sun Growth Fund	10,224.65	1.000 *	10,224.65	0.00	10,224.65
Ace Software	472.75	24.940 *	10,549.23	1,241.16	11,790.39
Penny Technologies	4,052.53	1.000	4,052.53	0.01	4,052.54
DataPlus Corp.	252.32	26.170 *	5,992.79	610.63	6,603.42
-Cash-	2,819.58	1.000	2,819.58	0.00	2,819.58
Total Investments			33,638.78	1,851.80	35,490.58

Number of shares (to the nearest 0.01).

Investment performance

The investment performance report shows the average annual total return of your securities during a specified time period. This return takes into account dividends, interest, and other payments you receive as well as increases and decreases in the market value of your securities. Generally, if the average annual return on an investment is 10%, that investment is performing as well as a bank account that pays 10% interest.

When the average annual total return is greater than 10,000% or less than -99.9%, or when the timing of cash flows prevents Quicken from calculating a figure, Quicken displays a message that one or more calculations appear as N/A (not available).

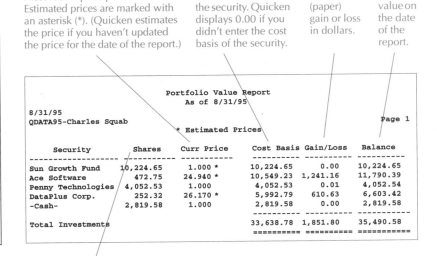

See page 156 for an explanation of the internal rate of return.

The average annual total return is the internal rate of return (IRR) for your investment. Technically, it equals the discount rate at which all the cash flows associated with the investment have a net present value of zero.

Initial settings for this report	
Subtotal by:	Don't subtotal
Cash flow detail:	Yes
Investment accounts to report on:	Current
Tax-related transactions only:	No
Select to include	All securities, security types, and investment goals

```
                         Investment Performance Report
                            5/1/95 Through 8/31/95
  8/31/95                                                              Page 1
  QDATA95-Charles Squab

                                                                   Avg. Annual
   Date  Action Description      Investments      Returns       Tot. Return
   ----- ------ ------------- -------------- ------------ -------------
              5/1/95 - 8/31/95

4/30/95          Beg Mkt Value              0.00
5/1/95    ShrsIn 100 Sun Growth Fund      800.00
5/15/95   DivX   Sun Growth Fund                          30.42
5/15/95   BuyX   39.2773 Sun Growth Fund 304.40
8/31/95          End Mkt Value                         1,114.22
                                        ---------      ---------         --------
TOTAL 5/1/95 - 8/31/95                  1,104.40       1,144.64            12.0%
```

Capital gains

A capital gains report shows long-term and short-term capital gains for securities sold during a specified period. (For capital gains distributions from a mutual fund, use the investment income report.)

See "Entering prior history for investments" on page 158.

To get an accurate capital gains report, you must specify the date or dates you bought the shares you sold and the actual cost basis of those shares. If you haven't already done so, enter this information in the investment register after you make the sale.

See "Selling securities" on page 139.

If you sold only part of your shares of a security in one account, Quicken assumes that the ones you sold are the ones you've held the longest, unless you specifically identified some other lot for selling.

Initial settings for this report	
Subtotal by:	Short- vs. Long-term
Maximum short-term gain holding period:	365 days
Organization:	Income and expense
Investment accounts to report on:	Current
Include unrealized gains:	No
Tax-related transactions only:	No
Select to include	All securities, security types, and investment goals

Quicken doesn't distinguish "wash sales" from other sales. (A "wash sale" is a sale at a loss within 30 days of acquiring the same security. Special tax rules apply.)

```
                              Capital Gains Report
                             1/1/95 Through 5/31/95
5/31/95
QDATA95-Charles Squab                                                   Page 1

Security   Shares    Bought    Sold   Sales Price   Cost Basis     Gain/Loss
--------- ---------- -------- -------- ------------ ------------ ---------------
         LONG TERM

Penny Tech    400    7/6/93   3/31/95     3,840.00     3,148.00        692.00
Ace Software 1,000   2/20/93  4/6/95      4,450.00     3,750.00        700.00
                                        ------------------------   ----------
           TOTAL LONG TERM                 8,290.00     6,898.00      1,392.00
                                       =========== =========== ==========
```

After creating this report, you can export the report to a file to use with tax preparation software. See "Creating tax schedule reports" on page 218.

To use this report for Schedule D (after you've entered all prior history for any security you've sold), subtotal by short-term vs. long-term gain. Select only those accounts that have taxable capital gains (for example, exclude IRAs).

Investment income

The investment income report shows dividend income (taxable and tax-exempt), interest income (taxable and tax-exempt), capital gains distributions, realized gain or loss, unrealized gain or loss (as an option), and margin interest and other investment expenses during a specified time period.

To use this report to gather information for Schedule B, be sure you've entered all investment transactions for the year. Select only those accounts for which you must report income (for example, exclude IRAs). Subtotal by security. Create one report for all your reportable income, both taxable and tax-exempt. Then create a second report, selecting only securities that generate reportable but tax-exempt income. Again, subtotal by security. Don't select the option to include unrealized gains.

Initial settings for this report (a type of summary report)	
Subtotal by:	Don't subtotal
Organization:	Income and expense
Investment accounts to report on:	Current
Include unrealized gains:	No
Tax-related transactions only:	No
Transfers:	Include all

```
                         Investment Income Report
                         5/1/95 Through 8/31/95
8/31/95
QDATA95-Charles Squab                                              Page 1
                                                      5/1/95-
            Category Description                      8/31/95
            ---------------------                     -------
            INCOME/EXPENSE
              INCOME
                _DivInc                                 30.42
                                                      -------
              TOTAL INCOME                              30.42

                                                      -------
            TOTAL INCOME/EXPENSE                        30.42

            TRANSFERS
              TO Savings                               -30.42
              FROM Savings                             304.40
                                                      -------
            TOTAL TRANSFERS                            273.98

            Balance Forward
              Sun Growth Fund                          800.00
                                                      -------
            Total Balance Forward                      800.00

                                                      -------
            OVERALL TOTAL                            1,104.40
                                                     ========
```

Investment transactions

Initial settings for this report (a type of transaction report)	
Subtotal by:	Don't subtotal
Organization:	Income and expense
Investment accounts to report on:	Current
Include unrealized gains:	No
Tax-related transactions only:	No
Transfers:	Include all

The investment transactions report shows how transactions during a specified time period have affected either the market value or the cost basis of your investments and the cash balance in your investment accounts.

If you don't include unrealized (paper) gains, the report shows the change in cost basis of your investments between the beginning and the end of the period. If you choose to include unrealized gains, the report shows the change in the market value of your investments between the beginning and the end of the period.

You may subtotal the report by period, account, category, security, security type, or investment goal.

A reinvested dividend shows up as a buy transaction on one line, followed by an income transaction on the next line. In general, complex transactions appear on several lines, with one line for each component of the transaction.

The Cash column shows the change in the cash balance of your account or accounts as a result of each transaction.

For each transaction, the Invest. Value column shows the change in cost basis of the security if unrealized gains aren't included, or the change in market value if unrealized gains are included. The balance is the current cost basis or market value of all the securities.

For each transaction, the Cash + Invest. column shows the sum of the amounts in the Cash and Invest. Value columns.

Investment Transactions Report
5/1/95 Through 6/30/95

6/30/95
QDATA95-Charles Squab | Page 1

Date	Action	Secur	Categ	Price	Shares	Commssn	Cash	Invest. Value	Cash + Invest.
BALANCE 4/30/95							0.00	0.00	0.00
5/1/95	XIn	-Cash-	[Savings]				8,000.00		8,000.00
5/2/95	Buy	Ace Software		25 3/8	150		-3,806.25	3,806.25	
5/3/95	Div	Ace Software	_DivInc				13.50		13.50
5/7/95	Buy	Penny Technologies		12 1/4	200		-2,450.00	2,450.00	
5/8/95	Buy	Sun Growth Fund		45.000	15		-675.00	675.00	
5/11/95	ReinvDiv	Sun Growth Fund		10.568	10.568		-111.68	111.68	
			_DivInc				111.68		111.68
5/15/95	Buy	DataPlus Corp.		10.000	100		-1,000.00	1,000.00	
5/18/95	Buy	DataPlus Corp.		9 1/2	100		-950.00	950.00	
6/3/95	Buy	DataPlus Corp.		9 1/4	45		-416.25	416.25	
TOTAL 5/1/95 - 6/30/95							-1,284.00	9,409.18	8,125.18
BALANCE 6/30/95							-1,284.00	9,409.18	8,125.18

Business reports

This section describes each of Quicken's business reports. To see which business reports are available, click the Reports icon on the iconbar and select the Business report family.

The basic procedure to create a report is in "Creating a report" on page 183.

More information about creating Quicken reports for your small business finances is in the *Quicken Business User's Guide*. To purchase this guide from Intuit, see "Quicken Business User's Guide" on page 320.

P&L Statement	Summarize profit and loss by category
P&L Comparison	Compare two periods for profit and loss by category
Cash Flow	Summarize income and expense by category
A/P by Vendor	Summarize bills-to-pay, by creditor
A/R by Customer	Summarize payments due, by customer
Job/Project	Summarize income and expense by class
Payroll	Summarize payroll income and expenses by employee
Balance Sheet	Calculate equity based on assets and liabilities

P&L statement

A profit and loss (P & L) statement summarizes the revenue and expenses of a business by category (first income, then expenses).

Initial settings for this report (a type of summary report)	
Row headings:	Category
Column headings:	Don't subtotal
Organization:	Income and expense
Accounts to report on:	All accounts
Transfers:	Exclude all

```
                         Profit & Loss Statement
                          1/1/95 Through 3/31/95
3/31/95
DESIGN-All Accounts                                                  Page 1
                                                   1/1/95-
          Category Description                     3/31/95
  ---------------------------------------  ----------------------
  INCOME/EXPENSE
    INCOME
      Design                                                 31,627.75
      Interest Inc                                              383.66
      Production                                             17,628.83
                                                           -----------
    TOTAL INCOME                                             49,640.24

    EXPENSES
      Ads                                                     1,005.87
      Auto:
        Gas                                        279.81
        Insurance                                  301.73
        Service                                     59.95
        Tickets                                     23.00
                                              -----------
      Total Auto                                                664.49
      Computer                                                  458.69
      Fed Ex                                                    580.07
      Insurance                                                 559.05
      Meals & Enter                                             271.02
      Mech Prep                                               1,479.25
      Paper                                                   1,456.89
      Payroll:
        Comp FICA                                1,117.76
        Comp FUTA                                  280.00
        Comp MCARE                                 261.45
        Comp SUI                                   140.00
        Gross                                   18,027.59
                                              -----------
      Total Payroll                                          19,826.80
      Photocopying                                              607.06
      Photostats                                                341.70
      Postage                                                   424.32
      Printing                                                5,075.66
      Ref. Materials                                            132.16
      Rent Paid                                               1,600.00
      Telephone                                                 347.73
                                                           -----------
    TOTAL EXPENSES                                           34,830.76

                                                           -----------
  TOTAL INCOME/EXPENSE                                       14,809.48
                                                           ===========
```

If you run your business using cash-basis accounting, you want your income to show up when you receive it, not when you issue invoices. Use a cash flow report instead of a P & L statement for income and expense reporting.

P&L comparison

It is similar to the home comparison report described on page 168, except that there are no difference columns.

This report compares profit and loss for the month to date to the year to date.

Cash flow

See page 162.

This report is identical to the home cash flow report. Remember that cash flow reporting and cash-basis accounting are different ideas: you don't have to use cash-basis accounting to create a cash flow report.

A/P by vendor

An accounts payable (or A/P) report summarizes the dollar amount of all unprinted checks in your bank accounts by payee name.

If you aren't using Quicken to print checks, the A/P report still works if you enter all your payables as printable checks. When you pay the bill, go back to the register and record the actual check number in the Num field (just type right over the word "Print").

Initial settings for this report (a type of summary report)	
Row headings:	Payee
Column headings:	Month
Organization:	Income and expense
Accounts to report on:	Bank, cash, credit card
Transaction types:	Unprinted checks only
Transfers:	Include all

A/P (Unprinted Chks) by Vendor
3/1/95 Through 4/30/95
4/30/95
DESIGN-Bank,Cash,CC Accounts Page 1

Payee	3/95	4/95	OVERALL TOTAL
Chris Jacobson	0.00	-961.15	-961.15
First Statewide Bank	0.00	-4,950.00	-4,950.00
Richard Long	0.00	-1,058.20	-1,058.20
State Board of Equalization	0.00	-3,265.28	-3,265.28
Valley Real Estate	0.00	-400.00	-400.00
OVERALL TOTAL	0.00	-10,634.63	-10,634.63

A/R by customer

To limit a report to a single account, see "Selecting accounts to include" on page 189.

The accounts receivable (or A/R) report summarizes uncleared transactions in all your Quicken asset accounts by payee. You might want to restrict the report to the asset account for receivables.

Initial settings for this report (a type of summary report)	
Row headings:	Payee
Column headings:	Month
Organization:	Income and expense
Accounts to report on:	Asset accounts only
Transaction types:	All
Transaction status:	Blank cleared status only
Transfers:	Include all

A/R by Customer
3/1/95 Through 4/30/95
4/30/95
DESIGN-Selected Accounts Page 1

Payee	3/95	4/95	OVERALL TOTAL
Ace Computer Sales	438.70	1,959.1	2,397.80
Balloon Adventures	0.00	1,426.85	1,426.85
Blaine Associates	1,417.75	1,037.90	2,455.65
Computer Waves	843.16	1,926.00	2,769.16
Engineering Control	0.00	920.20	920.20
Osborne Studios	736.70	2,874.02	3,610.72
Reynolds Markets	2,316.55	0.00	2,316.55
Robinson Shoes	1,257.25	2,889.00	4,146.25
Tower Concerts	1,653.15	0.00	1,653.15
OVERALL TOTAL	8,663.26	13,033.07	21,696.33

If you use the balance forward method of recording payments, the accounts receivable report includes *all* transactions in your report: unpaid invoices, paid invoices, and payments.

Job/project

A job/project report summarizes your income and expenses for each job, property, client, project, or other Quicken class. The report shown here summarizes income and expenses for two projects. To get a report like this, set up each project name as a class; then categorize each project-related transaction with an income or expense category and identify it with a project name as the class.

See "Setting up classes and subclasses" on page 16 for information about setting up classes.

If you manage properties and have set up properties as class names, you can use this report to show income and expenses by property.

Initial settings for this report (a type of summary report)	
Row headings:	Category
Column headings:	Class
Organization:	Income and expense
Accounts to report on:	All accounts
Transfers:	Include all

```
                              Job/Project Report
                          1/1/95 Through 3/31/95
3/31/95
DESIGN-All Accounts                                                      Page 1

                                                                        OVERALL
   Category Description         Ace Computer Co Blaine Associat           TOTAL
------------------------------- --------------- --------------- ---------------
INCOME/EXPENSE
  INCOME
    Design                              3,602.0         3,917.5        7,519.50
    Production                         1,234.85         2,483.9        3,718.82
                                 --------------  --------------  --------------
  TOTAL INCOME                         4,836.85         6,401.4       11,238.32

  EXPENSES
    Contracto                              0.00          140.00          140.00
    Mech Prep                             17.00          124.75          141.75
    Photocopyin                           57.44            0.00           57.44
                                 --------------  --------------  --------------
  TOTAL EXPENSES                          74.44          264.75          339.19

                                 --------------  --------------  --------------
TOTAL INCOME/EXPENS                    4,762.41        6,136.72       10,899.13
                                 ==============  ==============  ==============
```

Payroll

The payroll report summarizes income and expenses by category and has a separate column for each payee. The report is restricted to transactions categorized with payroll categories and transfers to payroll liability accounts. (The report is set up to limit transactions to category or transfer account names that start with "Payroll.")

Initial settings for this report (a type of summary report)	
Row headings:	Category
Column headings:	Payee
Organization:	Income and expense
Accounts to report on:	All accounts
Transfers:	Include all
Matching:	Categories and transfer accounts that start with "payroll"

The TRANSFERS TO rows show decreases in your accrued payroll liabilities. For example, each time you record a FICA payment in your checking account, Quicken automatically transfers the amount to the Payroll-FICA account, where it decreases the balance you owe.

The TRANSFERS FROM rows show increases in your accrued payroll liabilities. For example, each time you record a paycheck, Quicken automatically transfers the FICA contribution amount from your checking account to the Payroll-FICA account, where it increases the balance you owe. In the same way, the report can track your liability for items like FUTA, SUI, and Federal Withholding.

See page 316 for a description of QuickPay.

If you have employees to pay as part of your business, you need to do payroll tasks such as make calculations, write checks with numerous deductions, track data for payroll taxes, and fill out payroll tax forms. The easiest way to do payroll tasks is to use the program QuickPay together with Quicken. To use Quicken without QuickPay to track payroll, see the *Quicken Business User's Guide*, which you can purchase from Intuit. See "Quicken Business User's Guide" on page 320 for the phone number.

This row shows gross wages.

This column shows the total increase in your accrued payroll liabilities.

Payroll Report
1/1/95 Through 4/15/95

4/15/95
DESIGN-Selected Accounts
Page 1

Category Description	Chris Jacobson	First Statewide	Richard Long	OVERALL TOTAL
INCOME/EXPENSE				
EXPENSES				
Payroll:				
Comp FICA	610.48	0.00	666.96	1,277.44
Comp FUTA	160.00	0.00	160.00	320.00
Comp MCARE	142.80	0.00	156.00	298.80
Comp SUI	80.00	0.00	80.00	160.00
Gross	9,846.16	0.00	10,756.80	20,602.96
Total Payroll	10,839.44	0.00	11,819.76	22,659.20
TOTAL EXPENSES	10,839.44	0.00	11,819.76	22,659.20
TOTAL INCOME/EXPENS	-10,839.44	0.00	-11,819.7	-22,659.20
TRANSFERS				
TO Payroll-FIC	0.00	-1,500.00	0.00	-1,500.00
TO Payroll-FUT	0.00	-300.00	0.00	-300.00
TO Payroll-FWH	0.00	-2,500.00	0.00	-2,500.00
TO Payroll-MCAR	0.00	-300.00	0.00	-300.00
TO Payroll-SU	0.00	-150.00	0.00	-150.00
TO Payroll-SWHC	0.00	-200.00	0.00	-200.00
FROM Payroll-FIC	1,220.94	0.00	1,333.92	2,554.88
FROM Payroll-FUT	160.00	0.00	160.00	320.00
FROM Payroll-FW	1,304.32	0.00	1,337.28	2,641.60
FROM Payroll-MCAR	285.60	0.00	312.00	597.60
FROM Payroll-SUI	80.00	0.00	80.00	160.00
FROM Payroll-SWHC	99.36	0.00	130.96	230.32
TOTAL TRANSFERS	3,150.24	-4,950.00	3,354.16	1,554.40
OVERALL TOTAL	-7,689.20	-4,950.00	-8,465.60	-21,104.80

How transfers appear in payroll reports

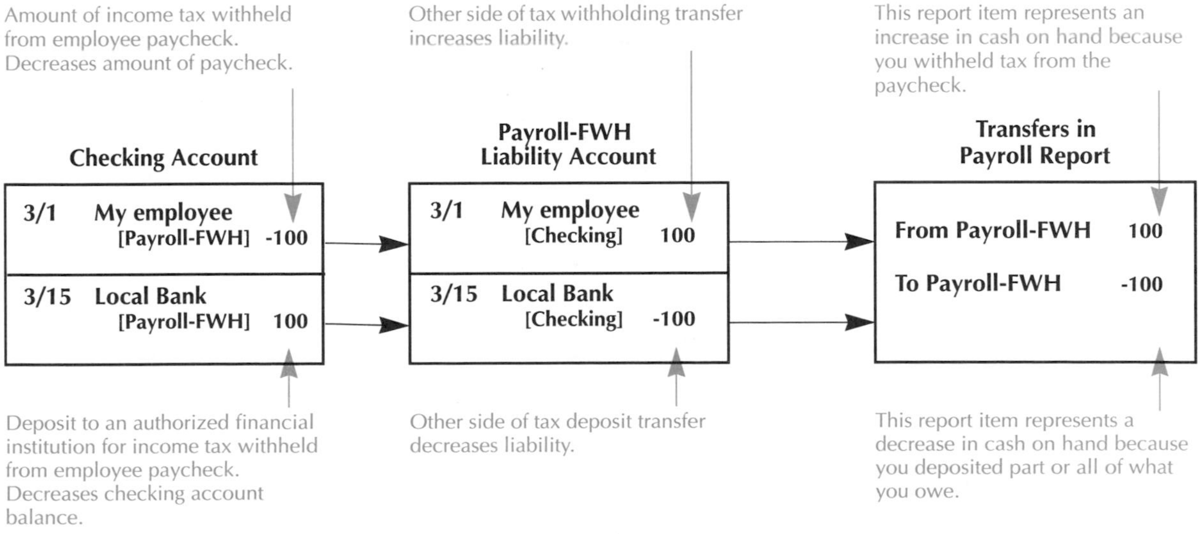
Amount of income tax withheld from employee paycheck. Decreases amount of paycheck.
Other side of tax withholding transfer increases liability.
This report item represents an increase in cash on hand because you withheld tax from the paycheck.
Checking Account
3/1 My employee [Payroll-FWH] -100
3/15 Local Bank [Payroll-FWH] 100
Payroll-FWH Liability Account
3/1 My employee [Checking] 100
3/15 Local Bank [Checking] -100
Transfers in Payroll Report
From Payroll-FWH 100
To Payroll-FWH -100
Deposit to an authorized financial institution for income tax withheld from employee paycheck. Decreases checking account balance.
Other side of tax deposit transfer decreases liability.
This report item represents a decrease in cash on hand because you deposited part or all of what you owe.

Balance sheet

A balance sheet shows the assets, liabilities, and equity (or capital) of a business as of a specific date.

Initial settings for this report (a type of account balances report)	
Report at intervals of:	None
Organization:	Balance sheet format
Accounts to report on:	All accounts
Include unrealized gains:	Yes

If your bank accounts include any unprinted or postdated checks, Quicken adds them to your bank balance and also lists them as a liability.

You can see subtotals by class in an account (or by security if it's an investment account).

Create the report, and then click Customize. Click Report Layout under "Customize." Select the Account Detail checkbox under "Show." (For more information, see "Changing the report layout" on page 186.)

Quicken calculates equity as the difference between your total assets and total liabilities.

```
                         Balance Sheet
                  (Includes unrealized gains)
                         As of 4/15/95
4/15/95
DESIGN-All Accounts                                              Page 1
                                                  4/15/95
                         Acct                     Balance
    ------------------------------------------ ----------------------
    ASSETS

      Cash and Bank Accounts
        First Statewide
          Ending Balance                           11,978.01
          plus: Checks Payable                     10,634.63
                                               -----------
        Total First Statewide                          22,612.64
                                                     -----------
      Total Cash and Bank Accounts                     22,612.64

      Other Assets
        AR                                             21,696.31
        Cap Equip                                       9,960.00
                                                     -----------
      Total Other Assets                               31,656.31

      Investments
        Mutual Fund                                     3,600.00
                                                     -----------
      Total Investment                                  3,600.00

                                                     -----------
    TOTAL ASSETS                                       57,868.95
                                                     ===========
    LIABILITIES & EQUITY

      LIABILITIES
        Checks Payable                                 10,634.63

        Credit Cards
          Amer Express                                      0.00
                                                     -----------
        Total Credit Cards                                  0.00

        Other Liabilities
          AP                                            2,582.34
          Payroll-FIC                                   1,054.88
          Payroll-FUTA                                     20.00
          Payroll-FWH                                     141.60
          Payroll-MCAR                                    297.60
          Payroll-SU                                       10.00
          Payroll-SWHC                                     30.32
          Sales Tax                                       853.57
                                                     -----------
        Total Other Liabilities                         4,990.31

                                                     -----------
      TOTAL LIABILITIES                                15,624.94

      EQUITY                                           42,244.01
                                                     -----------
    TOTAL LIABILITIES & EQUITY                         57,868.95
                                                     ===========
```

Missing checks

It is identical to the home missing checks report on page 167.

This report shows you missing and duplicate check numbers.

Comparison

It is identical to the home comparison report on page 168.

With this report, you can compare your income and spending for two different periods.

Standard reports ("Other")

This section describes each of Quicken's standard reports. All other Quicken reports are based on one of these five standard reports. You can create one of these standard reports and customize it to your needs. To create any report, see "Creating a report" on page 183. To customize any report, see "Changing report settings" on page 185.

To see the standard reports available, click the Reports icon on the iconbar and select the Other report family.

Transaction	List transactions from all/some accounts (subtotal optional)
Summary	Summarize transactions by category (or other item)
Comparison	Compare two transaction periods by category (or other item)
Budget	Compare actual income and expense to budget
Account Balances	Summarize account balances

Transaction

A transaction report lists transactions from one or more registers. Unlike a summary report, it shows individual transactions. To see a running total of balances, print your register and preview it onscreen.

See "Printing the register," on page 36.

Initial settings for this report	
Subtotal by:	Don't subtotal
Sort by:	None
Organization:	Income and expense
Accounts to report on:	Current
Include unrealized gains:	No
Transfers:	Include all
Subcategory display:	Show all

```
                          Transaction Report
                        5/1/95 Through 5/31/95
5/31/95
QDATA95-Checking                                                   Page 1

Date     Num   Description      Memo  Category                Clr  Amount
----     ---   -----------      ----  --------                ---  -------

5/1/95         Paycheck               Salary                   *   3,000.00
5/2/95   ATM   ATM Withdrawal         [Cash]                   *     -40.00
5/2/95         Northern Bell          Telephone                *     -34.22
5/5/95         123 Oak St. HomeownersHousing                   *    -250.00
5/9/95   ATM   ATM Withdrawal         [Cash]                   *     -60.00
5/10/95        SafeCar Insurance      Insurance                *     -62.22
5/10/95        Valley Gas & Electric  Utilities:Gas & Electric*      -58.00
5/15/95        SouthVision Cable      Utilities:Cable          *     -18.55
5/16/95  ATM   ATM Withdrawal         [Cash]                   *     -40.00
5/16/95        Paycheck               Salary                   *   3,000.00
5/23/95  ATM   ATM Withdrawal         [Cash]                   *     -40.00
5/31/95        American Excess        [American Excess]        *  -5,763.77
                                                                   --------
TOTAL 5/1/95 - 5/31/95                                              -366.76


                                                                   --------
TOTAL INFLOWS                                                      6,000.00
TOTAL OUTFLOWS                                                    -6,366.76

                                                                   --------
NET TOTAL                                                           -366.76
                                                                   ========
```

Summary

A summary report summarizes transactions from your accounts by category, or whatever else you choose for the row headings. Unlike a transaction report, it doesn't show individual transactions.

A summary report groups income and expense items in separate sections, followed by transfers and balances forward, unless you select the cash flow report organization option (see "Changing report settings" on page 185).

Initial settings for this report	
Row headings:	Category
Column headings:	Don't subtotal
Organization:	Income and expense
Accounts to report on:	Current
Transfers:	Include all

Quicken groups all transfers to and from the current account.

If an included account has an Opening Balance during the period, Quicken calls it a "balance forward" because you brought an existing balance into Quicken.

A summary report usually displays category or class names rather than category or class descriptions, but you can change the report to display descriptions; see "Changing report options" on page 196. (Then, if a category or class has no description, the category or class name appears.)

Summary Report
5/1/95 Through 7/31/95

7/31/95
QDATA95-Checking — Page 1

Category Description		5/1/95-7/31/95
INCOME/EXPENSE		
INCOME		
Salary		18,000.00
Income - Other		12,962.22
TOTAL INCOME		30,962.22
EXPENSES		
Clothing		112.52
Dues		435.00
Housing		750.00
Insurance		186.66
Int Exp		3,997.31
Tax:		
Fed	5,312.52	
Soc Sec	197.22	
State	102.48	
Total Tax		5,612.22
Tax Spouse:		
Medicare	1,699.98	
Total Tax Spouse		1,699.98
Telephone		102.66
Utilities:		
Cable	55.65	
Gas & Electric	174.00	
Total Utilities		229.65
Expenses - Other		700.88
TOTAL EXPENSES		13,826.88
TOTAL INCOME/EXPENSE		17,135.34
TRANSFERS		
TO American Excess		-6,389.02
TO Cash		-460.00
TO Home Loan		-1,405.28
TO Savings		-2,800.00
TOTAL TRANSFERS		-11,054.30
Balance Forward		
Checking		10,000.00
Total Balance Forward		10,000.00
OVERALL TOTAL		16,081.04

Comparison

A comparison report compares your income and spending for two different periods. For example, you can see if, and in which areas, you are spending more or earning more than a year ago. The report shows a breakdown of your finances by category, and lets you define two different periods to display side by side.

You can display the difference between the two periods in dollars, or as a percentage of the first figure, or both.

See "Comparison" on page 168.

See "Changing report settings" on page 185.

This comparison report has the same initial settings as the home comparison report. However, it reports on the current account only, and the home comparison report includes all your bank, cash, and credit card accounts. You can select different accounts by customizing the report.

Budget

See "About budgets" on page 235.

The budget report compares your actual expenses with your budgeted expenses for each category. Before creating a budget report, set up budget amounts for each category.

Initial settings for this report	
Column headings:	None
Organization:	Income and expense
Accounts to report on:	All accounts
Include unrealized gains:	No
Transfers:	Include all
Categories:	Budgeted categories only

If your budget is organized by supercategories, then the budget report is also. Otherwise, it is organized like a cash flow report: income categories are shown at the top under INFLOWS and expense categories are shown below them under OUTFLOWS.

The budget report prorates budget amounts in the Budget column, according to the report period. For example, a monthly budget amount of $50 would appear in the Budget column as $25 if the report period was 4/1/95 - 4/15/95.

See "Monthly budget" on page 163 for more information on the different parts of the report.

```
                          Budget Report
                     5/1/95 Through 7/31/95
7/31/95
QDATA95-All Accounts                                          Page 1
                                  5/1/95      -     7/31/95
     Category Description         Actual        Budget        Diff
   ---------------------------- -------------------------------------
     INCOME/EXPENSE
       INCOME
        Salary                  18,000.00     24,000.00   -6,000.00
                                ---------     ---------   ---------
       TOTAL INCOME             18,000.00     24,000.00   -6,000.00

       EXPENSES
        Auto:
         Fuel                       79.86        160.00       80.14
         Rental                    332.31        200.00     -132.30
                                ---------     ---------   ---------
        Total Auto                 412.17        360.00      -52.17
        Clothing                   349.61        300.00      -49.61
        Dining                     281.88        320.00       38.12
        Household:
         Furniture               1,687.02      1,200.00     -487.00
         Garden                     67.04         40.00      -27.04
                                ---------     ---------   ---------
        Total Household          1,754.06      1,240.00     -514.00
        Insurance                  186.66        248.00       61.34
        Recreation                 278.97        200.00      -78.97
        Tax:
         Fed                     5,312.52      6,000.00      687.48
         Soc Sec                   197.22        200.00        2.78
         State                     102.48        120.00       17.52
                                ---------     ---------   ---------
        Total Tax                5,612.22      6,320.00      707.78
        Telephone                  102.66        140.00       37.34
        Utilities:
         Cable                      55.65         76.00       20.35
         Gas & Electric            174.00        232.00       58.00
         Utilities - Other           0.00         12.00       12.00
                                ---------     ---------   ---------
        Total Utilities            229.65        320.00       90.35
        Vacation                    98.37        392.00      293.63
                                ---------     ---------   ---------
       TOTAL EXPENSES            9,306.25      9,840.00      533.75

                                ---------     ---------   ---------
     TOTAL INCOME/EXPENSE        8,693.75     14,160.00   -5,466.20

     TRANSFERS
       TO Home Loan             -1,405.28     -4,540.00   -3,134.70
       TO Savings               -2,830.42     -8,000.00   -5,169.50
       FROM Home Loan                0.00          0.00        0.00
       FROM Savings                304.40          0.00      304.40
                                ---------     ---------   ---------
     TOTAL TRANSFERS            -3,931.30    -12,540.00    8,608.70
                                ---------     ---------   ---------
     OVERALL TOTAL               4,762.45      1,620.00    3,142.40
                               ==========    ==========  ==========
```

Account balances

An account balances report lists and totals the balances for all accounts in the current file. If you have investment accounts, the balances for those accounts include unrealized gains. The result shows the net worth of your Quicken accounts.

To include "Checks Payable" (unprinted checks) under LIABILITIES in an account balances report, enter an ending date for the report that is later than any of your postdated checks in the register.

Initial settings for this report	
Report at intervals of:	None
Organization:	Net worth format
Accounts to report on:	All accounts
Include unrealized gains:	Yes

```
                    Account Balances Report
                 (Includes unrealized gains)
                        As of 7/29/95
7/29/95
QDATA95-All Accounts                                Page 1

                                              7/29/95
                Acct                          Balance
       ---------------------------        -------------
       ASSETS
         Cash and Bank Accounts
          Cash                                   102.10
          Checking
           Ending Balance                     11,581.04
           plus: Checks Payable                  625.25
                                              ---------
          Total Checking                      12,206.29
          Savings                              8,526.02
                                              ---------
         Total Cash and Bank Accounts         20,834.41

         Other Assets
          Home Equity                        350,000.00
                                              ---------
         Total Other Assets                  350,000.00

         Investments
          Charles Squab                       12,894.52
          Sun Growth Fund                      2,089.16
                                              ---------
         Total Investments                    14,983.68

                                              ---------
       TOTAL ASSETS                          385,818.09

       LIABILITIES
         Checks Payable                          625.25

         Credit Cards
          American Excess                      2,764.12
                                              ---------
         Total Credit Cards                    2,764.12

         Other Liabilities
          Home Loan                          198,594.72
                                              ---------
         Total Other Liabilities             198,594.72

                                              ---------
       TOTAL LIABILITIES                     201,984.09

                                              ---------
       OVERALL TOTAL                         183,834.00
                                           ============
```

You can see subtotals by class in an account (or by security if it's an investment account).

Create the report, and then click Customize. Click Report Layout and select the Account Detail checkbox. (For more information, see "Changing the report layout" on page 186.)

14 Creating and customizing reports

Creating a report

Follow these steps to create a Quicken report.

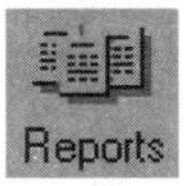

1 **Click the Reports icon on the iconbar.**

Or choose any item from the Reports menu.

See "Changing report options" on page 196.

You can skip the Create Report window altogether, so that when you select a report from the menu bar, the report appears immediately. Select the Skip Create Report Prompt option in the Report Options window.

Select a date range for the report to cover.

Select the type of report you want to see:

First select a report family.

Then select a report name.

Quicken shows you an example of the type of report you've selected. (This isn't your real data.)

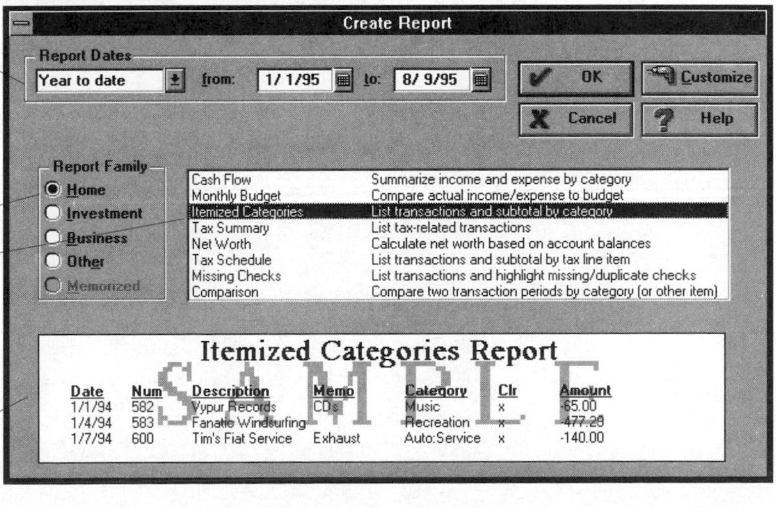

2 **Select a date range for the transactions to be included in the report.**

If the report is an "as of" report (for example, a net worth report), the closing date is today. For comparison reports, enter two date ranges for comparison. Either:

If you regularly need a date range that isn't shown in Quicken's preset list, customize the preset date range that appears when you first open this window—see "Changing report options" on page 196.

- Select a preset date range from the drop-down list by the left field.

OR

- Enter dates in the From and To fields (month/day/year). Use the pop-up calendar to help you select dates by clicking the drop-down buttons by the date fields.

You can select a preset date range and then modify the start or end date.

See the illustration on page 298.

To define a fiscal year instead of using the calendar year in the preset date ranges, turn on Fiscal Year and specify the start month of the fiscal year in the General Options window.

For example, if the fiscal year starts in April, and it's now January, 1995, then Last Year is April 1, 1993 to March 31, 1994.

3 **Select a report family, then a report name.**

For examples of all Quicken's reports, see Chapter 13, *Sample reports,* on page 161.

Most of Quicken's home, investment, and business reports are based on standard reports listed under "Other." If the preset reports don't give you what you want, start with one of the standard reports and customize it.

You can customize any report by changing its layout, the accounts covered, the type of transactions it includes, and various other aspects. You can do that now, before creating the report, or after it is displayed on your screen.

For more information, see "Changing report settings" on page 185.

4 **(Optional) Click Customize to change the report settings before creating the report.**

5 **Click OK.**

Quicken searches the current file for transactions within the date range and displays the report on the screen. The search may take several seconds, depending on the size of your accounts.

With the report displayed, you can click the buttons at the top of the report (the Report button bar) to change your report or save it.

Save your report settings. See "Memorizing and recalling reports" on page 194.

Print the report or save it to a file. See "Printing reports" on page 213.

Sort the transactions in a different order. (See page 187 for details.) The Sort button appears only for transaction reports.

Close the Report window.

Change the report to your liking. See "Changing report settings" on this page.

Copy the report to the clipboard. This is an easy way of transferring your Quicken data to other programs, such as a spreadsheet program. For details, see "Transferring report data to other programs" on page 198.

(The tax schedule report has an additional Export button for transferring tax data to other tax preparation software. See page 220 for details.)

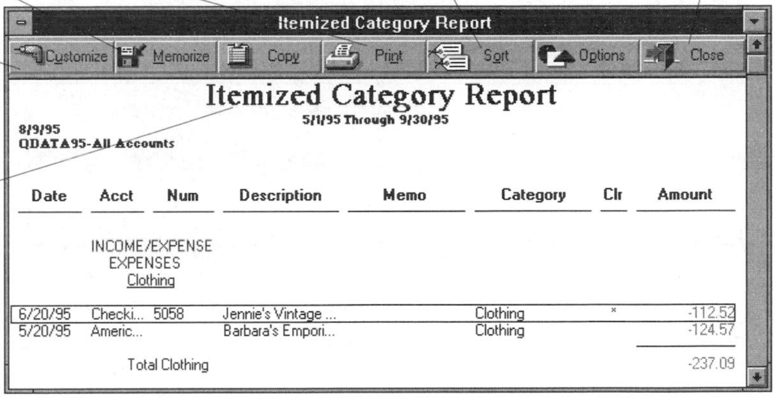

Creating QuickReports

Some Quicken windows show a Report button that gives you an instant transaction listing (a QuickReport) relevant to that window. For example, with the Category & Transfer list displayed, select a category and click the Report button for a quick listing of all transactions (in all accounts) with that category. You can display QuickReports for the:

- Category & Transfer list See page 13.
- Class list See page 16.
- register, to list all transactions for a certain payee See page 33.
- Memorized Transaction list (a payee report) See page 45.
- Portfolio View window, to list all transactions for a certain security See page 148.

These QuickReports are actually standard transaction reports that have been filtered to include only the transactions you're interested in. With the report displayed, you can change the report settings as you can for any Quicken report.

Changing report settings

Quicken gives you great flexibility in creating your reports. You can change the layout, the date range, the accounts to be included, and various other settings. You can also filter the report, for example to include only certain payees or categories. After customizing a report you can *memorize* it for future use.

1. **Create a report as described on page 183.**
2. **Either click Customize in the Create Report window or click OK to create the report and then click the Customize button on the report button bar.**

First click the area you want to customize.

Then set up the detailed settings as you want them.

Quicken tells you what changing each area does.

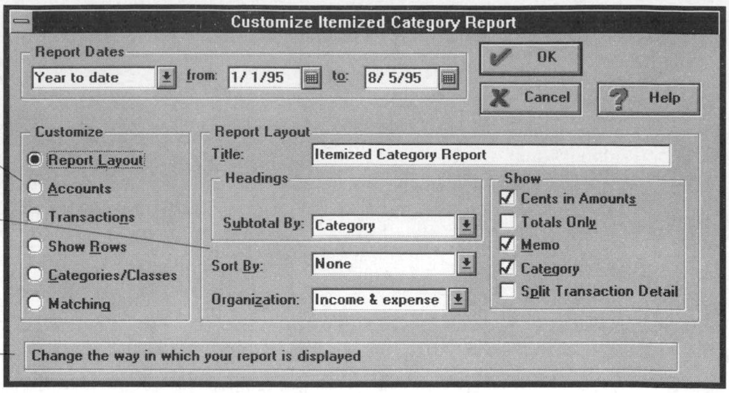

See page 184, step 2, for instructions on how to choose a date range.

3 **(Optional) Change the date range.**

4 **In the Customize section, click the area of the report you want to change.**

5 **Change the settings for that area in the right part of the window.**

The rest of this section gives you complete details of all the options.

6 **Click OK.**

Quicken applies your new settings to the report.

You can change the title, date range, or accounts to report on while the report is displayed on your screen. Move the mouse pointer over the title and heading information at the top of the report. (The pointer changes to a magnifying glass.) Now double-click on the item. You can then change the item in the Customize Report window.

Double-click the title to change it, or the dates to change the date range.

Double-click the accounts label to select other accounts.

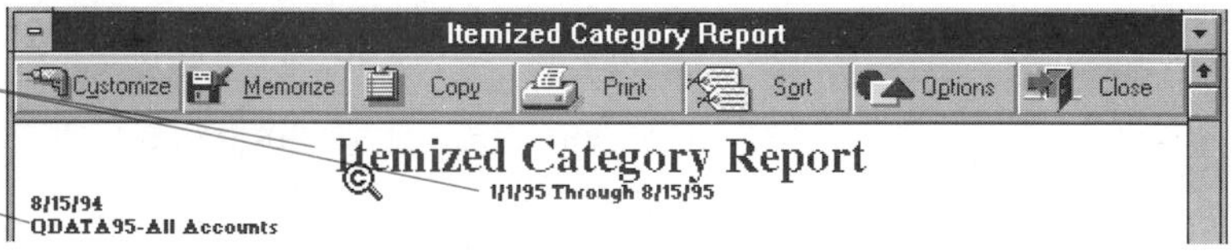

Changing the report layout

Click Report Layout in the Customize Report window.

The right part of the window lets you rename the report, rearrange the report with different row and column headings, or change the accounting organization.

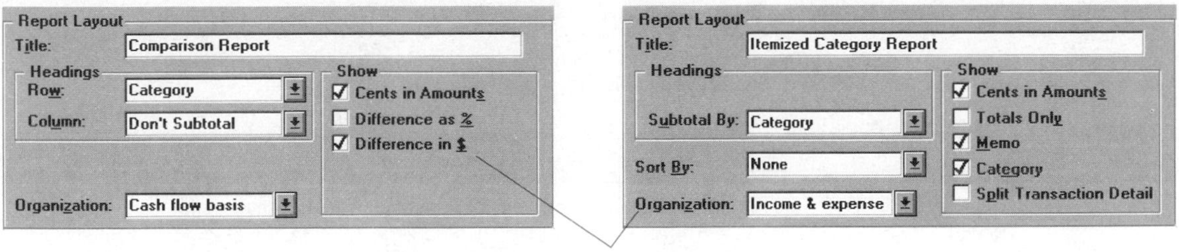

What you see in the Report Layout area depends on the type of report you are customizing. Not all options may be offered.

The next table shows all the report layout settings in Quicken reports. The settings available vary for each report type.

Name of setting	Choice	Results
Title	(Your choice)	Displays and prints the report with the title you enter.
Row headings (summary reports)	Category Class Payee Account	Creates a row for each category, class, payee, or account.
Column headings (summary, budget, and account balances reports)	Don't subtotal (Various periods) Category Class Payee Account	Creates a column for each week, two weeks, half month, month, quarter, half year, year, category, class, payee, or account. (See "How Quicken defines report periods" on page 189.) If you choose Don't Subtotal, Quicken creates a report with a single column.
Subtotal By (transaction reports)	Don't subtotal (Various periods) Category Class Payee Account Tax schedule	Groups and totals transactions by week, two weeks, half month, month, quarter, half year, year, category, class, payee, account, or tax schedule. (See "How Quicken defines report periods" on page 189.) If you choose Don't Subtotal, Quicken doesn't subtotal amounts in the report.
Interval (account balances reports)	None	Includes one total for account balances based on the ending date you enter at the top of the window.
	(Various periods)	Creates a column and totals account balances for each week, two weeks, half month, month, quarter, half year, or year.
Sort by (transaction reports)	None	Sorts transactions first by account type, then by account name, and then by date.
	Date/Acct	Sorts transactions first by date, then by account type, and then by account name.
	Acct/Chk #	Sorts transactions first by account type, then by account name, and then by check number.
	Amount	Sorts transactions from smallest to largest amount.
	Payee	Sorts transactions alphabetically by payee name.
	Category	Sorts transactions alphabetically by category.

Name of setting	Choice	Results
Max Short-Term Gain Holding period (investment capital gains reports)	Enter a number	This number defines how many days you must have held a security before selling it for the resulting capital gain to qualify as a long-term gain.
Organization	Income and expense	Totals income, expense, and transfer transactions in separate sections of your report.
	Cash flow basis	Groups and totals inflows and outflows (including expenses and transfers out of the account). For example, if you have an asset account called "House," and you treat home improvement transactions as transfers to that account, choosing cash flow basis lets you treat those transfers as spending, giving you a more accurate picture of your total expenditures.
	Net worth format	(Account balances reports) Prints your net worth as the last item.
	Balance sheet format	(Account balances reports) Prints net worth as a liability ("equity") with total liabilities and equity last.
	Supercategory	(Budget reports) Groups and totals budget amounts by supercategory instead of inflows and outflows. (See page 235.)
Show Cents in Amounts	Select	Displays amounts in dollars and cents.
	Clear	Displays amounts in dollars (Quicken rounds to the nearest dollar).
Amount as % (summary reports)	Select	Shows amounts in relative terms, as percentages of the total.
	Clear	Shows amounts only as dollars (and cents).
Difference as % (comparison reports)	Select	Shows the difference between the two column amounts as a percentage of the first column amount. (Unfavorable amounts are shown in red as negative amounts.)
	Clear	Hides the percentage differences.
Difference in $ (comparison reports)	Select	Shows the dollar difference between the two column amounts. (Unfavorable amounts are shown in red as negative amounts.)
	Clear	Hides the dollar differences.
Show Totals Only (transaction reports)	Select	Displays only the total dollar amount of transactions that meet the criteria you've specified.
	Clear	Lists all the transactions that meet the criteria you've specified.
Show Memo (transaction reports)	Select	Include a column for memos.
	Clear	Hide memos in the report.
Show Category (transaction reports)	Select	Include a column for categories.
	Clear	Hide categories in the report.
Show Split Transaction Detail (transaction reports)	Select	Include the detail from the Splits window.
	Clear	Hide the detail from the Splits window in the report.
Account Detail (balance sheet, net worth, and account balances reports)	Select	Display subtotals by class (or security) for all selected accounts.
	Clear	Hide subtotals by class (or security if it's an investment account) for all selected accounts.
Show Cash Flow Detail (investment performance reports)	Select	Show all transactions that contribute to the Average Annual Total Return figure.
	Clear	Show only the Average Annual Total Return figure.

How Quicken defines report periods

You can subtotal certain reports by period. You can use the following periods (next page) as row headings for transaction reports and as column headings for summary, transaction, and budget reports.

These definitions are for whole periods. Your report will include a partial period if your starting or ending date doesn't fall on the first or last day of a period as defined here.

Period	Quicken definition
Week	Starts on Sunday, runs through Saturday.
Two weeks	Starts on Sunday, runs for 14 days (ends on Saturday).
Half month	Runs from the 1st through the 15th or from the 16th through the last day of the month.
Month	Starts on the 1st of the month, ends on the last day of the month.
Quarter	Includes three consecutive calendar months. If you have Calendar Year selected, the first quarter is January, February, and March. if you choose Fiscal Calendar and define the fiscal year to start in June, for example, then the first quarter is June, July, and August.
Half year	Starts on the starting date and ends on the last day of the month five months later; for example, January 2 through June 30.
Year	Starts on the starting date, runs for 365 days (366 days for leap years).

The starting dates for quarters will be different if you have defined a fiscal year. See "Customizing other Quicken features" on page 297.

Selecting accounts to include

Click Accounts in the Customize Report window.

The right part of the window lets you select which accounts to include in the report. Simply click on an account to select it.

Depending on what type of report you have displayed, certain accounts may be preselected. For example, a cash flow report preselects all your bank, cash, and credit card accounts. Standard transaction and summary reports include only the current account.

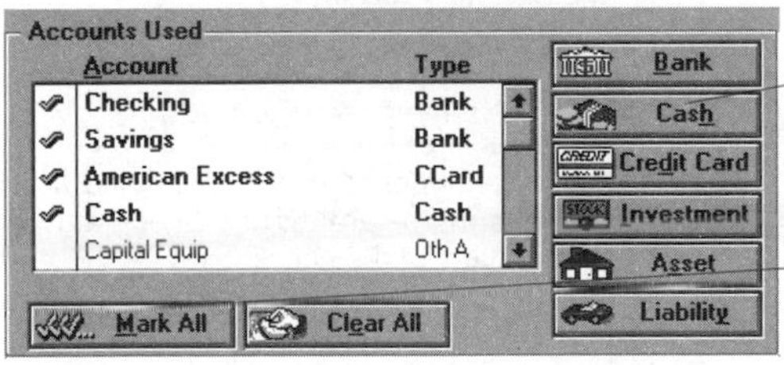

Click an account type button to select all the accounts of that type.

Click Mark All to select all accounts at once, or click Clear All to deselect all accounts.

Selecting transactions to include

Click Transactions at the Customize Report window.

The right part of the window lets you select only certain transactions for the report by filtering on the transaction amount or type. For example, you can report only on payments from your accounts or only on deposits. Or you can create a report limited to transactions assigned to tax-related categories.

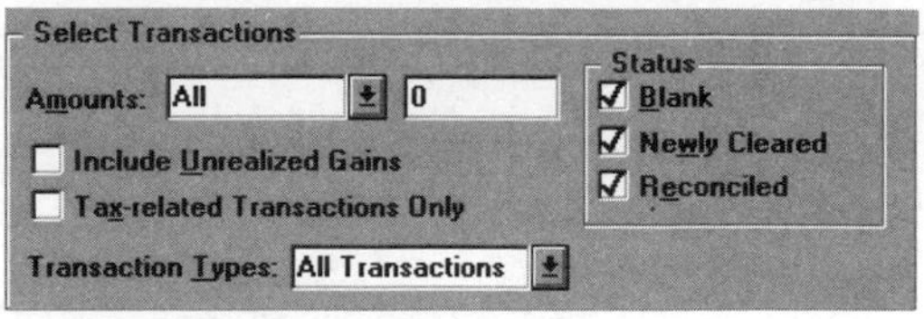

Name of setting	Choice	Results
Amounts	All	Includes all transaction amounts.
	less than	Includes amounts less than the amount you enter.
	equal to	Includes amounts equal to the amount you enter.
	greater than	Includes amounts greater than the amount you enter.
Include Unrealized Gains	Select	Include unrealized gains.
	Clear	Determine whether Quicken generates additional transactions (in transaction reports) or income/inflow lines (in summary reports) to represent the impact of price increases and decreases for securities. Appears only if you have set up investment accounts. If the checkbox is cleared, Quicken doesn't include unrealized gains.
Tax-related Transactions Only	Select	Include only transactions that have been categorized with tax-related categories.
	Clear	Include both tax-related and non-tax-related transactions.
Transaction Types	Payments	Includes payments only (including checks). For nonbank accounts, payments are decreases to cash and other asset accounts, and increases to credit card and other liability accounts.
	Deposits	Includes deposits only.
	Unprinted Checks	Includes unprinted checks only.
	All Transactions	Includes all transactions.
Status	Blank Newly cleared Reconciled	Refers to a transaction's entry in the Clr (Cleared) field. Quicken reports include all transactions, regardless of cleared status, unless you change this filter. Don't change or clear any of the checkboxes for these choices unless you are creating a report specifically to show which of your transactions are cleared or uncleared.

Showing row information

Click Show Rows at the Customize Report window. The right part of the window lets you show or hide transfer and category information in the row heading.

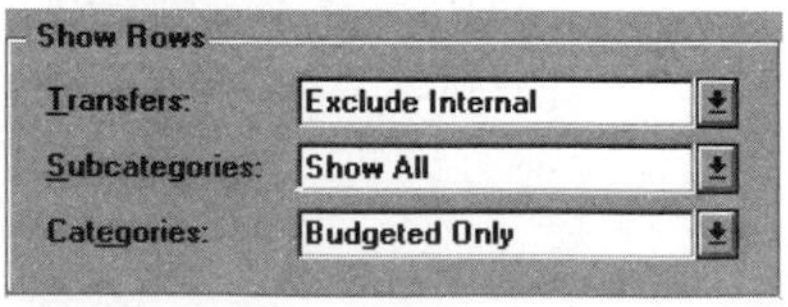

Name of setting	Choice	Results
Transfers	Include All	Includes all transfers in the report.
	Exclude All	Excludes all transfers in the report. Use for a report showing income and expenses without transfers (similar to Quicken's business profit and loss statement).
	Exclude Internal	Excludes transfers between accounts that are included in the report. Essentially, these are transfers that cancel each other out in the report.
Subcategories	Show All	Displays subcategories and subclasses grouped under their main categories.
	Hide All	Doesn't display subcategory or subclass information.
	Show Reversed	Displays subcategories with the main categories grouped under them. For example, if you have transactions assigned to Car Repairs:Honda and to Insurance:Honda, you can use the reversed option to generate a report totaling expenses for Honda.
Categories (budget reports only)	Include All	Includes all categories from the current list, regardless of whether you've used them yet in a transaction.
	Non-Zero Actual/ Budgeted	Includes any categories that you have already used in transactions, and also all categories to which you have assigned budget amounts in the Set Up Budgets window.
	Budgeted Only	Includes only the categories to which you have assigned budget amounts in the Set Up Budgets window.

Selecting categories, transfers, supercategories, and classes to include

Click Categories/Classes in the Customize Report window. (For investment reports, this is named Select to Include.)

The right part of the window lets you select which categories, classes, or supercategories to include in the report. For investments reports, you can select actions, categories, securities, security types, and investment goals. Click on a category, class, or supercategory (or investment item) to select or deselect it.

Click on an item to select or deselect it.

(Select Not Categorized to include transactions with no category assigned.)

Click Mark All to select all items, or click Clear All to deselect all items.

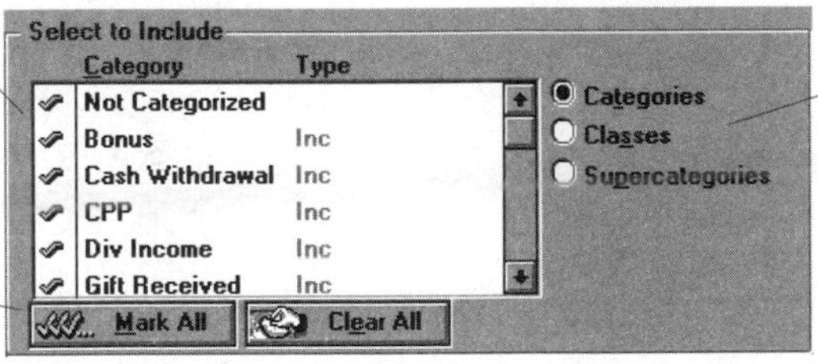

Click Categories, Classes, or Supercategories (budget reports only) to display the list to select from. For investment reports, click the investment item.

(To match investment actions and categories to transaction types, see the table on page 137.)

See also the Transfers option listed on this page.

The list of categories also includes, at the bottom of the list, the names of all your accounts. By selecting or deselecting these names, you can include or exclude transfers between specific accounts and the accounts you're reporting on.

If you use classes, you may find it useful to create a report with only certain classes selected, to report on the finances for particular jobs or projects.

For budget reports, you might want to create a report with only certain supercategories selected.

Using matches to filter transactions

Click Matching at the Customize Report window.

The right part of the window lets you further define or limit the transactions to be included in your reports, depending on the details of each transaction. You can define what must be true about a transaction for it to be included in a report. For example, you can include only transactions with a specific payee. Just type the payee's name in the Payee Contains box.

Enter the exact name, using QuickFill or the drop-down lists to help you, or a partial name, using two periods (..) to represent characters you're not sure of.

Case (capitals or non-capitals) doesn't matter, and Quicken ignores any spaces before or after the phrase you type.)

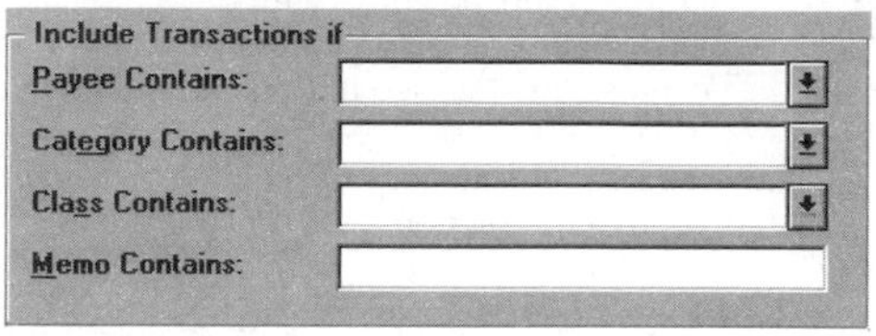

For investment reports, you can filter your reports by the security or the memo contents.

In the Category Contains box, you can type a category name or an account name to report on transfers to a specific account. For a category or class match, Quicken also searches through entries in the Splits window.

In addition to typing an entire payee, category, class, memo, or security name, you can use special *match characters* to limit a report.

Match character	Type of match
= (equal sign)	An exact match (include only transactions that match the text you type exactly)
.. (two periods)	A match that contains unspecified characters where you type .. (at the beginning, in the middle, or at the end of the text you type)
? (question mark)	A match with one unspecified character
~ (tilde)	The report excludes all matches for the text that follows

If you type ~.. (a tilde and two periods), Quicken excludes all transactions except those that are empty in the specified field. For example, if you type ~.. in the Category Contains box, Quicken includes only those transactions that are uncategorized. Uncategorized transactions show up as "Other" in reports.

For an investment report, if you type ~.. in the Security Contains box, the report includes only cash transactions, which don't have a security. If you type .. in the box, the report will exclude all cash transactions.

The following chart shows some examples of what your report can include with and without using special match characters.

Example	The report includes	The report doesn't include
=tax	tax, Tax, TAX	taxable, tax deduction, Tax:State, surtax, new tax loss, rent, utilities
tax	tax, Tax, TAX, taxable, tax deduction, Tax:State, surtax, new tax loss	rent, utilities
tax..	tax, Tax, TAX, taxable, tax deduction, Tax:State	surtax, new tax loss, rent, utilities
..tax	tax, Tax, TAX, surtax, property tax	taxable, tax deduction, Tax:State, new tax loss, rent, utilities
~=tax	taxable, tax deduction, Tax:State, surtax, new tax loss, rent, utilities	tax, Tax, TAX
~tax	rent, utilities	tax, Tax, TAX, taxable, tax deduction, Tax:State, surtax, new tax loss
t..x	trix, tx, tkx, t—x, tax, Tax, TAX	taxable, tax deduction, Tax:State, surtax, new tax loss, rent, utilities
=t?x	tkx, tax, Tax, TAX	trix, tx, t—x, taxable, tax deduction, Tax:State, surtax, new tax loss, rent, utilities
..	tax, rent, utilities, and so on	*blank*
~..	*blank*	tax, rent, utilities, and so on
.. in the Security Contains field	All transactions for which the Security column is filled in	All cash transactions and totals that aren't associated with a security

Investigating report items with QuickZoom

Use QuickZoom to examine the transaction detail in most Quicken reports (in summary, transaction, budget, comparison, investment income, and investment transactions reports). For example, to examine the individual transactions that are represented by an "Actual" amount in a budget report or an uncategorized "Other" amount in a summary report, double-click the amount to see a list of the transactions that make up that amount.

Or press Ctrl+Z

1 **Select an amount in the report and double-click it.**

You can QuickZoom an item when the arrow pointer turns into a magnifying glass:

Quicken displays a QuickZoom report, which is a list of the transactions that make up that amount. (Or, if you use QuickZoom in a transaction report, the register appears.)

Click Print on the Report button bar or press Ctrl+P to print the list of transactions.

You can sort the transactions in a QuickZoom report by clicking the Sort button.

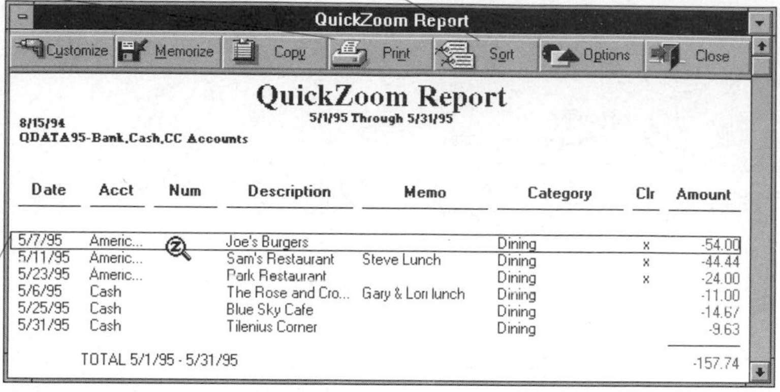

To examine or change a transaction, double-click it to go to the account register with that transaction selected.

Or press Ctrl+Z again

2 **(Optional) To examine a transaction in the register or make any changes, double-click the report line.**

Quicken displays the register and selects the transaction.

Windows Tip
To minimize a window to an icon, click the minimize button (▼) in the upper right corner. The window appears as an icon on the Windows desktop. To restore a minimized icon, double-click it.

To modify a large number of transactions in the register, it's best to close or minimize (to an icon) the Report window to avoid the delay that would be caused by recalculation. (This recommendation also applies when you are changing budget amounts while a budget report is open.) When you're ready to see your changes, double-click on the report icon to open and update your report.

3 **To return to the QuickZoom report from the register, close or minimize the register, or click in the QuickZoom report window.**

If you used QuickZoom to move directly from a transaction report to the register, Quicken returns you to the transaction report when you close or minimize the register.

Memorizing and recalling reports

Once you customize a report, you can memorize it for future use. This feature is most useful for reports that filter out transactions, for example, those that use matching criteria.

Memorizing a report

1 **Create and display a report as described in "Creating a report" on page 183.**

Or press Ctrl+M

2 **Click Memorize on the Report button bar.**

Or choose Memorize Report from the Edit menu.

If you use the same title as an existing memorized report, Quicken warns that you are about to overwrite an existing memorized report.

This option is available only if you selected a preset date range in the Create Report window.

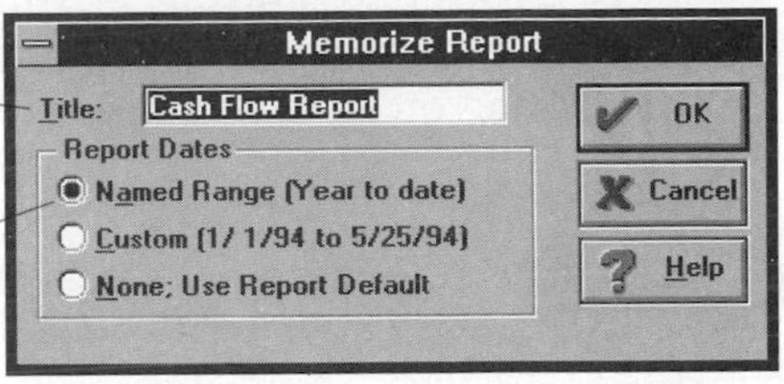

3 **(Optional) Change the title of the memorized report.**

For example, type "Inv. Transactions - Current Quarter."

4 **Choose an option for report dates.**

Named Range. (Available only if you used a preset date range when creating the report.) Instead of memorizing actual dates, Quicken will calculate the dates, depending on when you recall the report. For example, if you memorize a report with the date range "Month to date," the report will cover the period from the beginning of the current month to the day when you recall the report.

Custom. Quicken memorizes the actual dates that were used in the report.

To change the preset starting and ending dates for all reports, see "Changing report options" on page 196.

None. Quicken will use the preset starting and ending dates that appear in the Create Report window when you recall the report.

5 **Click OK to memorize the report.**

Quicken adds the report to the Memorized Report list.

Recalling a memorized report

After you have memorized a report, you can recall it. When you recall a report, it's really the report definition you are recalling (including all the settings and sort criteria you've specified).

To recall a report:

- Click the Reports icon on the iconbar, select Memorized as the report family, then select a memorized report from the list.

OR

- Choose Memorized Reports from the Reports menu, select a report from the list of your memorized reports, and click Use. At the Create Report window, click OK.

To display this list, choose Memorized Reports from the Reports menu.

To rename a memorized report, select it and click Edit.

To delete a memorized report, select it and click Delete.

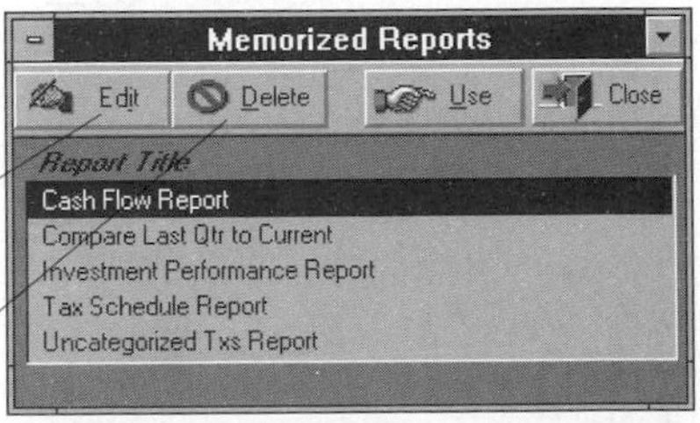

Quicken searches for transactions and prepares the report as usual.

If you change the settings for a memorized report, you can rememorize it with the same title or you can give the altered report a new title and memorize it again. If you don't rememorize a report whose definition you have changed, it retains the original definition.

Changing report options

You can change certain aspects of Quicken's reports from the Options menu item.

1 **From the Edit menu, choose Options (or click the Options icon on the iconbar).**

Or click Options on the button bar of any report.

2 **Click the Reports icon.**

This illustration shows the options that are selected when Quicken is installed.

Click a button to select it.

Click a checkbox to select or clear it.

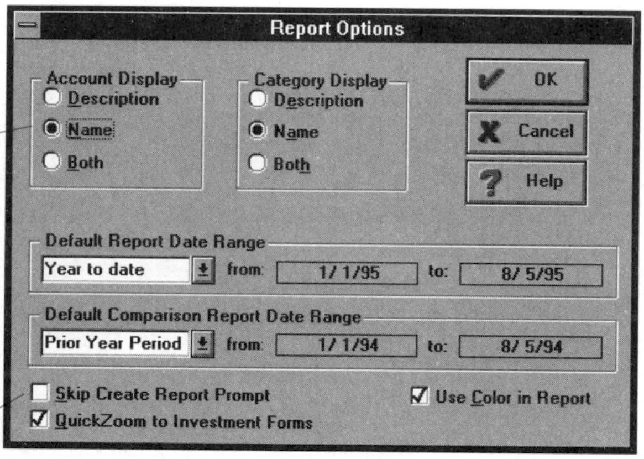

3 **Choose the options you want to use and click OK.**

Quicken updates all opened reports so you can see your changes immediately.

Quicken displays report text on your screen in Helvetica and uses Times Roman for report headings. These display fonts can be modified by editing your QUICKEN.INI file. For more information, press F1, click Search, type "fonts," press Enter, and double-click "Changing the font in reports displayed onscreen."

Report option	Effect on reports
Account Display	**Description** shows the account description only. If an account has no description, Quicken uses the account name. **Name** shows the account name only. **Both** shows both the name and description.
Category Display	**Description** shows the category/class description only. If a category or class has no description, Quicken uses the category or class name. **Name** shows the category/class name only. **Both** shows both the name and description.
Default Report Date Range	The initial date range for all reports (which you can change when creating a report). Select the date range you use most often for your reports. If you want to use some other date range that isn't listed, see "Setting up your own default date range" next.
Default Comparison Report Date Range	The second default date range for comparison reports. Select the date range you use most often for comparison reports.

Report option	Effect on reports
Skip Create Report Prompt	Select to create reports from the Reports menu without first displaying the Create Report window. The default date range shown in this window will be used. If necessary, you can change any settings by clicking the Customize button on the Report button bar after the report is created.
QuickZoom to Investment Forms	From an investment income or investment transactions report, QuickZoom to the entry forms instead of to the investment register.
Use Color in Report	Select to display text and positive amounts in blue and negative amounts in red.

Setting up your own default date range

In the Report Options window, you can select the date range to use as the starting (or default) date range when you create reports. You can also set up your own default date range. Quicken then displays that as the starting date range each time you create a report.

1 **In the Report Options window, click the drop-down button in the Default Report Date Range field.**

2 **Select Custom Date at the bottom of the list.**

3 **Select From and To dates from the drop-down lists.**

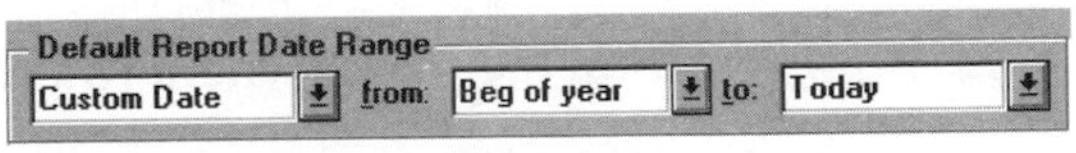

These lists contain more dates than are available from Quicken's preset date ranges. If you select a From date such as "May 1," Quicken always uses the previous May 1. For example, if you set up a date range of May 1 to August 1, and run a report on January 20, 1994, the report will run from May 1, 1993 to August 1, 1993.

4 **Click OK to record your changes.**

See page 194 for more information about date ranges in memorized reports.

A memorized report won't remember your own default date range as "floating" dates.
If you memorize a report after using your own default date range to create the report, Quicken doesn't offer you the date range as a "Named Range". For example, if you set up a default date range of "Beginning last month" through "Today," Quicken converts this to (for example) 4/1/94 through 5/19/94 when you create the report. If you memorize the report, you can memorize only the fixed custom dates 4/1/94 through 5/19/94 or the report default options.

Transferring report data to other programs

Use the Copy button to easily transfer Quicken data to other programs, such as Microsoft Excel for Windows, Lotus 1-2-3 for Windows, other spreadsheet software, or a word processor.

1 **In Quicken, display the report with the data arranged exactly as you would like to copy it to the other program.**

Customize the report if necessary, as described in this chapter.

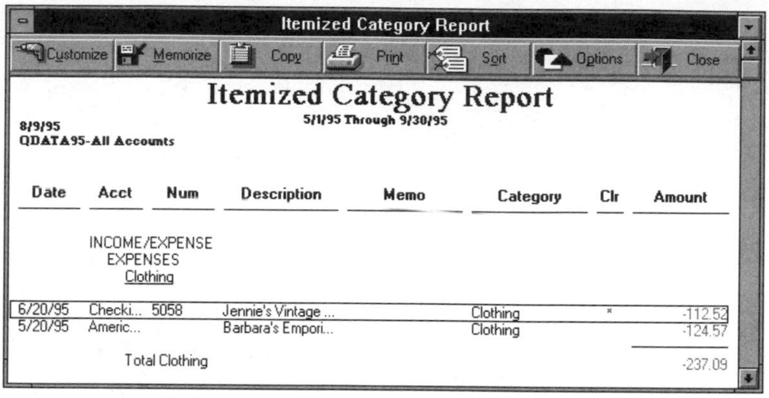

The report data is copied in a tab-delimited format compatible with many spreadsheet programs.

2 **Click Copy.**

3 **Switch to the other program.**

Click in the other program's window if it is visible, or press Alt-Tab to select the program. If it wasn't already running, start it now.

4 **Position the cursor where you would like the data to be read in.**

5 **Use the program's Paste function to copy the Quicken data in.**

The Paste function is usually found on the Edit menu. The data is read from the clipboard into the program.

This example shows a Microsoft Excel worksheet.

If you paste the report data into a word processor document, you may need to set tabs in the document to format the report attractively. The figures in the Quicken report are separated by tabs. However, you may prefer to print the report to an ASCII file on disk (see page 213), and then import the file. Then, the report columns are separated by spaces.

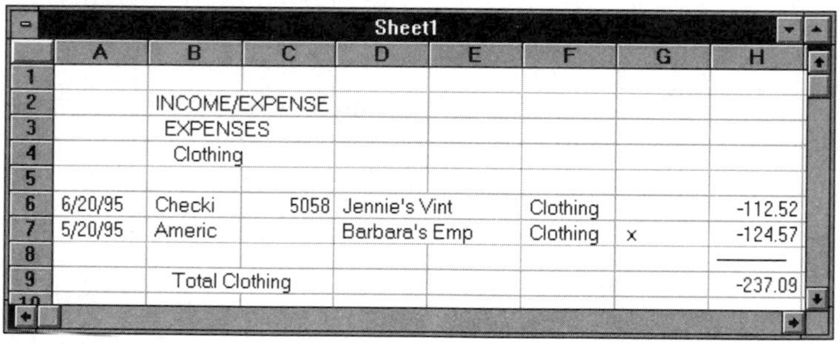

15 Creating graphs

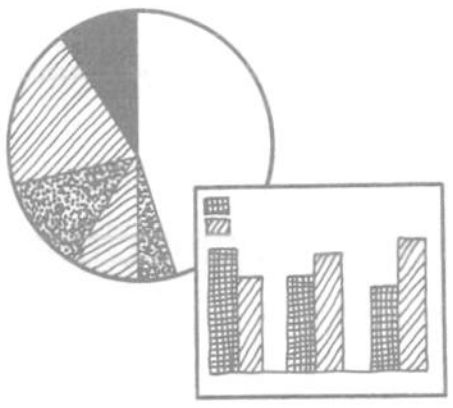

About graphs

Graphs help give you a visual summary of your finances. Quicken creates four types of graphs:

- Income and Expense
- Budget Variance
- Net Worth
- Investment

Creating a graph

Follow these steps to create a Quicken graph.

1 **Click the Graphs icon on the iconbar.**

Or select Graphs from the Reports menu.

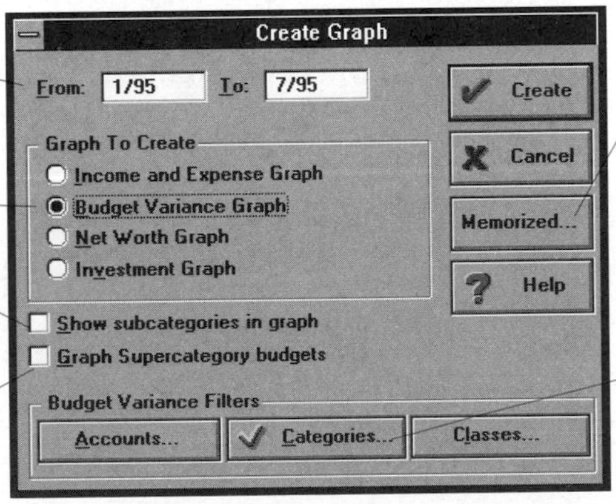

(Optional) Type a date range. Graphs may be too cluttered and difficult to understand if you enter a date range longer than a year.

Choose the type of graph.

(Optional) Select this checkbox to show the extra detail that subcategories allow you.

(Optional) Select this checkbox to organize the budget graph by supercategories instead of categories. (Budget Variance Graph only.)

Click here to select a previously memorized graph. (See "Memorizing and recalling graphs" on page 202.)

(Optional) Click the filter buttons to include or exclude specific accounts, categories, or classes (or securities for the investment graph). When the Select Items To Include window appears, mark the items you want to include. The checkmark on the button tells you when some items are excluded.

2 **Complete the Create Graphs window and click Create.**

Unless you specify otherwise, the graph includes all accounts, categories, and classes. The selection of items for graphs works the same way it does when you customize reports. You can select accounts, categories, and classes for income and expense, budget variance, and net worth graphs. You can select accounts and securities for investment graphs.

See Chapter 17, *Printing reports, graphs, and Snapshots,* on page 211.

To print the graph, choose Print Graph from the File menu, or click the Print button on the Graph button bar.

Viewing graph windows

Each segment of a graph is shaded with a different color (or pattern if you don't have a color monitor).

Change the dates, accounts, categories, or classes for your graph. See the Create Graphs window on page 199.

Save your graph settings. See "Memorizing and recalling graphs" on page 202.

Print the graph or save it to a file. See "Printing graphs" on page 214.

Quicken displays two graphs in one window. To view the graphs in separate windows, you can change this setting. See "Changing graph options" next.

Change graph settings. For example, you can view graphs in patterns instead of colors. See "Changing graph options" next.

In bar graphs, Quicken displays dollar amounts on the y-axis and months, accounts, or categories on the x-axis.

The title of each individual graph appears above the graph.

In pie charts, if you have more than ten categories, Quicken displays the largest ten categories first. It groups the rest of the categories in the eleventh slice of the pie, called "Other." To see the rest of your categories, click Next 10 or double-click the "Other" slice.

A legend to the right of each graph shows what the patterns or colors represent.

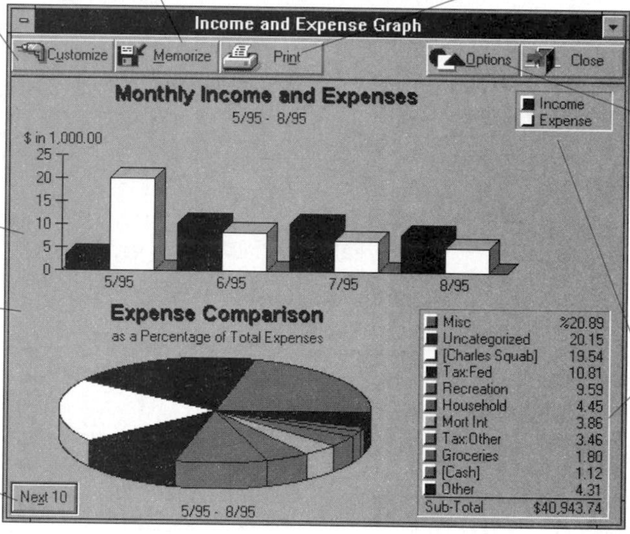

Changing graph options

If you are using a color monitor and some of the colors in your graphs are very similar to other colors, turn up the brightness or contrast on your monitor. Each color becomes vivid and distinct.

You can change three graph display settings.

1 **Click the Options button on the Graph window button bar.**

Select this option to display patterns instead of colors. (If you have a monochrome monitor, Quicken turns this option on automatically.)

Select this option to display each graph in its own window instead of two graphs per window.

Select this if your computer takes a long time to display three-dimensional graphs.

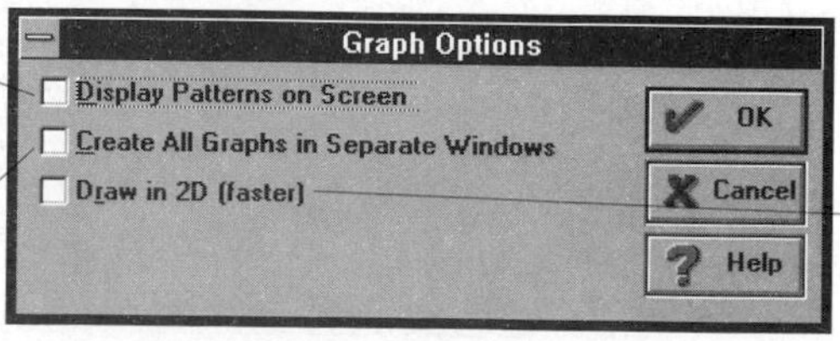

2 **Select the options you want to use and click OK.**

Investigating items in graphs

You have three ways to investigate the information in a graph. Whenever you see the arrow cursor turn into a magnifying glass, you can create a more detailed graph about the item under the magnifying glass, or see the exact value. Or you can remove the item from the graph to look more closely at other items.

- **QuickZoom.** As with Quicken reports, you can QuickZoom from a graph to examine transaction details in a report. To get more information about a particular element in a graph, double-click any pie slice or bar. Double-click again to see even more detail in a report.

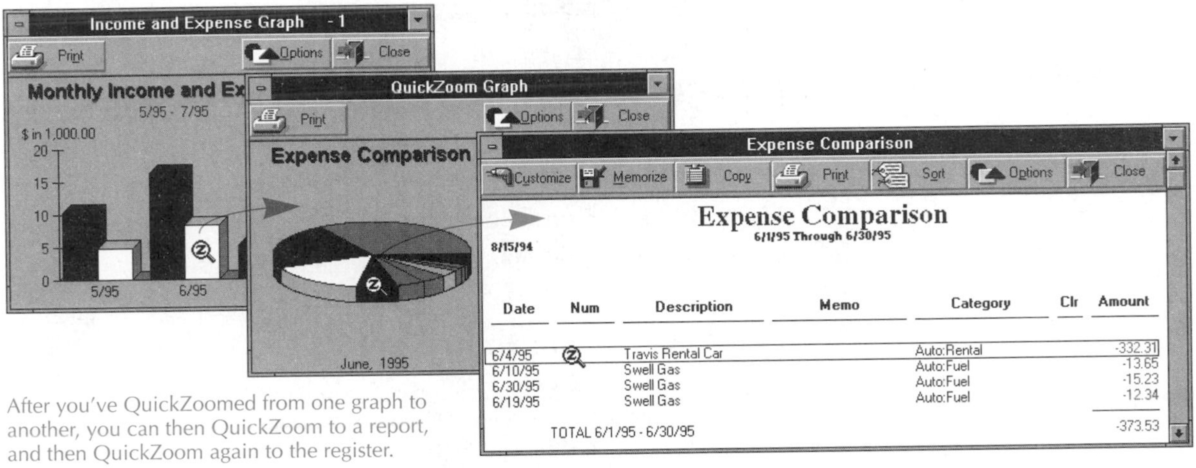

After you've QuickZoomed from one graph to another, you can then QuickZoom to a report, and then QuickZoom again to the register.

- **Data labels.** To see the exact value of a pie slice or bar, click and hold down the right or left mouse button.

Whenever you see the mouse pointer turn into a QuickZoom magnifying glass, you can see the exact value of the element that is below the magnifying glass by holding down the right mouse button.

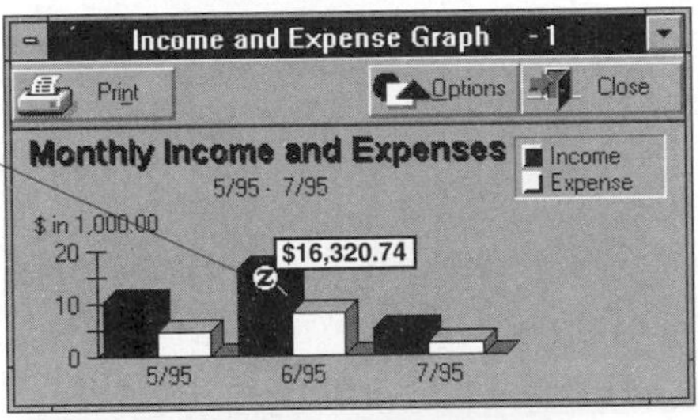

- **Hide data.** To hide a pie slice or bar from the graph, hold down the shift key and click the slice or bar with the left mouse button. To *unhide* an item, create the graph again.

In the first graph, the Tax category is one of the largest slices of the pie. You can hide this category so that you can see other pieces of the pie more clearly.

Hiding categories isn't the same as filtering them. When you filter categories, Quicken doesn't include them in its analysis. When you hide them, Quicken still calculates their value in the graph, but doesn't display the value.

After *hiding* the tax slice, Quicken displays a subtotal instead of a total at the bottom of the legend.

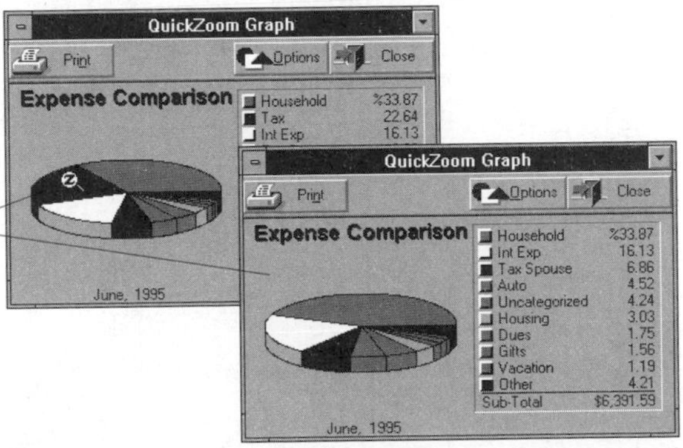

Memorizing and recalling graphs

Once you customize a graph, you can memorize it for future use.

Memorizing a graph

1 **Create and display a graph as described in "Creating a graph" on page 199.**

Or press Ctrl+M

2 **Click Memorize on the Graph button bar.**

Or choose Memorize Graph from the Edit menu.

If you use the same name as an existing memorized graph, Quicken warns that you are about to overwrite an existing memorized graph.

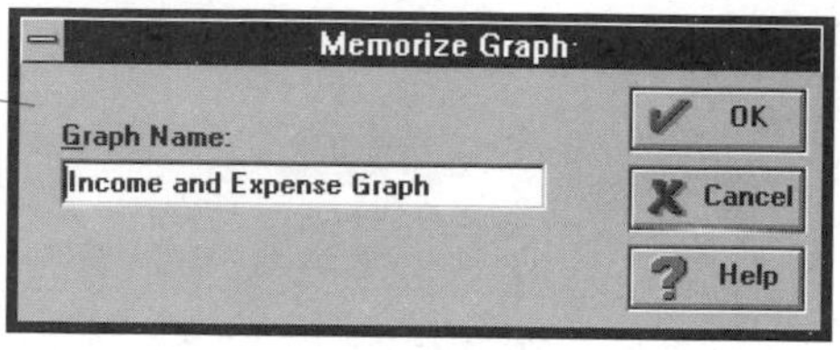

3 **Click OK to memorize the graph.**

Quicken adds the graph to the Memorized Graphs list.

Recalling a memorized graph

After you have memorized a graph, you can recall it.

Choose Memorized Graphs from the Reports menu, select a graph from the list of your memorized graphs, and click Use. At the Recall Memorized Graph window, change any of the graph information that you want to, and then click OK.

To display this list, choose Memorized Graphs from the Reports menu.

To rename a memorized graph, select it and click Edit.

To delete a memorized graph, select it and click Delete.

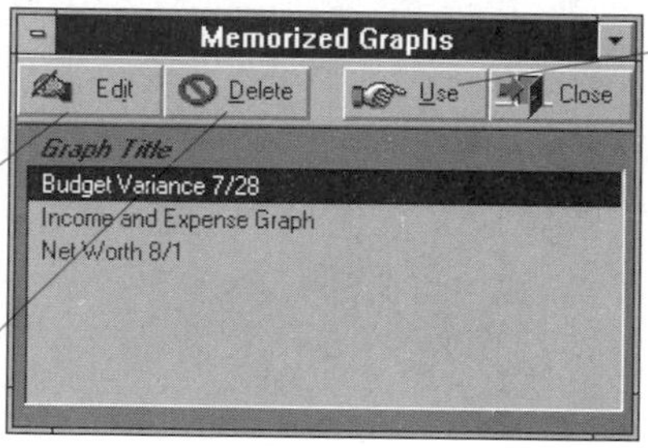

To recall a memorized graph, select it and click Use.

Quicken searches for transactions and prepares the graph as usual.

If you change a memorized graph, you can rememorize it with the same name or you can give the altered graph a new name. If you don't rememorize a graph whose definition you have changed, it retains the original definition the next time you recall the graph.

Income and expense graphs

Income and expense graphs can help you spot spending patterns, highlight your top ten expenses, warn about overspending, and provide comparisons of historical data.

These graphs use the categories you assigned when you entered transactions. Quicken ordinarily includes the value of any subcategory within its parent category; however, when you create the graph, you can select the Show Subcategories in Graph checkbox to break down the graph into subcategory amounts. To break down subcategories after you've created the graph, click Customize and then select Show Subcategories in Graph.

Income and expense graphs help answer these questions:

- Is my income changing over time?
- Is my income covering my expenses?
- Where does my money come from?
- Where does my money go?

The bar graph compares income and expense over time.

This example shows that income was greater than expenses for most months in the date range. Both income and expenses fluctuate from month to month in this household.

If your income was greater than your expenses in the time period covered by the graph, this pie chart shows your top ten expenses relative to (as a percentage of) your total income. The Net Savings slice represents the amount of money that you received and didn't spend.

If your expenses were greater than your income in the time period covered by the graph, this pie chart will show your top ten expenses as a percentage of your total expenses and the Net Savings slice won't appear in the graph. (Graphs don't display negative amounts.)

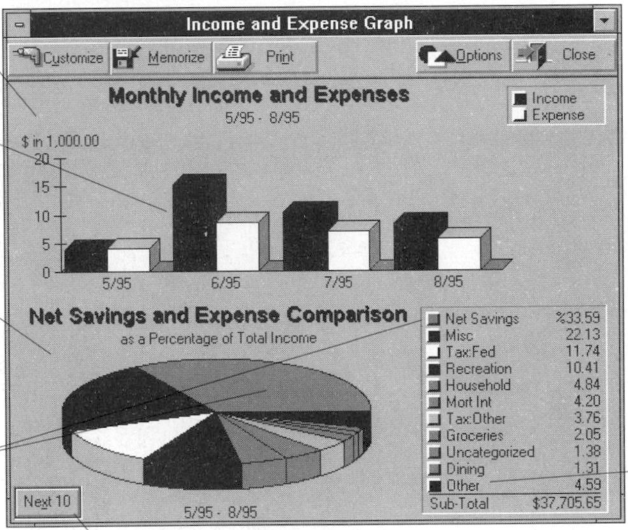

Double-click Other to create a QuickZoom graph of the next ten highest expense categories.

Click the Next 10 button to show the next ten highest expense categories.

Budget variance graphs

Budget variance graphs compare actual spending and income with budgeted spending and income. Quicken calculates the difference in dollars between the two so you can see how you are actually doing compared with your budget.

To create a budget, see Chapter 21, *Creating a budget or savings goal,* on page 235.

You can create budget variance graphs that quickly alert you to potential problem areas such as expenses that are over budget or income that is under budget. Determining how successfully you budgeted this year can help you prepare next year's budget.

Budget graphs help answer these questions:

- Am I staying within my budget from month to month?
- How well do I estimate what I will earn and spend?
- In which categories do I overspend or underspend?
- In which supercategories do I overspend or underspend?

This example shows the budget variance in June through August as favorable.

Favorable means that either actual income was more than budgeted income or actual expenses were less than budgeted expenses.

Unfavorable means that either actual income was less than budgeted income or actual expenses were more than budgeted expenses.

Using the information in this graph, you can pursue the reasons for overspending or underearning by category.

The top graph shows actual net income less budgeted net income.

The bottom graph shows the five categories that are furthest from budget (both over and under).

Favorable actual amounts are displayed in green, and actual amounts which are over budget are displayed in red.

Budget amounts are displayed in yellow.

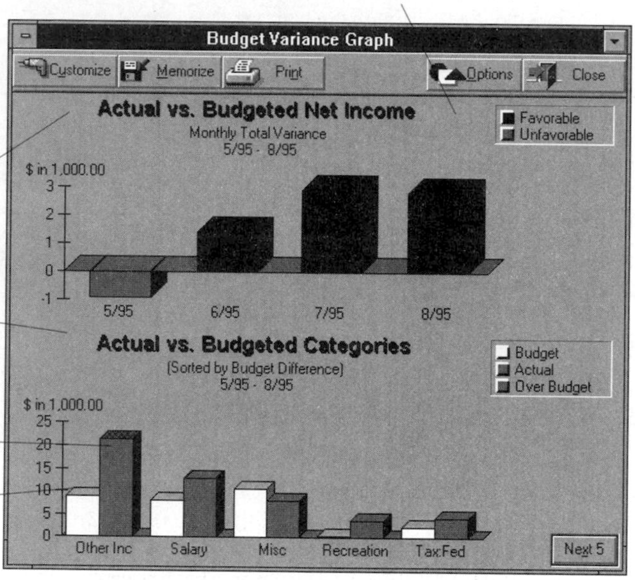

Net worth graphs

Net worth graphs are similar to income and expense graphs, except they use account balances rather than category data. Net worth graphs are also similar to account balance reports.

Create net worth graphs to show the balance of your credit cards or other debts and your bank accounts or other assets over time, or to show if your net worth is changing.

Net worth graphs help answer these questions:

- Do I own more than I owe?
- In what assets do I have most of my money?
- What are my largest debts?
- How is my net worth changing over time?

The graph shows your assets in bars above the x-axis and your liabilities in bars below the x-axis.

Your net worth is the difference between your assets and liabilities.

This example shows that net worth is positive (above zero) and increasing slightly over the date range of the graph.

Double-click a liability bar to see a liability comparison graph as of that month. It shows a breakdown of your individual liabilities as a percentage of your total liabilities.

Double-click an asset bar to see an asset comparison graph as of that month. It shows a breakdown of your individual assets as a percentage of your total assets.

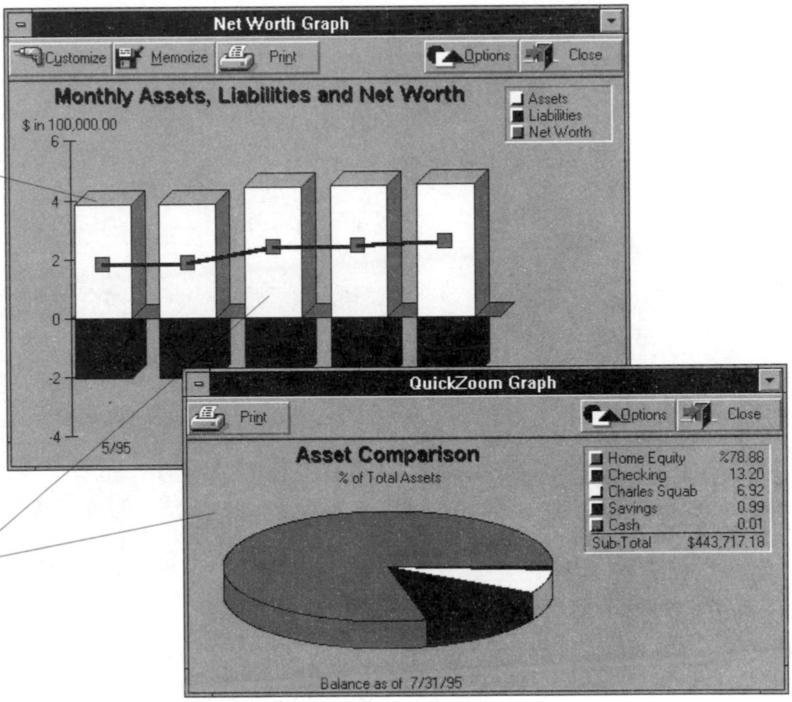

Investment performance graphs

Investment graphs help to evaluate your investment portfolio and the price history of your securities.

Four portfolio value graphs summarize the market value of each security you own, either by type (such as bond, CD, or mutual funds), goal (such as college, retirement, growth, or income), security (such as IBM, Exxon, AT&T, or Intuit), or Quicken investment account (such as Mike's IRA, Karen's IRA, or Merrill Lynch).

The average annual total return graph is a measure of how well your securities are performing.

To update security prices, see "Updating the values of your investments" on page 153.

The price history graph, available from the Portfolio View window, displays the trends in the prices and market value of a particular security.

Investment graphs help answer these questions:

- Is my portfolio value increasing?
- How is my portfolio allocated?
- How are my stocks and bonds doing?

The monthly portfolio value graph shown here is summarized by security. To see the graph summarized by security type, goal, security, or account, click the appropriate button.

This graph summarizes the market value of each security you own.

The total internal rate of return (IRR) is shown on this line. IRR is the annual total return of your securities during the time period you specified for the graph. This value takes into account dividends, interest, and other payment you receive, including increases and decreases in the market value of your securities.

The average annual total return graph measures how well your securities are performing. Taller bars indicate better performance.

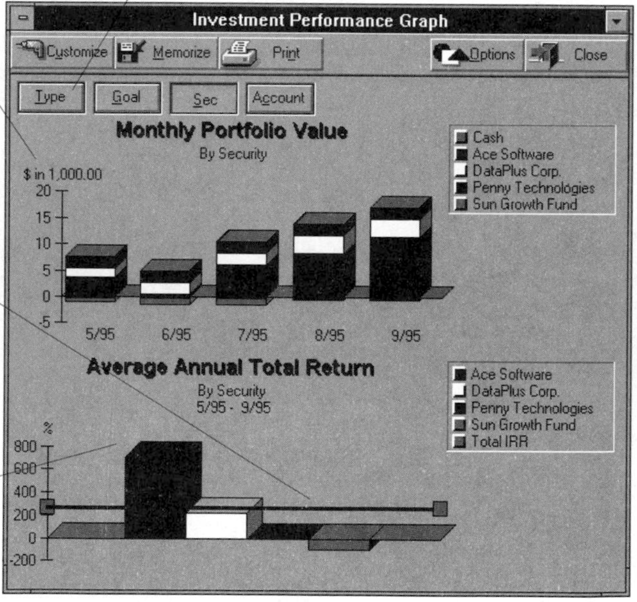

16 Displaying Snapshots of your financial picture

About Snapshots

Quicken Snapshots summarize different aspects of your finances on a single screen, or *page*. Snapshots provide an instant overview of your finances, showing exactly what you want to keep track of. For example, you can create a Snapshot page that displays your current net worth, your monthly income and expenses, and your progress on meeting a savings goal of $4,000 for a vacation to Europe six months from now.

You can display three types of information in Quicken Snapshots:

- Graphs (page 199)
- Calendar notes (page 59)
- Budget, savings, and supercategory budget goals (page 235)

Snapshot graphs can be customized by date range, accounts, and categories.

Creating Snapshots

From the Reports menu, choose Snapshots.

The default Snapshot page appears, named First Page. The default page includes an expense comparison graph, a monthly income and expenses graph, a net worth graph, a dining budget graph, a portfolio value graph, and any calendar notes.

See "Creating a budget from your forecast" on page 254.

If you create a forecast, you can use the Track feature to automatically create a Snapshot page. The Track button creates a budget from your forecast, and also creates a Snapshot page containing your six biggest budget goals.

You can print the Snapshot page. See "Printing Snapshots" on page 215.

Select the Snapshot page to display here.

Snapshots can be graphs, notes, budget goals, supercategory budget goals, and savings goals. You can also display any of the graphs in text format.

Click this button to open a full-size version of the selected Snapshot. Or, double-click directly on the Snapshot.

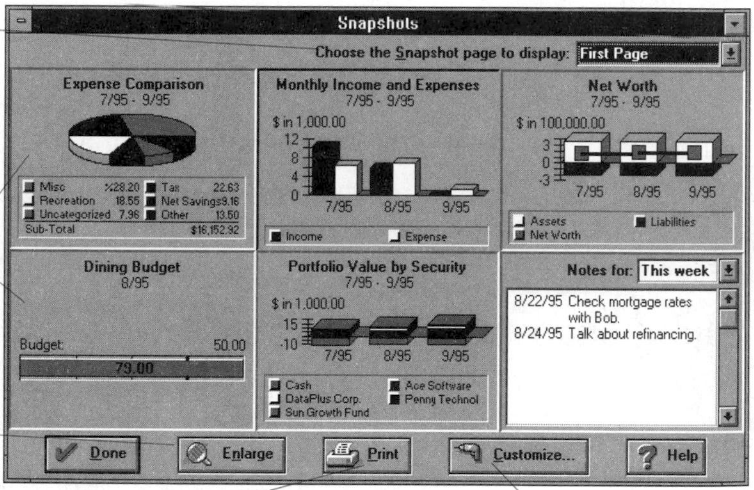

Click here to print the Snapshot page. See "Printing Snapshots" on page 215.

Click here to customize the Snapshot page or add a new page. See "Customizing Snapshots" on page 209.

Customizing Snapshots

From the Quicken Snapshots window, click Customize. You can change the number of Snapshots per page, the placement of the different Snapshots, and the types of Snapshots you want to display.

Select the number of Snapshots to display on the current page.

Select a Snapshot position, and then click the graph or report type below.

You can display most Snapshots in either graph or text format.

Click here to customize dates and filters for graph Snapshots. For savings, budget, or supercategory budget goals, click this button to select a goal.

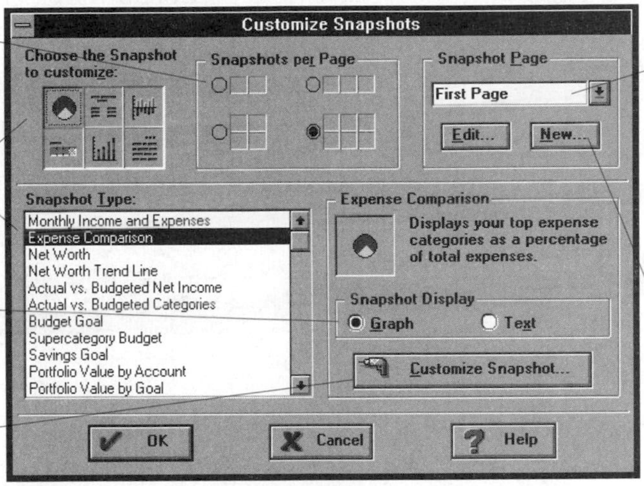

Select the Snapshot page to display.

Click New to create a new Snapshot page, or click Edit to rename or delete the current page.

Adding a Snapshot page

1 **From the Customize Snapshots window, click New under the Snapshot Page list.**

The New Snapshot Page window appears.

2 **Enter a name for the page, and then click OK.**

3 **Select the number of Snapshots per page.**

You can display two, three, four, or six Snapshots on one page. The number selected applies only to the current page. You can select a different number of Snapshots for other pages you define.

4 **Define each Snapshot on the page.**

- Click on the location you want in the upper left corner of the window.
- Select a Snapshot type from the Snapshot Type list.

  Select Graph to display the information as a graph or Text to display a text report. (This doesn't apply to Calendar Notes, Budget Goal, Supercategory Budget Goal, or Savings Goal.)

  You must create Calendar Notes, savings goals, or budgets before you can display them in Snapshots.

See Chapter 15, *Creating graphs,* on page 199.

- (Optional) Click Customize Snapshot to customize the dates and filters for the Snapshot.

5 **Click OK.**

Editing and deleting Snapshot pages

From the Customize Snapshots window, click Edit under the Snapshot Page dropdown list. The Edit Snapshot Pages window appears.

First, select a Snapshot page.

Then:

click New to create a new page,
click Edit to change the name of the selected page, or
click Delete to delete the selected page.

Click OK when you're done.

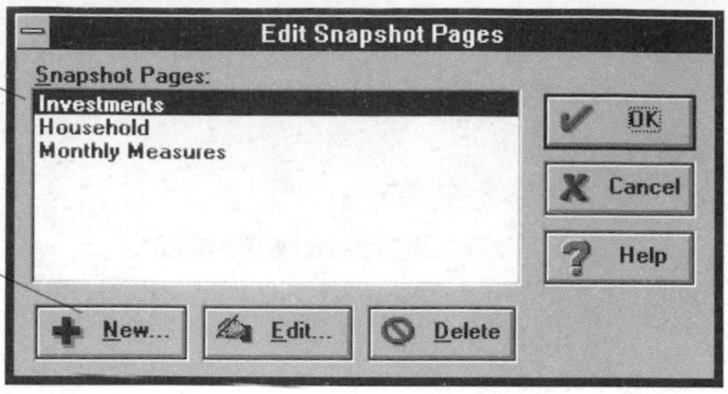

Displaying Snapshots

To display Snapshots, choose Snapshots from the Report menu. The Snapshot page you last selected appears.

For easier access, you may want to add a Snapshots icon to the iconbar. See "Adding an icon to the iconbar" on page 294.

17 Printing reports, graphs, and Snapshots

About printing

Quicken enables you to print your reports, graphs, and Snapshots to many kinds of printers and offers several styles of printing, depending on the capabilities of your printer. You can also print a report to a disk file in one of several different formats.

Setting up your printer

Before you print a report, graph, or Snapshot, you need to select the printer you're going to use. Depending on the capabilities of your printer, you can also select options for printing reports, including fonts, paper size, and page orientation.

When you set up a report printer,* Quicken remembers your settings and uses them whenever you print a report. Printer settings for reports have no effect when you print checks and vice versa. However, Quicken uses your report printer settings when you print graphs, Snapshots, and budget spreadsheets.

---

* Setting up your printer and changing the fonts affect printed reports, not reports as they are displayed onscreen. Report text appears onscreen in Helvetica, and report titles appear onscreen in Times Roman. To change these onscreen fonts, see instructions in Help. (Press F1, click Search, type "fonts," press Enter, and double-click "Changing the font in reports displayed onscreen.")

1 **From the File menu, choose Printer Setup and then choose Report/ Graph Printer Setup.**

Click Settings to select the paper size and page orientation.

Quicken can automatically detect whether your printer is continuous-feed or page-oriented.

Select this checkbox if you want to print negative report amounts in red and graphs in color (if you have a color printer).

To indent your printed text, enter the margins here.

Click Head Font or Body Font to select the fonts Quicken uses when it prints your reports.

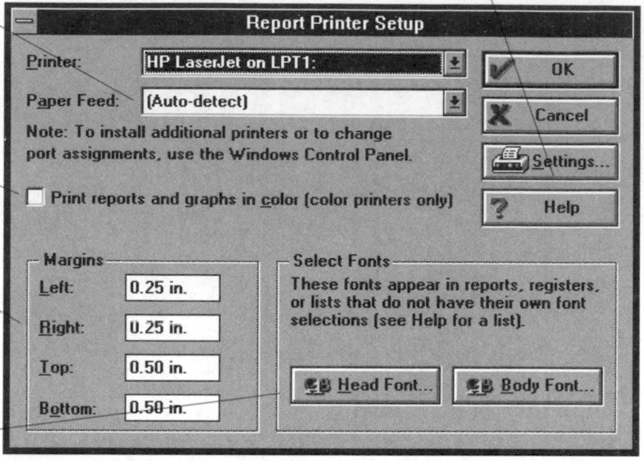

2 **Select the printer you want to use from the Printer drop-down list.**

See your *Microsoft Windows User's Guide* for instructions on installing a printer.

If your printer isn't listed, use the Windows Control Panel to install the printer driver for your printer.

3 **(Optional) Change the paper-feed option for your printer from the Paper Feed drop-down list.**

With Auto-detect selected, Quicken automatically detects whether your printer is continuous-feed or page-oriented. You can force Quicken to use one or the other by selecting another option.

4 **To allow more space or less space between the printed text and the edges of the paper, change the margin measurements.**

5 **To change the font settings for report titles and headings, click Head Font, select the settings you want to use, and then click OK.**

The fonts you can use in your Quicken reports are determined by the fonts available to your printer.

Select the font, font style, and size you want to use for report titles and headings.

For the best printing results, select a font with either a printer icon or a True Type icon (TT) next to it. If you have a dot matrix printer, your reports will print faster if you use a font with the letters CPI after the font name.

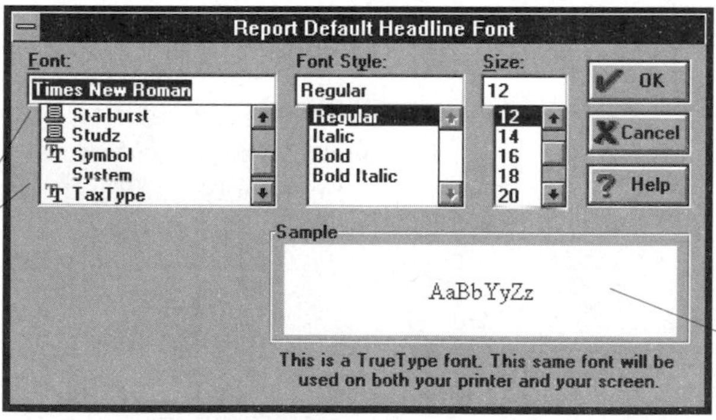

The Sample box shows the currently selected font and size.

6 **To change the font settings for report and graph text, click Body Font, select the settings you want to use, and then click OK.**

Select the report text font settings in the same manner that you selected the report heading font settings.

7 **(Optional) To change the settings for paper size and page orientation, click Settings, select the settings you want to use, and then click OK.**

The options you see on your screen may be different from this illustration, depending on the type of printer you are using.

Use the Paper Size drop-down list to set up the correct size for the paper you want to use.

These options appear only if your printer provides a choice of page orientations. Click Portrait to print your report across the width of the page. Click Landscape to print across the length of the page (which is useful for wide reports). Snapshots only print Landscape.

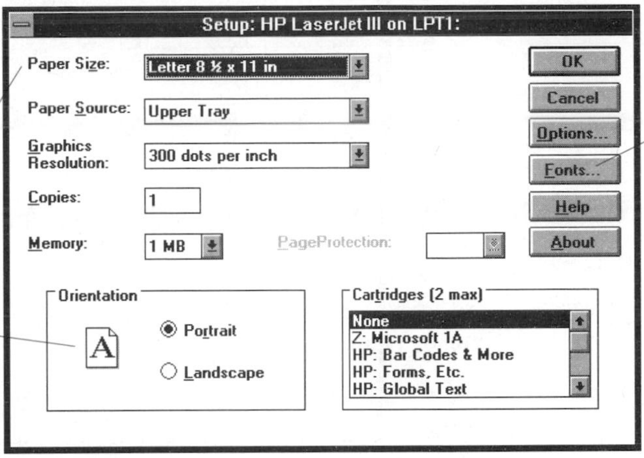

If you see a Fonts button, you can click the button to install fonts for your printer. (Then click Help for instructions.)

8 **Click OK to save the settings for printed reports and graphs.**

Printing reports

Print a report when you want a paper copy or when you want to save the report in a file on your disk.

1 **If you're printing on paper, check that your printer is turned on, is online, and is loaded with paper.**

2 **Create the report you want to print.**

Or press Ctrl+P

3 **Click Print on the report button bar.**

Or, from the File menu, choose Print Report.

4 **Complete the Print Report window, and then click Print.**

Select Printer to print the report on your printer.

Or print to:
A file on disk that you can read into your word processor or other program.

A tab-delimited disk file that can be read by spreadsheets (such as Microsoft Excel).

A comma-delimited disk file that you can read into Lotus 1-2-3 and other spreadsheets.

Enter a page range if you don't want to print all pages.

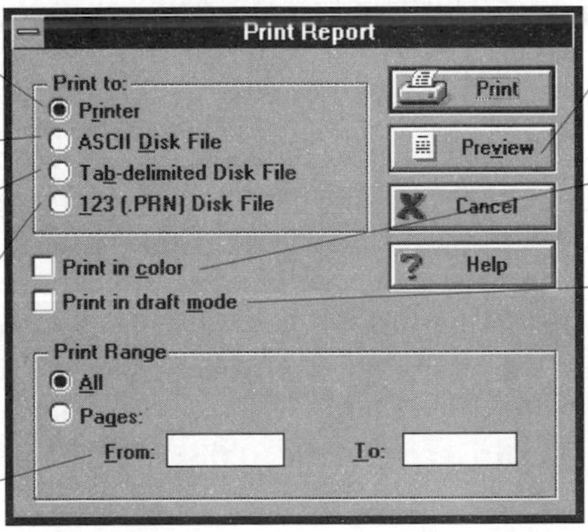

Click Preview to see a preview of what your report will look like when you print it.

Select this if you have a color printer and want negative amounts to print in red.

Select draft mode for faster but less attractive printing.

(You also see this window if you are printing your budget spreadsheet, your registers, your forecast, or any of Quicken's printable lists.)

To preview the printed report, click Preview.

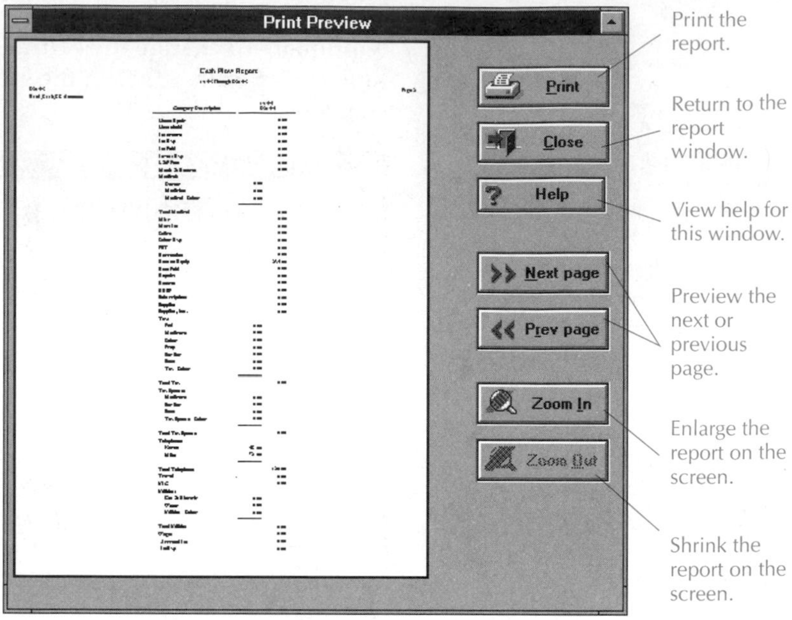
Print Preview
Print
Close
Help
Next page
Prev page
Zoom In
Zoom Out
Print the report.
Return to the report window.
View help for this window.
Preview the next or previous page.
Enlarge the report on the screen.
Shrink the report on the screen.

Printing wide reports

Some reports have too many columns to print completely on a single sheet of paper. Depending on the capabilities of your printer, you may be able to fit the report on a single page by selecting different report printer options:

See "Setting up your printer" on page 211 to change report printer options.

- Select a smaller font size for the report text.
- Select landscape orientation to print horizontally on the page.
- Reduce the left and right margins.

Printing graphs

When you print a graph, Quicken uses the same settings you selected for printing reports. It prints the text in your graph using the report text (body) font settings.

Your printer needs sufficient memory to print a graph successfully at a resolution of 300 dpi (dots per inch) or higher. To set your printer's resolution to 150 dpi or lower to avoid errors from insufficient memory, see "Setting up your printer" on page 211 (step 7). Note: This procedure displays the printer driver window, but you may need to go to an auxiliary window to change the resolution. For example, you may need to click an Options button in the printer driver window to display the auxiliary window.

1 **Make sure your printer is turned on, is online, and is loaded with paper.**

2 **Create the graph you want to print.**

Or press Ctrl+P

3 **From the File menu, choose Print Graph.**

Quicken prints the graph. A printed graph typically looks a little different from the onscreen graph.

Printing graphs in color

If you have a color printer, select the Print reports and graphs in color option in the Report Printer Setup window, as described on page 212.

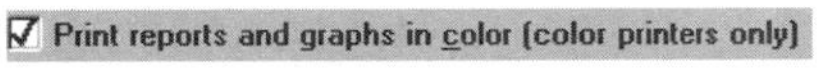

If you don't have a color printer, leave this option unchecked. Quicken prints fill patterns to distinguish between different segments in the graph. However, if you prefer, you can print shades of gray instead of fill patterns by selecting the option.

If monochrome graph printing seems very slow:
If it takes you more than 20 minutes to print a graph on a monochrome printer, try selecting the Print Reports and Graphs in Color setup option. With some printers, this speeds up graph printing.

Printing Snapshots

You can print any page of Snapshots that you create. If you have calendar notes on your Snapshot page that are longer than will fit in the Snapshot, Quicken prints only what fits. Snapshots will only print in landscape orientation.

1 **Check that your printer is turned on, is set to online, and is loaded with paper.**

2 **Display the Snapshot page you want to print.**

Or press Ctrl+P

3 **Click the Print button on the button bar.**

Or, from the File menu, choose Print Snapshots.

Report and graph printing problems and solutions

This section describes some common printing problems and their solutions. If you continue to have problems, see your printer manual or call Intuit's technical support group. (See "Phone numbers" on page 318.)

Problem	Solution
Printer doesn't print.	Check your equipment: • Make sure your printer is turned on and online, and that the cable connection between the printer and the computer is secure. • From the File menu, choose Printer Setup and then Check Printer Setup. Make sure that the correct printer is selected. • Try to print a Windows Write document. Look for Write in the Accessories Program Group. Open it and type a few words. Then, from Write's File menu, choose Print. If the document prints OK, the problem probably lies with your check printer setup.
Printer prints strange characters instead of report text.	From the File menu, choose Printer Setup and then Report/Graph Printer Setup. Make sure the correct printer is selected. If there is a choice of an IBM or an Epson driver, try both, as your printer may be set for the other one.
Printer prints blank pages instead of report text.	Check your settings. • From the File menu, choose Print Report. Make sure draft mode isn't selected. • If you are using Adobe Type Manager, turn it off.
Large fonts aren't aligned on the report page.	Use the same style and size fonts for the headings and the body text.
Printer error occurs before the graph is completely printed. (The printer may report an "out of page memory" error or error 20; Windows may report an "out of paper" error.)	This is common with laser printers that have less than 1 megabyte of memory. Change your graphics resolution setting to 150 dpi (dots per inch) or less. This setting is in the printer driver window. See "Setting up your printer" on page 211. Note: This procedure displays the printer driver window, but you may need to go to an auxiliary window to change the resolution. For example, you may need to click an Options button in the printer driver window to display the auxiliary window.
Some columns of the report print on a different page.	Try changing the font size and the margins, or print in landscape orientation instead of portrait. See "Setting up your printer" on page 211 to change printer options.

18 Preparing your income taxes

Preparing your personal income taxes

Quicken can greatly simplify the preparation of your Federal Income Tax Return (Form 1040) and related tax schedules. Using Quicken helps whether you prepare your own returns or gather the information to submit to a tax preparer. If you categorize your transactions with Quicken income and expense categories throughout the year, you can create reports with the tax information you need in seconds.

See "Transferring Quicken data to tax preparation software" on page 220.

You can also transfer Quicken data directly to Windows or DOS tax software programs, eliminating the need to re-enter financial information when you prepare your taxes.

Setting up categories with tax time in mind

You can set up your income and expense categories in several ways, depending on how you want to report your tax information.

To get these kinds of reports	Set up your category like this
Tax summary reports that group and subtotal transactions in your accounts by tax-related category.	Mark the category as tax related.
Tax schedule reports and capital gains reports that group and subtotal your transactions by tax schedule line item.	Make sure you're set up to use tax schedules and then assign the category to the correct tax schedule line item.
Both tax summary and tax schedule reports.	Mark the category as tax related *and* assign the category to a tax schedule line item. See the Use Tax Schedules with Categories option on page 298.

The tax schedule line items Quicken uses include these forms and schedules:
Form 1040
Schedule A
Schedule B
Schedule C
Schedule D
Schedule E
Schedule F
Form 2106
Form 2119
Form 2441
Form 3903
Form 4137
Form 4684
Form 4952
Form 6252
Form 8606
Form 8815
Schedule K-1
W-2
1099R

Quicken's standard home and business categories are already set up with appropriate tax schedule assignments. Whenever you create a new category, you may need to assign it to a tax schedule line item.

1 **If you want to create tax schedule reports, make sure you've set Quicken to use tax schedules with categories.**

From the Edit menu, choose Options and then choose General.

Make sure that the Use Tax Schedules With Categories checkbox is selected. If it isn't selected, click the checkbox.

2 **From the Lists menu, choose Category & Transfer.**

Or click the Cat List icon on the iconbar.

3 **Select the category or subcategory that you want to be tax related and click Edit.**

If the category isn't already in the list, click New.

4 **If you want to create tax summary reports, select Tax-related.**

5 **If you want to create tax schedule reports, select the tax schedule line item for that category from the Form drop-down list, and then click OK.**

If you want to create tax schedule reports, select the tax schedule line item that the category should report to from the Form drop-down list.

If you want to create tax summary reports, select the Tax-related option.

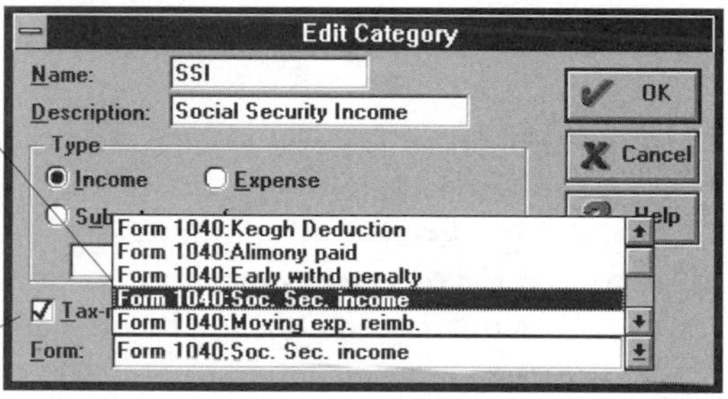

Quicken automatically assigns some categories to tax schedule line items, but if you create your own categories, you may need to assign line items yourself.

Creating tax summary reports

When you want a report that shows the total amount of tax-related income and expenses, create a tax summary report. See "Tax summary" on page 165 for a sample tax summary report. This report initially includes all accounts in the current file except tax-deferred investment accounts (such as 401(k) and IRA accounts).

See Chapter 14, *Creating and customizing reports,* on page 183, for full details of running reports.

Creating tax schedule reports

The tax schedule report lists the exact figures you need to fill in on your 1040 tax form and schedules, with the qualifications listed below. This is the report you should run if you plan to export the information to tax software.

- Check the figures against any limits defined by the IRS, for example, the maximum deduction allowed for IRA contributions. The Quicken tax schedule report simply gives you your personal totals.
- Have already recorded all relevant transactions in Quicken. (If you assign the investment categories _DivInc and _IntInc to Schedule B, the tax schedule report subtotals the amount for each category by investment account but not by security.)

The report gathers figures from all accounts in the current file except tax-deferred accounts (for example, 401(k) and IRA accounts) and from all categories that have been assigned to a tax form and line. Several categories or accounts can contribute to the same figure in the report. For example, the line "Salary" on Form W-2 can include both regular salary and bonuses.

You can run this report at the end of each year or tax period. You can also export tax schedule reports to tax preparation software.

1. **Click the Reports icon on the iconbar.**
2. **Enter a date range that covers the tax period.**
3. **Choose Home and then choose Tax Schedule.**
4. **(Optional) To restrict the report to certain accounts, click Customize and then click Accounts.**

   Select the accounts you want to use. You may need to do this if, for example, your file contains checking accounts for you and your spouse and you are filing separate tax returns. If you exclude an account for which you defined tax form information (for example, your IRA account), the report still lists transfers made into or out of the account if the account at the other end of the transfer is included.
5. **Click OK to create the report.**

   See "Tax schedule" on page 166.

   The resulting report lists your transactions, subtotaled for each tax line on each tax form.

   See "Transferring Quicken data to tax preparation software" on page 220 if you are using software to prepare your tax return.

Creating capital gains reports for Schedule D

If you have investment accounts with realized capital gains (following buy and sell transactions), the tax schedule report doesn't show these realized gains. To obtain figures for your realized gains, run a capital gains report. To get income by security, run an investment income report as described on page 171.

The capital gains report lists your long-term and short-term capital gains transactions in a format suitable for Schedule D.

You can also export capital gains reports to tax preparation software.

1. **Click the Reports icon on the iconbar.**
2. **Enter a date range that covers the tax period.**

3 **Choose Investment and then choose Capital Gains.**

4 **Click Customize.**

5 **In the Report Layout section, select "Short- vs. Long-Term" in the Subtotal By box.**

6 **Click OK.**

See "Capital gains" on page 170 for a sample report.

If you are using software to prepare your tax return, see "Transferring Quicken data to tax preparation software" next.

Transferring Quicken data to tax preparation software

If you use Windows or DOS tax software to prepare your Form 1040, you can use data from Quicken's tax schedule or capital gains report in the program that calculates your tax and prints completed tax forms.

Exporting Quicken for Windows tax data to TurboTax for Windows

See the *TurboTax for Windows User's Guide.*

If you use TurboTax for Windows, you don't need to create the tax schedule report or capital gains report or export it into TurboTax. TurboTax for Windows can read and import Quicken for Windows data without any work on your part.

If you use another type of tax preparation software, you need to follow the steps below.

Exporting Quicken for Windows data to other tax preparation software (including DOS TurboTax)

Quicken writes your tax data to a TXF (Tax Exchange Format) file with a standard format compatible with several major tax preparation programs. Exporting your Quicken tax schedule report or capital gains report to a TXF file eliminates the need to re-enter financial data when you prepare your taxes.

1 **Display the tax schedule or capital gains report as described earlier in this chapter.**

2 **Click the Export button on the Report button bar.**

3 **Enter a filename for the tax schedule or capital gains report in the File Name field.**

The filename must follow the usual DOS rules for filenames (maximum eight characters).

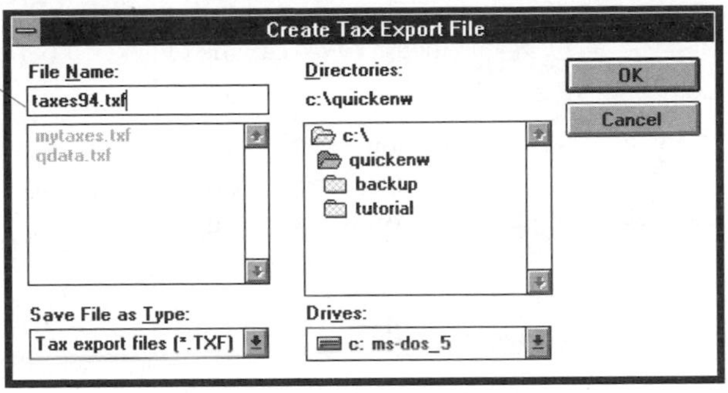

If you created both a tax schedule report and a capital gains report, you must print each report to disk so that you have a separate TXF file for each report.

4 **Click OK.**

Quicken writes the data to the file and closes the Report window. See the instructions that accompany your tax preparation program to use the data file.

Updating your tax form information

Occasionally the IRS changes the information required on IRS tax forms and schedules. When this happens, Intuit provides an updated list of tax form assignments (the TAX.SCD file) to the manufacturers of tax preparation software.

Most changes to IRS tax forms occur in January and very often affect only specialized forms that most people don't need to file. If the IRS makes any changes to the forms you file, however, you will need to obtain a new copy of the TAX.SCD file.

Canadian users: The TAX.SCD file for Canada includes Canadian tax forms and links to WinTax.

If you are a TurboTax for Windows user, your Final Edition will include an updated TAX.SCD file in time for you to file your annual returns.

All you need to do is copy the file to your Quicken directory. (The directory is QUICKENW if you used Quicken's Express Installation to install Quicken.)

Estimating your taxes with Quicken Tax Planner

Quicken Tax Planner lets you:

- Estimate the amount of tax you will owe at year-end.
- Determine if you are withholding the correct amount of tax during the year.
- Determine if you should file quarterly estimated taxes.
- Evaluate the tax impact of major decisions such as buying a home or filing taxes jointly versus separately.
- Analyze your taxes for 1994 or 1995.
- Use tax-related data that you've already entered.

To update the Tax Planner with changes in 1994/1995 tax rates that occur after August 1994, call the Quicken Tax Rate Information line at (415) 858-6081.

Remember that you and your tax accountant are responsible for staying current on tax laws and interpreting their impact on your personal tax situation.

Displaying the Tax Planner window

To open Tax Planner, choose Tax Planner from the Plan menu.

Get your tax-related data into the Tax Planner automatically. You can preview the data first.

Print tax estimates and scenarios.

Calculate and copy values into Tax Planner fields.

Reset values in scenarios to zero.

Create and compare different tax scenarios.

Change tax rates to keep current with tax law changes.

Select the appropriate Filing Status and Tax Year.

These recessed fields are filled in by you.

These fields are automatically calculated by Tax Planner.

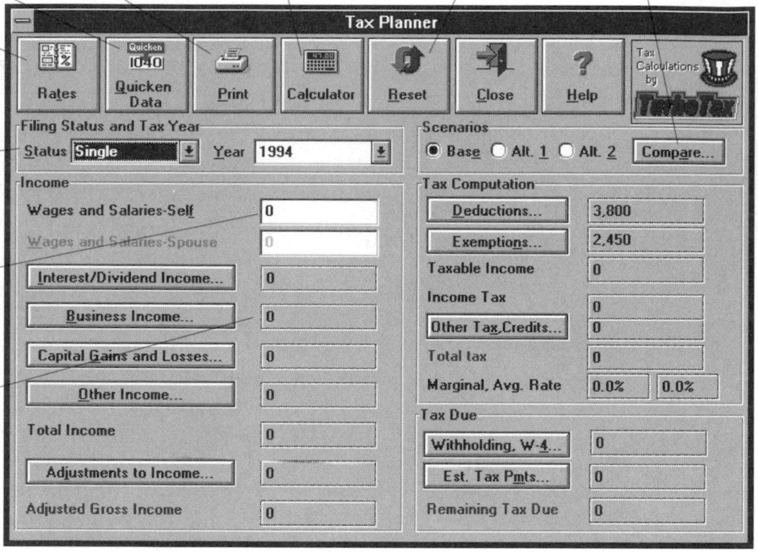

Using the Calculator

To display the calculator, click the Calculator button.

To keep the calculator always on top of the window, click here, then select Always on Top.

Click C to clear the display panel to start a new calculation.

Click Paste to paste the result into the selected field.

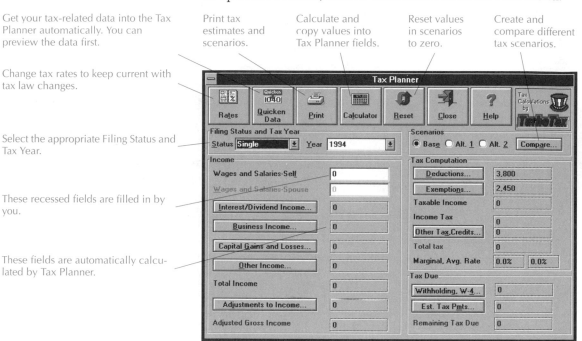

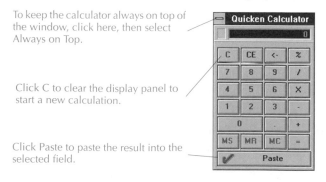

Assembling your tax information

Before you enter information into Tax Planner, assemble all your tax-related "paper" information so you can be sure your tax estimation is comprehensive. This includes:

Income records. Paycheck stubs are usually your best source of income information, particularly in mid-year, since most paycheck stubs show both current and year-to-date earnings and deductions. If you are estimating at year-end, you will also want to assemble your W-2, W-2G, and 1099 wage forms.

Itemized deductions and tax credits records. These include:

- Medical and dental payment records
- Real estate and personal property tax receipts
- Interest payment records for your home mortgage
- Records of payments for child care
- Dependent expenses that may be tax related
- Charitable contribution receipts

Tax publications. You can get them from the IRS, public libraries, and your tax accountant. Most bookstores stock a variety of commercial tax instruction and information books.

Previous tax returns. Copies of your returns from prior years may be helpful for reference. Remember, some figures won't be valid for 1994 or 1995.

See "Tax schedule" on page 166, and "Capital gains" on page 170.

Quicken tax schedule report and/or capital gains report. Run these reports to help you check whether all your tax-related financial information is included in your Quicken files. Otherwise, you'll need to enter some or all information into Tax Planner manually.

Getting tax information from Quicken

Tax Planner uses data from your Quicken file. Open the Tax Planner window by selecting Tax Planner from the Plan menu.

To estimate your 1995 taxes during 1994, you should select Tax Year 1994 in the Planner, and then get your 1994 data. Then change to Tax Year 1995.

---

1 **Click Quicken Data.**

The Preview Quicken Tax Data window appears. Tax Planner imports year-to-date data through the end of the previous month. For example, if you import data on August 4, 1994, Tax Planner imports data from 1/1/94 through 7/31/94.

The tax schedule attached to the imported item. Tax schedules are assigned to categories in Quicken. For example, Schedule A: Charity Contributions is attached to the Quicken category named "Charity." To assign tax schedules to Quicken categories, see "Setting up categories with tax time in mind" on page 217.

The year-to-date amount currently assigned to the item in Quicken.

The field in Quicken Tax Planner where the imported item will go.

Double-click a line to change Annualize from Yes to No, or vice-versa.

The final amount imported into Tax Planner, depending on whether you annualize or not.

Annualize all items or no items.

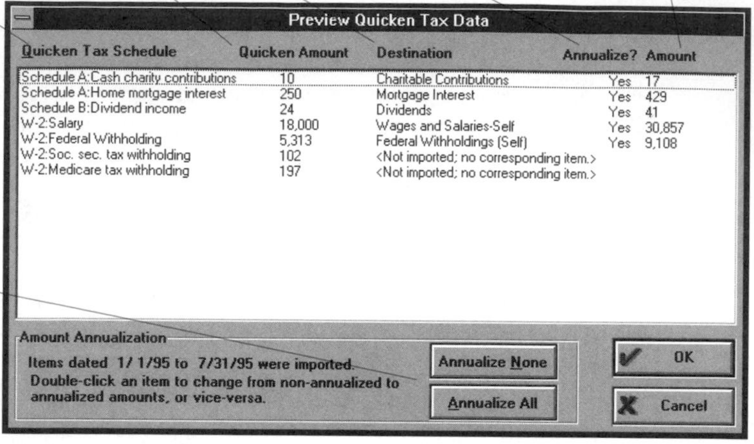

2 **Choose whether to annualize imported items, and then click OK.**

What does annualizing mean?

- If an item shows $10,000 earned through April 31, 1994, annualizing this amount gives you a year-end income estimate of $30,000.
- On the other hand, if you earned $10,000 through April 31, 1994, but don't expect that income to continue at the same rate for the rest of the year, don't annualize that item.

Some tax schedules appear on the Preview Quicken Tax Data window with this note: *Not imported; no corresponding item.* These fields are tax-related Quicken categories that don't affect your 1040 federal tax bill. In the example above, Medicare Tax Withholding is a tax withheld from your paycheck that isn't deducted or otherwise taken into account for your federal taxes.

---

3 **The Quicken Tax Planner window appears with your tax-related information in the appropriate fields.**

4 **Select the appropriate Filing Status and Tax Year.**

5 **Click each of the buttons such as Interest/Dividend Income, Deductions, and Payments and review the information displayed.**

The lower right section of the Tax Planner window indicates either:

- Remaining Tax Due: the tax you are estimated to owe at year end
- Refund Due: the refund you are estimated to receive at year end

Getting help

Detailed instructions for each window are in the onscreen Help. At any window, press F1 for information.

19 Planning with Quicken – an overview

About Quicken's planning tools

Some people want to see what expenses are coming up next month. Others like to plan 20 years ahead to their retirement, or to putting their children through college. Some people like to spend an evening analyzing their budget for the next year. Others just want a simple reminder to pay the rent.

Whatever your planning needs, Quicken offers a complete suite of planning tools, from quick loan calculators to forecasting graphs that can project your account balances for years ahead.

Financial planning calculators
The calculators let you try out "what-if" scenarios for loan planning and refinancing, investment savings planning, college planning, and retirement planning.

See Chapter 20, *Using financial planning calculators,* on page 229.

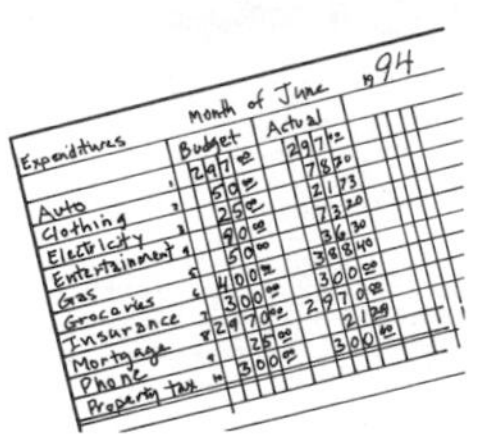

Budget spreadsheet
To keep track of where your money goes, set up a budget spreadsheet. Enter estimated amounts of your income and expenses, and then track them against your plan. A budget lets you plan a whole year ahead at a time. Special graphs and reports show how well you are keeping to your budget.

See Chapter 21, *Creating a budget or savings goal,* on page 235.

Forecasting graph
Project your spending patterns forward up to two years and display your account balances in a graph. Now you can make the right medium-term decisions such as when to buy a new car and how much you can afford to borrow for a new home.

See Chapter 22, *Creating a forecast,* on page 247.

Savings goal account
Put aside some of your earnings for a vacation or other major purchase by setting up a savings goal account, in which you can track how much you have saved.

See "Creating a savings goal" on page 241.

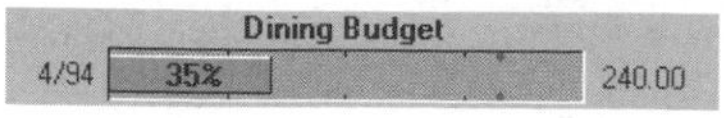

Progress bar
Track how well you've kept to your budget for a particular category or supercategory or how far along you are in attaining your savings goal, with the Quicken progress bar. After setting up a budget spreadsheet or savings goal account, use the progress bar to show your progress wherever you are in Quicken.

See "Tracking your goals with the progress bar" on page 246.

Loan and mortgage tracking
Quicken amortizes your home or car loan and shows you the complete payment schedule. See how much interest and principal you are paying and track the varying payment amounts on an adjustable-rate mortgage. Automatically record the payments in your register each month if you set up the payment as a scheduled transaction.

See Chapter 10, *Tracking loans and mortgages,* on page 105.

Financial Calendar
The Financial Calendar can record your bill payments for you and project your account balances. Schedule either once-only future transactions or recurring transactions such as your paycheck deposit or your house payment. See exactly what's coming up month-by-month.

See Chapter 5, *Using the Quicken Financial Calendar,* on page 49.

Reports, graphs, and Snapshots
Your best aid in planning the future may be to analyze the past. Use Quicken's reports and graphs to help you understand your present situation. Set up Snapshots of your most frequently used graphs so you can see your financial picture at a glance.

See Chapters 13, 14, 15, and 16.

Deciding which tools to use

A good starting point is to decide what you want to get out of Quicken. Try to answer these questions:

- Over what sort of period am I interested in planning? A month? A year? Ten years?
- Do I need to make a detailed analysis of the period ahead? For example, would I like to differentiate between household expenses and leisure expenses? Or is it just the overall financial picture I'm interested in?
- Do I want to improve my money management, for example to plan to make a regular transfer to a mutual fund or savings account?
- Do I have specific goals in mind, such as:
  - saving toward a home loan down payment?
  - affording a higher monthly rent?
  - putting my children through college?
  - planning my investments for retirement?

The following table describes some typical aims of planning, and how best to use Quicken to achieve those aims.

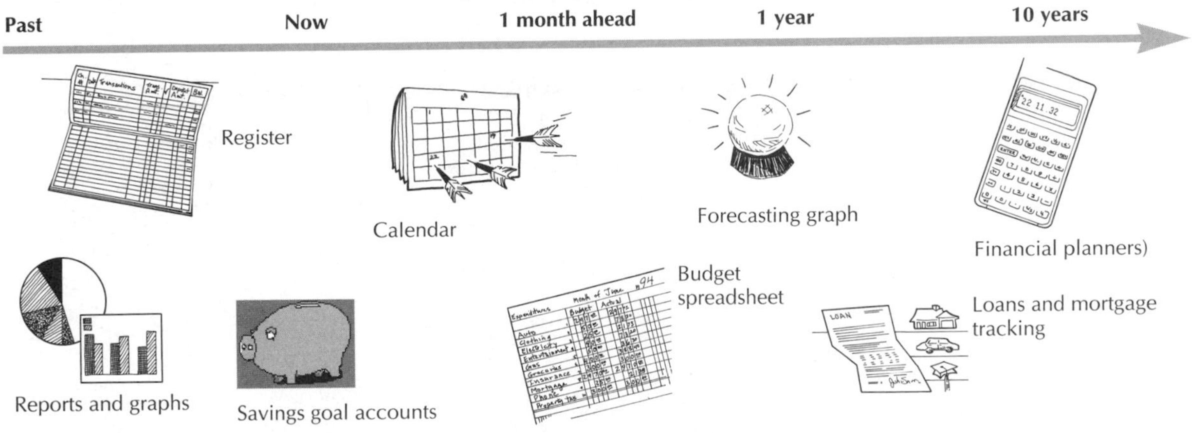

To do this	Use Quicken in this way
Decide what you can afford over the next year or so	Keep your **registers** up to date. Use the **budget spreadsheet** to plan your spending for the next year. Set up the **progress bar** to track your most crucial budget categories. Schedule major income and expenses on the **Financial Calendar**; use the **forecast graph** to view your account balances and future cash flow.
Determine what size loan you can afford	Use the **Loan Planner** (calculator) to play with the numbers. You can also set up the loan in the **View Loans window**, add the loan payment transaction to the forecast, and see the effect on the **forecast graph**. For an adjustable-rate loan, try adjusting the rate for future dates, to see the effect on the payment schedule.
Estimate how much you can set aside each month for long-term investment	Enter figures in **forecasting** and see the results on the **forecast graph**. Select only your cash flow accounts (bank, credit card, and cash accounts). Save different **scenarios** to compare spending and saving habits. Also try using the **Investment Savings Planner** (calculator).

To do this	Use Quicken in this way
Save towards a specific medium-term goal, such as a car, a vacation, or a down payment on a house	Use the **forecast graph** to predict when you will have the money available, or to estimate your spending allowance. To track how much you are managing to put aside, set up a **savings goal account**.
Save towards a specific long-term goal, such as retirement or putting your children through college	Use the **financial planning calculators** to see how much you need to save now.
Automate entry of future transactions as much as possible	Set up recurring **scheduled transactions** for all regular deposits and expenses such as paychecks, rent, insurance. Set up **loans** for all amortized loan payments. **Memorize** any other transactions to ease transaction entry (see Chapter 4, *Memorizing transactions,* on page 41).
Enter transactions in advance; remind yourself to pay bills	First set up amortized **loans** and recurring **scheduled transactions** as described above. Enter once-only future transactions on the **Financial Calendar**.
Leave reminders for yourself (not necessarily finance-related)	Attach notes to the **Financial Calendar**.
Compare current spending to past spending patterns	Create a **comparison report** to compare two periods on a dollar or percentage basis (see page 168 for an example). If you previously set up a budget spreadsheet, create a **monthly budget report** or a **budget variance graph**.

20 Using financial planning calculators

About financial planning calculators

Quicken has five financial planning calculators that let you answer questions such as:

- If I take out a mortgage with a 9.25% interest rate, what will my monthly payments be?
- Is it worth refinancing my mortgage if I plan to move within five years?
- If I invest $10,000 of my savings and receive an annual yield of 12%, what will the value be in five years?
- If I set aside $3,000 each year until my child is 18, will I have enough to pay for a good four-year college?
- If I retire in ten years and put $2,000 into my IRA account every year until then, how much money will I have available?

The formulas Quicken uses to calculate values for the Financial Planning Calculators are in Help. Press F1, click Search, type "formulas", and press Enter.

Calculating loan payments and principal

From the Plan menu, choose Financial Planners and then choose Loan.

Click Payment Per Period to calculate what your payments would be for a loan of a given amount.

For example, if you want to take out a second mortgage on your home to complete some remodeling, you can learn how much your payments would be if you borrow $20,000 for 30 years at a 9% interest rate.

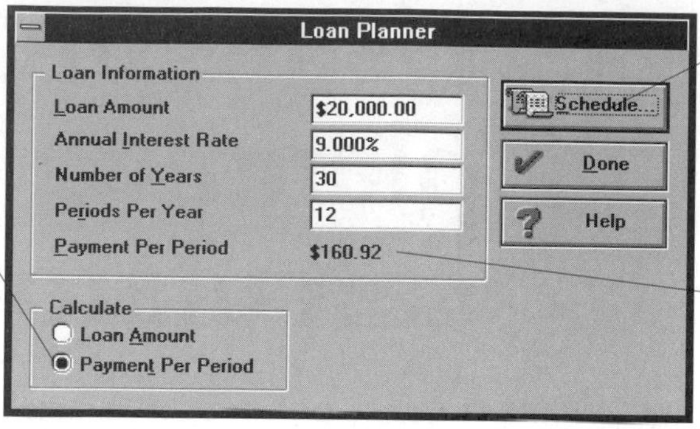

Click to display a payment schedule.

Quicken calculates the payment and displays it here.

Click Loan Amount to calculate how much you can afford to borrow, given a particular payment amount and interest rate.

For example, if you want to buy a new car and can afford to pay $300 a month on a car payment, you can learn how much the total amount (not including a down payment) will be if you borrow for 5 years at a 10.125% interest rate.

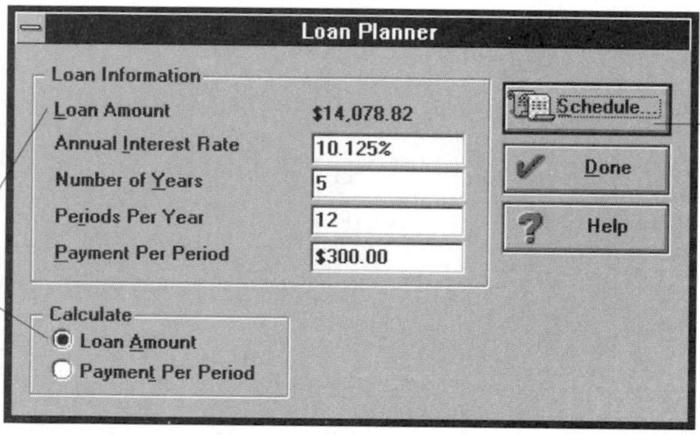

You can see how much of your payment is interest and how much is principal by clicking Schedule.

Scroll in this window to see more of the schedule, or press PgUp or PgDn to move up or down one screen.

Click this button to print the complete payment schedule.

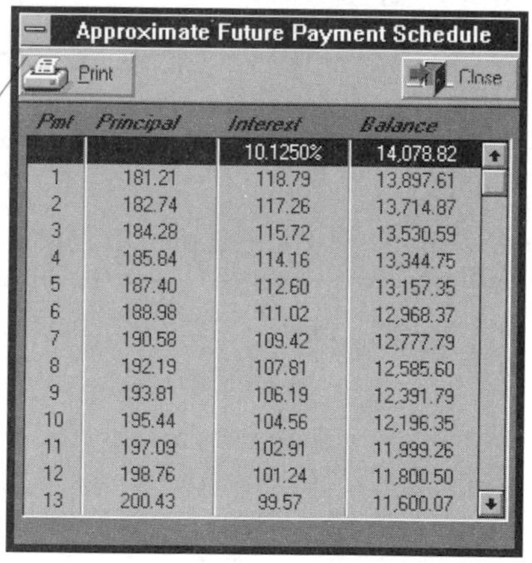
Approximate Future Payment Schedule

Print Close

Pmt	Principal	Interest	Balance
		10.1250%	14,078.82
1	181.21	118.79	13,897.61
2	182.74	117.26	13,714.87
3	184.28	115.72	13,530.59
4	185.84	114.16	13,344.75
5	187.40	112.60	13,157.35
6	188.98	111.02	12,968.37
7	190.58	109.42	12,777.79
8	192.19	107.81	12,585.60
9	193.81	106.19	12,391.79
10	195.44	104.56	12,196.35
11	197.09	102.91	11,999.26
12	198.76	101.24	11,800.50
13	200.43	99.57	11,600.07

How many more loan payments?

If you prepay the principal on a loan, you may wonder how long it will take to pay off the loan. Follow these steps:

- In the Approximate Payment Schedule window, scan down the Interest column until you find the interest amount that most closely matches the interest due on your next payment.
- Notice the number of that payment.

- Subtract that payment number from the number of the last payment to get the number of payments left.
- Divide by twelve (Periods Per Year) to get the number of years remaining.

Calculating the cost of refinancing a loan

From the Plan menu, choose Financial Planners and then choose Refinance.

Quicken's refinance planner determines whether it makes sense to refinance your current mortgage. Although the new mortgage may have a lower interest rate, you also need to look at the points charged by the lender and how long you plan to stay in the house. If you plan to stay only one more year, the lower interest rate may not offset the cost of getting the new loan.

For example, suppose you are currently paying $1,750 each month, and you want to apply for a new mortgage with an 8% interest rate. The lender is charging 1.75 points (1.75%), and your loan broker has estimated closing costs of $3,000. You plan to stay in the house at least two more years.

Quicken compares your current mortgage with the new mortgage and tells you how long it will take to break even—that is, recoup your costs.

Enter your total payment here, including any impound or escrow amount.

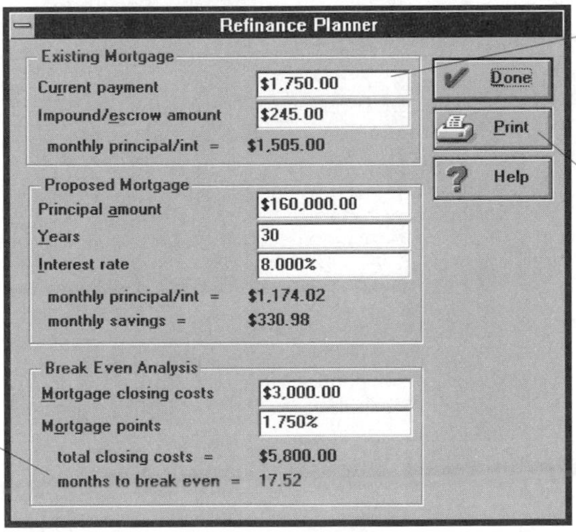

Click Print to print the contents of this window.

Quicken calculates that it would take you 17.52 months to break even. Because you plan to be in the house for at least 24 months, refinancing looks like a good deal.

Planning your investment savings

From the Plan menu, choose Financial Planners and then choose Savings.

Click Opening Savings Balance to calculate how much money you need to begin with to reach a financial goal.

Click Regular Contribution to calculate how much you need to contribute to your savings to reach your goal (the number you enter in the Ending Savings Balance field).

Click Ending Savings Balance to calculate the future value of your savings, given a certain period of time, a consistent level of contributions, and an expected inflation rate.

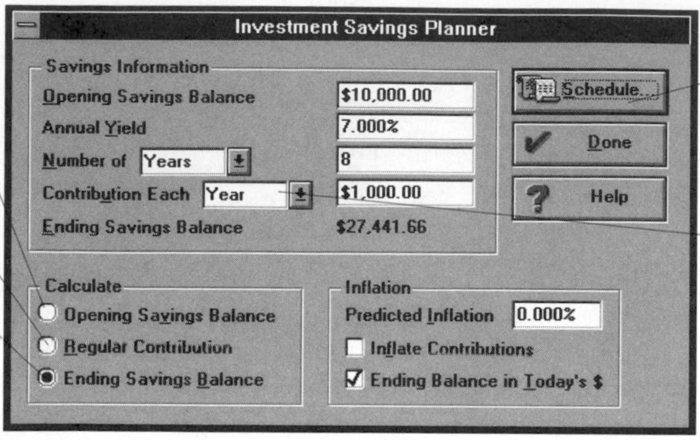

Click to display a deposit schedule.

Calculate the contributions on a weekly, monthly, quarterly, or yearly basis.

The Ending Savings Balance shows the amount in today's dollars. Because of the effects of inflation, ten dollars buys more today than ten dollars will buy thirty years from now.

For example, if you currently have $10,000 saved and you contribute $1,000 to your account each year (with a 7% yield), your investment grows to $27,441.66 in eight years. However, if you estimate that inflation will average 4%, that amount will buy only $20,051.36 worth of goods (in today's terms).

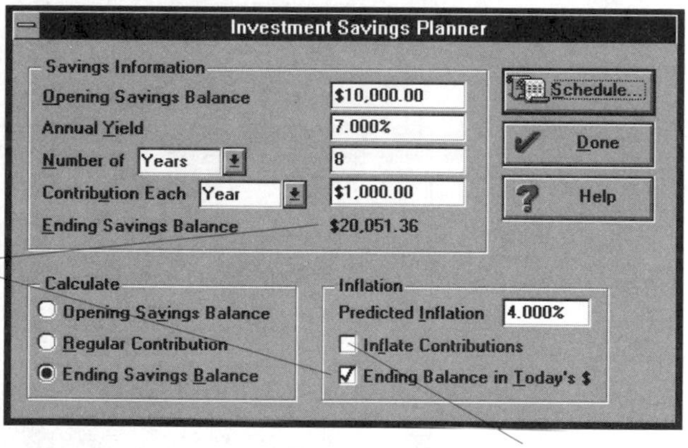

The rate of inflation affects what each of your contributions is really worth. To counteract the effects of inflation on your contributions, you may want to increase your contributions to the investment account by the same rate of inflation. Select Inflate Contributions.

After selecting Inflate Contributions, click Schedule to see how the contributions are adjusted. To keep up with a projected 4% inflation rate, you must increase your $1,000 contribution every year to $1,315.93 by the end of eight years.

Click this button to print the complete deposit schedule.

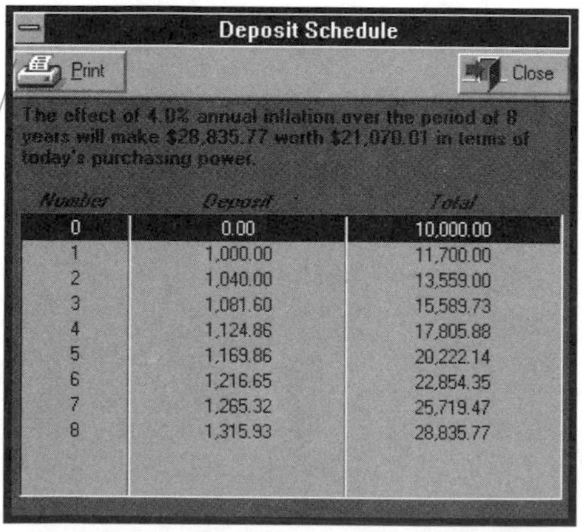

Planning for college expenses

From the Plan menu, choose Financial Planners and then choose College.

Select Annual College Costs to calculate the level of tuition you can afford given your present savings and the number of years until your child goes to college.

Select Current College Savings to calculate what you need to have put away already today given a certain tuition, annual yield on your investment, and the number of years until your child attends.

Select Annual Contribution to calculates how much you need to save each year to pay college expenses when your child is ready to attend.

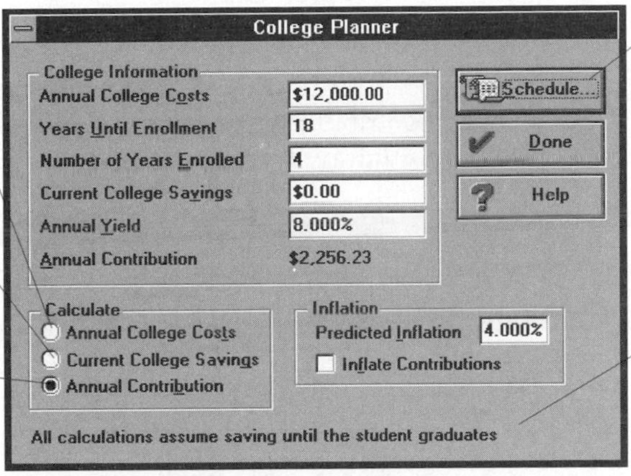

Click to display a deposit schedule.

Quicken expects you to continue saving while the student is attending college.

For example, suppose your child is four years away from attending college. You have $12,000 already saved and figure you can contribute $5000 per year for the next eight years (four years before your child attends college, and four years while your child is in college). Enter these numbers into the College Planner and Quicken calculates that you can afford an annual tuition of over $13,000 in today's dollars.

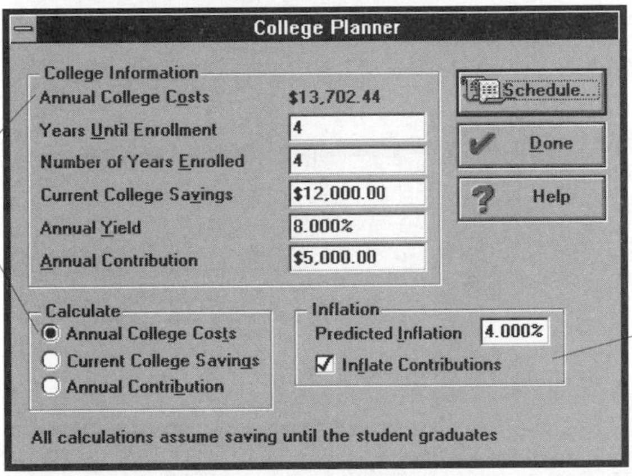

You can inflate contributions like you can in the Investments Savings Planner. See "Planning your investment savings" on page 232.

The Deposit Schedule shows the deposits you need to make while your child is in high school and in college.

All of Quicken's calculations are conservative: this Deposit Schedule assumes that each deposit isn't made until the end of the year, and that each tuition payment is made at the beginning of the year.

Click the Print button to print the complete deposit schedule.

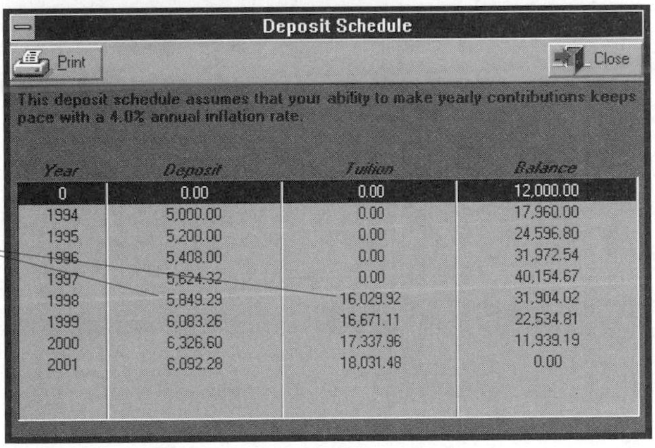

Saving for retirement

From the Plan menu, choose Financial Planners and then choose Retirement. The Retirement Planner looks at one retirement account at a time to project how much income that account will provide in your retirement.

For example, suppose you are 38 years old and plan to retire at age 65. Your IRA account currently has $20,000 in it and you plan to contribute $2,000 to it annually until you retire. You plan to withdraw from the account until age 85.

If this retirement account is tax-sheltered (for example, an IRA or Keogh account), click Tax-Sheltered Investment. Quicken presets the Retirement Tax Rate at 15%.

If it isn't tax-sheltered, click Non-Sheltered Investment. Quicken presets the Retirement Tax Rate at 15% and the Current Tax Rate at 28%.

Click Current Savings to calculate the amount you need to start with to meet your retirement goal.

Click Annual Contribution to calculate how much you need to contribute to your retirement account each year to meet your goal.

Click Annual Retirement Income to calculate how much a particular investment will be worth given your estimated tax rate and all contributions.

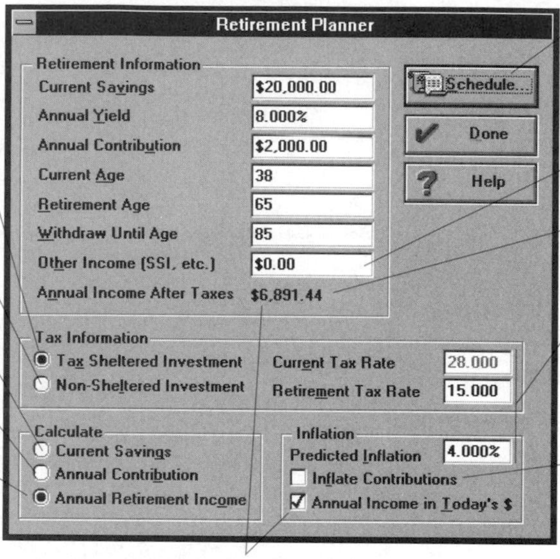

Click to display a deposit schedule.

Enter the annual (not monthly) amount of other retirement income you expect to receive.

Quicken shows the after-tax income in today's dollars.

You can change these preset percentages.

You can inflate contributions like you can in the Savings Planner. See "Planning your investment savings" on page 232.

Clear this bottom checkbox to show the income in future dollars.

When Quicken calculates your pre-tax income, it shows the amount in future dollars. Because of the effect of inflation, each dollar you receive in the future is worth less (has less buying power) than a dollar you receive today. Consider this when you are planning retirement income. What sounds like a huge sum of money may be reduced to a moderate sum when you account for inflation.

Click this button to print the complete deposit schedule.

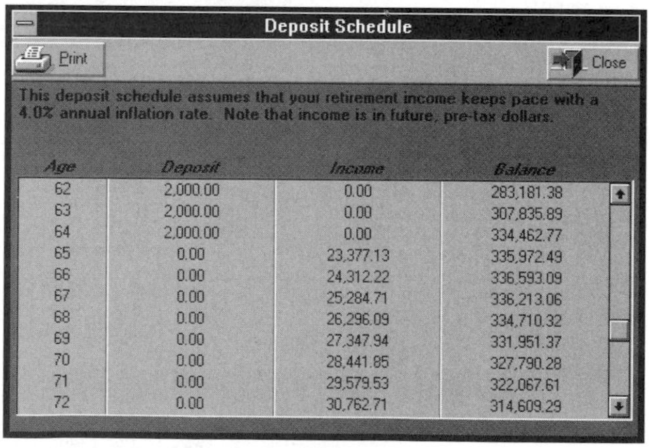

Age	Deposit	Income	Balance
62	2,000.00	0.00	283,181.38
63	2,000.00	0.00	307,835.89
64	2,000.00	0.00	334,462.77
65	0.00	23,377.13	335,972.49
66	0.00	24,312.22	336,593.09
67	0.00	25,284.71	336,213.06
68	0.00	26,296.09	334,710.32
69	0.00	27,347.94	331,951.37
70	0.00	28,441.85	327,790.28
71	0.00	29,579.53	322,067.61
72	0.00	30,762.71	314,609.29

This approximate schedule shows how your contributions grow and how much income you can withdraw given your estimated life span.

21 Creating a budget or savings goal

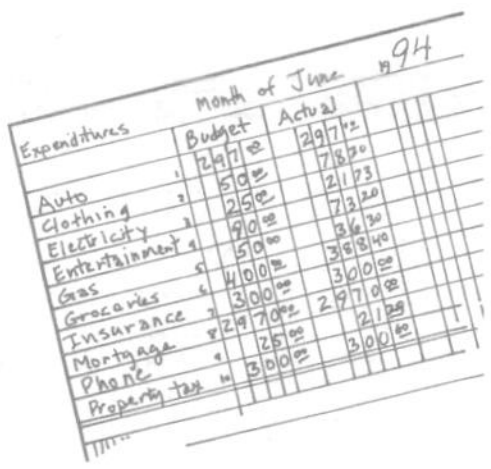

About budgets

A *budget* lets you set a goal for the amount of money you want to spend in a particular category (for example, $200 for dining per month), and then compare it to the actual amount you spend.

Before you create a budget in Quicken, you must first set up categories (see "Setting up categories and subcategories" on page 10).

Follow these steps to create a budget:

- **Enter budget amounts.** See the next section.
- **(Optional) Set up supercategories.** See page 239.
- **(Optional) Customize the budget display.** See page 240.

After you create a budget, you can create budget reports and graphs to track your progress. See page 241.

Entering budget amounts

You can enter budget amounts by hand (see below), or have Quicken automatically create them by using data from your accounts (see the next section).

1 **From the Plan menu, choose Budgeting.**

Depending on the number of categories you use, you probably need to scroll to see the entire list.

Your income categories appear at the top of the Budget window. Your expense categories appear below (not shown here).

The total budgeted amounts *for all categories each month* are in the Total rows at the bottom of the window.

The total budgeted amounts *for each category* are in the Totals column on the right side of the window.

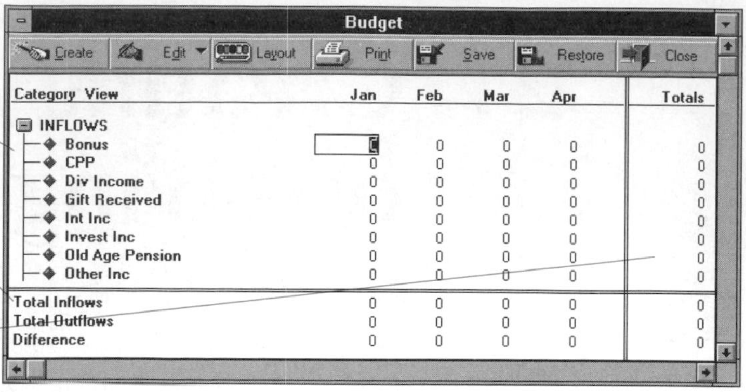

2 **To enter a budget amount by hand, select its cell and type an amount. Use these keys:**

Key	Action
Home	Move cursor to the beginning of the current cell
End	Move cursor to the end of the current cell
Enter	Move down one category (same period)
Shift+Tab, Left Arrow	Move left one column in the same category
Tab, Right Arrow	Move right one column in the same category
Ctrl+Left Arrow	Move left by page within the budget data
Ctrl+Right Arrow	Move right by page within the budget data
Home+Home	Move left to the first column in the same category
End+End	Move right to the last column in the same category
Up Arrow	Move up one category in the same column
Down Arrow	Move down one category in the same column
Ctrl+Home	Move up to the first category in the same column
Ctrl+End	Move down to the last category in the same column
PgUp	Move up by page within the budget data
PgDn	Move down by page within the budget data
Esc	Undo the last entered amount

Budget amounts appear in different colors:

To budget $200 a month to be *spent* in the category Dining, select a cell in the Dining row and type 200. When you Tab to another cell, the Dining amount changes to -200 and is shown in red on the screen.

To budget $100 a month to be *received* in the category Bonus, select a cell in the Bonus row and type 200. This amount remains positive and black on the screen.

3 **Click Save on the Budget button bar to save your changes.**

4 **To print the budget, click Print on the Budget button bar.**

Automatically creating budget amounts

Instead of entering budget amounts by hand, you can have Quicken automatically enter them, using data that you've already entered into your account registers.

Caution: If you autocreate budget amounts and then save the budget, Quicken overwrites any budget amounts you have already entered for the selected categories.

1 **Click Create on the Budget button bar.**

2 **Complete the Automatically Create Budget window.**

Round off values to the nearest $1, $10, or $100.

Click Use Monthly Detail to copy actual income, expense, and transfer amounts from any number of months up to 12 to the same months in the budget. If you are budgeting by quarter or year, Quicken copies the actual monthly amounts to their corresponding periods. For example, Quicken copies actual data for January, February, and March to Q1 of a quarterly budget.

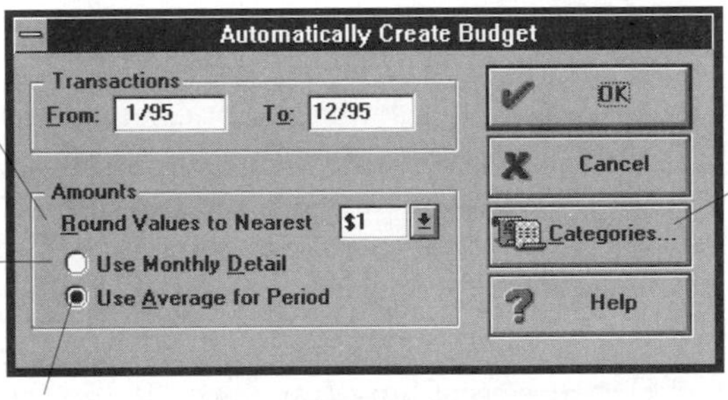

(Optional) Click here to restrict the budget to specific categories. Otherwise, Quicken copies amounts for all categories.

Click Use Average for Period to copy monthly averages for income, expense, and transfer amounts based on the months you specified in the date range. If you are budgeting by month, Quicken enters the average amount in every month. If you are budgeting by quarter (or year), Quicken enters three (or 12) times the monthly average in every period.

3 **Click OK.**

Quicken overwrites any budget amounts you entered with data from your accounts. To restore the budget to the way it was when you first opened the Budget window, click Restore in the Budget button bar.

4 **Click Save on the Budget button bar to save your changes.**

Setting up an item that recurs at two-week intervals

You may have a category or transfer item that you enter into Quicken every two weeks, such as the deposit of your paycheck in a checking account. Quicken can budget your salary income at the correct two-week intervals.

1 **Select the category row for the recurring item.**

2 **Click Edit on the Budget button bar and choose 2-Week.**

Make sure the correct income or expense category is displayed. If not, click Cancel and go back to step 1.

Enter the amount you receive or spend every two weeks.

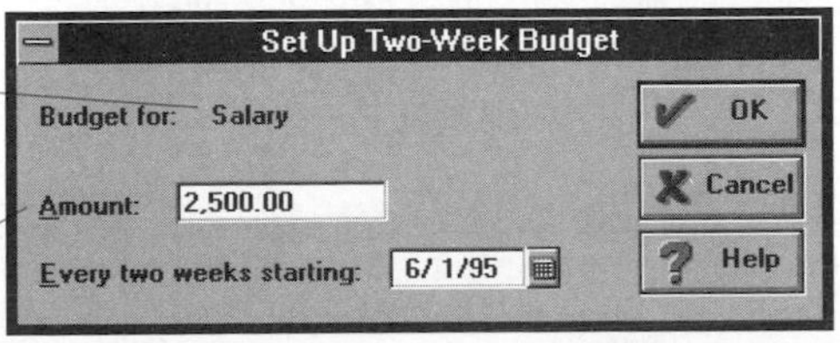

3 **Enter the amount you want to budget in two-week intervals for the selected category.**

4 **Enter the starting date for the first two-week interval.**

To set up Salary as a two-week budget category for the rest of the year, enter the date of your next payday. To budget at two-week intervals for the entire year, enter the date of the first payday in January.

5 **Click OK.**

Quicken fills in budget amounts calculated at two-week intervals from the starting date to the end of the year in the same row.

Setting up budget amounts for a transfer

Besides setting up budget amounts for categories, you can also set up budget amounts for transfers between accounts. For example, you can enter a budget amount for a transfer from a checking account to a savings account. Budgeting transfers can give you a more complete picture of your cash flow.

To show transfers, click Layout on the Budget button bar and then select Show Transfers. (To hide transfers, clear Show Transfers.)

Then to budget a monthly transfer of $200 from an account called Checking to an account called Savings, scroll down the Budget window until you see FROM Checking. Enter 200 for its amount. Then scroll down to the bottom of the Budget window until you see TO Savings, and enter 200 for its amount.

Editing budget amounts

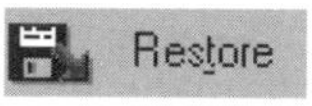

Use the Edit and Restore buttons on the Budget button bar to enter or change budget amounts.

To do this	Do this
Copy a budget amount from the current cell to all cells to the right in the same category	Select the amount you want to copy, click Edit, and choose Fill Row Right.
Copy all budget amounts in the current column to all the columns to the right	Place the insertion point in the column to be copied, click Edit, and choose Fill Columns. For example, you can copy all amounts for January to the rest of the months of the year when you click Fill Columns. If your insertion point is in the March column when you click this button, the amounts in January and February won't be affected.
Erase all amounts for the currently selected category	Click Edit and choose Clear Row.
Erase all amounts for all categories, and start with a blank budget	Click Edit and choose Clear All Budgets.
Restore the budget to the way it was when you last saved the budget	Click Restore.
Copy budget amounts to another Windows program, such as Microsoft Excel for Windows	Click Edit and choose Copy All. The data is copied in a tab-delimited format, compatible with many spreadsheet programs. Switch to the other program and use the program's Paste function to copy the data in.

Using supercategories

For a greater level organization in your budget, use *supercategories*. A supercategory is simply a grouping of categories. This is useful, for example, if you want to group the categories Dining and Groceries under the supercategory Food. You can then enter a single budget amount for Food. Or, you can track both the income and expenses of a small hobby with a single supercategory.

Displaying supercategories

In the Budget window, click Layout. Select Show Supercategories and click OK.

This shows you are in supercategory view.

Supercategories

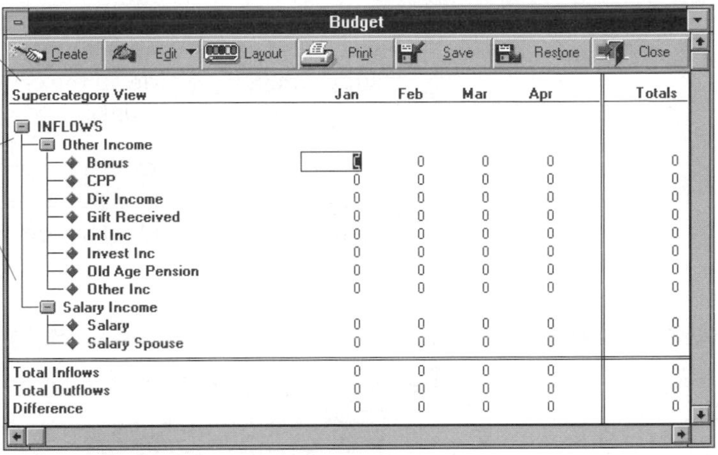

Editing the supercategory list

The preset list of supercategories is:
Discretionary
Non-Discretionary
Other Income
Salary Income

You can customize the list of supercategories by adding new supercategories, deleting unused ones, or renaming existing ones.

1 **Click Edit on the Budget button bar, and choose Supercategories.**

2 **Complete the Manage Supercategories window, then click OK.**

See "Setting up supercategories" on page 14 for more information.

The first category you assign to a new supercategory determines the supercategory type; if the first category is an expense category, then the supercategory becomes an expense supercategory.

Assigning a category to another supercategory

Quicken presets the list of categories that are assigned to each supercategory. To reassign a category to another supercategory:

You can also assign categories to supercategories in the Manage Supercategories window. From the Budget window, click Edit and choose Supercategories.

1 **In the Budget window, click on the name of the category you want to reassign, and hold the left mouse button down.**

If you don't see the category you want, scroll down the Budget window until you see Unassigned. All categories not assigned to a specific supercategory are listed there.

Categories are listed under a supercategory in this order:
Supercategory - Other
Income categories
Expense categories
Account transfers

2 **Move the cursor to the supercategory where you want to assign the category, and release the mouse button.**

The category appears under the new supercategory.

3 **Click Save on the Budget button bar to save your changes.**

You can also use the procedure above to move supercategories between INFLOWS and OUTFLOWS. All categories and subcategories assigned to a supercategory move with it.

Setting up a budget amount for a supercategory

You may want to budget a single amount for a supercategory, instead of entering an amount for each category in it. Click the supercategory to hide all the categories beneath it. Then enter a budget amount as usual.

If you hide categories in a supercategory, and then change the budget amount for that supercategory, the difference appears in the "Other" category in that supercategory.

Changing the display of a budget

You can change the way your budget looks in several ways.

Click Layout on the Budget button bar.

If you enter budget amounts by quarter or year, and then switch to monthly format, Quicken distributes the budget amounts evenly across the months in the period, with any remainder included in the last month. For example, if you budget $301 for the first quarter of the year and then switch to monthly format, Quicken distributes $100 each to January and February, and $101 to March.

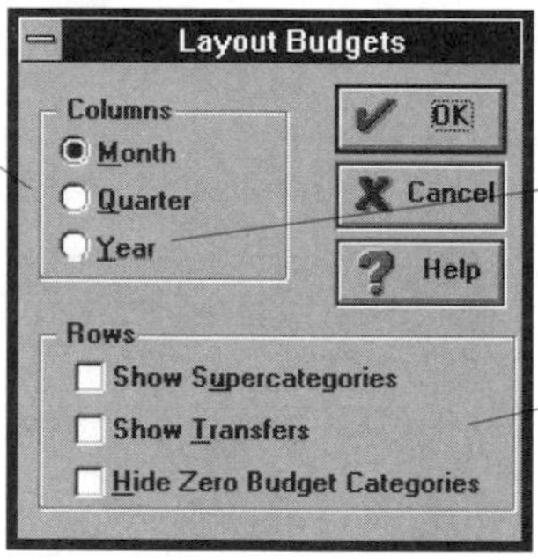

To specify a fiscal year instead of a calendar year, see page 298.

Show or hide supercategories, transfers, and zero budget categories. These options help you "tidy up" your budget to show only the data you want to see.

Collapse and expand rows. In the Budget window, you can collapse (hide its categories) or expand (show its categories) any supercategory by clicking it.You can also collapse and expand INFLOWS, OUTFLOWS, and categories with subcategories in the same way.

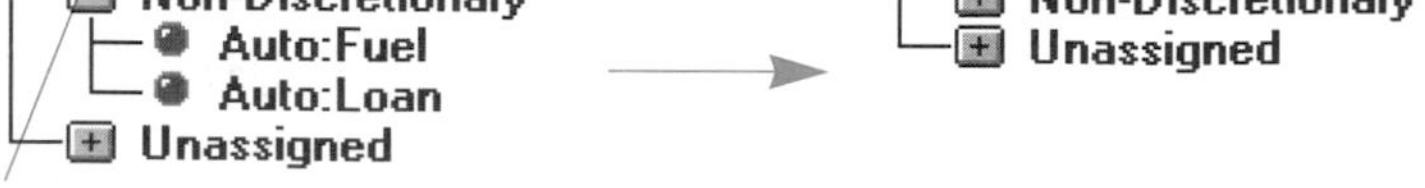

Click any row with a minus sign... ...to hide a supercategory's categories. Click any row with a plus sign to display the categories.

QuickScroll. In the Budget window, drag the scroll box in the scroll bar to show a box in which the names of categories appear and disappear as you scroll. When you see the category name you want in the box, release the scroll bar. The category row will appear at the top of the window.

If your screen looked like the one below, releasing the mouse button would make the line "Groceries" appear at the top of the Budget window.

QuickScroll displays categories in your budget as you drag the scroll box.

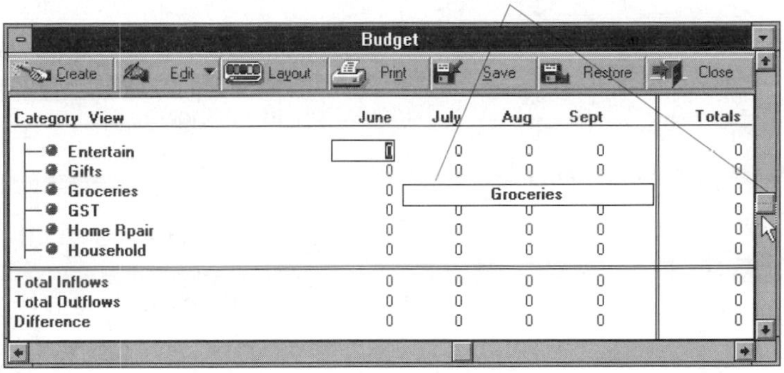

Creating budget reports and graphs

To use budget reports and graphs, you must first categorize your transactions (see "Assigning categories to transactions" on page 21), enter budget amounts for those categories (see page 235), and enter transactions with those categories.

You can print the budget spreadsheet by clicking Print on the Budget button bar. You can also print a budget report or graph that compares the amounts you entered in the budget with the actual amounts you've spent or received.

Quicken has two types of budget reports:

Budget report (Custom)	Monthly budget report (Home)
Is a variation of the basic summary report. See page 181 for an example.	Is a variation of the basic budget report. See page 163 for an example.
Compares the money you spend and receive in a specific date range with your budget amounts for each category and transfer account.	Compares the money you spend and receive in a specific date range with your budget amounts for each category and transfer account.
Calculates the difference between the actual and budgeted amounts for each category and transfer account.	Calculates the difference between the actual and budgeted amounts by month.
Doesn't subtotal by month.	Subtotals by month.
Includes all accounts.	Includes only bank, cash, and credit card accounts.
Is organized by income and expense.	Is organized by cash flow.

If your budget is saved with supercategories on, then budget reports and graphs will display in supercategory organization. See the report setting organization by supercategory on page 188.

Quicken also uses the budget data you enter to create a budget variance graph.

For more information, see "Budget variance graphs" on page 204.

Creating a savings goal

A Quicken *savings goal* lets you "hide" money for something you want to save for—for example, a vacation or a new car. Although the money really is in your bank account, you mark it as unavailable for other spending purposes.

When you create a savings goal, Quicken automatically creates a savings goal account—it helps you track how much money you've contributed to your goal and how much money you have spent on your goal.

It's important to understand that a savings goal account doesn't represent a real account and there is no real money in it! It's just a way of hiding and tracking money towards a specific goal.

Setting up a savings goal

1 **From the Plan menu, choose Savings Goals.**

The Savings Goals window appears.

2 **Click New.**

3 **Complete the Create New Savings Goal window, then click OK.**

Enter a name for this goal.

Enter the total amount of money you want to save towards this goal.

Enter when you want to achieve this goal.

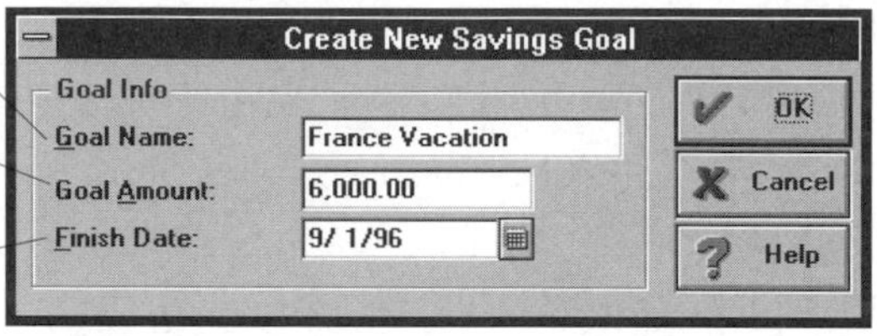

Your savings goal appears in the Savings Goals window. The example shows a savings goal of $6000 for a vacation to France, to be achieved in 12 months. This calculates to a monthly contribution of $500.

Click a savings goal name and then click Delete to delete it.

Click a savings goal name and then click Edit to edit it.

Click a savings goal name here to see its progress bar here.

Quicken automatically enters today's date as the goal start date.

Click Contribute to contribute money to a savings goal account. Click Withdraw to spend money from your savings goal account.

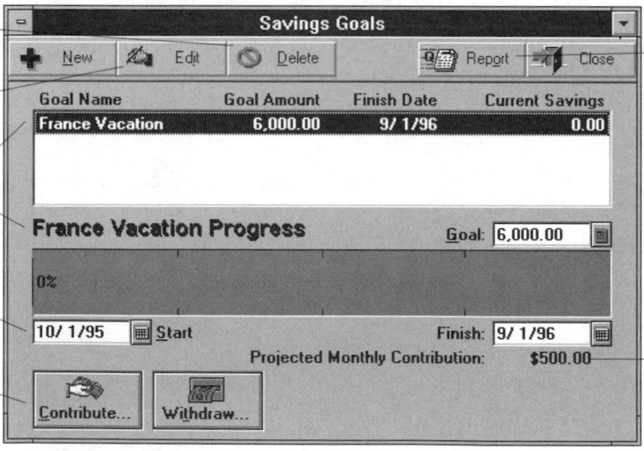

Click a savings goal name from the list and then click Report to show a list of contributions you've made toward the goal.

This number is based on the start and end dates, and goal amount.

Contributing money to a savings goal

1 **From the Savings Goals window, click the Contribute button.**

2 **Complete the Contribute To Goal window.**

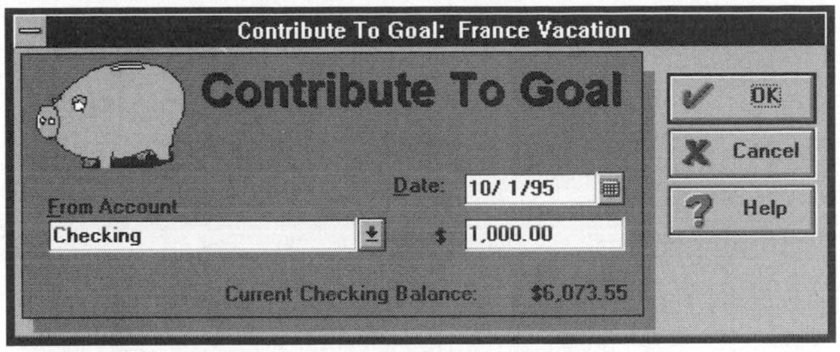

When you complete the Contribute To Goal window, Quicken adds the transfer to your checking account (shown below) and to your savings goal account.

This example shows $1,000 being set aside for a France vacation savings goal.

Transferring money to a savings goal account doesn't affect your overall net worth (as shown in a net worth report).

This checkbox appears when the account contains a transfer to a savings goal account.

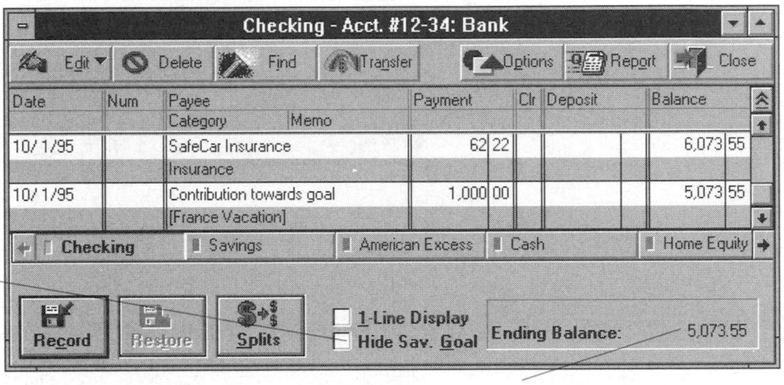

When the Hide Savings Goal checkbox is clear, the Ending Balance shows how much money is available once you have set aside money for your savings goal.

With the Hide Savings Goal checkbox clear (as shown above), the account balance appears, including transfers to any savings goal accounts. *The Ending Balance isn't the true balance of your checking account* (because the money has not really left the checking account). Instead, it shows how much money is available in the account once you have put aside money for your savings goal. To stay on target for your savings goals, you shouldn't let this balance fall below zero.

If you click the Hide Savings Goal checkbox, Quicken hides the transfer to the savings goal account, and displays the true Ending Balance for the checking account.

When the Hide Savings Goal checkbox is selected, any transfers to the savings goal account aren't displayed. (They aren't "real" transactions.)

When the Hide Savings Goal checkbox is selected, the Ending Balance shows the account's true balance.

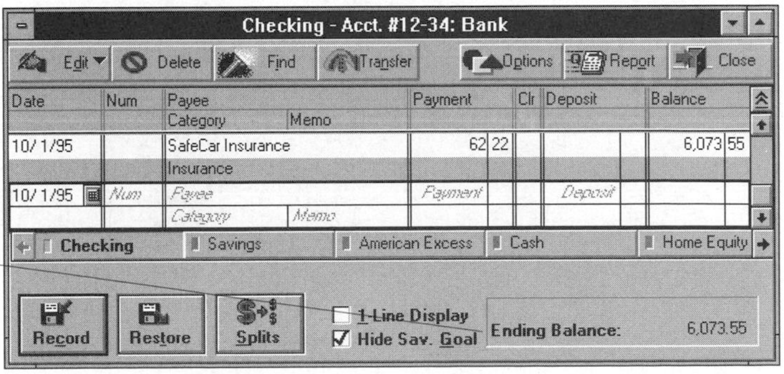

Spending money out of your savings goal account

To spend money that you've already contributed toward your savings goal, you need to do two things: transfer the money back from your savings goal account into the checking account, and then record the payment transaction in your checking account.

1 **From the Savings Goals window, click the Withdraw button.**

2 **Complete the Withdraw From Goal window.**

First: transfer the money to be spent back to your checking account.

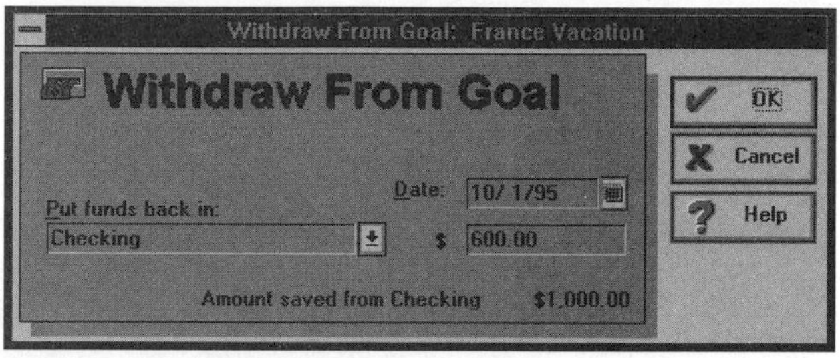

When you complete the Withdraw from Goal window, Quicken adds the transfer to your savings goal account (shown below) and to your checking account.

(Note that you can transfer money from more than one account into the savings goal account, as shown here.)

The Ending Balance in your savings goal account shows how much money you still have put aside for this goal.

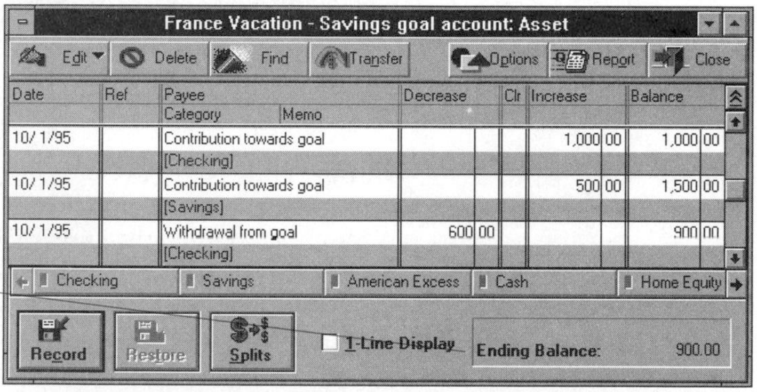

Second: record the expense transaction in your checking account as you normally would.

The net result of these two transactions (here dated 10/1/95) is to decrease the balance of your savings goal account by $600, and to decrease the *true* balance of your checking account by $600 (click Hide Savings Goal to see the true balance).

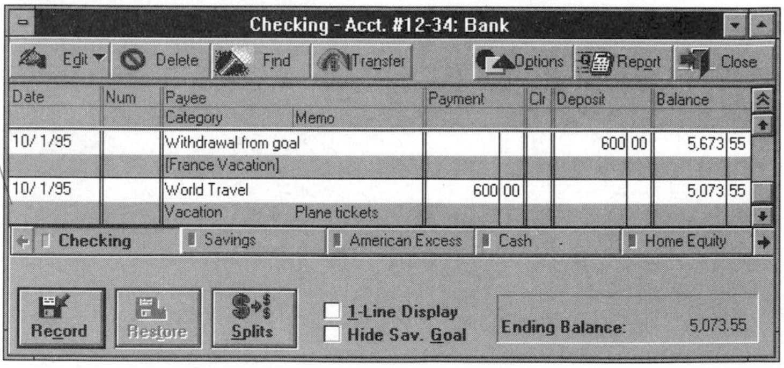

Don't record payments in a savings goal account.
Quicken doesn't let you spend directly from your savings goal account. As the previous example illustrates, you must transfer the money back to a regular bank account first, and then spend it from the bank account.

Checking your progress on meeting a savings goal

To check how much you have saved toward a savings goal, choose Savings Goals from the Plan menu. The goal bar shows your progress:

The tick marks show how much you should have contributed as of today, assuming you made regular contributions from the goal start date. In the example here, the goal bar shows you've made 75% of your goal, and the tick marks show you are ahead of schedule, and can decrease your monthly contributions to $250 in order to make the goal by the finish date.

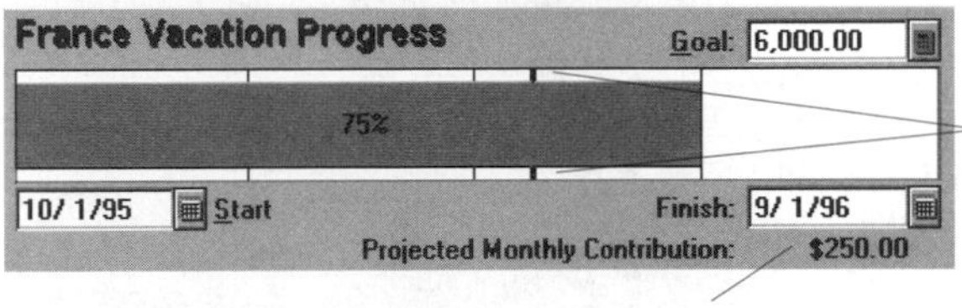

Tick marks (they're red onscreen).

After each contribution you make, Quicken recalculates the projected monthly contribution for the remaining months.

You can also see the Ending Balance of your savings goal account in the Account list.

If you keep several savings goal accounts, you can run a net worth report to show how much you've saved toward each goal.

To run this net worth report, click the Reports icon from the iconbar, and choose Net Worth from the Home report family.

In reports, the balances of your checking accounts don't include the money you've set aside (transferred to the savings goal accounts).

The money you've set aside for savings goals is shown separately under the asset accounts.

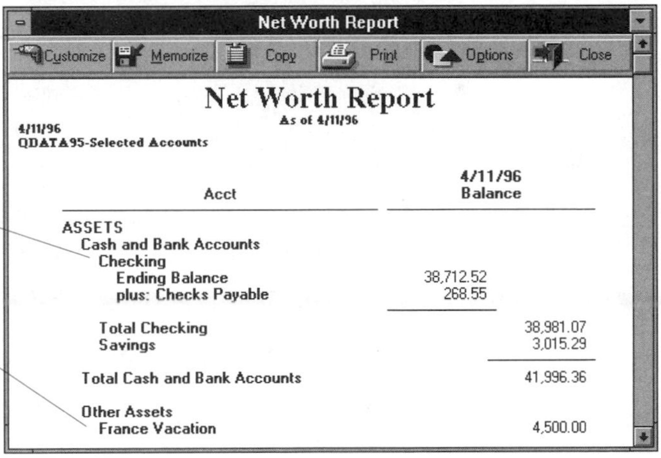

Net Worth Report
As of 4/11/96
4/11/96
QDATA95-Selected Accounts

Acct	4/11/96 Balance	
ASSETS		
Cash and Bank Accounts		
Checking		
Ending Balance	38,712.52	
plus: Checks Payable	268.55	
Total Checking		38,981.07
Savings		3,015.29
Total Cash and Bank Accounts		41,996.36
Other Assets		
France Vacation		4,500.00

Deleting a savings goal

When your savings goal account has served its purpose (for example, you've taken that vacation to France), simply delete the account by selecting the goal in the Savings Goals window and clicking Delete. Quicken removes all the transfer transactions from your checking account(s), and the checking account Ending Balance once again shows the true balance.

Tracking your goals with the progress bar

After you create a budget, supercategory budget, or savings goal, use the Quicken progress bar to display your progress towards your two most important goals, no matter where you are in Quicken.

1 **From the Plan menu, choose Progress Bar.**

The progress bar appears at the bottom of the screen. It shows a left gauge and a right gauge.

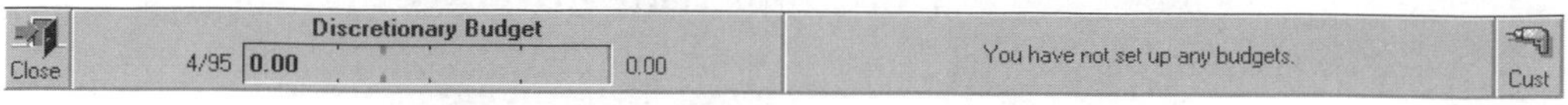

2 **Click the Customize button at the right end of the progress bar.**

Depending on the gauge type you choose, the button below changes. See the table below.

Clear this checkbox to hide icon and goal labels on the progress bar.

Select this option to always display the progress bar, no matter where you are in Quicken.

3 **For the left gauge, choose a gauge type from the list.**

If you choose this for the gauge type	The button below the gauge type drop-down list is labeled
Savings Goal	Choose Goal
Budget Goal	Choose Category
Supercategory Budget	Choose Supercategory

4 **Click Choose Goal, Choose Category, or Choose Supercategory to choose a specific goal, category, or supercategory.**

5 **(Optional) Repeat steps 3 and 4 for the right gauge.**

6 **Choose the display options you want, then click OK.**

As you make progress on your goals, the progress bar may look like this:

The tick marks (shown in red onscreen) show where your progress should be as of today's date. For example, if today is 9/8/94, the tick marks in the Dining Budget gauge show you're over budget, and the tick marks in the France Vacation Goal gauge show you are ahead of schedule in contributions.

22 Creating a forecast

About forecasts

You've kept your Quicken registers up to date with your past transactions. You're using the Financial Calendar to keep track of upcoming bills and receipts. With this information, you're now ready for the "big picture," the illuminating view of how your financial future is shaping up.

Forecasting and budgeting are two of Quicken's tools for planning your spending. Budgeting allows you to create budget amounts and then track how well you are staying within those amounts. Forecasting allows you to project your cash flow for the future, based on scheduled transactions and estimated amounts.

See "Creating a budget from your forecast" on page 254.

You can use your budget amounts to create a forecast, or vice versa, or you can create the two separately. You can also have Quicken create a forecast from the transactions in your register, or from the transactions on the Financial Calendar.

Quicken's forecast graph is a feature to experiment with. Take your time, adjust the figures, and see the results in the graph. You can't do any harm, so play with this feature until you feel comfortable with your setup.

Projecting your account balances

The forecast graph projects forward the balances of your accounts on the basis of three sources of information:

- Your income and spending behavior up to today (Quicken can get this information automatically from your registers, or from your budget spreadsheet, or from estimates you enter manually).
- Any additional transactions you have scheduled on your Financial Calendar; recurring transactions are projected forward for the range of the graph, if you let Quicken create your forecast automatically.

Other amounts you enter for the purposes of forecasting. For example, you might want to create a forecast with a higher salary item, to see what getting a raise would do to your finances.

Quicken can show your account projections from one month up to two years ahead. With the ability to look ahead, you can:

- See when you'll be able to afford the new jacuzzi or skiing trip.
- Look for danger zones when your accounts might fall below zero.
- Plan your spending and map out your savings more clearly.
- Experiment with Quicken's projections to do "what-if" planning. For example, you can alter the rent amount and see what happens to your account balance over the next six months to find out what level of rent you can afford.

For example, Quicken can display what you're likely to save if you continue to spend and earn money as your forecast data indicates.

Click Create to have Quicken automatically get amounts from the Calendar, your registers, or your budget.

This graph shows your projected account balances for the next year.

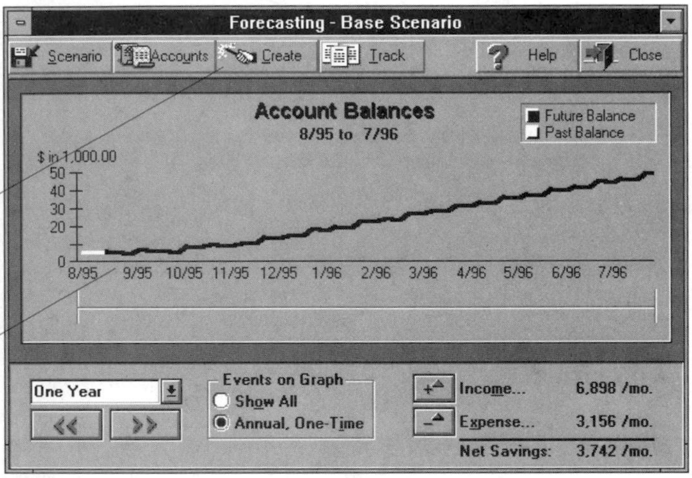

Creating a forecast graph

Quicken's projections will be as accurate as *you* make them. The graph can include average income and expense amounts to cover all the transactions not included as regularly scheduled events. This chapter shows you how to build the greatest accuracy into your forecast graph.

Two different kinds of amounts make up your forecast: income items and expense items. Expense and income amounts include both Known and Estimated items. Known items are regularly scheduled transactions, such as a paycheck or a car payment. If you know a transaction occurs at regular intervals, and you know the amount, enter it as a Known Item. Estimated items are the amounts you think you'll spend over a certain period of time. Estimated items have no specific date, but are averaged over a period of time. Quicken gets the known items from your scheduled transactions, and can get the estimated amounts from your budget or your register.

You can create expense and income amounts just for your forecast, or you can automatically create these amounts from other data that you have already entered in Quicken.

1 **Choose Forecasting from the Plan menu.**

The Automatically Create Forecast window appears. To display this window from the Forecasting window, click Create.

2 **Complete the Automatically Create Forecast window.**

Enter a historic date range you want Quicken to look in for your forecast amounts.

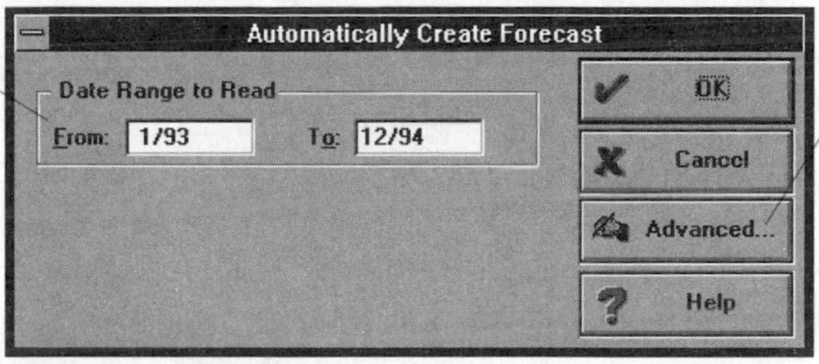

(Optional) Click Advanced to specify where Quicken should get amounts from.

3 **(Optional) Click Advanced to specify what items Quicken should create, and to limit the forecast to certain accounts and categories.**

Select the options you want and then click Done.

Select Known Items to get scheduled amounts and events from your Calendar, register, and Scheduled Transaction list.

Select Estimated Items to create new average amounts from your register or your budget.

Select Create Both to create new Estimated and Known Items.

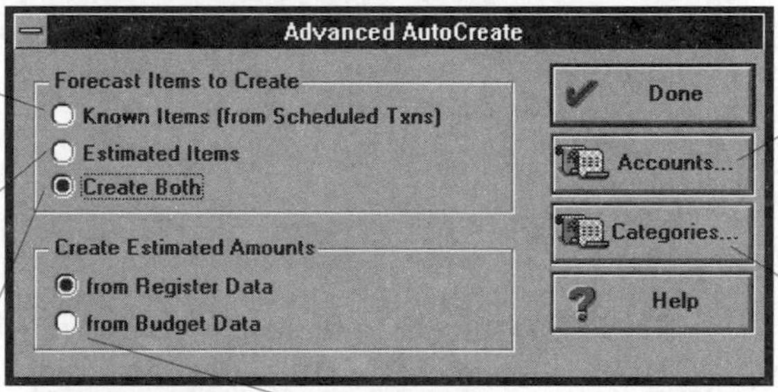

Click Accounts to specify which accounts you want Quicken to get amounts from.

Click Categories to create Estimated Items only for certain categories.

Choose whether you want Quicken to create Estimated Items from your register, or from your budget.

4 **Click OK to create your Forecast.**

Quicken creates Known Items from your scheduled transactions and estimated items from your register and budget.

Any category that appears in the Known Items section of the forecast won't be included in the Estimated Items section, even if it is in your register or budget. For example, if you scheduled your paycheck with the category Salary and also included that amount in your budget under Salary, then the forecast will automatically put Salary in the Known Items section, but not in the Estimated Items section. After you create your forecast, check to make sure the amounts are realistic and that all the amounts you want to include are there.

The graph shows you the balance of the selected accounts for the current month, the next six months, the next year, or the next two years. You can display previous or future months by clicking << or >>, or you can change the range of the graph by selecting from the date drop-down list.

Click Accounts to select which account balances you want to include. See "Selecting accounts for your graph" next.

Click Scenario to create a different set of forecast amounts, or to compare different possibilities. See "Creating multiple scenarios" on page 252.

Projected future balances are shown in blue (darker).

Balances before today are shown in yellow (lighter).

These triangles represent items in your forecast. Click them to see the details.

Select a date range from this drop-down list.

Click << or >> to see the next or previous months.

Click Create to recreate your forecast amounts.

Click Track to create a budget from your forecast. See page 254.

Click the mouse button to see the exact balance.

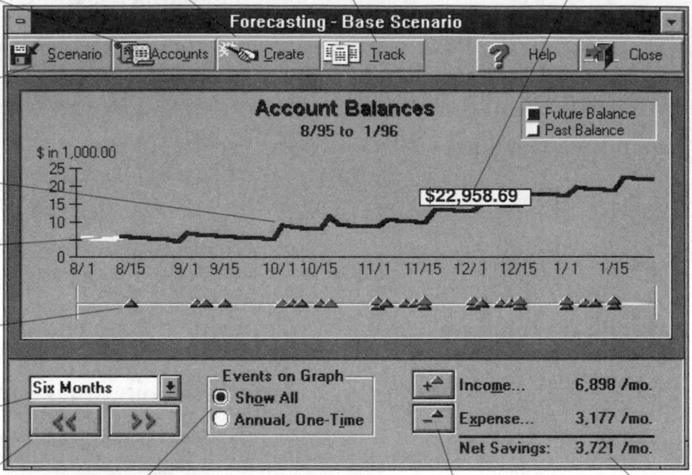

Click Show All to display all scheduled events as green or red triangles, or click Annual, One-Time to display only annual or one-time scheduled events.

Click one of these buttons to view and edit your income and expense amounts.

This is the total income minus the total expenses for each month.

Typically, a planning graph will show a gradual rise or decline in the balance, due to your underlying financial trend, disturbed by sharp jumps and falls resulting from your Known Items.

Printing the forecast graph

See "Setting up your printer" on page 211.

1 **Set up your printer.**

2 **Create your forecast.**

Or press Ctrl+P

3 **Select Print Forecast from the File menu.**

Quicken prints the forecast graph.

Selecting accounts for your graph

You can select which account balances to include in your forecast. For example, if you are interested in forecasting cash flow, include all your bank accounts, cash accounts, and credit card accounts, but not investment, asset, or liability accounts.

1 **To change the account balances that are included in your projection, click Accounts on the Forecasting button bar.**

2 **Mark the accounts to include and click OK.**

To mark or unmark an account, click it, or select it and then press the spacebar. Click Mark All or Clear All to mark or clear all accounts.

Modifying your forecast

Now that you have reasonable data in your forecast, it might look something like this one. If you didn't have much data to create the amounts from, your forecast might be considerably simpler. Click the Income or Expense buttons to display your forecast amounts.

Click Income Items or Expense Items.

These are regularly scheduled items. If you let Quicken create your forecast automatically, Quicken gets these from your Financial Calendar or your Scheduled Transaction list.

These are estimated average expenses that aren't associated with a specific date.

Click New to create a new amount. Amounts you create here won't be recorded in your register.

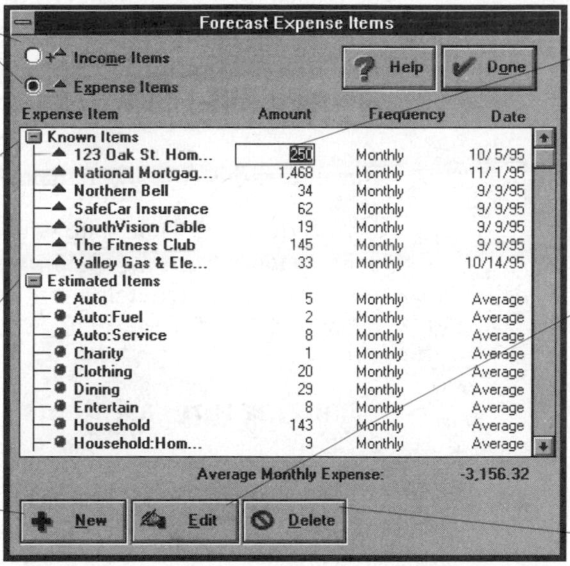

You can edit these amounts directly by typing in this field.

Click Edit to change existing item information, such as description, date, or frequency.

Click Delete to delete an item.

You can change any figures in this summary at any time and see the result immediately in the forecast graph. Remember that if you change scheduled amounts, they won't change in the Scheduled Transaction list or the Financial Calendar. If you change scheduled transactions elsewhere, click Create again to see the changes in your forecast. If you click Create again, however, you will lose any changes you made since the last time you created your forecast.

Creating a new forecast amount

Amounts you create manually won't be recorded in your register. To add a forecast amount:

Or click on the horizontal line at the bottom of the Forecasting window.

1 **Click Income or Expense in the bottom right part of the Forecasting window, and then click New.**

2 **Enter the item information.**

Items created in forecasting are for planning only. They are never actually entered in your register.

Enter a description, amount, and frequency here.

Click Average Amount to enter an estimated item rather than a scheduled item. If you click Next Scheduled Date, enter a date in the field.

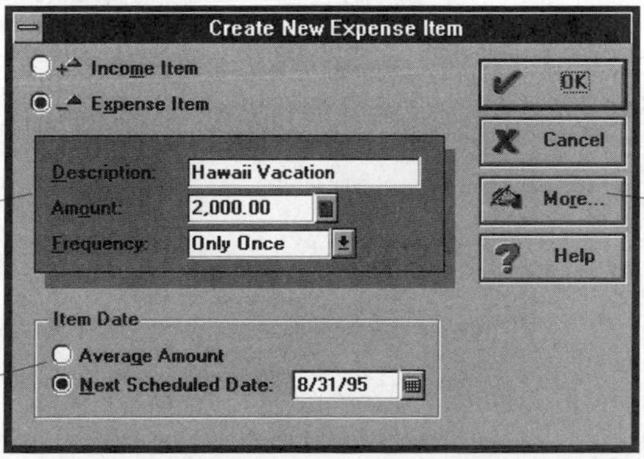

Click More if you want to include a category, number of payments, or transfer information with this item.

3 **(Optional) Click More to include a category, number of payments, or transfer information.**

4 **Select an Item Date option.**

Select Average Amount to create an Estimated Item. The amount is averaged over the period selected in the Frequency field.

Select Next Scheduled Date to create a Known Item.

5 **Click OK.**

Remember this rule when making changes:

If you add a Known Item to your forecast, remember to subtract the same amount from the appropriate Estimated Item. For example, if you set up a Known Item for your paycheck, you shouldn't have an estimated item for Salary.

Changing forecast items

You can change the description, amount, frequency, and advanced information of a forecast item by clicking Edit in the Forecast Items window. You can also change Known Items to Estimated Items, and vice versa:

1 **Select the item you want to change in the Forecast Items window.**

2 **Click Edit.**

3 **Change the Item Date:**

- To change a Known Item to an Estimated Item, select Average Amount instead of Next Scheduled Date.
- To change an Estimated Item to a Known Item, select Next Scheduled Date instead of Average Amount.

4 **Click OK.**

Creating multiple scenarios

You can create different forecast scenarios and compare them. You can also compare your current forecast to a past forecast. To manage your scenarios, click the Scenario button in the Forecasting window.

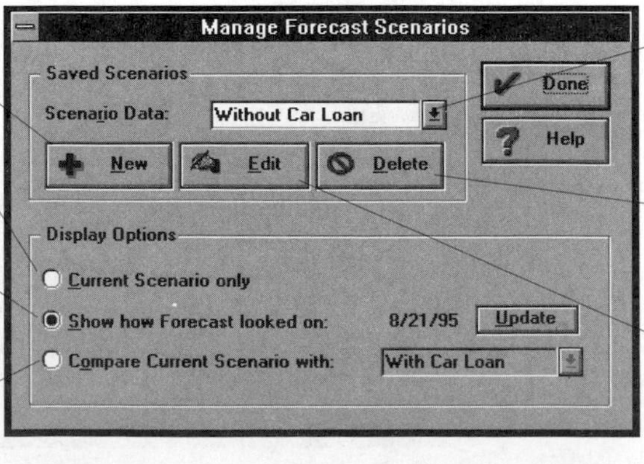
Manage Forecast Scenarios
Saved Scenarios
Scenario Data:
Without Car Loan
New
Edit
Delete
Done
Help
Display Options
Current Scenario only
Show how Forecast looked on:
8/21/95
Update
Compare Current Scenario with:
With Car Loan
Click New to save the current forecast data.
Select this option to display just the current forecast scenario.
Select this option to display the current scenario and the saved forecast graph from this date. To save the current graph, click Update.
Select this option to compare the current scenario with another scenario that you select from the drop-down list.
Select a scenario from this list.
Click Delete to delete the selected scenario.
Click Edit to change the name of the selected scenario.

Once you've created several scenarios, you can compare them. See "Comparing two scenarios" on page 254 for details.

Saving a graph

After a month or two, you may want to compare what has *actually* happened to your account balances with what you *thought* was going to happen. Quicken lets you save a forecast's graph so that you can look back at it later and see how accurate it was.

When you have finished setting up your planning worksheet, so that you believe the graph shows your best guess at the future, save the graph as follows.

1 **With the forecast displayed, Click Scenario.**

2 **Under Display Options, select Show how Forecast looked on, and click Update.**

Quicken saves the current graph, and displays the date of the saved graph next to the Update button.

When you click Done, notice the additional line on the graph—this is your saved graph.

To get rid of the line from your graph, click Scenario, select Current Scenario only under Display Options, and click Done.

Retrieving a saved graph

Let's say you now wait a month and want to see how close to reality your saved graph was. To retrieve your saved graph:

1 **Click Scenario.**

2 **Select Show how Forecast looked on, and click Done.**

Quicken superimposes your previously saved graph over the actual history of your account balances.

The green line shows your previously saved graph.

The blue or yellow line shows what actually happened to your account balances, or your latest projection of what you think will happen.

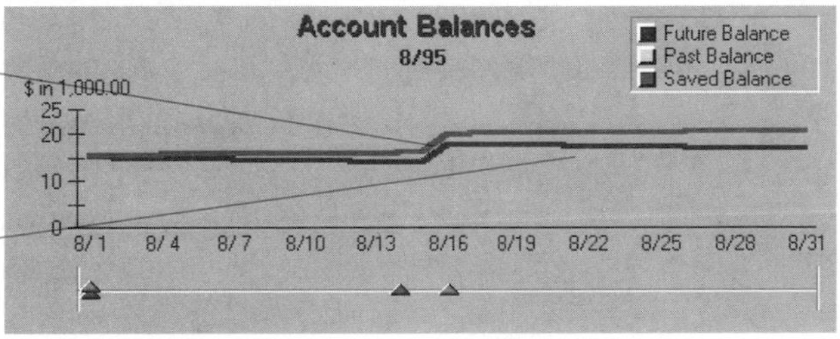

Comparing two scenarios

1 **Display the first scenario you want to compare.**

2 **Click Scenario.**

Select the first scenario here.

Select this option to compare the current scenario with the one you selected from the drop-down list.

Select the second scenario here.

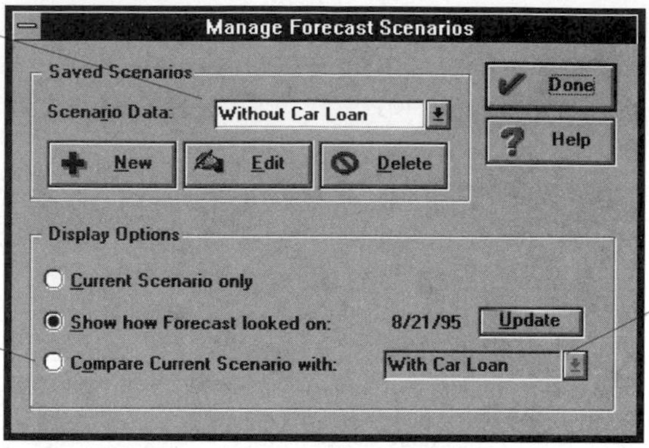

3 **Select Compare Current Scenario with under Display Options.**

4 **Select the second scenario from the drop-down list under Display Options.**

5 **Click Done.**

Creating a budget from your forecast

Once you've set up a forecast that you like, you can use it to create a budget. Do this if you want to know what kind of a budget you'll have to stick to in order to achieve your forecast.

1 **Select Forecasting from the Plan menu.**

2 **Make sure the scenario you want is displayed.**

3 **Click Track.**

4 **Click OK to replace your current budget.**

See Chapter 21, *Creating a budget or savings goal,* on page 235.

Caution:
Creating a budget from your forecast will overwrite your existing budget.

Quicken creates a budget from your Estimated Items only. Select Budgeting from the Plan menu to see your new budget.

See Chapter 16, *Displaying Snapshots of your financial picture,* on page 207.

Quicken also creates a Snapshot page of your six biggest budget goals. Click Snapshot to see the page now, or select Snapshots from the Reports menu.

23 Setting up your modem

About modem setup

To register your Quicken software online or use the online services in Quicken, your modem must be set up correctly. (A modem is a device that lets your computer send and receive information over a telephone line.)

The modem setup procedures for Intuit online services and the CheckFree service are different.

- For Intuit online services (online software registration, Portfolio Price Update, IntelliCharge, and Intuit Marketplace), Quicken sets up your modem *automatically.* If these settings work for your modem and you are able to make an online connection, you don't have to change your modem settings manually. See "Letting Quicken set up your modem for Intuit services" on page 256.

  If Quicken is unable to set up your modem correctly, you need to make changes to individual modem settings in the Set Up Modem window (and possibly the Advanced Modem Setup window.) See "Setting up your modem to use Intuit services" on page 256.
- For the CheckFree service, you must set up your modem yourself. See "Setting up your modem to use CheckFree" on page 258.

To work with Quicken, your modem must support the industry standard AT command set used by Hayes and Hayes-compatible modems. To confirm that your modem supports the AT command set, check your modem manual.

Letting Quicken set up your modem for Intuit services

Quicken automatically sets up your modem for Intuit online services.

1 **Be sure your modem is turned on.**

2 **From the Online menu, choose Set Up Modem. Or initiate an online activity–Update Portfolio Prices, Get IntelliCharge Data, Intuit Marketplace, or Software Registration.**

Note: Automatic modem setup happens only the first time you choose Set Up Modem or initiate one of the online activities.

Quicken queries your modem and makes the modem settings it determines are correct. Automatic modem setup typically takes about 20 seconds.

To test Quicken's automatic modem settings, try online software registration. If you are able to register online, the modem settings are correct.

If the automatic modem settings are correct, Quicken is able to make an online connection to Intuit. If the settings aren't correct, you see an error message when Quicken tries to connect to Intuit. In this case, you need to change one or more modem settings yourself.

Setting up your modem to use Intuit services

Check each setting and change any that is incorrect.

1 **From the Online menu, choose Set Up Modem.**

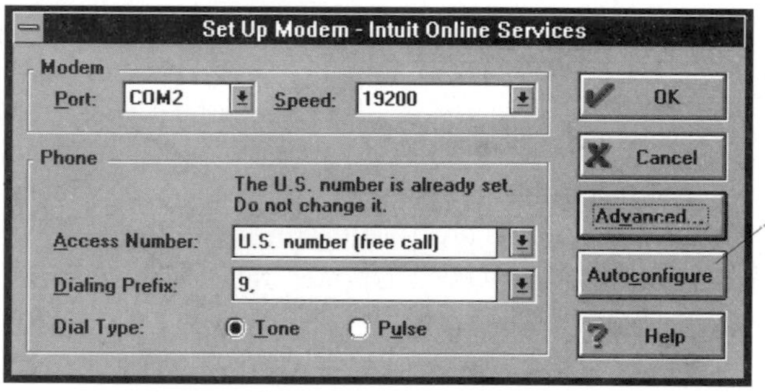

Click Autoconfigure to re-run Quicken's automatic modem setup at any time.

2 **From the Port drop-down list, select the serial port to which your modem is connected.**

If you are unsure which port to select, try COM2 first. If you have a mouse that uses COM2, try COM1 for your modem.

3 **From the Speed drop-down list, select the speed (baud rate) of your modem.**

Your modem can probably run at a higher speed than you think. For a 9600 or 14,400 baud modem, set the speed to 19,200.

4 **The access number for U.S. calls is already set. *Don't change it.***

If the local number isn't available in your area, Quicken automatically dials a second toll-free number.

A free local number, represented by the text **U.S. number (free call)**, is already set in the software. This number works for most locations in the United States (including Alaska, Hawaii, and Puerto Rico). If you change any of the phone number text, you need to restore it by choosing **U.S. number (free call)** from the drop-down list.

If you need to connect to an Intuit online service from outside the United States, you must enter a series of numbers in the Access Number box. These may include numbers required to dial out from a hotel, a country code to dial to the U.S., and a calling card number, as well as the Intuit international access number (415-328-1725). First delete all the text in the Access Number box, and then enter the numbers you need in their required order. The international Intuit number is a toll call.

You can select a dialing prefix from the drop-down list. Two of the prefixes disable call-waiting services, so your online connection won't be interrupted. (Use "*70," for a touch-tone or "1170," for a rotary-dial phone.) The "9," prefix is often used to obtain an outside line when you make a phone call from an office. (Don't include the quotation marks when entering the prefixes.)

5 **(Optional) In the Dialing Prefix box, enter any prefix (such as "9,") required to reach an outside line.**

The comma tells the modem to pause for two seconds.

6 **Select Tone if you have a touch-tone phone line or Pulse if your phone line works only with rotary-dial phones.**

7 **Click OK.**

Autoconfigure

If you change Quicken's automatic modem settings and then wish to restore them, you can do so with Autoconfigure. (You should also run Autoconfigure if you install a new modem.)

1 **From the Online menu, choose Set Up Modem.**

2 **In the Set Up Modem window, click Autoconfigure.**

Quicken queries your modem and makes the modem settings it determines are correct. This process takes about 20 seconds.

Advanced modem setup

Quicken's automatic setup enters advanced settings for your modem; you can adjust them if necessary.

Caution: Don't change the advanced modem settings unless you understand the changes you are making. If you have modem problems, try the solutions in "Communications problems with Intuit online services" on page 260 *before* you change the advanced settings. If you change these settings accidentally, you can use Autoconfigure to restore them to their original values.

1 **In the Set Up Modem window, click Advanced.**

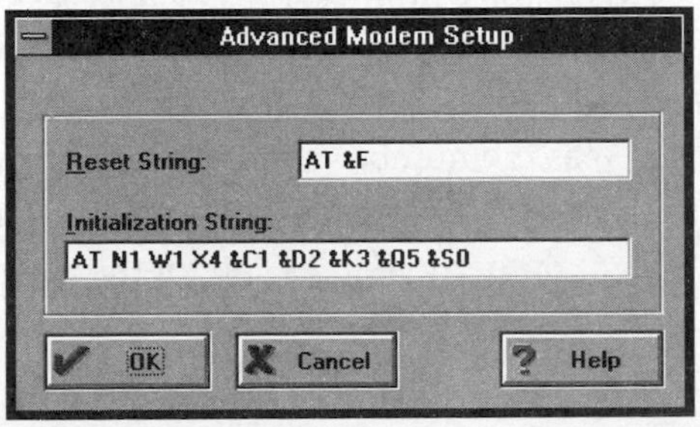

2 **Set or change the reset string, if necessary.**

The reset string can reset your modem to its factory settings or to the "power on" settings (settings that take effect when your modem is turned on).

3 **Set or change the initialization string, if necessary.**

You can change the initialization string to customize your modem for your preferences and your system. Refer to your modem documentation for codes specific to your modem.

4 **Click OK.**

Setting up your modem to use CheckFree

Before you can pay bills through CheckFree, you must sign up for the CheckFree service. See the booklet in your Quicken package for information and an enrollment form. If you need a new enrollment form, call the CheckFree Corporation. For the phone number, see CheckFree Corporation Technical Support on page 319.

1 **If your modem is external, turn it on.**

2 **From the Activities menu, choose CheckFree and then choose Set Up Modem.**

Most newer modems support 9600 baud. You may need to use a slower speed if you have an older modem.

Enter the telephone number CheckFree sent you in the welcome kit. Omit the area code if it's a local number.

```
┌─────────────────────────────────────────────────────────────┐
│  ─             Set Up Modem - CheckFree                      │
│  ┌─Dial Type─┐   Port:    [COM2 ▲▼]                          │
│  │ ● Tone    │                              [ ✔  OK  ]       │
│  │ ○ Pulse   │   Speed:   [9600 ▲▼]                          │
│  └───────────┘                              [ ✘  Cancel ]    │
│  CompuServe Local Access Number:  [802 0130        ]         │
│  (for CheckFree Access)                     [ ?  Help  ]     │
│  Initialization String:  [AT&F&C0&D0L0X4          ]          │
│  (optional)                                                  │
└─────────────────────────────────────────────────────────────┘
```

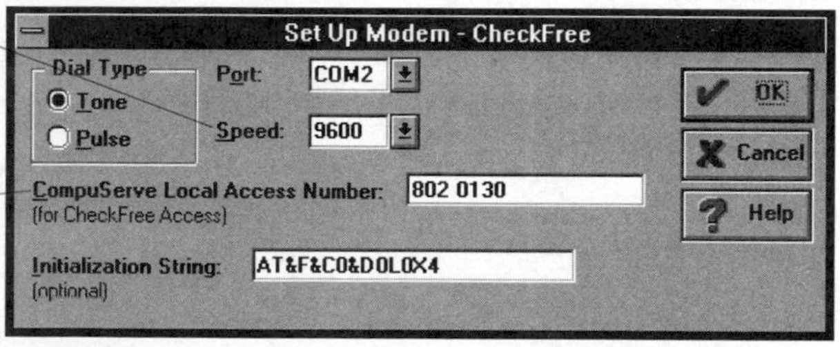

Most telephone lines are touch-tone lines.

3 **Select Tone if you have a touch-tone phone line or Pulse if your phone line works only with rotary-dial phones.**

4 **From the Port drop-down list, select the serial port to which your modem is connected.**

If you are unsure which port to select, try COM2 first. If you have a mouse that uses COM2, try COM1 for your modem. Or ask your computer dealer which port your modem is connected to.

5 **From the Speed drop-down list, select the highest baud rate supported by CheckFree and your modem.**

You may want to enter a dialing prefix. Two prefixes disable call-waiting services, so your online connection won't be interrupted. (Use "*70," for a touch-tone or "1170," for a rotary-dial phone.) The "9," prefix is often used to obtain an outside line when you make a phone call from an office. (Don't include the quotation marks when entering the prefixes.)

6 **In the CompuServe Local Access Number box, enter the telephone number you received in your CheckFree welcome kit.**

Omit the area code if the number is local (it has the same area code as the number you are calling from).

If the number is outside your local calling area, your telephone company charges you for the phone call when you send information to CheckFree.

7 **In the Initialization String box, enter any special letters, digits, or other characters to send to the modem.**

For more information, look in your modem user's guide. (Most modem commands must begin with the prefix AT.)

8 **Click OK.**

Communications problems and solutions

If you have problems with your modem or problems connecting to an Intuit online service or CheckFree, consult the following tables. Also check your modem user's guide for troubleshooting suggestions particular to your modem.

General communications problems

These problems may occur when you are trying to connect to either Intuit online services or CheckFree.

Problem	Solution
No response from the modem.	**Check the modem itself:** • If you have an external modem, make sure it is turned on and securely plugged in to your computer. • If you have an older modem that has switches, check the switch settings. Your modem manual describes the function of each switch. With the modem turned off, set the switches to originate a call (not to answer), to respond to DTR (data terminal ready), and to recognize commands. **Check the settings in the Set Up Modem window:** • In the Set Up Modem window, change the port setting to see if you've been using the wrong port. • Make sure the modem speed isn't set too high (above 19,200). If you set the speed to a higher rate than your modem can handle, the modem may fail to respond. **Close other communications programs:** • If you have other programs that use your modem (such as FAX software, online services such a CompuServe and America Online, or other communications software), close those programs.
Modem responds but you can't connect.	**Check the modem itself:** • Check to see that the phone cable is securely connected to your modem and to the wall outlet. Be sure that the cable is connected to the line outlet on the back of your modem, not the phone outlet. **If the first phone number doesn't work, wait for Quicken to dial the second phone number:** • Although the local, toll-free number set in the software works in most locations, it may not work in yours. If you hear a recording after the modem dials the first number, wait while the modem dials a second toll-free number. Be patient; it may take as long as 45 seconds for the modem to redial.
Quicken freezes while initializing modem connected to COM4.	• If there is no device connected to COM2, move your modem to COM2. • If you have devices connected to both COM1 and COM2 and you have no COM3, leave your modem connected to COM4 and add the following items to the [386Enh] section of your Windows SYSTEM.INI file: **COM3IRQ=-1** **COM4Base=02E8** **COM4IRQ=3** Then, reboot Windows and start Quicken.

Communications problems with Intuit online services

If you are using an Intuit online service and the suggestions in the first table haven't solved your problem, try these additional steps.

Problem	Solution
Modem responds, but you can't connect.	**Change settings in the Set Up Modem window:** • Change the Speed setting to match the speed (baud rate) of your modem. (Speeds over 19,200 can result in unreliable behavior for some modems.) • Change the Dial Type setting for tone or pulse dialing. • Enter a dialing prefix, if necessary. **Change settings in the Advanced Modem Setup window:** • In the Initialization String box, you may need to include a different sequence of commands for Quicken to send to the modem before dialing the access number. Enter any special letters, digits, and other characters to be sent to the modem. To find out what codes you need, look in the modem user's manual. Most modem commands must begin with the prefix AT.) *Don't change this setting unless you understand the change you are making.*

Communications problems with CheckFree

If you are having problems transmitting to CheckFree, wait a few minutes and try transmitting again. The system may simply have been busy the first time you tried to transmit. If transmitting again doesn't work, try the steps in the table under "General communications problems" on page 259, then try the troubleshooting steps in the following table.

Problem	Solution
Modem responds but doesn't connect to CheckFree. 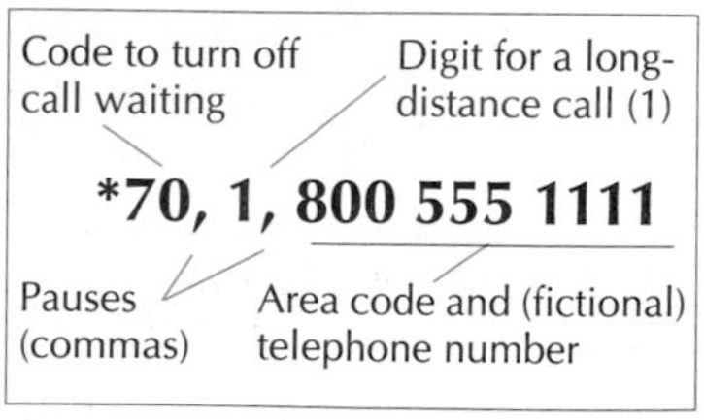 	**Dial the service number yourself:** • Dial the number that the modem dials to be sure that you're getting a dial tone and that when you dial the access number, the CheckFree Processing Center answers with a high-pitched tone. Your service number is supplied by CheckFree for your particular modem speed and geographic location. • Write down the sequence of digits, characters, and pauses you dialed. An example of a character is an asterisk (*), which some phone systems use as a signal for a special phone feature. • Translate what you've written down into the sequence of numbers, commas, and characters you need to enter in the CompuServe Local Access Number box in the Set Up Modem window. (Use a comma for each pause, or several commas for longer pauses. For example, if you need to dial 9 to get an outside line and then need to wait a second to hear a dial tone, enter 9 and then enter a comma in this field.) • Change the setting for the modem speed and check that the access number is correct for the modem speed. If possible, change to a slower speed.
Modem appears to be operating correctly, but the CheckFree Processing Center doesn't respond.	**Call CheckFree Corporation:** • For the phone number, see CheckFree Corporation Technical Support on page 319. **Please don't call Intuit**; we have no control or knowledge in these areas. Note any error messages exactly as they appear.

24 Tracking credit card transactions online

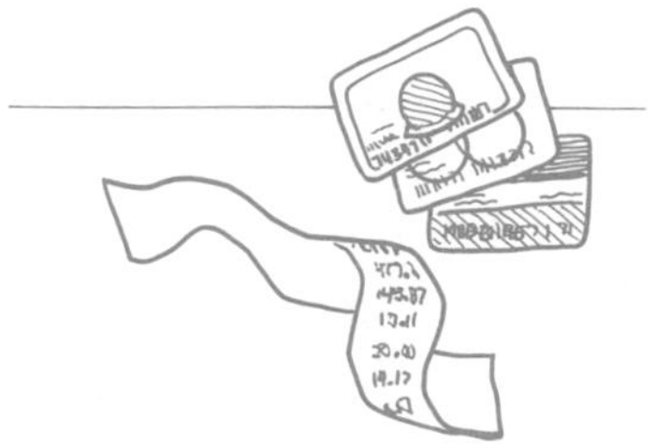

About IntelliCharge

If you have a Quicken credit card, you can use IntelliCharge to automatically enter the data from your charge statement (which Intuit sends you via modem or disk) into your Quicken register.

IntelliCharge can automatically categorize your transactions based on merchant codes or based on your previously selected categories.

Setting up a credit card account to use IntelliCharge

To use an IntelliCharge account, you must have a Quicken credit card. To apply for a Quicken credit card, see the application included in your Quicken package, or if you need a new application, see "Intuit Customer Assistance for IntelliCharge" on page 320.

1 **Set up a Quicken credit card account as you normally would. See "Setting up additional Quicken accounts" on page 1 for more information.**

2 **If you selected the Guide Me checkbox in the Create New Account window, click Yes to the question, "Have you signed up for Intelli-Charge for this credit card through Intuit?". Or, select the Enable IntelliCharge checkbox in the Create Credit Card Account window.**

See "Letting Quicken set up your modem for Intuit services" on page 256.

If you choose modem as the delivery method, you must enter your social security number and your IntelliCharge password, and set up your modem.

After you set up your account for IntelliCharge, look in the Account List window: IntelliCharge accounts are marked with a lightning bolt in the Type field.

Updating credit card accounts with IntelliCharge

Each month, Intuit either mails you an IntelliCharge statement disk or makes an electronic statement available for you to download via modem. The statement contains all the transactions for your credit card that occurred in the current statement period. These transactions include credit card purchases, finance and cash advance charges, credits from merchants, and payments.

Intuit won't send you an electronic statement if your Quicken credit card account is closed or if there was no activity during the billing period. (If the bank sends you a paper statement, Intuit sends you an electronic statement; if the bank sends no statement, Intuit doesn't either.)

Getting your IntelliCharge statement by modem

Your electronic statement is available for you to download by modem at approximately the same time you receive your paper statement in the mail. After you get your first electronic statement, Billminder and Quicken Reminders let you know when new information is ready for you to download.

To save yourself repeated modem calls, wait until your first paper statement arrives before trying to download your statement.

See "Letting Quicken set up your modem for Intuit services" on page 256. If you have modem problems, see "Communications problems and solutions" on page 259.

1 **From the Account List window, open the IntelliCharge account register.**

2 **Make sure your modem is turned on (if it is external) and the phone or modem line is plugged in.**

3 **From the Online menu, choose Get IntelliCharge Data.**

The Get IntelliCharge Data window appears and tells you that Quicken is about to use your modem.

4 **Click OK to download your data, then review your transactions in the IntelliCharge Statement window.**

See "Reviewing transactions in the IntelliCharge Statement window" on page 263.

Getting your IntelliCharge statement from a disk

Disk delivery is available only in the U.S.

1 **From the Account List window, open the credit card register.**

2 **From the Online menu, choose Get IntelliCharge Data.**

3 **Insert your IntelliCharge statement disk in your floppy drive, and type the letter of that drive (for example,** A **or** B**).**

The number shown here is the account number you entered when you set up the IntelliCharge account in Quicken.

4 **Click OK to load your statement data, then review your transactions in the IntelliCharge Statement window.**

Reviewing transactions in the IntelliCharge Statement window

If IntelliCharge reads a transaction whose category isn't in your list, it asks whether you want to set up a new category or select a different one.

- Click Set Up to add the new category to the list.

OR

- Click Select to select an existing category from the list.

In this example, the category "Travel" isn't set up in the current Quicken file. Add this new category to Quicken's Category & Transfer list, or pick an existing category instead.

After Quicken reads your statement, it displays the IntelliCharge Statement window.

1 **Review the transactions in the IntelliCharge Statement window.**

This onscreen statement is similar to the paper statement you receive from a bank.

Use the Mark button to mark a transaction for further review. See "Handling credit card disputes with IntelliCharge" on page 266.

A credit or a payment appears as a negative number in the Amount column. These transactions decrease the balance due on your Quicken credit card.

Cancel saves the statement to disk but doesn't record transactions to your register. Any changes to the categories are lost. The statement is reloaded from disk next time you choose Get IntelliCharge Data.

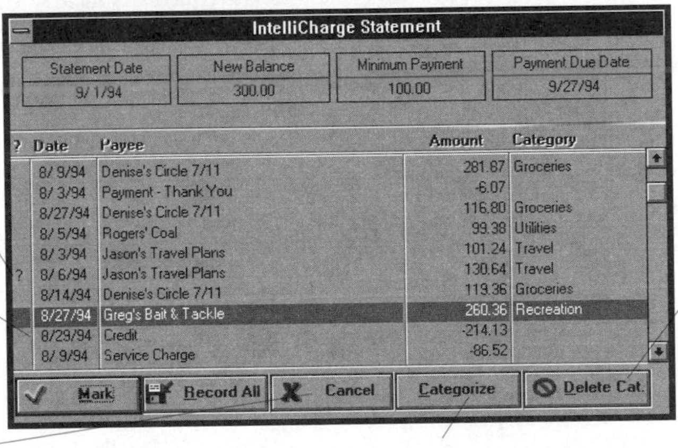

To delete the category assigned to a transaction, select the transaction and click Delete Cat.

To enter or change the category assigned to a transaction, click Categorize and choose a category from the list.

2 **(Optional) Change the categorization of any transaction.**

See "How IntelliCharge categorizes your transactions" next for more information.

IntelliCharge searches for previous transactions with the same payee and categorizes your new transactions the same way. If IntelliCharge finds no previous transaction with the same payee, it uses Quicken's standard category list to categorize the transactions.

3 **(Optional) Select any transaction and click Mark (or press the spacebar) to mark the transaction for special attention.**

Mark a transaction if you want to:

- Check or change the payee information
- Split the transaction
- Add text in the Memo field of the transaction
- Compare a transaction with your credit card receipt or charge slip and possibly dispute it

For each transaction you mark, IntelliCharge places a single question mark in the left column of the IntelliCharge Statement window. It also puts five question marks (?????) in the Ref field of the register, so you can find a marked transaction easily after IntelliCharge has recorded all the transactions.

4 **Click Record All to record the transactions in the register.**

See "Paying credit card bills with IntelliCharge" on page 265.

IntelliCharge records the transactions and displays the Make Credit Card Payment window.

How IntelliCharge categorizes your transactions

The first time IntelliCharge updates your register with transactions from your electronic statement, it categorizes the transactions according to Quicken's standard category list and the merchant codes contained in your electronic statement.

After your first IntelliCharge update, you can change the categories assigned to transactions at any time. When you make changes, you teach IntelliCharge how to categorize future transactions.

If IntelliCharge finds this while categorizing a new transaction	It does this
No matching payee	Assigns a category to the new transaction from its own list of credit card categories. Your IntelliCharge statement contains a list of standard credit card industry code numbers that it maps to Quicken category names. For example, IntelliCharge assigns the Quicken category "Medical" to a credit card transaction you charged to "Dr. Louise Fernandez."
A transaction with a matching payee	Copies the category information from the most recent transaction with a matching payee.
A split transaction with a matching payee	Copies the category information from the first line of the Splits window.

Keep IntelliCharge in mind when you make changes to past transactions. If you change the information in the Payee field after IntelliCharge records the transactions in your register, it won't be able to match payees and categories correctly the next time you update your register.

Note: IntelliCharge's use of payee information may also affect your decision whether to use Quicken's Start New Year option. This option removes the previous year's transactions from your accounts (including payee information). When payee information is removed, IntelliCharge may not be able to match payees and categories correctly the next time you update your register.

Entering transactions manually

IntelliCharge records all the transactions in the IntelliCharge Statement window that aren't already in the current register. If you have recorded any transactions in the register manually, IntelliCharge tries to match the amount of the transaction with a transaction from the electronic statement. If it is successful, IntelliCharge marks the transaction as cleared in the register. (An X in your IntelliCharge register means that the transaction appeared on your credit card statement and was cleared.) If IntelliCharge can't match a transaction by amount, IntelliCharge doesn't change the transaction in the register, since the matching transaction may appear on a future electronic statement.

Caution: If you enter a transaction manually but the amount differs from what is on the electronic statement, IntelliCharge won't match the transaction and your balance won't be correct. Because of this possibility, we strongly recommend that you *don't* enter transactions manually. Let IntelliCharge enter the transactions.

Paying credit card bills with IntelliCharge

You can pay your Quicken credit card bill with a check you print from Quicken, a handwritten check that is automatically entered in your register, or an electronic payment.

1 **Complete the Make Credit Card Payment window.**

If you don't want to pay your bill at this time, click Cancel.

Choose the bank account from which you will pay the credit card bill.

Electronic payment is an option only if you already have an electronic account set up.

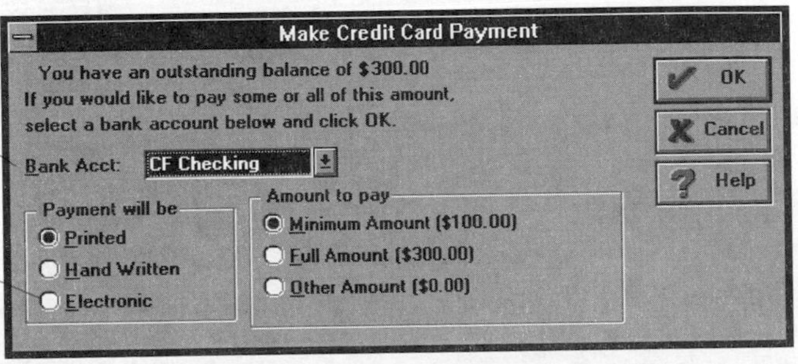

2 **Click OK.**

The Register window appears if you are paying with a handwritten check.

If you pay your bill electronically with CheckFree, the payment date is either the due date from the statement or five days from today, whichever is later.

The Write Checks window appears if you are paying with a check printed with Quicken or through CheckFree. For a printed check, Quicken inserts the name and address of the bank.

3 **(Optional) Make any necessary changes to the transaction in the register or the Write Checks window, and click Record.**

Handling credit card disputes with IntelliCharge

Your paper and electronic statements should always match. If there is ever any discrepancy between the statements, the bank always considers the paper statement to be correct.

You can use IntelliCharge to help single out a charge that you don't recognize or an amount that doesn't match the charge amount on your credit card receipt.

1 **Use the Mark button in the IntelliCharge Statement window to mark the disputed item.**

Five question marks (?????) will appear next to the disputed transaction in the register.

2 **Click Record All to let IntelliCharge record all transactions in the register.**

3 **Find each disputed transaction in the register so you can review it.**

Don't delete the disputed transaction! Whatever the reason the charge has appeared on your credit card statement, you must notify the bank and follow the bank's instructions to dispute the charge. If the charge was an error, a credit will appear on a subsequent statement to correct the balance of your account.

See "Travelers Bank" on page 320 for the phone number

4 **Call the bank immediately about the disputed charge.**

Check the Revolving Loan Agreement and Disclosure Statement that you received from the bank, or consult the back of your paper credit card statement to find out how the bank advises you to handle a disputed transaction.

5 **Notify the bank of the disputed item *in writing*.**

25 Updating your portfolio prices online

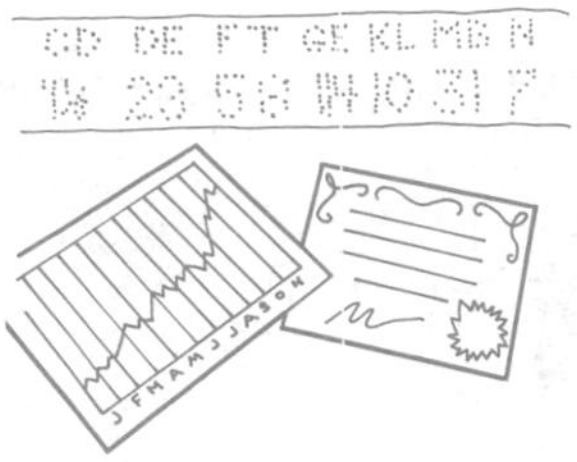

About Portfolio Price Update

Portfolio Price Update is a service that updates the prices of the stocks and mutual funds in your Quicken investment portfolio. The service can update prices of all stocks and mutual funds traded on the New York Stock Exchange, American Stock Exchange, and NASDAQ.

The Portfolio Price Update service is available 24 hours a day, 7 days a week.

Portfolio Price Update includes only "last price" information; high, low, and volume aren't included.

- If you update stock prices while the market is open, prices are delayed by at least 15 minutes.
- If you update stock prices while the market is closed, prices reflect the most recent closing price.
- Mutual fund prices are always quoted at the most recent closing price. They are updated once a day at 5:30 p.m. EST.

You may use Portfolio Price Update three times at no charge. Then you need to sign up for the service to continue using it. When you sign up, you provide your name, address, and credit card information that Intuit uses to bill you for the service. You also set up a password that protects access to your account.

Pricing

Charges for using Portfolio Price Update are billed monthly to your credit card. The monthly billing cycle begins on the day you sign up, rather than on the first day of the month.

Once you sign up for Portfolio Price Update, you are charged the basic monthly fee, whether or not you use the service.

For current pricing information, call Intuit. See "Intuit Online Services Technical Support" on page 319 for the phone number.

Using your free updates

1 **From the Online menu, choose Update Portfolio Prices.**

The first time you use Portfolio Price Update, a message appears advising you of your three free updates.

This message tells how many free updates you have used.

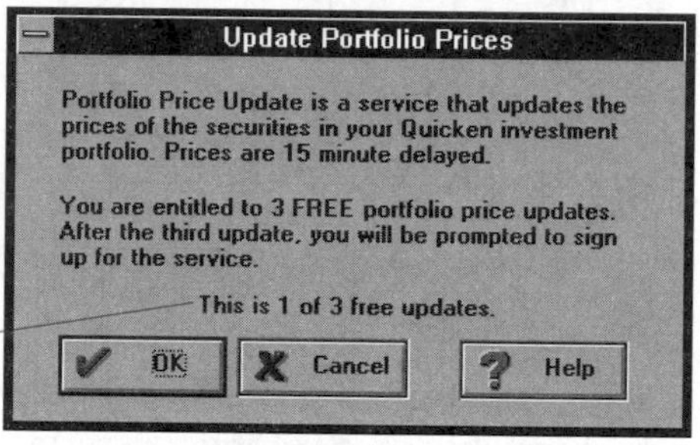

2 **Click OK to update your portfolio prices at no charge.**

See "Using Portfolio Price Update" on page 271. (You won't need to enter a password.)

Signing up for Portfolio Price Update

The fourth time you request a price update, Quicken prompts you to sign up for the Portfolio Price Update service.

To sign up for Portfolio Price Update, use the top half of this window.

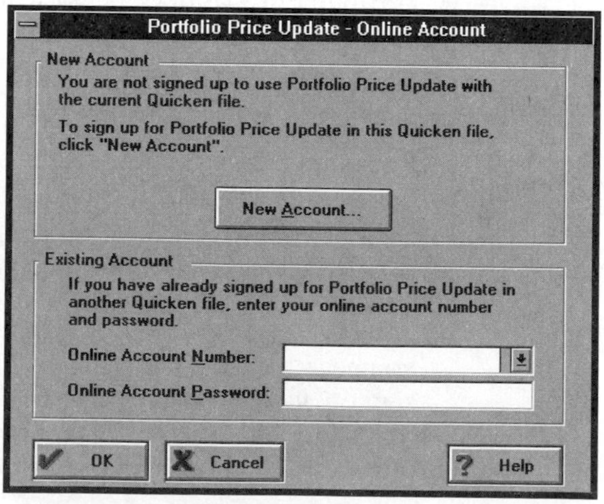

1 **Click New Account.**

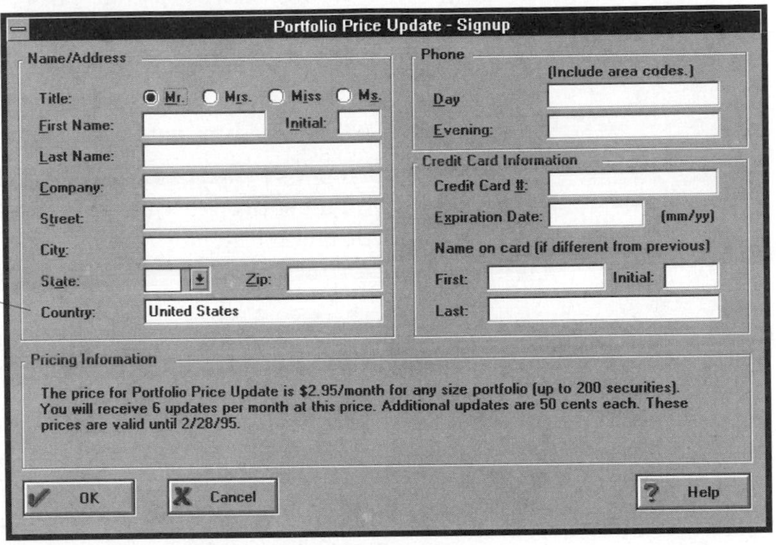

At this time, Portfolio Price Update is available only to residents of the United States (including Alaska, Hawaii, and Puerto Rico).

2 **Complete the Portfolio Price Update Signup window and click OK.**

Your monthly charges will be billed to the credit card you specify in this window. Intuit keeps your credit card information confidential. Intuit accepts the MasterCard, Visa, American Express, and Discover cards.

Setting your account password

After you click OK in the signup window, the Set Password window appears. In this window, you set up a password to protect your online account from unauthorized use.

Your password can contain between 4 and 16 characters and can include any combination of numbers, letters, and symbols.

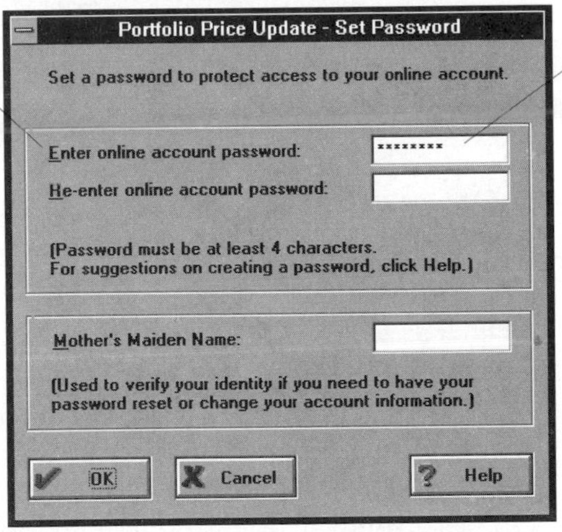

When you enter a password, you see only asterisks (for security).

We suggest that you use a combination of at least eight letters and numbers for your password. Don't use common words or names (especially yours). If you enter blank spaces as the leading or trailing characters in your password, Quicken removes them.

Passwords aren't case-sensitive, so it doesn't matter whether you use uppercase or lowercase letters.

1 **In the first box, enter a password.**

2 **In the second box, enter the password again.**

Whatever you enter must match the first password exactly.

Caution: Make a note of your password and keep it in a safe place. If you lose your password, you must call Intuit to have it reset. See "Intuit Online Services Technical Support" on page 319 for the phone number.

3 **In the third box, enter your mother's maiden name.**

If you lose your password or wish to change your online account, you must provide this information to confirm your identity when you call Intuit.

4 **Click OK.**

Quicken now dials Intuit, establishes an online connection, and sends the information you entered.

Note: If Quicken is connecting to Intuit for the first time, it attempts to set up your modem automatically. If the online connection fails, a message may instruct you to change your modem settings. See "Setting up your modem to use Intuit services" on page 256.

After your signup is complete, Quicken ends the online connection and displays a confirmation message with your online account number.

This number identifies your personal Intuit online account. Be sure to write it down.

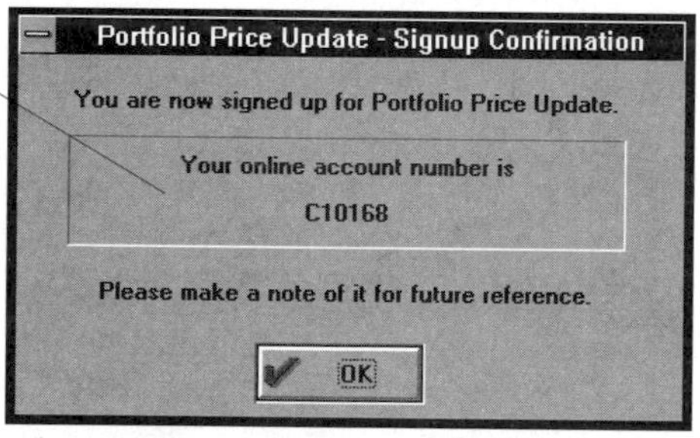

5 **Click OK to close the confirmation window.**

A window appears in which Quicken asks whether you want to update your portfolio prices now.

6 **Click Yes to update prices, or click No to close the window without updating.**

Your online account number

When you sign up for Portfolio Price Update, Intuit creates an online account for you. This account is identified by the unique number you see in the confirmation window. You need this number if you want to use your online account with another Quicken file. See "Using Portfolio Price Update with more than one Quicken file" on page 274.

See "Changing your password" on page 273.

If you lose or forget your online account number, you can find it displayed in the Change Password window.

Using Portfolio Price Update

Once you have signed up for Portfolio Price Update, you can update your investment portfolio prices quickly and easily.

If you use Portfolio Price Update more than once during a Quicken session, you don't need to re-enter your password.

1 **In the Portfolio View window, click Update. Or, from the Online menu, choose Update Portfolio Prices.**

2 **Enter your online account password and click OK.**

Quicken does the following:

- Dials a phone number and establishes an online connection.
- Retrieves and updates prices for the stocks and mutual funds in your Quicken portfolio (in the current Quicken file only).
- Disconnects the phone line.
- Displays a message confirming the price update.
- Displays the Portfolio View window for the account that is currently open. If no account is open, Quicken displays the Portfolio View window for the last account you had open.

Note: Even though you see updated prices for only the current investment account, all the prices in your security list have been updated.

Ticker symbols required

To update the price of a security, Quicken needs its ticker symbol. The ticker symbol is a letter combination that uniquely identifies the security. Often, it is the truncated or abbreviated name of the company, fund, or group issuing the security.

In the Portfolio View window, the ticker symbol appears in a column labeled Sym to the right of the Security column. *If you haven't entered a ticker symbol for a security, Quicken can't update its price.*

Most ticker symbols aren't case-sensitive. You can enter them in either uppercase or lowercase letters. For information about exceptions, press F1 in Quicken, click Search, type "case-sensitive", and press Enter.

When you start a portfolio price update, Quicken checks to see if all the securities in your portfolio have ticker symbols. If any securities are missing symbols, Quicken displays a message telling you which securities can't be updated.

- Click OK to update the rest of your portfolio–those securities that have ticker symbols.

OR

- Click Cancel to return to the Portfolio View window, where you can add ticker symbols to those securities that don't have them. See "Setting up securities for a regular investment account" on page 127.

Finding ticker symbols

If you don't know the ticker symbol for a stock or mutual fund, you can find it:

- In your brokerage or mutual fund account statement.
- In the Wall Street Journal or other financial publications, such as Barron's or the Investor's Business Daily.
- By calling your broker or mutual fund company.

Note: Quicken updates certain stock market indices if you include them in your investment portfolio. For more information, press F1 in Quicken, click Search, type "indices", and press Enter.

If Quicken can't update a security price

If Quicken can't update prices for one or more securities in your investment portfolio, it displays a window that lists those securities. Quicken may be unable to update a price for the following reasons:

- The ticker symbol for the security is incorrect.
- The ticker symbol can't be found in the database of securities.
- The security is no longer being traded.

Preventing a price update for a security

You may want to prevent Quicken from trying to update the price of a security if:

- You don't have the symbol and don't want to get a "missing ticker symbol" message from Quicken.
- You want to reduce total update time by preventing updates for securities that you don't track frequently.
- You have more than 200 securities in your portfolio and want to exclude one or more from the update. (Quicken can update up to 200 securities per access.)

See "Setting up securities for a regular investment account" on page 127.

To tell Quicken *not* to update the price of a security, type an asterisk (*) in front of its ticker symbol. (Examples: *NOVL, *PAC)

If you don't know a security's ticker symbol and want to avoid the "missing ticker symbol" message, type an asterisk (*) in the Symbol box instead of a ticker symbol.

Changing your online account information

Once you have signed up for Portfolio Price Update, you may wish to make changes to the information you provided to Intuit. For example, you may wish to change:

- Name, address or phone number information.
- Billing information (a different credit card or a new expiration date).

To make any change to your online account information, you must call Intuit. See "Intuit Online Services Technical Support" on page 319 for the phone number. When you call, you need to provide your mother's maiden name to verify your identity. (You entered it in the window where you set your online account password.)

Changing your password

For maximum protection of your Intuit online account, we recommend that you change your password at regular intervals.

1 **From the Online menu, choose Change Online Account, and then choose Change Password.**

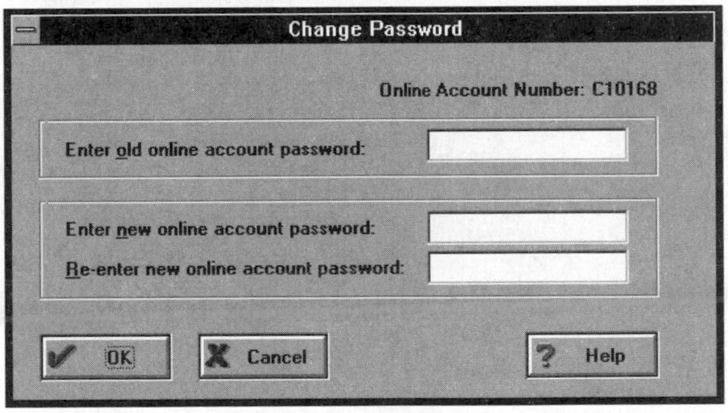

2 **In the first box, enter your current online account password.**

When you enter a password, you see only asterisks (for security).

3 **In the second box, enter a new online account password.**

4 **In the third box, enter the new online account password again. Then click OK.**

The new and re-entered passwords must match exactly.

Canceling Portfolio Price Update

If you no longer wish to use Portfolio Price Update, you can cancel the service.

1 **From the Online menu, choose Change Online Account, and then choose Cancel Service.**

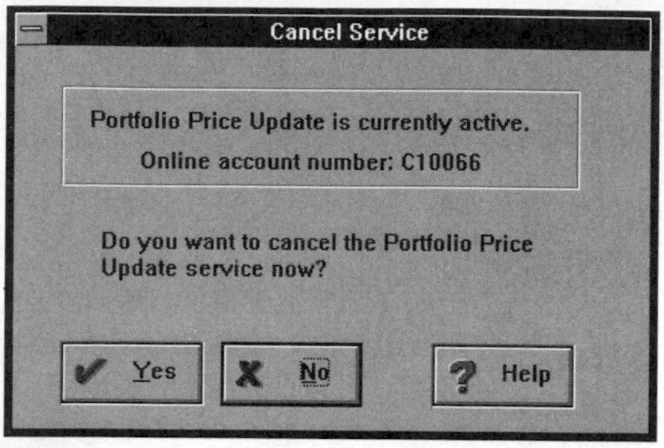

2 **Click Yes to cancel the Portfolio Price Update service.**

Note: You don't receive additional free price updates if you cancel Portfolio Price Update and then sign up again.

Advanced options

Most people use one Portfolio Price Update online account with one Quicken file on one computer. However, for people who need more options, Portfolio Price Update has additional flexibility. Read this section to learn how to:

- Use Portfolio Price Update with more than one Quicken file.
- Sign up for an additional Portfolio Price Update account.
- Use Portfolio Price Update on more than one computer.

Using Portfolio Price Update with more than one Quicken file

When you sign up for Portfolio Price Update, the Quicken file you are currently using is linked to your new online account. (The name of the current file appears in the Quicken window's title bar.) You can sign up for Portfolio Price Update only once in any Quicken file.

While most people use only one Quicken file, others use multiple Quicken files to separate home and business data, data for different years, and data for different people.

If you want to use Portfolio Price Update with another Quicken file, you have two choices:

- Use your *existing* online account with the other Quicken file.

OR

- Sign up for an *additional* online account to use with the other Quicken file.

Using an existing online account

1 **Open the Quicken file that doesn't have an online account.**

2 **From the Online menu, choose Update Portfolio Prices.**

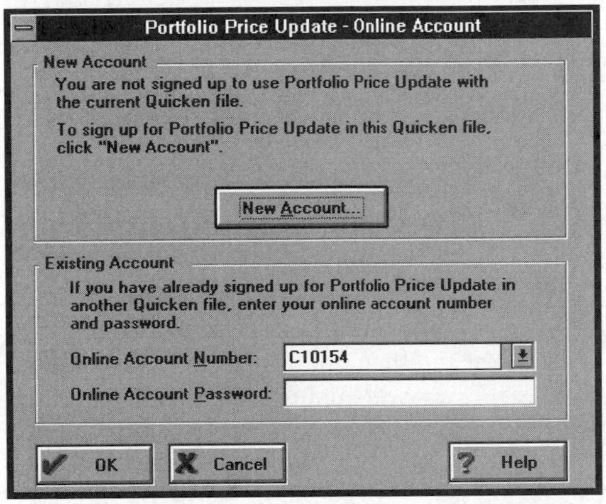

For Portfolio Price Update advanced options, use the bottom half of this window.

3 **Enter your online account number, or select it from the drop-down list.**

This number appeared in the confirmation window that displayed when you signed up for Portfolio Price Update. It is also displayed in the Change Password window.

4 **Enter your online account password.**

5 **Click OK.**

Quicken makes an online connection and updates prices for the securities in the current Quicken file. That file is now linked to the online account you specified.

Signing up for an additional online account

Although a single online account will probably meet your needs, you can sign up for more than one online account, if you wish. Portfolio Price Update usage is billed separately for each account.

1. **Open a Quicken file that you haven't yet used with Portfolio Price Update.**
2. **From the Online menu, choose Update Portfolio Prices.**
3. **In the Online Account window, click New Account.**
4. **Complete the Portfolio Price Update Signup window and click OK.**
5. **Set a password for your new account and click OK.**

When your signup is complete, Quicken displays your new online account number.

Using Portfolio Price Update on more than one computer

You can use your Portfolio Price Update online account on more than one computer. The account is linked to the Quicken file you were using when you signed up, not the computer you were using it on.

If you copy your Quicken file from one computer to another, you must use your existing online account. Quicken recognizes that you already have an online account linked to that file, and it prompts you for the password.

If you use a different Quicken file on the second computer, you can either use your existing online account with that file or sign up for a new one. See "Using an existing online account" on page 275 and "Signing up for an additional online account" on this page.

Communications problems and solutions

If you have problems with your modem or problems connecting to Portfolio Price Update, see "Communications problems and solutions" on page 259. (In most cases, you will find the symptoms described and the solution outlined there.)

26 Paying bills online

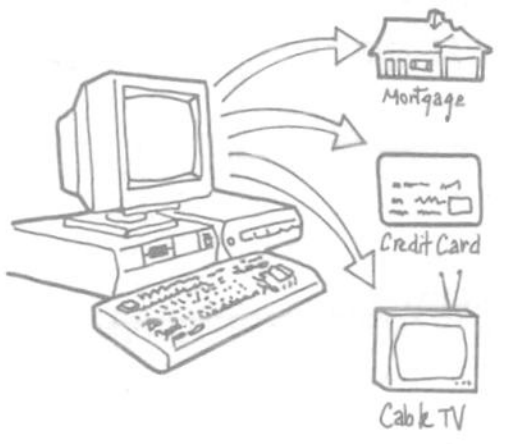

How CheckFree works

See the information booklet and enrollment form included in your Quicken package.

CheckFree* is an electronic bill-payment service. You set up payments in Quicken and then send them to CheckFree via modem. CheckFree then pays your payees from the account you specify.

CheckFree works for any household or business with a computer, a modem, and Quicken. If you are undecided about the benefits of paying bills through CheckFree, give it a try. The first month is free.

The following overview describes the basic CheckFree process.

1 **You enter an electronic payment transaction in Quicken, much as you enter transactions in the register or in the Write Checks window.**

See page 285 for payment scheduling guidelines.

Your transaction includes the payment date (the date the payee receives payment from CheckFree).

2 **Using your modem and Quicken, you transmit your payment instructions to CheckFree before the payment date.**

Quicken dials the CheckFree Processing Center and transmits your instructions.

---

* You can use CheckFree for payments in the United States regardless of where you transmit from. The bank account used for CheckFree must also be in the United States. CheckFree is an independently owned company, not part of Intuit.

The CheckFree Processing Center returns a confirmation number for each transmission, which Quicken stores in the register when the transmission is successfully completed.

3 **The CheckFree Processing Center makes the payment.**

See the table on page 288 for details.

Some payees receive electronic payments, and others receive a printed check.

4 **You receive verification of the payment both in your bank statement and in the statement you receive from the payee (if the payee sends statements).**

Signing up for CheckFree service

You can send electronic payments as soon as CheckFree processes your signed CheckFree enrollment form and voided check, and you receive your CheckFree welcome kit.

Call CheckFree for current pricing. For the telephone number, see "CheckFree Corporation Technical Support" on page 319.

As of October 1994, the monthly fee for the service is $9.95, with added charges for more than 20 monthly transactions. The first month of service is free.

Setting up an account to use CheckFree

After you have received your CheckFree welcome kit and set up your modem, set up your bank account for electronic payment. CheckFree allows you to use one bank account with one CheckFree account.

If you are already using CheckFree with software other than Quicken, you can switch to using CheckFree through Quicken. (In Quicken Help, search for "Importing data from an existing CheckFree account" under the keyword "importing".)

1 **From the Activities menu, choose CheckFree, and then choose Set Up Account.**

2 **From the Account List window, choose the bank account to make CheckFree payments from, and click Set Up. (This must be the account you specified on the enrollment form.)**

The Electronic Payment Setup window lists all of your bank accounts.

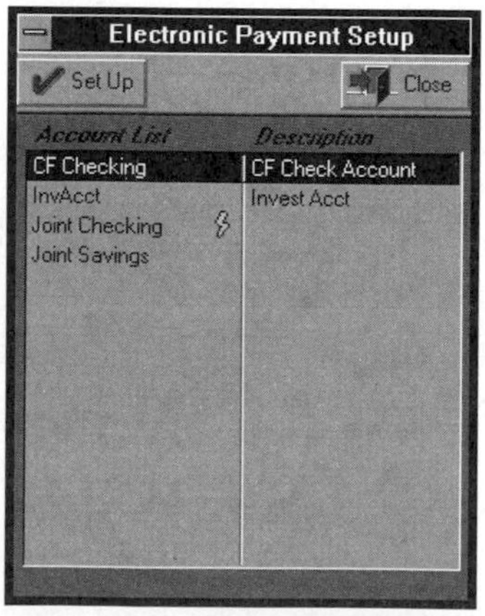

3 **Ensure that the Enable Electronic Payments checkbox is checked and the bank account you want to set up is displayed.**

This checkbox should already be selected, and the bank account you selected is displayed.

Enter your telephone number, beginning with the area code. You don't have to type hyphens or parentheses.

Enter the CheckFree Account Number that you provided in your enrollment form. (In most cases, this number is your Social Security number.)

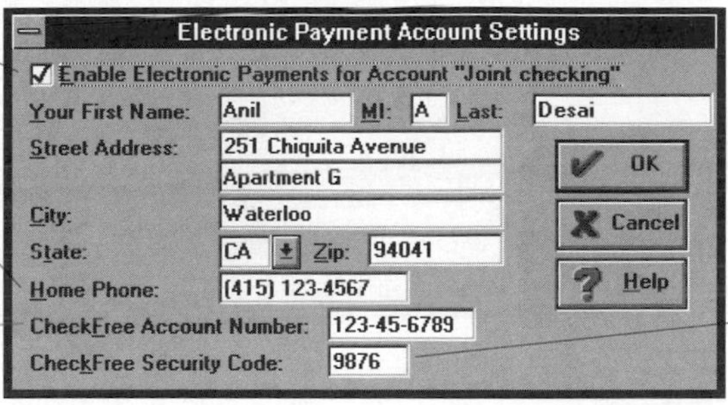

Enter the four-digit Personal Security Code you selected when you signed up for CheckFree.

4 **Complete the Electronic Payment Account Settings window, and then click OK.**

Quicken returns to the Account List window. Note that a lightning bolt appears next to the accounts that are electronically enabled in both this Account List window and in the Quicken Account List window.

To discontinue CheckFree service, select the account again (steps 1 and 2) and clear the Enable Electronic Payments checkbox. Then notify CheckFree Corporation in writing that you are canceling the service.

5 **Close the Account List window.**

6 **Set up your modem.**

See "Setting up your modem to use CheckFree" on page 258.

Setting up electronic payees

For Quicken to record an electronic payment, you must first add the payee to the Electronic Payee list. (CheckFree calls electronic payees "merchants," but you can send an electronic payment to any business or individual.)

Add a payee to the Electronic Payee list only once; all accounts in a Quicken file share the same list. You can add payees before you begin writing electronic payments or as you write payments. (The next time you transmit to CheckFree, Quicken sends any changes you've made to the Electronic Payee list.)

You can set up a payee for individual payments or for recurring payments of the same amount. For example, credit card payments are individual payments of varying amounts, while loan payments are typically recurring payments of the same amount.

Setting up payees for individual payments

1 **From the Activities menu, choose CheckFree and then choose Electronic Payee List.**

If Electronic Payee List is dimmed on the CheckFree menu, no accounts have been set up for electronic payments.

Your list is initially empty. From this window, you can add, edit, and delete payees.

Once you've set up electronic payees, you can use the list to print a mailing list of payees, including phone numbers. To print the Electronic Payee List window, press Ctrl+P while the list is displayed.

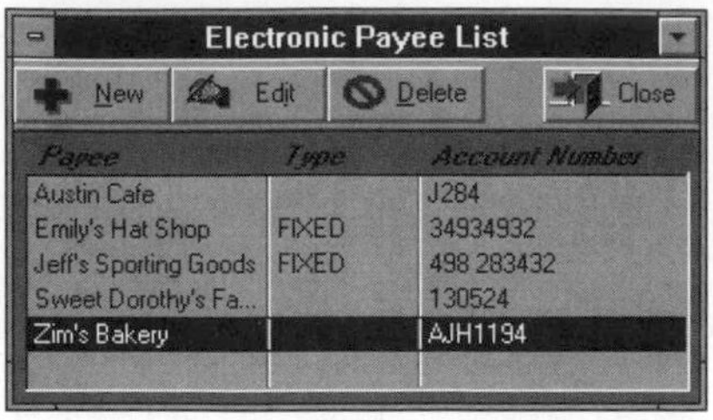

2 **Click New.**

3 **Select Normal Payee and click OK.**

Choose this if the amount or timing of the payments vary.

Choose this to have CheckFree automatically send regular, recurring payments of the same amount.

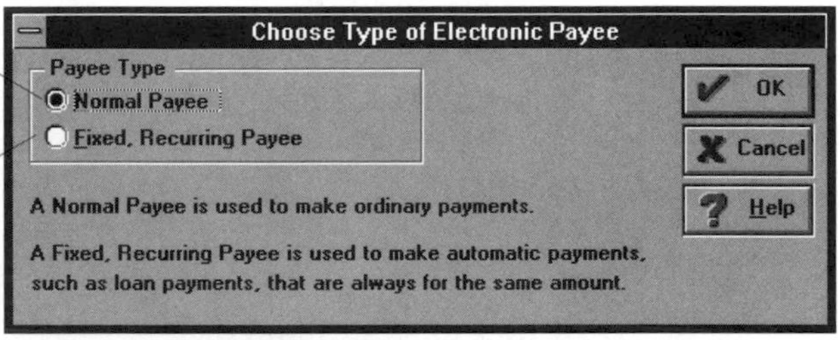

4 **Complete the Set Up Electronic Payee window.**

CheckFree may need the address to mail your payment to the payee.

Enter the number the electronic payee uses to identify you (account number, policy number, or loan number). If you don't know the number, enter your last name. The payee needs the account number to credit your account for the payment.

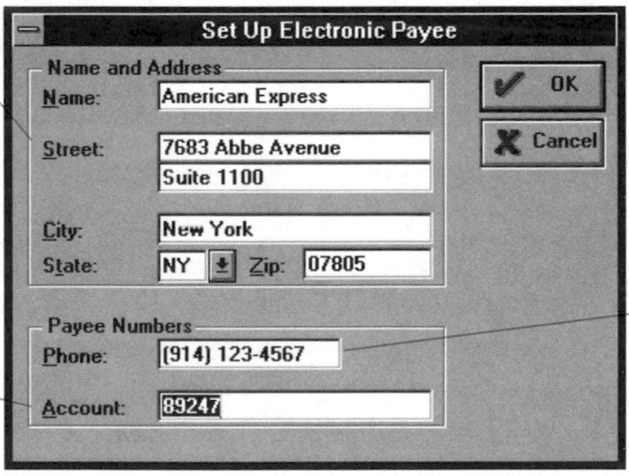

Enter the phone number you would call if you had a billing question, beginning with the area code. CheckFree must have the correct phone number to route your payments correctly.

5 **Click OK to record the information.**

You can set up more electronic payees or begin entering payments.

See "Entering electronic payments" on page 283.

Setting up payees for fixed payments

You can authorize CheckFree to make a series of fixed, recurring payments from your bank account to an electronic payee. You specify payment frequency and other details, and Quicken sets up as many payments as you need.

You set up this payment once, CheckFree takes care of paying all the bills at the frequency you specify, and Quicken automatically enters the transactions in your account register. (For example, you may want to schedule 36 months of car payments, to be paid on the third day of each month, starting 1/3/95.)

Future CheckFree fixed payments show up in your Financial Calendar too. (See page 54.)

You can't change a normal payee into a fixed payee, and you can't change a fixed payee into a normal payee. To make fixed payments to a payee you have already set up as a normal payee, you need to delete the normal payee from the Electronic Payee list, transmit the deletion to CheckFree, and then set up the payee as a fixed payee.

1 **From the Activities menu, choose CheckFree and then choose Electronic Payee List.**

2 **Click New.**

The Choose Type of Electronic Payee window appears.

3 **Select Fixed, Recurring Payee and click OK.**

4 **Complete the Set Up Electronic Payee window.**

This shows the account from which electronic payments will be drawn. If you have only one electronic account, it appears here automatically. If you have more than one electronic payment account, choose the account from a drop-down list here.

Enter information here as you would to set up normal electronic payees. See step 4 on page 280.

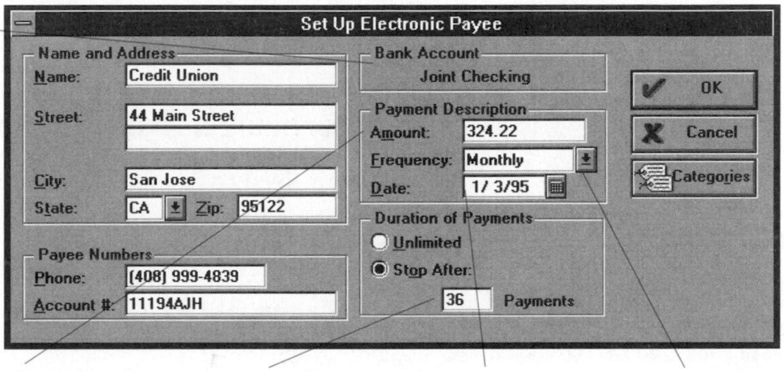

Enter the amount of the fixed payment.

Enter the length of time you expect the fixed payments to continue.

Enter the payment date of the first fixed payment.

From the drop-down list, choose how often CheckFree should make the payments.

5 **Click Categories.**

Enter a category here. Click Splits if you want the fixed payment transaction to cover more than one category or class.

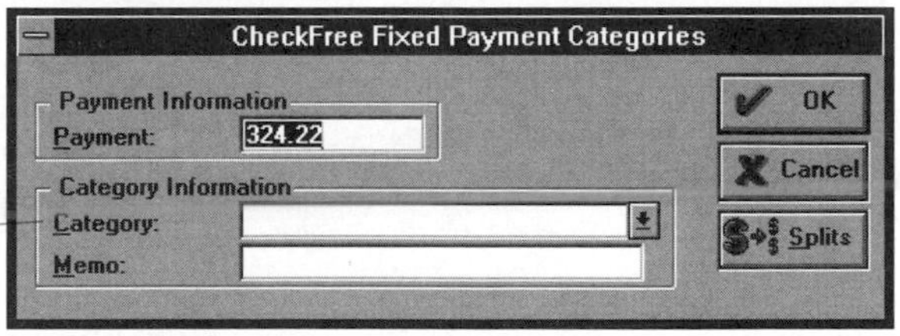

6 **(Optional) Enter a category and memo, and click OK.**

7 **Click OK to close the Set Up Electronic Payee window.**

CheckFree doesn't know about a fixed payment until you transmit it.

If you are ready to send the information to CheckFree, "Transmitting electronic payments" on page 287.

Setting up more than one account for a payee

You can set up multiple accounts with one payee, but the account numbers you enter must differ. (For example, use a homeowner's insurance policy number and life insurance policy number from the same insurance company.)

If you set up more than one account for the same payee, Quicken asks you to add extra characters to the name to make the name unique. You can edit an existing payee by adding characters in braces at the end.

Quicken doesn't transmit the characters within the braces to Check-Free. The braces help to distinguish the two accounts in the Electronic Payee list and in Quicken reports.

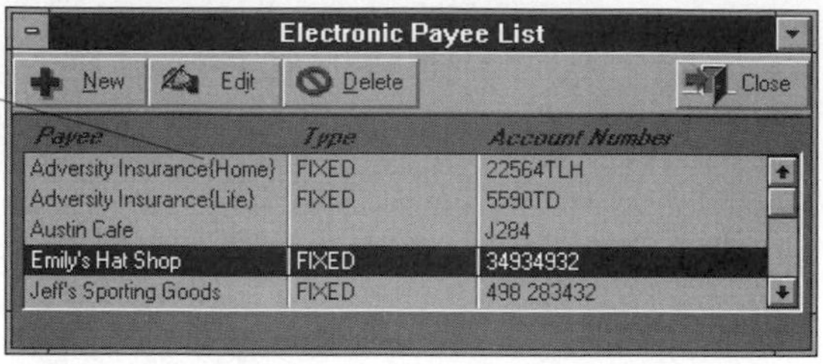

If you change an electronic transaction to a paper check transaction and then print checks, Quicken won't print the characters after the first brace or the brace itself. You may find this feature useful for paper checks as well as for electronic payments.

Amortizing a fixed payment

If your fixed payment is for an amortized loan, such as a mortgage, set up the loan details in Quicken's View Loans window. With each payment, Quicken automatically calculates the split between principal, interest, and any impound items, and then enters the details as a split transaction in your register. You can then analyze your loan amortization in the View Loans window.

For full details of Quicken's loan handling features, see Chapter 10, *Tracking loans and mortgages,* on page 105.

To amortize a CheckFree fixed payment:

See page 280.

1 **Set up the payee for the fixed payment.**

2 **Set up the loan in the View Loans window.**

See ""Setting up a loan" on page 106. In step 6 on page 108, click Method of Pmt and select CheckFree Fixed Payment. Select the payee from the drop-down Fixed Payee list, and click OK to return to the Set Up Loan Payment window.

Quicken uses the total amount from your loan in the fixed payment transaction it sends to CheckFree. If you change the total payment amount in the View Loans window (for example, if the rate changes for an adjustable rate mortgage), Quicken sets up a change transaction to transmit to CheckFree, instructing CheckFree to alter the payment amount. Remember that CheckFree won't change the payment amount until you actually transmit the change transaction.

See "Stopping fixed payments" on page 289.

If you delete the loan from the View Loans window, Quicken doesn't delete the payee from the Electronic Payee list, nor does it create a stop payment transaction. If you want to stop the payment, you must do it as a separate action.

Entering electronic payments

Entering electronic payments in the Write Checks window or in the register is similar to entering any other kind of payment. See the following sections, "Entering individual electronic payments in Write Checks" and "Entering individual electronic payments in the register."

Entering individual electronic payments in Write Checks

After you have set up a normal payee, each time you want to send a payment to that payee, enter the payment in your Quicken account.

To enter payments in the Write Checks window:

Or click the Check icon on the iconbar

1 **From the Activities menu, choose Write Checks.**

2 **Click an account button to select the correct account.**

3 **Select the Electronic Payment checkbox to display the screen in electronic payment format.**

Quicken automatically postdates any electronic payment by five business days from today. You can change the date to postdate this check even further. See "Scheduling electronic payments" on page 285.

Enter a payee name or choose it from the Electronic Payee list.

When you have electronic payment set up for an account and select the Electronic Payment checkbox, Quicken clearly labels the window.

Quicken doesn't transmit the contents of the Memo field to CheckFree. This information is for your records only.

Clear the Electronic Payment checkbox to write and print a paper check.

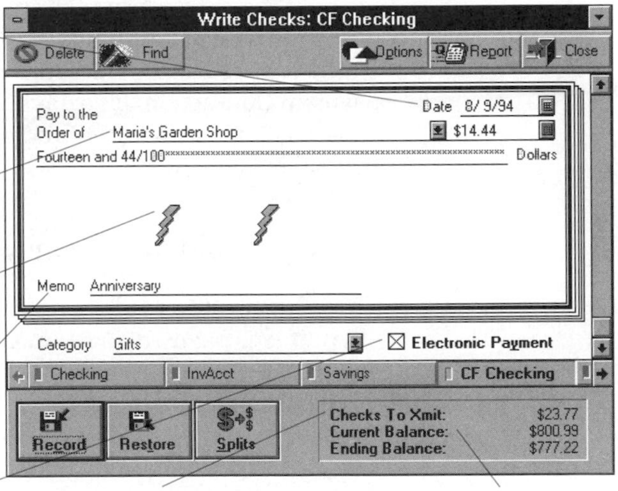

Checks To Xmit tracks the total amount of electronic payments you have written and have yet to transmit.

The Current Balance doesn't include postdated transactions; the Ending Balance does.

4 **Complete the information in the Write Checks window.**

5 **Click Record to record the payment.**

See "Transmitting electronic payments" on page 287.

Quicken records the payment in the check register with XMIT in the Num field. Quicken doesn't transmit the payment until you tell it to.

Entering individual electronic payments in the register

You can enter electronic payments in the register instead of in the Write Checks window. Open the register and enter the transaction. Type XMIT in the Num field (or choose it from the drop-down list) to show that this is an untransmitted electronic payment. Record the payment as usual.

Type XMIT in the Num field of a transaction to tell Quicken that this transaction is an electronic payment. XMIT indicates that the transaction *will be* transmitted.

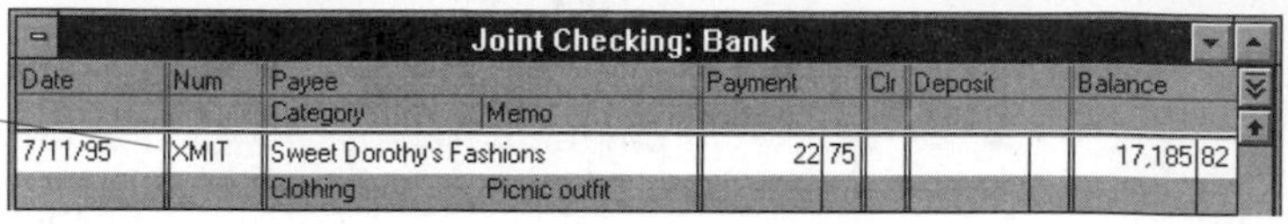

Joint Checking: Bank
Date
Num
Payee
Category
Memo
Payment
Clr
Deposit
Balance
7/11/95
XMIT
Sweet Dorothy's Fashions
Clothing
Picnic outfit
22 75
17,185 82

Entering fixed electronic payments

See "Transmitting electronic payments" on page 287.

If you set up fixed payments, just transmit the first fixed payment to CheckFree.

After that, CheckFree automatically sends the payments to the payee at the intervals you've specified, and Quicken automatically enters the transactions into your register. In the check register, Quicken inserts the word FIXED in the Num field of any fixed payment transaction. Five days before the payment date, Quicken replaces FIXED with E-PMT and enters the next FIXED payment to that payee.

Making duplicate payments on the same day

CheckFree won't process a payment that appears to be a duplicate of a previous payment (a payment that has the same payee, amount, and payment date). Although you receive a confirmation number for the duplicate payment, only the first payment is processed. If you need to send a second payment to the same payee, you must vary the amount or payment date.

Scheduling electronic payments

Using CheckFree doesn't mean you can pay your bills at the last moment. CheckFree requires lead time between the date you transmit your payment instructions and the date your payment is due. The *first time* you make a payment to each payee, use this table to determine how to schedule the payment.

Date	Definition	Calculation
Transmission date	Date you send payment instructions from Quicken to CheckFree	Five business days before the payment date, ten business days before the due date
Payment date	Date that you've entered in the Date field in Quicken; it's the date the payee receives payment from CheckFree	Five business days before the due date
Due date	Due date on the statement from the payee	

For example, suppose you have a bill due on November 15. *If this is the first electronic payment to the payee,* you would transmit the payment on November 1, ten business days before the due date.

The transmission date is November 1, five business days before the payment date.

The payee receives payment from CheckFree on the payment date, November 8, five business days before the due date.

The due date of the bill is November 15.

Shaded areas on this calendar are nonbusiness days.

If a payment is due on or after a holiday like Thanksgiving, be sure you still allow a minimum of five business days between the transmission date and the payment date.

To decide how to schedule your future payments, examine the next statement from the payee to see how promptly the payee was able to process the payment. To adjust the schedule for your next payment, see the guidelines below. The latest possible date you can transmit a payment from Quicken to CheckFree is five business days before the bill is due.

Guidelines to avoid late payments

Enter the correct telephone number, account number, and address for the payee when you set up an electronic payee in Quicken.

After you have made several payments to an electronic payee, use the table below to determine when to transmit the payment to CheckFree.

Date	Definition	Calculation
Transmission date	Date you send payment instructions to CheckFree	Five business days before the payment date (can be no less than five business days, but may be more)
Payment date	Date that you've entered in the Date field in Quicken; it's the date the payee receives payment from CheckFree	Five business days before the due date (if the payee always processes the payment immediately, the payment date may be the same day as the due date)
Due date	Due date on the statement from the payee	

You can't decrease the length of time required between the transmission date and the payment date (five business days).

But, after you have made several payments to the electronic payee and you determine how quickly the payee can process a CheckFree payment, you may be able to decrease the length of time between the payment date and the due date. You may even treat the payment date and the due date as the same date if you know that a particular payee always processes the payment from CheckFree immediately.

Deferring the transmission of an electronic payment

To defer the transmission of a recorded transaction to CheckFree, you can temporarily change the status of the transaction.

1 **In the register, select the transaction that you don't want to send right now.**

2 **In the Num field, delete** XMIT **and type** PRINT.

FIXED marks the next fixed payment in a series of recurring payments.

XMIT marks an individual electronic payment that has been entered but not transmitted yet.

E-PMT marks an electronic payment, either fixed or normal, that has already been transmitted.

Date	Num	Payee / Category	Memo	Payment	Clr	Deposit	Balance
11/17/95	FIXED	Adversity Insurance{Home}		250 00			17,208 57
7/11/95	XMIT	Sweet Dorothy's Fashions / Clothing	Picnic outfit	22 75			17,185 82
7/11/95		**VOID**Zim's Bakery / Catering	Stopped{Confirm:TE				17,185 82
7/11/95	E-PMT	Sweet Dorothy's Fashions / Clothing	Dress for Jeff's party	26 55			17,159 27

Joint Checking: Bank

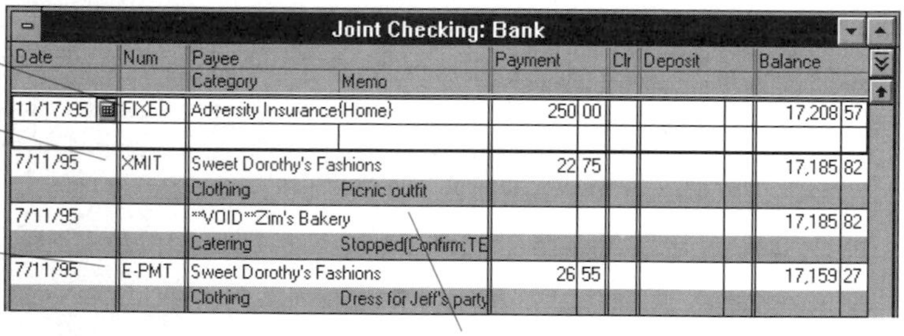

To void an E-PMT transaction, see "Stopping individual electronic payments" on page 289. To cancel a FIXED payment transaction, see "Stopping fixed payments" on page 289.

3 **Click Record to record the transaction.**

When you want to transmit the transaction, delete Print and type XMIT in the Num field.

Transmitting electronic payments

The transactions you transmit to CheckFree can include payments, changes to the Electronic Payee list (payees that are edited, added, or deleted), stop payments, payment inquiries, and E-mail messages to the CheckFree Processing Center.

Previewing and transmitting transactions

1 **Start in the Write Checks window or in the register.**

If you have more than one account enabled for use with CheckFree, make sure the correct account is active.

2 **From the Activities menu, choose CheckFree and then choose Transmit.**

Quicken tells you how many payments are ready to be transmitted.

3 **Click Preview to preview the transmission.**

Quicken places electronic payments to be transmitted at the top of the window in the payment date order. All electronic payments are indicated by the abbreviation "Pmt" or "Fxd."

These are updates you have made to the Electronic Payee list since the last time you transmitted payments to CheckFree. Whenever you add, edit, or delete a payee, or set up a fixed payment, the action appears in this list. CheckFree uses this information to update your records at the CheckFree Processing Center.

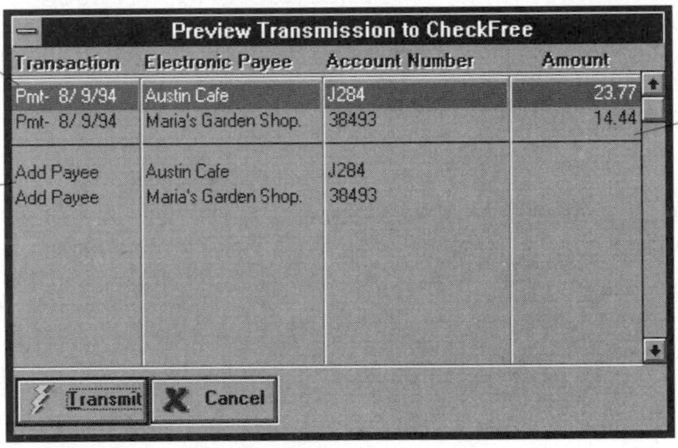

Payments to be transmitted appear above this line.

Changes to the Electronic Payee list appear below the line. (Fixed payments appear in both places.)

4 **(Optional) To modify or defer transactions or to edit payee information, click Cancel.**

See "Deferring the transmission of an electronic payment" on page 286.

5 **Click Transmit.**

Quicken initializes the modem and dials the CheckFree Processing Center. As it transmits, Quicken displays messages indicating progress. If you see an error message, try the procedure again.

If you have problems with your modem, "Communications problems and solutions" on page 259.

How payments appear on your bank statement

The way the CheckFree Processing Center makes the payment depends on what the payee can accept. The payment method determines how a payment appears on your bank statement.

Payment method	Description	Payment verification
Electronic-to-check	CheckFree mails a check on your behalf to the payee and then receives funds electronically from your bank on the payment date you specified.	Your bank statement will list the payee name, payment amount, and date for this type of transaction, instead of attaching a canceled check as a receipt.
Laser-printed draft	CheckFree mails a check drawn on your bank account to the payee. The check contains your account number and address.	If your checks are returned with your bank statement, this laser-printed check from CheckFree will be returned like any other paper check.
All electronic	If the payee is set up to receive electronic payments via one of CheckFree's payment networks, CheckFree initiates an electronic payment directly from your bank account to the payee's bank account.	Your bank statement will list the payee name, payment amount, and date for this type of transaction, instead of attaching a canceled check as a receipt.

Unposted payments

You should allow at least 10 business days from the payment date for a payee to post your payment. If a payee doesn't post your payment within this period, you should:

- Call the merchant directly. In most cases, the payment will be posted by the time you call, and any questions can be cleared up easily. If this isn't the case, follow the next step.
- Contact CheckFree Corporation. Provide a contact name and phone number for the payee, and CheckFree will provide proof of payment remittance to the payee. If the posting problem is due to a CheckFree error, CheckFree will resolve the situation directly with the payee (including paying any late fees up to a maximum of $50).

For the telephone number, see "CheckFree Corporation Technical Support" on page 319.

Getting a confirmation number

CheckFree sends a confirmation number back to Quicken for each transaction. Quicken stores this confirmation number and automatically uses it if you send an inquiry or a stop payment request regarding the transaction.

1. **Select the transaction in the check register.**
2. **From the Activities menu, choose CheckFree and then choose Electronic Payment Info.**

   Quicken displays the confirmation number you received from CheckFree.

Stopping electronic payments

After Quicken transmits an electronic payment, you can stop payment on the transaction if you don't wait too long. On the basis of the five days it can take CheckFree to make a scheduled payment, Quicken determines whether you are likely to be able to stop the payment and tells you if it's clearly too late.

Caution: Don't void an electronic payment. If you delete or void an electronic payment, Quicken can't get the confirmation number needed to stop the payment or transmit a status inquiry to CheckFree. Use the Stop Payment command instead.

Stopping individual electronic payments

1 **Select the transaction in the check register.**

2 **From the Activities menu, choose CheckFree and then choose Stop Payment.**

Quicken tells you when the payment is scheduled to be made. If it is possible to stop payment, Quicken asks if you want to do so. If it's too late to stop the payment or the payment has not yet been transmitted, Quicken lets you know.

Quicken determines whether you can stop a payment, taking into account the usual five business days between the transmission date and the payment date. CheckFree Corporation doesn't assess a charge for stop payments performed this way. If Quicken tells you that it is too late to transmit the stop payment, call CheckFree Corporation to try to stop the payment manually. CheckFree does assess an additional fee to stop payments manually.

For the telephone number, see "CheckFree Corporation Technical Support" on page 319.

3 **Click OK if it's still possible to stop the payment.**

Quicken immediately transmits your request to CheckFree. If the transmission is successful, Quicken marks the payment VOID in the register and records the stop payment confirmation number received from CheckFree in the Memo field of the transaction.

Stopping fixed payments

There are two ways to stop fixed payments. Either way, if you stop one payment to a payee, you stop them all.

- If you use the Stop Payment command described in the previous section, "Stopping individual electronic payments," Quicken stops all future fixed payments to that payee and saves all the payee information you entered.

- If you delete a fixed payee from the Electronic Payee list and transmit the deletion to CheckFree, Quicken stops all future fixed payments to that payee and deletes all the information about that payee, including confirmation numbers from previous transactions.

FIXED payees become INACTIVE payees when you either finish paying all the fixed payments or stop the fixed payments before you finish the payments. Keep inactive payees in the Electronic Payee list if you think you may need access to any of the payee or payment information in the future.

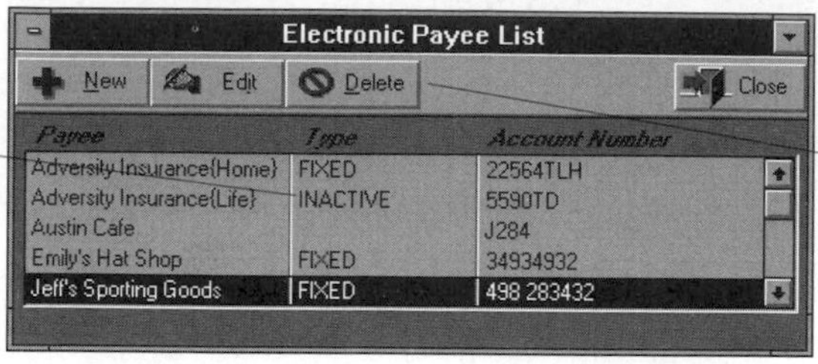

Click Delete to delete a payee from the list.

Editing or deleting a payee

If you edit payee information or delete a payee from the Electronic Payee list, Quicken waits to send the changes to CheckFree until the next time you transmit payments.

	Individual payments untransmitted	**Individual payments pending at CheckFree**	**Fixed payments**
Can you edit payee information?	No	Yes	Yes
Can you delete the payee?	No	No	Yes

Changing or deleting payees

1 **Select the name in the Electronic Payee list.**

2 **Click Edit to edit the payee or click Delete to delete the payee.**

Deleting a payee also deletes any confirmation number history for that payee.

3 **If you're editing the payee, enter the changes and click OK.**

Quicken transmits the change or deletion the next time you transmit a payment.

Changing a normal payee with pending payments

If you have pending (transmitted but not paid) payments to a normal payee, Quicken waits to transmit the change until Check-Free has processed all pending payments to that payee.

1 **Set up a new payee with the correct information.**

2 **Select the pending payment in the check register and double-click the new payee name from the Electronic Payee list.**

Repeat if there are multiple untransmitted payments to this payee.

Quicken transmits the payee changes the next time you transmit a payment.

3 **After CheckFree pays the pending transaction, delete the payee from the Electronic Payee list.**

Communicating with CheckFree

You can send electronic messages directly to CheckFree to make a payment inquiry or for general information. See "CheckFree Corporation Technical Support" on page 319.

Inquiring about electronic payments

CheckFree knows nothing about a payment until you transmit it to them. To get information about an untransmitted payment from Quicken, view it in the check register or preview it before transmission.

To find out the status of a transaction that you've already transmitted to CheckFree:

1 **In the Quicken register, select the payment transaction.**

2 **From the Activities menu, choose CheckFree and then choose Inquiry.**

Quicken displays a window showing the selected transaction's transmission date, payment date, account number, and confirmation number. Quicken then asks if you want to transmit an inquiry to CheckFree regarding this transaction.

3 **Make sure this transaction is the one you want to inquire about. If it is, click OK.**

4 **Enter information in the Transmit Payment Inquiry to CheckFree window.**

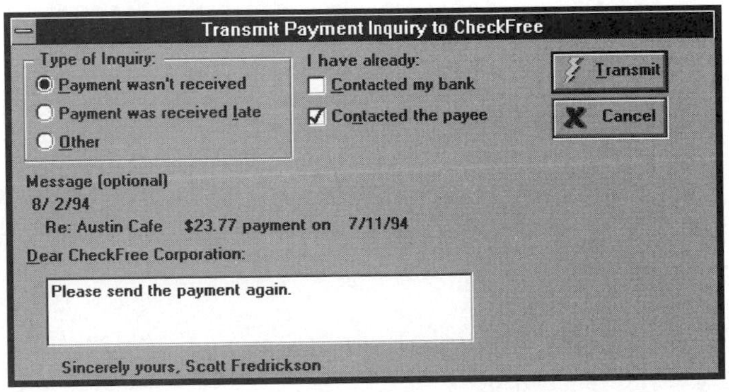

5 **Click Transmit to send the inquiry to CheckFree.**

CheckFree responds to your message by electronic mail (CheckFree E-Mail) or by U.S. mail. To view your electronic mailbox in Quicken, see "Sending or receiving electronic mail" next.

Sending or receiving electronic mail

You can send CheckFree a message that isn't specific to a payment. CheckFree replies to your message by E-Mail that you can read in Quicken or by U.S. mail.

1 **From the Activities menu, choose CheckFree and then choose E-Mail.**

2 **Choose either to create or retrieve a message.**

- Click Create to prepare a message. The Transmit Message to Check-Free window appears. Type your message in the text area, and click Transmit to send the message. Quicken transmits the message to CheckFree immediately.
- Click Retrieve to read a message from CheckFree. Quicken connects to the CheckFree Processing Center and looks for new messages that are addressed to you. Quicken displays all the messages you've already received from CheckFree in chronological order. (It also displays messages you've sent to CheckFree.) If there is a new message from CheckFree, it appears at the top of the list. Select the message you want to read. The text of the message appears in the Message window.

Handling the CheckFree service charge

You pay a monthly service charge to use CheckFree, which the CheckFree Corporation automatically charges to your bank account. You will see this charge on your bank statement.

Note: Don't use electronic payments to pay CheckFree Corporation directly for the service charge.

See "Scheduling a transaction on the Financial Calendar" on page 56.

To keep your Quicken register up to date for the CheckFree service charge, set up the fee as a recurring, scheduled transaction so that Quicken automatically enters it into your register once a month.

Alternatively, add the CheckFree charge to the Service Charge field in the Reconcile Bank Statement window each time you reconcile your account.

A Customizing Quicken

Rearranging the iconbar

To rearrange the order of the icons in the iconbar, simply drag and drop each icon where you want it to go. For example, to move the Register icon so that it appears to the right of the Graphs icon:

Click the Register icon and hold the mouse button down.

Then, move the cursor over the Graphs icon and release the mouse button.

Removing an icon from the iconbar

To reinstate the icon to the iconbar, see "Adding an icon to the iconbar" on page 294.

To remove an icon from the iconbar, move the cursor to the icon, and then hold down the Shift key and click the left mouse button. (You can also remove it by clicking Delete in the Customize Iconbar window—see the next section.)

Changing the iconbar display

Each icon is displayed with a label. You can display just the icon, just the label, or hide the iconbar altogether.

1 **From the Edit menu, choose Options.**

2 **Click Iconbar.**

3 **Click Show Icons or Show Text, and then click OK.**

To turn off the icons in the iconbar so that only text appears on the buttons, clear the Show Icons checkbox.

To turn off the text in the iconbar, clear the Show Text checkbox.

To hide the iconbar entirely, clear both checkboxes.

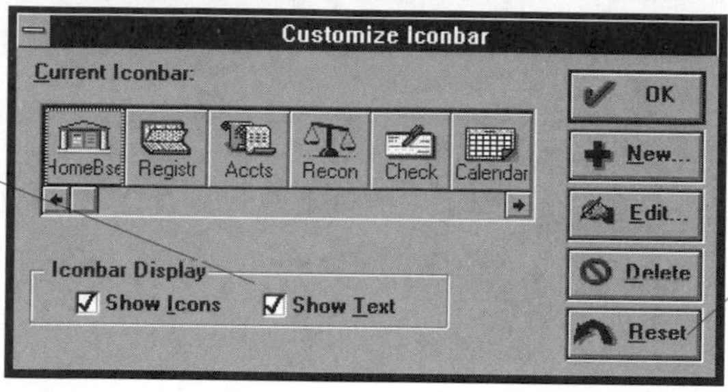

Click Reset to reset the iconbar back to when Quicken was first installed.

Important: Quicken can't restore your custom settings if you reset the settings this way.

Adding an icon to the iconbar

In addition to the icons you initially see in the iconbar, Quicken has a store of other icons you can add, each with its own specific action.

1 **From the Edit menu, choose Options.**

2 **Click Iconbar.**

Or hold down the Ctrl key and click in an empty position on the iconbar.

3 **Click New.**

The Add Action to Iconbar window appears.

4 **From the Icon Action list, select the action you want to assign to the icon.**

For example, select File Backup from the list.

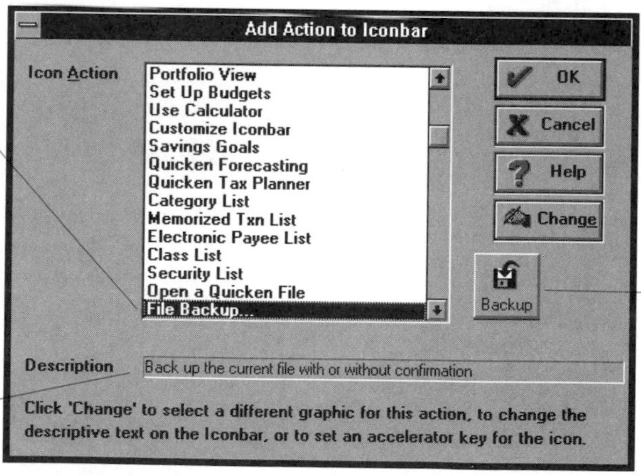

Quicken displays the icon for the selected action here.

Quicken displays a description of the selected icon here.

5 **(Optional) Click Change to change the icon, icon text, or Speed Key.**

Click another icon if you don't want to use the icon that Quicken has assigned for the action.

For example, to set up a transaction that involves a credit purchase, click one of the credit card icons.

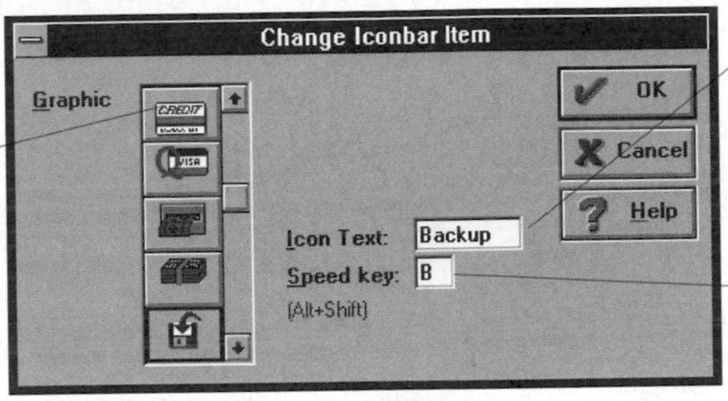

Change the icon's text label here.

Set up a Speed Key, so that you can perform this action by pressing the Speed Key.

In this example, pressing Alt+Shift+B has the same effect as clicking the icon.

6 **Click OK three times.**

When you click the new icon (or press the assigned Speed Key combination), Quicken performs the assigned action.

Editing the icons in the iconbar

You can change the action of any icon in the iconbar, or change the icon associated with an action.

Or hold down the Ctrl key and click an icon on the iconbar to edit it.

1 **From the Edit menu, choose Options.**

2 **Click Iconbar.**

3 **Select an icon and click Edit.**

4 **Continue with step 4 on page 294.**

Assigning an icon to open an account

Instead of displaying the account list to open an account, you can set up an icon to open an account you use frequently. For example, you can set up the Use Account icon so that it opens a credit card account named "American Excess." Or you can set up an icon to open an investment account with the Portfolio View window displayed instead of the register.

1 **From the Edit menu, click Options.**

2 **Click Iconbar.**

3 **Click New.**

4 **From the Icon Action list, select Use a Specific Account (it's at the bottom of the list).**

5 **Click OK.**

The Assign Account to Icon window appears.

6 **Scroll the Account to Load drop-down list to see all available accounts and select the account you want to set up.**

Windows tip
Click the drop-down arrow to display the list. Then click the down arrow at the bottom of the scroll bar.

7 **Select an option for the type of window you want to open for this account from the Register, Reconcile/Pay Credit Card, Write Checks, or Portfolio View options.**

Not all options are available for all accounts. For example, on a credit card account you can't write checks or see an investment portfolio, so those options are dimmed for a credit card account.

Scroll the Account to Load drop-down list to select the account.

Click Register if you want the account register to open when you click the icon, or choose one of the other available options.

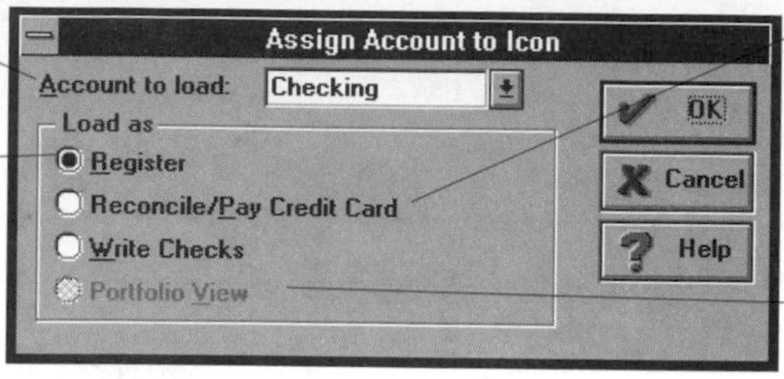

Click this if you want the reconcile window to open when you click the icon.

Click this to open an investment account with the Portfolio View window displayed.

8 **Click OK.**

Now when you click the icon, the account you selected opens and displays the window you specified.

To set up an additional icon to open another specific account, see "Adding an icon to the iconbar" on page 294, and select the action "Use a Specific Account" from the Icon Action list.

Reassigning the Use Account icon

1 **From the Edit menu, choose Options.**

2 **Click Iconbar.**

3 **Select the Use Account icon (UseAcct) and click Edit.**

4 **Select Use a Specific Account and click OK.**

The Assign Account to Icon window appears. Change the setup as described in the previous steps.

Assigning an icon to enter a transaction

The following example shows how to set up the Use Transaction icon so that, when you click it, Quicken enters a transaction you use frequently (such as an ATM withdrawal for $300) into your checking account register. The transaction must already be in your Memorized Transaction list.

1 **From the Edit menu, choose Options.**

2 **Click Iconbar.**

3 **Click New.**

4 **From the Icon Action list, select Use a Specific Memorized Txn and click OK.**

5 **Complete the Assign Memorized Transaction to Icon window.**

Select the memorized transaction you want to set up from this drop-down list.

Select the account in which you usually enter this transaction from this drop-down list.

If you select this, clicking the icon automatically records the transaction.

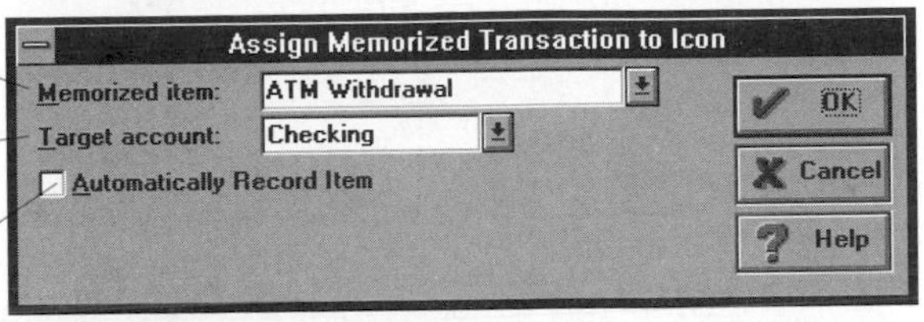

6 **Click OK twice, then click Close.**

Now when you click the icon, the register for the account you selected opens and Quicken inserts the memorized transaction you selected into the register. Check the amount and change it if necessary, then click Record.

When you click the Use Txn icon or press its Speed Key (see how to create Speed Keys on page 295), Quicken enters the memorized transaction.

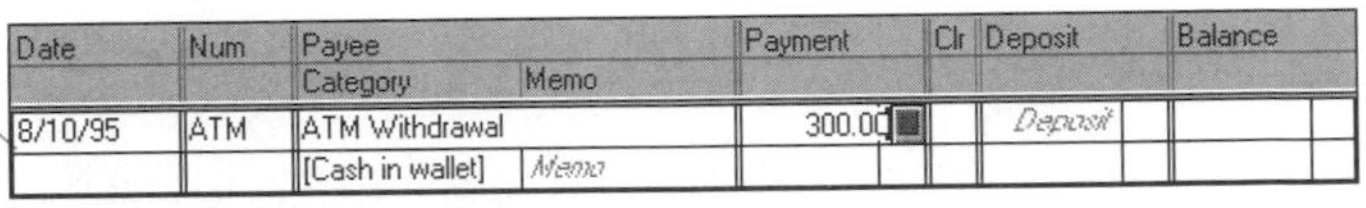

Date
Num
Payee
Category
Memo
Payment
Clr
Deposit
Balance
8/10/95
ATM
ATM Withdrawal
300.00
Deposit
[Cash in wallet]
Memo

To change the transaction assigned to the Use Transaction icon, see "Reassigning the Use Account icon" on page 296 (but select the Use Txn icon in step 3.)

To set up an additional icon to enter another specific transaction, add a new icon to the iconbar as described in "Adding an icon to the iconbar" on page 294, and select Use a Specific Memorized Txn from the Icon Action list.

Customizing other Quicken features

At any time, you can change the settings for many of Quicken's features through the Options window. In this way, you can make Quicken look and behave more to your own liking.

From the Edit menu, choose Options. Or click the Options icon on the iconbar. Then click one of the Options buttons.

Customize the appearance of Quicken checks (page 66).

Change the kinds of fonts and colors used in account registers and lists, the way account registers behave when you enter transactions, and how Quicken memorizes and completes transactions in account registers (page 37).

Set up a fiscal year calendar and other general settings (see the next page).

Change how accounts, categories, and dates appear in reports (page 196).

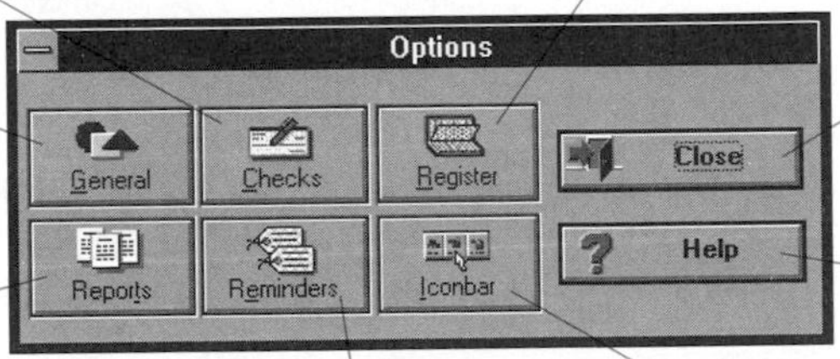

Click here to save the settings.

Click here to learn about what each option does.

Change the way Billminder and Reminders work (page 62).

Change the appearance of the iconbar or the way the icons behave (page 293).

Here are the options you can set when you click the General button from the Options window:

Display Quicken windows with a gray background to give them a 3-D effect. This overrides the background color in the Windows Control Panel.

Have Quicken ask you to confirm a transaction you've entered on an investment form before entering it in your investment register.

If you use Quicken for DOS, you can save your price history in Quicken for DOS format. Then when you update prices in DOS, the price history you've been recording in Quicken for Windows will be converted and available for you to use.

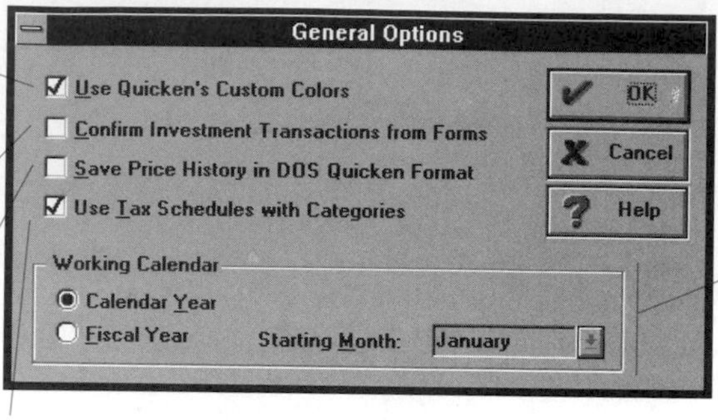

Choose whether you want your working calendar to be based on a calendar or fiscal year.

If you choose Fiscal Year, then choose the first month of the fiscal year.

This option lets you assign a tax schedule form to each tax-related category you set up (see "Setting up categories with tax time in mind" on page 217 for more information).

Here are other parts of Quicken that you can customize:

To do this	Do this
Customize how your Quicken desktop will appear the next time you open the current file	Choose Save Desktop from the File menu. The Save Desktop window appears. • Click Save Current Desktop to save the *current* window positions and display them in the same position each time you open the current file. • Click Save Desktop on Exit to save the window positions *at the time you exit Quicken,* and display them in the same position the next time you open the file.
Turn Qcards on or off	Choose Show Qcards from the Help menu. A checkmark next to the Show Qcards menu item shows that Qcards are on.
Change the display options for graphs	See "Changing graph options" on page 200.
Set up a modem to use Quicken online	See Chapter 23, *Setting up your modem,* on page 255.

B Managing and archiving your data files

Setting up additional files

In most cases, you will have a single Quicken data file containing all your accounts. This file is probably called QDATA, the one Quicken automatically creates during installation.

Each Quicken file can contain up to 255 accounts. All the accounts in a single file share the same categories, classes, and memorized transactions. Reports can show data from all or selected accounts in a file. You can transfer amounts from one account to another within the same file.

While accounts in the same data file share data, each data file is separate and distinct, unrelated to any other data file. Given that, you might create additional files if you want to keep:

- Your home finances separate from your business finances for tax reasons.
- A separate file for each year's accounts.

1 **From the File menu, choose New.**

To set up a new account within your existing Quicken file instead, click New Account and click OK. See "Setting up additional Quicken accounts" on page 1.

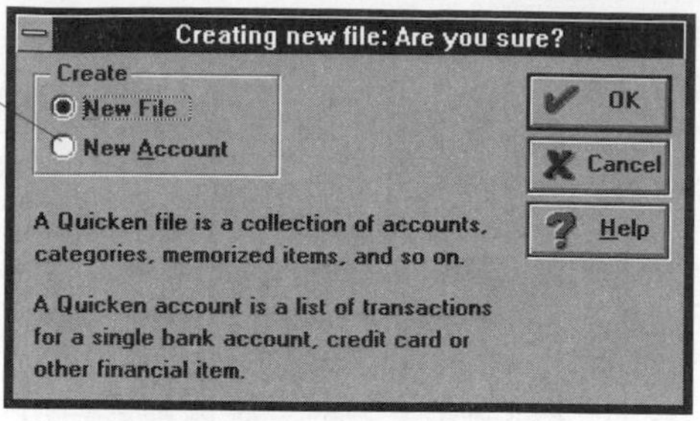

2 **Click OK if you are sure you want to create a new file.**

3 **Complete the Create Quicken File window.**

Type a DOS filename (up to eight characters) for your new Quicken file. Quicken adds the .QDT extension.

Quicken will create the file on this drive and in this directory. To create the file elsewhere...

...double-click the directory you want in this list (you can double-click c:\ to see other directories on the C: drive) or select the drive you want from this drop-down list.

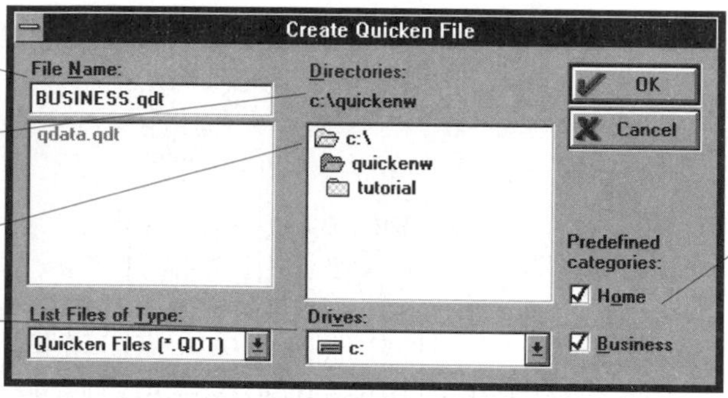

Clear the Home and/or Business checkboxes if you don't want to use these predefined categories. You can always add, edit, or delete categories later.

4 **Click OK.**

Quicken creates the new file and opens the Select Account Type window.

To set up accounts within this file, see "Setting up additional Quicken accounts" on page 1.

Choosing a file

When you start Quicken, it opens the last file you used. To work in another file, open it.

Or press Ctrl+O

1 **From the File menu, choose Open.**

2 **Complete the Open Quicken File window, then click OK.**

Type the name of the Quicken file you want to open. Don't delete or type over the .QDT extension.

Or, select the file from this list to automatically enter its name in the File Name box.

If the file you want to open isn't in this directory or drive...

...double-click the directory you want in this list (you can double-click c:\ to see other directories on the C: drive) or select the drive you want from this drop-down list.

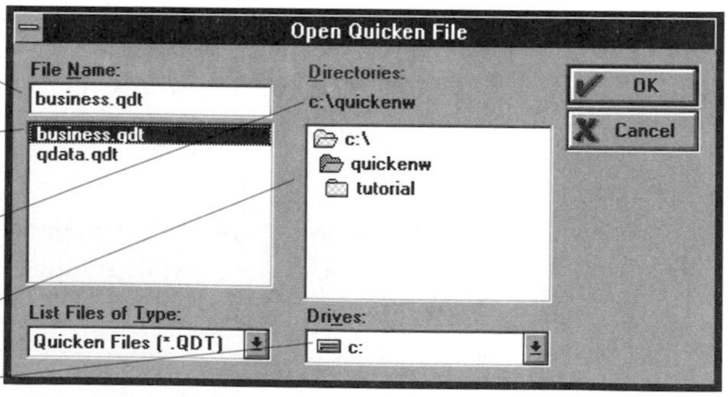

Windows Tip
You can double-click the filename from the file list instead of selecting it and clicking OK.

3 **Enter a password if you have assigned one to this file, then click OK.**

Quicken closes all the open account windows of the current file before it opens the new file.

Creating icons for additional files

You can set up a Windows icon for each file you have. You can then double-click the icon to open the file, instead of using the File Open command.

1 **In Windows, click the Quicken for Windows icon to select it.**

2 **From the File menu in the Program Manager window, choose Properties.**

This is the current name of the Quicken icon.

This is the command line Windows uses to start Quicken.

This is the directory where Quicken looks first for its data files.

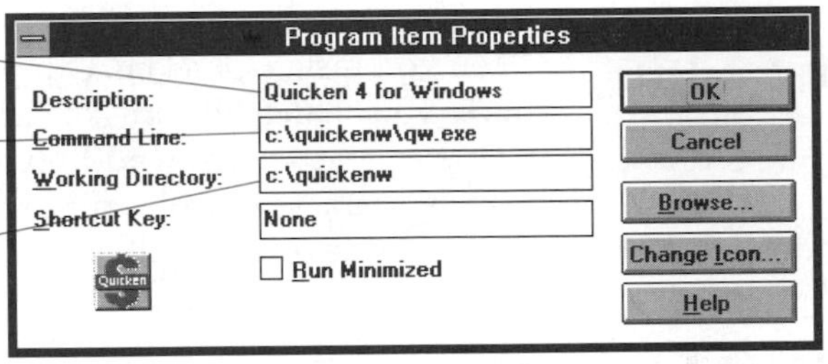

3 **In the Description box, enter a name for the first Quicken icon you want to create.**

For example, type Personal Accounts.

4 **In the Command Line box, type a space after the existing text, and then enter the name of your data file with the .QDT extension.**

For example, if you named the data file for your personal accounts PA and stored it in the working directory (in this example, the QUICKENW directory on the C: drive), type a space after C:\QUICKENW\QW.EXE, and then type PA.QDT.

This is the new label for one of your Quicken icons.

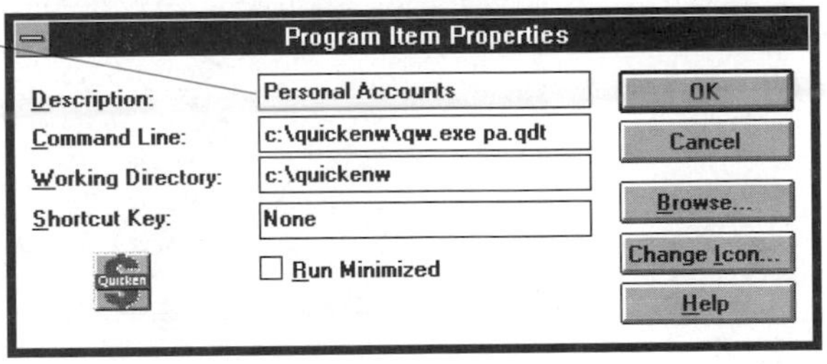

5 **In the Working Directory box, enter the drive and directory where your data file is located. Then click OK.**

The Quicken icon is now labeled with the name you entered in the Description box (in this example, Personal Accounts). Double-clicking this icon now opens the file PA.QDT in Quicken.

6 **To create another Quicken icon that opens a different Quicken file (for example, your business accounts), select the icon you just created.**

Windows Tip
Instead of using the Copy command, you can hold down the Ctrl key and drag the Quicken icon to the group where you want the copy to be located.

7 **From the File menu in the Program Manager window, choose Copy.**

The Copy Program Item window appears.

8 **Select the group where you want the new Quicken icon to be located from the drop-down list and click OK.**

Now you have two Quicken icons with the same name in Windows.

9 **Click one of the Quicken icons to select it.**

10 **From the File menu in the Program Manager window, choose Properties.**

11 **Repeat steps 3-5, except use a different description and filename.**

Renaming a file

When you install Quicken, Quicken names your data file QDATA unless you change that preset name. If you keep your personal data in QDATA and set up an additional file named BUSINESS for your business data, you may want to rename QDATA to PERSONAL or another more meaningful name.

When you rename a Quicken data file, you actually change the names of the five DOS files that make up the Quicken file (or six DOS files if you use Check-Free). You must not change the extensions of these DOS files when you rename the Quicken data file, so use Quicken's Rename command (not DOS or Windows commands) to rename files.

---

1 **From the File menu, choose File Operations and then choose Rename.**

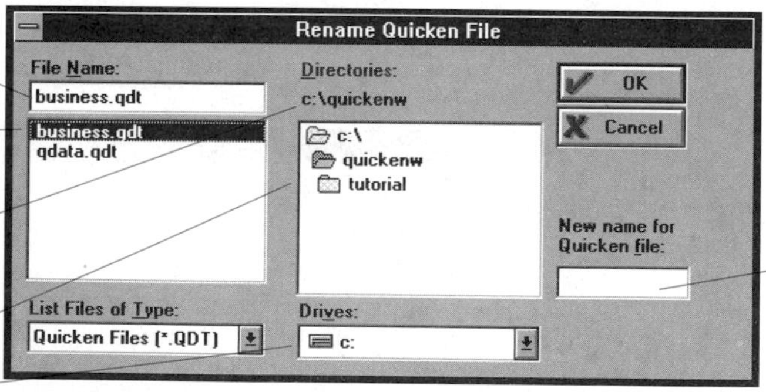

Enter the name of the Quicken file you want to rename. You don't need to enter the .QDT extension.

Select the file from this list to automatically enter its name in the File Name box.

If the file you want to rename isn't in this directory or drive...

...double-click the directory you want in this list (you can double-click c:\ to see other directories on the C: drive) or select the drive you want from this drop-down list.

Enter the new name for the file.

2 **Use the files, directories, and drives lists to select the file you want to rename.**

The file to be renamed appears in the File Name box.

3 **In the New Name For Quicken File box, enter the new name for the file.**

Don't enter an extension for the file. Quicken automatically gives the file the extension .QDT, even if you enter a different extension.

4 **Click OK.**

The renamed file appears with its new name in the File Name list. To see the File Name list: from the File menu, choose Open.

Deleting a file

Deleting a Quicken file permanently removes all of the records in that file from your disk. Once you've deleted records, there is no way to get your account data back except by using your backup disk. Be certain you want to delete a file before doing so.

1 **From the File menu, choose File Operations and then choose Delete.**

2 **Select the file you want to delete, and then click OK.**

Windows Tip
You can double-click the filename in the file list instead of selecting it and clicking OK.

Quicken warns that you are about to permanently remove the accounts in that file.

3 **To delete the selected file, type** YES **and click OK.**

Otherwise, click Cancel to return to the Quicken window.

Copying part or all of a file

You can copy all or part of a file to create a new file. You might copy part of a file if:

- You want to copy transactions within a certain date range to start a new file for a new fiscal year.
- Your data disk is full.
- You want to copy your scheduled transactions, memorized transactions, transaction groups, and categories to a new file without copying any transactions.
- You want to increase the maximum number of accounts that can be created in the file to 255.

Don't confuse copying a file with copying an account. To copy transactions in one account to another account, see "Copying data from one account to another" on page 305. Or, to copy your Quicken data file from one computer to another, see "Moving a Quicken file between computers" on page 309.

Quicken doesn't change the original file in any way.

1 **Open the file you want to copy.**

2 **From the File menu, choose File Operations and then choose Copy.**

See "How Copy treats prior uncleared transactions" next before selecting or clearing this checkbox.

This option appears only if you have investment accounts in your file.

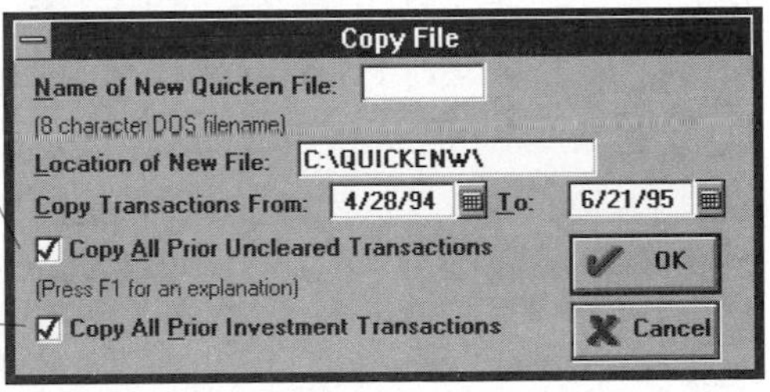

3 **Enter a name for the new Quicken file.**

4 **Enter the directory location for the new file.**

5 **(Optional) In the Copy Transactions From and To boxes, enter the date range of transactions to be included in the new file.**

By default, Quicken copies all transactions in the file by entering the dates of the oldest and newest transactions in the current file as the date range of transactions to be included in the new file. Change these dates if you want to copy only some transactions.

To create a new file that contains only your scheduled transactions, memorized transactions, transaction groups, and categories (but no transactions), enter dates that are later than the last transaction in the existing file. You must also perform steps 6 and 7.

For more information, see "How Copy treats prior uncleared transactions" below.

6 **(Optional) Clear the Copy All Prior Uncleared Transactions checkbox to *exclude* all transactions that occurred before the date range but haven't yet been cleared or reconciled.**

7 **(Optional) If your file includes investment accounts, clear the Copy All Prior Investment Transactions checkbox to *exclude* all investment transactions that occurred before the date range.**

8 **Click OK.**

9 **Choose the file you want to work in now.**

How Copy treats prior uncleared transactions

Prior uncleared transactions are transactions that occurred before the date range but haven't yet been cleared or reconciled (marked with an asterisk or X in the Clr (Cleared) column).

If you include prior uncleared transactions when you copy a file, Quicken transfers the information to the new file as follows:

- For each account in the original file, Quicken summarizes (that is, sums the amounts of) all prior cleared transactions. Quicken then uses this total amount as the opening balance of the corresponding account in the new file.
- Quicken copies all prior uncleared transactions from each account in the original file to the corresponding account in the new file.

When should you copy prior uncleared transactions?

Copy prior uncleared transactions to the new file to:

- Reconcile bank or credit card accounts.
- Track assets.
- Track business payables and receivables.

Include uncleared transactions in the new copy of the file, even when those transactions occur before the beginning of the current period. Make sure the Copy All Prior Uncleared Transactions checkbox is selected in the Copy File window.

If your cash, asset, or liability account contains prior cleared transactions, Quicken doesn't copy these transactions to the account in the new file. Instead, Quicken summarizes the transactions and uses this sum as the opening balance of the account in the new file.

Transfer transactions may include cases where one side of a transfer has cleared, but not the other. For example, a check to VISA might have appeared on a bank statement, but not on a VISA statement. If you then copy prior uncleared transactions and the check date is prior to the beginning date you specify, Quicken summarizes the bank account side of the transfer and copies the credit card account side. This partial summary causes the message "Transfer not present" to appear if you use the Go to Transfer (Ctrl+X) command in the VISA account transaction. Also, the TOTAL TRANSFERS line item in a summary report might not be zero.

When should you exclude prior uncleared transactions?

Exclude prior uncleared transactions from the new file only if you want the new file to include only transactions in the date range for the current period, regardless of their cleared status. Clear the Copy All Prior Uncleared Transactions checkbox in the Copy File window.

Copying data from one account to another

There are two ways of copying transactions from one account to another, depending on whether you want to copy one transaction at a time, or many transactions at once.

Copying a single transaction

1. **Select a transaction.**
2. **Click Copy to copy the transaction data to the Windows clipboard.**
3. **Go to the second account (which could be in a different file).**
4. **Select an empty transaction.**

   If you don't select an empty transaction, Quicken replaces the selected transaction with the copied transaction details.
5. **Click Paste to copy the transaction data in.**

Copying a range of transactions

You might copy a range of transactions if you want to:

- Merge transactions from two accounts into one account. For example, you may have been using Quicken on two different computers and now want to combine your data.

- Correct an account with the wrong account type. To rectify this, create a new account of the right type, and then copy all the transactions from the old account to the new.
- Move an account from one Quicken file to another. To do this, set up a new account in the second file, and then copy all the transactions from the old account to the new.

To copy a range of transactions from one account to another:

More information about QIF files is in Help. Press F1 and then click Contents. Click "Having Quicken work for you," then "Quicken technical information," and then "Information about Quicken's QIF format."

- ◆ **Export the transactions from the source account to a QIF (Quicken interchange format) file.**
- ◆ **Import the QIF file into a target account.**

How Quicken handles transfer transactions. Quicken copies the transfers that were made to or from the copied account. For example, if you export data from a checking account that contains transfers to a cash account and then import that data into a new file, Quicken creates a cash account in the new file's Account list. This new cash account is empty except for transfers from checking.

Copying lists

To set up a new file with your existing lists, use Export and Import to copy everything *except* the transactions from an existing file. After copying the list information, you can make changes to the lists at any time.

Besides copying transactions from an account, you can also include:

- Category & Transfer list
- Class list
- Memorized Transaction list
- Account list

Exporting transactions from an account to a QIF file

1 **Open the account you want to export data from.**

2 **From the File menu, choose Export.**

3 **Complete the QIF Export window, then click OK.**

Enter the directory path and name of a file to receive the exported data. You don't have to give the file any particular extension, but if you enter the extension .QIF, it will remind you what the file is for.

In this example, the filename is CHECKING.QIF, and will be created in the directory C:\QUICKENW.

This is the account you are exporting transactions from.

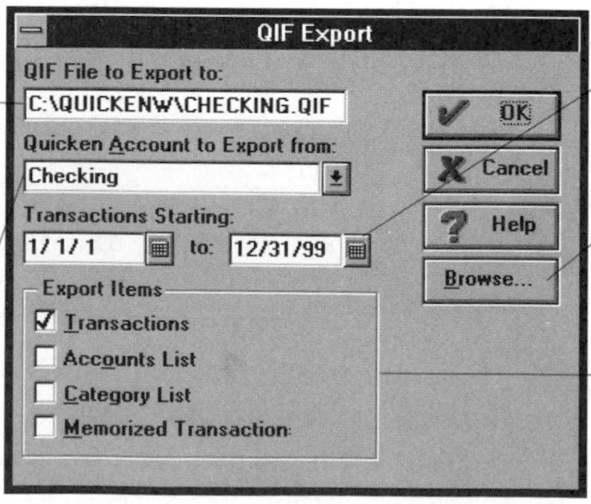

Leave these default dates to export all transactions. Otherwise, enter start and end dates.

Click Browse to specify a directory location and filename.

Select what else you want to export. If you select the Category list, Quicken also exports the Class list.

Importing transactions from a QIF file to an account

See "Setting up additional Quicken accounts" on page 1.

1 **If the account you want to import data into doesn't yet exist, set up the account.**

2 **From the File menu, choose Import.**

3 **Complete the QIF Import window, then click OK.**

Enter the directory path and name of the QIF file you are importing data from.

Or click Browse to specify a directory location and filename.

Select the account you are importing transactions into. Click the underscored down arrow to drop down the list. Click the down arrow to scroll the list. Then click the account you want.

Select what you want to import.

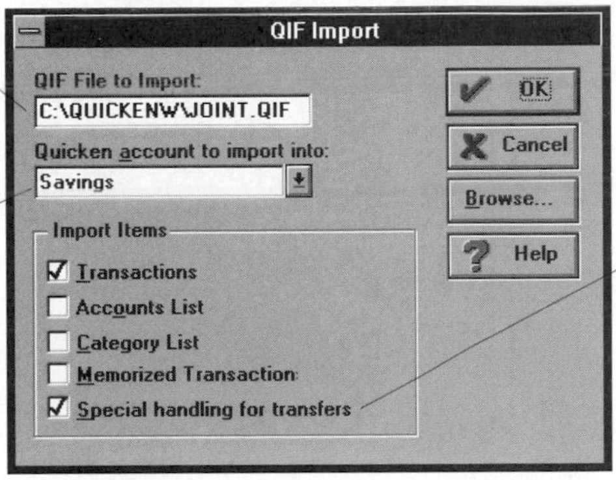

Select this checkbox only if you have exported from a number of Quicken accounts in the same file (to several QIF files) and will be using import to recreate all the transactions (by importing from several QIF files). Selecting this checkbox prevents duplicate transfer transactions when you import data from both the "to" and the "from" accounts involved with transfers.

See "Copying lists" on page 306.

Quicken imports the transactions and any additional import items you selected from the QIF file into the current account.

If the current account has a different name from the account you exported from, Quicken offers to create a new account with the same name as the exported account.

- Click Yes to create the new account and import the transactions into the new account
- Click No to import the transactions into the current account.

Setting up passwords

To protect transactions in a Quicken file from unauthorized changes, you can set up two kinds of passwords in Quicken:

- Discourage unauthorized access to your Quicken data by requiring a file password before your file can be opened.
- Set up a separate transaction password that protects all transactions before a certain date.

Setting up a file password

Use a file password to protect an entire file. After you set up a file password, you can't open the file unless you enter the password correctly. A file password doesn't protect your file from being copied, deleted, or renamed. (If your file is renamed or copied, the password remains in effect.)

When you set up a password, it protects only the current file. Make sure that the current file is the one you want to assign a password to.

1 **Open the file you want to protect with a password.**

2 **From the File menu, choose Passwords and then choose File.**

As you enter your password, Quicken displays an asterisk (*) in place of the character you typed to ensure privacy.

3 **Enter a password and click OK.**

Write down the password and keep it in a safe place in case you forget it.

Enter up to 16 characters, including spaces. You can use upper- or lower-case characters.

4 **Enter the password again to confirm it and click OK.**

From now on, Quicken prompts you for the password before allowing you to open this Quicken file.

Changing or removing a file password

1 **Open the file whose password you want to change or remove.**

2 **From the File menu, choose Passwords and then choose File.**

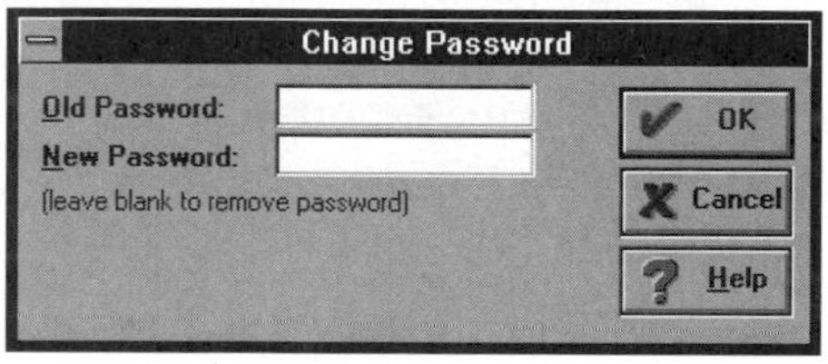

3 **In the Old Password box, enter the current password.**

4 **In the New Password box, enter a new password, or leave the box blank to remove the password for the file.**

5 **Click OK and enter the new password again to confirm it.**

6 **Click OK.**

Quicken activates the new password or removes the current password immediately.

Setting up a transaction password

When you set up a transaction password, you can't make changes to transactions prior to a given date unless you enter the correct password. For example, you can *close* an accounting period so that no accidental changes can be made to transactions in it.

1 **From the File menu, choose Passwords and then choose Transaction.**

As you type the password, Quicken displays an asterisk (*) in place of each character to ensure privacy.

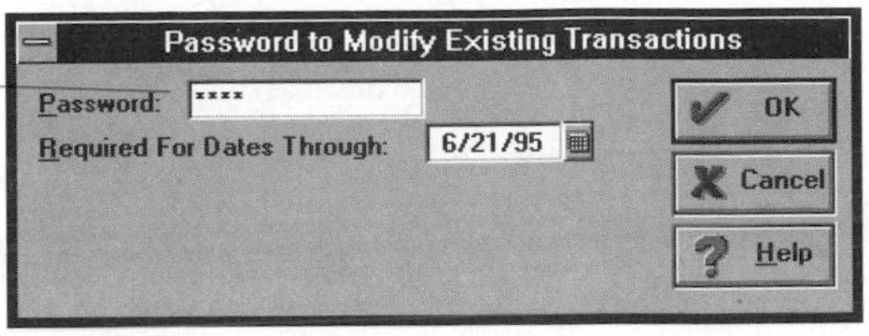

2 **In the Password box, type a password.**

Enter up to 16 characters, including spaces. Quicken passwords aren't case-sensitive.

3 **(Optional) Enter the date of the last transaction you want the password to protect.**

4 **Click OK.**

5 **Enter the password again to confirm and click OK.**

From now on, Quicken prompts you for the password before you can record changes to any of the transactions dated on or before the date you specified.

Changing or removing the transaction password

You can change or delete a password from a range of transactions, or change the date of the last transaction protected by the password.

1 **From the File menu, choose Passwords and then choose Transaction.**

2 **In the Old Password box, type the current password.**

3 **In the New Password box, type a new password or leave the box blank to remove the transaction password. Enter the current password if you want to change the protected date range.**

4 **(Optional) Change the date of the last transaction you want the password to protect.**

5 **Click OK.**

Quicken activates the new password, removes the current password, or changes the protected date range immediately.

Moving a Quicken file between computers

To move a Quicken file from one computer to another (for example, from your home computer to your business computer), use the Backup and Restore commands.

One Quicken data file actually comprises five DOS files (six DOS files if you use CheckFree). When you use the Backup and Restore commands, Quicken finds all of its files quickly and easily, and then backs up and restores the DOS files together. Don't try to back up and restore the DOS files individually.

1 **Install Quicken on any computer that doesn't already have Quicken installed on it.**

See the *Getting Started Guide* for complete installation instructions.

See "Backing up your Quicken files" on page 6.

2 **On the first computer, back up the Quicken file you want to move to a floppy disk.**

See "Restoring a Quicken file" on page 8.

3 **On the second computer, restore the Quicken file you backed up.**

Archiving your Quicken files

When you *close out* your accounts, you save all the information about completed transactions from the previous year in one file, and continue the new year with only those transactions that are still uncleared. This protects your data from changes.

See "Setting up a transaction password" on page 308.

Quicken doesn't require you to close out accounts. In fact, if you do close out a Quicken file, you can't create reports covering several years. If you're worried about protecting your data, you can protect a range of transactions by date with a password.

However, if you still want to close out a file in Quicken, you have two options: Archive and Start New Year.

Archiving the previous year's data

The Archive option makes a copy of all transactions in the current file dated earlier than the current year. You give the file copy its own name (for example HOME94) and this copy is for archiving only. The current file is untouched and remains your working file—it still contains all your past transactions.

If you select the Archive option once a year, you will eventually have a series of archive files, each containing all transactions up to the end of a certain year. You can give these archive files appropriate names.

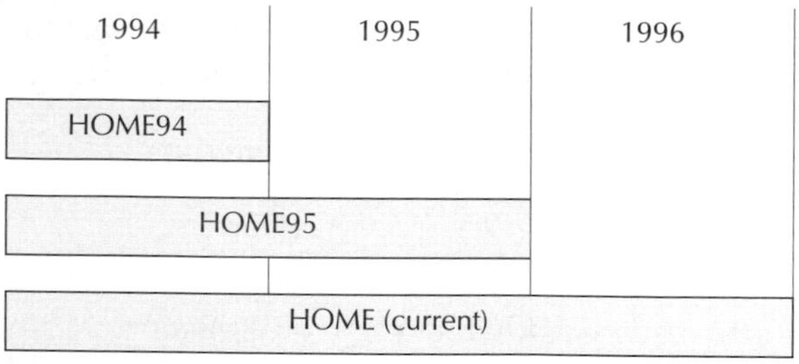

1 **From the File menu, choose Year-End Copy.**

2 **Click Archive in the Year End Action box and click OK.**

3 **Make any needed changes, then click OK.**

Quicken appends last year's date to the filename to create the archive filename.

Quicken presets the location for the archive file to your current Quicken directory.

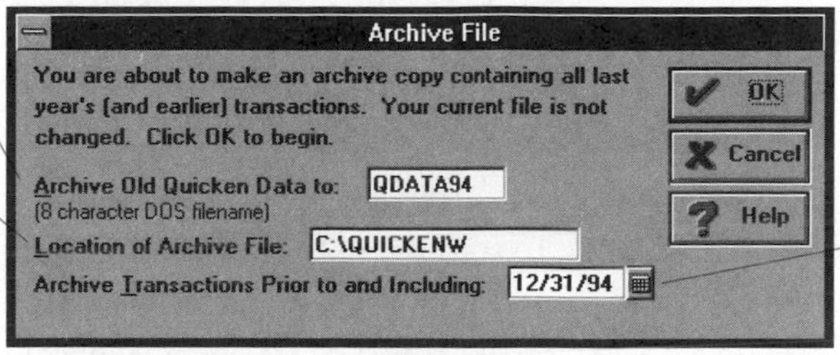

By default, Quicken archives transactions through the last day of the previous year.

Quicken creates the archive file, and then asks which file you would like to use, the current file or the archive file. The archive file appears in your list of files.

You should never need to make changes to an archive file. To ensure that nobody makes changes inadvertently, set a transaction password that lets you view the file but not make changes without entering the password. Or you can set a file password so that nobody else can view the file or make changes to it.

See "Setting up a transaction password" on page 308.

See "Setting up a file password" on page 307.

Reviewing the year

Quicken provides many reports for reviewing yearly finances. When creating reports with a date range, specify the entire year.

- To see how activity varies from one period to another, create a summary report (page 180) for the year with column headings set to the time period you prefer, for example, Month or Quarter.
- To review how funds have moved in and out of categories and asset or liability accounts, create a cash flow report (page 162) for the year.
- To see changes in your net worth, create a net worth report (page 165) with columns for the intervals you want to examine.

Starting a new year

The Start New Year option saves a copy of your current file, and then deletes any transactions in the current file that aren't in the current year. In other words, your current file will go back no earlier than January 1 of this year. However, investment transactions and uncleared transactions aren't deleted, regardless of how old they are. (If you have never used Reconcile, the Start New Year option won't work well, as your old transactions won't be cleared.)

If you select the Start New Year option at the beginning of each year, you will eventually have a series of archived files, each containing the transactions for just one year.

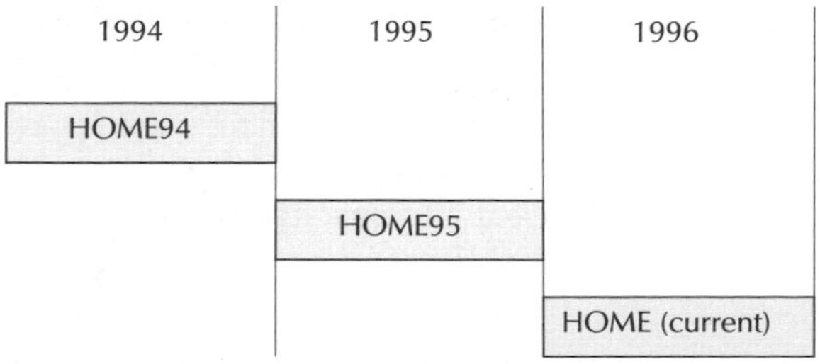

If you use IntelliCharge to update your credit card accounts, take note that the Start New Year option removes the previous year's transactions from your accounts (including payee information). When payee information is removed, IntelliCharge may not be able to match payees and categories correctly the next time you update your register.

To start using this method part way through a year, use Archive first and then use the Start New Year option, using your current file in both instances. Archive creates an archive file without any of the current year's transactions, and then Start New Year deletes previous years' transactions from your current file, except for investment transactions and uncleared transactions. Start New Year also creates an intermediate file containing all transactions: you can delete this file.

1 **From the File menu, choose Year-End Copy.**

2 **Click Start New Year in the Year End Action box and click OK.**

Enter the name of a DOS file to copy your current file to. Quicken puts the copy in your current Quicken directory.

The preset start date is the first day of the current year.

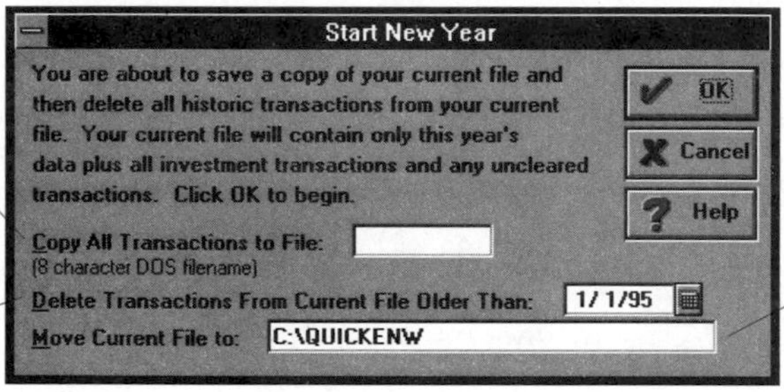

Quicken keeps your current file in the current Quicken directory, but you can move your current file to another directory if you want.

3 **In the Copy All Transactions To File box, type a name for the copy of your current file.**

For example, type HOME94. Don't include an extension.

4 **(Optional) Make any other needed changes, then click OK.**

Quicken doesn't delete any investment transactions or any uncleared transactions.

Quicken makes a copy of your current file, and then deletes all transactions in the current file earlier than the "Older Than" date.

5 **In the File To Use box, select the file you want to use, then click OK.**

Click here to use the copy of your original file with all transactions intact.

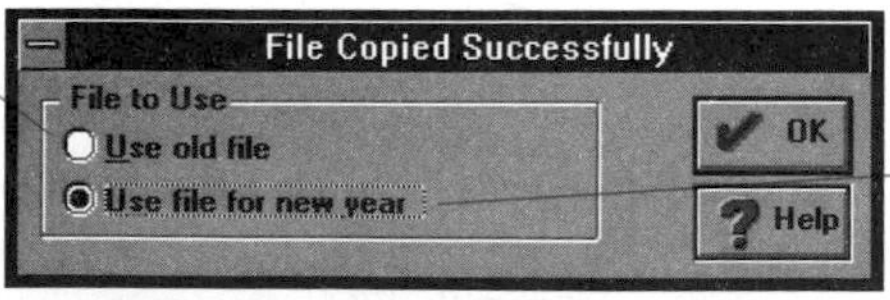

Click here to use your current file, which now contains only this year's transactions, plus all investment transactions and uncleared transactions.

Did Start New Year work as you expected? If not, it could be because you haven't reconciled your previous year's transactions. Start New Year doesn't delete any transactions that aren't cleared. You can clear a transaction by entering an x in the Clr field.

See Chapter 7, *Balancing your checkbook,* on page 83.

C Ordering Intuit software and supplies

About Intuit software and supplies

Intuit offers a complete line of checks and other time-saving products to meet both personal and business needs.

Besides checks, you can also purchase:

- Deposit slips
- Double-window envelopes
- Single-sheet forms leaders for printers
- Endorsement, message, and return-address stamps
- Imprinted stationery
- Intuit software products that work with Quicken

Using Intuit Marketplace to order products

You can use Intuit Marketplace to order Intuit checks, software, and supplies. Intuit Marketplace guides you through the ordering process and prints your order for you or sends your order to Intuit via modem.

For information about Intuit products, see the onscreen catalog in Intuit Marketplace.

To use Intuit Marketplace:

- If Quicken is already open, choose Intuit Marketplace from the Online menu.

OR

- If Quicken isn't open, double-click the Intuit Marketplace icon in your Quicken program group.

Follow the directions on the screen to create your order.

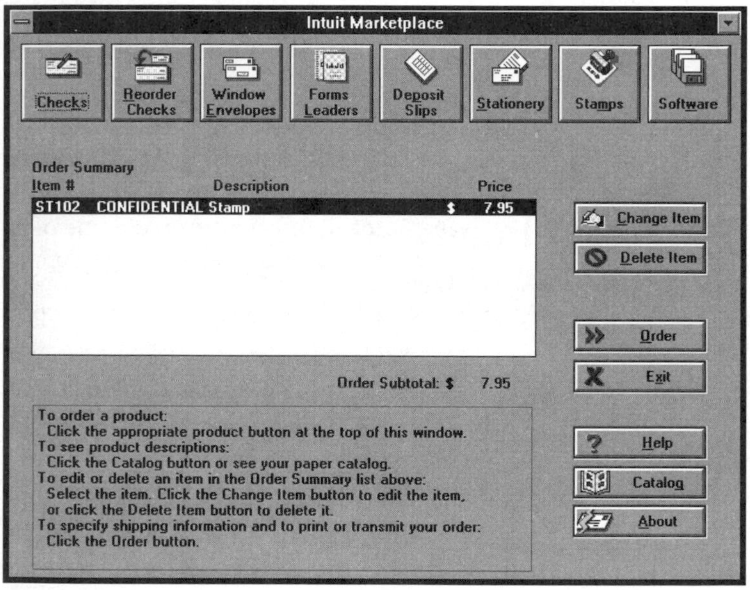

See "Setting up your modem to use Intuit services" on page 256.

After creating your order, you can print it out and mail or FAX it to Intuit, or you can use Intuit Marketplace to send your order to Intuit via modem.

Note: If you are ordering checks or deposit slips for the first time, you must send your order by mail or FAX and include a check marked "void."

Common questions and answers about Intuit checks

The following table contains the most common questions about Intuit checks. If you have other questions, or if you want another paper catalog, see "Intuit Supplies Customer Service" on page 319 for the phone number.

Why should I print checks with Quicken?	• It saves you time. Once you've entered your data in Quicken, click a button to print checks in just seconds. • Checks printed with Quicken are legible and attractive, which helps you look more organized and professional.
Can I order checks from Intuit instead of my bank?	**Yes.** Intuit checks are accepted everywhere other checks are accepted. They adhere to the standards of the American Banking Association and are pre-approved by all banks, savings and loans, credit unions, and brokers across the U.S. and Canada.
How do I write checks away from home?	For checks you write away from home, such as at the grocery store, just use the paper checks you already have, or write a Quicken check by hand. Then the next time you use Quicken, simply enter the transactions into your Quicken check register. When you order your Intuit checks, select a starting number that is considerably greater than your personal check numbers. That way, you avoid any confusion or possible duplication of numbers. For example, if your personal check numbers are in the 1000 range, begin your Intuit checks at 4001.
Is having two sets of check numbers a problem?	**No.** Quicken can easily manage two sets of check numbers in one account. Moreover, the bank has no concerns about which numbers you use on your checks. Check numbers are for your own records.
Why must I have check numbers printed on my Intuit checks?	Check numbers are printed with magnetic ink along the bottom of the check where they can be read electronically. When you place a stop payment on a check, the bank's automated equipment reads the check numbers to find and stop payment on the requested check.
What is the logo service?	Intuit has a selection of logos that you can print free on your Intuit checks. Just order by number from the catalog. If you want a custom logo, enclose black-and-white, camera-ready artwork with your order. There is a one-time $35 setup fee for custom logos. If touchup, typesetting, or rearrangement is required, you may incur additional charges. Custom logos can't be ordered by FAX or modem. Don't forget that you can use Quicken to print your own artwork on your checks without using our Logo Service. (See "Setting up continuous-feed printers" on page 74 or "Setting up page-oriented printers" on page 68.)

Intuit software products

To order any of these software products, use Intuit Marketplace or call Intuit Direct Sales at the phone number on page 320.

QuickPay

For business users of Quicken. By adding QuickPay to Quicken, you can integrate your payroll and business accounts into one financial system. QuickPay instantly calculates pay and withholdings, and tracks employee information. When you write payroll checks, QuickPay automatically updates your Quicken accounts and keeps track of your payroll liabilities. The Tax Table Update Service ensures that you keep abreast of any tax rate changes. And at the end of the year, QuickPay prints your W-2s.

QuickInvoice

For business users of Quicken. With QuickInvoice, writing invoices is as easy as writing checks with Quicken. QuickInvoice stores the details of your customers and sale items for easy completion of invoices. It helps you track your receivables in Quicken, retrieve customer information, and create useful accounts-receivable reports.

QuickBooks

The complete solution for small businesses, QuickBooks is a full-fledged accounting system with Quicken's ease of use. Using QuickBooks instead of Quicken, you can write checks *and* invoices. In addition, QuickBooks gives you great accounts-receivable management, so you always know who owes you money and when the money is overdue.

QuickBooks also has dozens of great business reports, handles sales tax automatically, does job costing and budgeting, and allows you to switch between cash and accrual accounting at the touch of a button. The bottom line is that QuickBooks is the *easy* way to control your business.

QuickBooks works with QuickPay. QuickBooks can also use any business data you've created in Quicken or QuickInvoice.

Quicken Deluxe 4 for Windows
(available on diskette or CD-ROM)

Quicken Deluxe adds to Quicken a comprehensive set of tools for managing personal finance. You get additional powerful programs that can pass or receive data from Quicken: Quicken Home Inventory, Quicken Quotes, and the Tradeline Electronic Stock Guide.

The Deluxe version also includes two more useful books: *101 Tips and Tricks for Quicken Users* and the *Quicken Tax Guidebook*.

Quicken Deluxe 4 for Windows CD-ROM gives you the tools mentioned above, plus multimedia effects, such as talking tutors who appear on your computer screen to step you through reconciling your checkbook or recording transactions.

Note: Please see the back of your Quicken package for a table describing the four versions of Quicken for Windows currently available.

TurboTax Federal
TurboTax State
TurboTax CD-ROM

All three TurboTax products can quickly read the tax information from your Quicken files. The TurboTax EasyStep system walks you through your entire return and makes money-saving suggestions. TurboTax also alerts you to items the IRS may question.

TurboTax State automatically reads the data from TurboTax Federal to further speed your tax preparation process.

D Contacting Intuit

Places to look for help

If you have a question about the way Quicken works, the best way to get an accurate, immediate answer is to look here:

Onscreen Help. Press F1 to get instant onscreen information while you're working in Quicken. If you want information about a specific task, make sure the window for that task is open and active.
Or, use the Search button in Help to look up topics the same way you do in a book's index. Help contains answers to many common questions. See "Getting onscreen Help" on page 23 in the *Getting Started Guide* if you're not sure how to use Quicken's Help system.

Index. Check the index beginning on page 321 for the topic you need. There are some topics in Help thac don't appear anywhere in this User's Guide, but these topics are included in the User's Guide index with instructions on how to find the information in Help.

Problem-solving tips. These tips are located at the end of three chapters in this book. Look for common symptoms that you may be experiencing and solutions that you may not have thought of.

If you are trying to	See
Print checks	"Check printing problems and solutions" on page 81.
Print reports or graphs	"Report and graph printing problems and solutions" on page 216.
Use your modem	"Communications problems and solutions" on page 259.

Troubleshooting on your own

If you still have a problem using Quicken, the best way to solve it is to try these self-help approaches first:

1 **Exit from Quicken, and then restart it.**

You should always choose Exit from the File menu or close the Quicken window to exit.

If Quicken tells you to reindex
Quicken normally reindexes automatically whenever it's required. Sometimes this reindexing can help you recover a damaged file, but don't do this unless Quicken tells you to. To make Quicken reindex a file: From the File menu, choose File Operations, and then choose Reindex.

When you restart Quicken, you may see a message explaining that Quicken is maintaining or reconstructing your index file. The index file improves access to your financial data. Sometimes Quicken doesn't have a chance to save the index file before you exit. By restarting, you give Quicken the opportunity to reconstruct its index file.

2 **Explore the problem a bit before you call.**

The key to troubleshooting is trying the most basic approach first. Even if you can't solve the problem yourself, exploring it will help you to explain it clearly if you must call for product support.

- Try the procedure again, starting at the beginning.

Make sure you are entering information in the appropriate window and are choosing the correct options for what you want.

For example, if a report doesn't include the information you want, check the date range and restrictions in the Create Report window.

Testing printing outside of Quicken
Look for Write in the Accessories Program Group. Open it and type a few words. Then, from the Write File menu, choose Print.

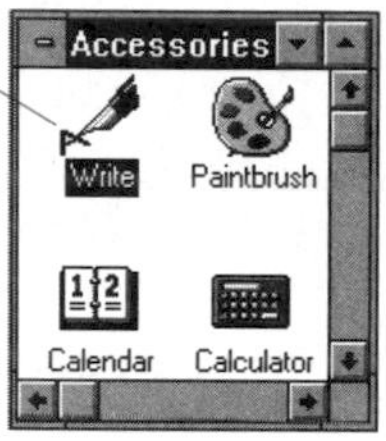

- Try a related procedure.

If you have trouble printing checks, try printing a report. If you can't print from Quicken, try printing from a word processor. If nothing prints, the problem may be related to the printer, not the software. Check the printer connections and the name of the printer selected in the Windows Control Panel.

- If something used to work, think about what has changed.

For example, if Billminder doesn't work, did you move BILLMNDW.EXE to a different location from QW.CFG? Both files must be in the same directory for Billminder to work.

Phone numbers

Before you call with a question on how to use Quicken, be at your computer with Windows and Quicken running, and have the following information handy:

- Quicken version number (from the Help menu, choose About Quicken to see the version number)
- If you receive an error message, exact wording of the message
- Online services account number, if applicable
- Hardware type and model and amount of memory (RAM) installed
- DOS version number and Windows version number
- Monitor type
- Printer manufacturer, type, and model (if relevant to your problem)
- Network configuration, if any

Writing to get product support
Calling for support is the quickest way to get an answer from us, but we can respond to a written request for support if you include this information in your letter:

- All the information we need from callers (listed beside this note).
- Your day and evening phone numbers.
- The best time to reach you at those numbers.
- A FAX number if available.

Send your letter to:
Technical Support Department,
Quicken for Windows
Intuit
P.O. Box 3014
Menlo Park, CA 94026

For product support

For questions about	Contact	At this number	During these hours
Quicken for Windows	**Quicken Technical Support** Talk to a representative during our business hours.	**415-858-6004**	Monday - Friday 5 am - 5 pm Pacific standard time
	QuickFax System Order and receive faxes about Quicken problems and solutions at any time.	**415-858-6090**	24 hours a day 7 days a week
	Quicken Online Forum Use your CompuServe or Prodigy membership to send your questions to us.	Connect to CompuServe; then enter GO INTUIT. Connect to Prodigy; then enter JUMP INTUIT.	Send your question any time. We'll respond within one business day.
IntelliCharge **Portfolio Price Update** **Online software registration** **Intuit Marketplace** Call this number if technical problems occur while using any Intuit online service with Quicken. (See the table below and on the next page for other support numbers or information about these services.)	**Intuit Online Services Technical Support**	**415-858-6070**	Monday - Friday 5 am - 5 pm Pacific standard time
CheckFree Call this number if problems occur within Quicken *before* you transmit transactions.	**Intuit Technical Support for CheckFree**	**415-858-6070**	Monday - Friday 5 am - 5 pm Pacific standard time
Call this number if problems occur with payment processing *after* you transmit transactions to CheckFree.	**CheckFree Corporation Technical Support**	**614-825-3500**	Monday - Friday 8 am - 8 pm Eastern standard time

For information about services

For information about	Contact	At this number	During these hours
Intuit checks, invoices, other supplies Call this number for information only. We can't accept orders over the phone.	**Intuit Supplies Customer Service**	**800-433-8810** (U.S. and International) **800-268-5779** (Canada only)	Monday - Friday 6 am - 5 pm Pacific standard time Monday - Friday 8 am - 8 pm Eastern standard time
Portfolio Price Update Call this number for pricing information, or to change your customer profile (e.g., name, address).	**Intuit Online Services Customer Service**	**800-245-2164**	Monday - Friday 6 am - 5 pm Mountain standard time
Tax Planner Call this number to find out if there are tax law changes that affect the way you use Tax Planner.	**Quicken Tax Update Hotline**	**415-858-6081**	24 hours a day 7 days a week

For information about	Contact	At this number	During these hours
IntelliCharge with Quicken credit card			
Call this number to get a Quicken credit card application.	**Intuit Customer Assistance for IntelliCharge**	**800-756-1855**	Monday-Friday 6 am - 5 pm Mountain standard time
Call this number for Quicken credit card limits, billing inquiries, and other Quicken credit card issues.	**Travelers Bank** (formerly Primerica Bank)	**800-772-2221**	Monday-Friday 8 am - 9 pm Eastern standard time
Call this number to report a lost or stolen Quicken credit card.	**Travelers Bank lost cards**	**800-426-2441**	24 hours a day 7 days a week
Call this number to get your Quicken credit card balance or last payment amount and date received.	**Travelers Bank Automatic Response Unit**	**800-262-9323** Call from a touch-tone phone, and then enter your Personal Identification Number.	24 hours a day 7 days a week

To place an order

To order	Contact	At this number	During these hours
Software upgrades **Intuit software products** ***Quicken Business User's Guide***	**Intuit Direct Sales**	**602-295-3220 Ext. 810006** (Before March 1995) **520-295-3220 Ext. 810006** (Beginning March 1995)	24 hours a day 7 days a week
Intuit checks, invoices, other supplies Send your order by FAX, mail, or modem. We can't accept orders over the phone.	**Intuit Supplies**	**FAX: 415-852-9146** (U.S. only) **FAX: 416-752-1140** (Canada only) **Mailing Address:** Intuit Supplies P.O. Box 50930 Palo Alto, CA 94303-9796	24 hours a day 7 days a week

Quicken customer forums and user groups

For more information about contacting Intuit's customer forum, accessing online customer forums, or joining a user group near you, press F1 to access Help, click Search, type 'forums', and press Enter.

If you have a modem and a membership to CompuServe or Prodigy, you can send your questions online to our support representatives. Also, many online services have product forums where their customers can post questions and answers about software. You can use these services to learn more about Quicken from other Quicken users. If you don't have a membership to an online service, contact the service you wish to join for membership and pricing information.

Personal computer user groups are a great way to learn more about computers and software. Some user groups even have special interest groups for Quicken users.

GS = *Getting Started Guide*

Index

A

* Open Quicken, choose Quicken Help from the Help menu, and then click Search. Type the keyword and press Enter.

B

C

* Open Quicken, choose Quicken Help from the Help menu, and then click Search. Type the keyword and press Enter.

D

* Open Quicken, choose Quicken Help from the Help menu, and then click Search. Type the keyword and press Enter.

E

* Open Quicken, choose Quicken Help from the Help menu, and then click Search. Type the keyword and press Enter.

G

H

I

J

K

* Open Quicken, choose Quicken Help from the Help menu, and then click Search. Type the keyword and press Enter.

L

M

N

O

* Open Quicken, choose Quicken Help from the Help menu, and then click Search. Type the keyword and press Enter.

P

Q

R

* Open Quicken, choose Quicken Help from the Help menu, and then click Search. Type the keyword and press Enter.

S

* Open Quicken, choose Quicken Help from the Help menu, and then click Search. Type the keyword and press Enter.

T

U

V

W

* Open Quicken, choose Quicken Help from the Help menu, and then click Search. Type the keyword and press Enter.

X

Y

Z

Symbols

Numbers